The Informit C++ Reference Guide
Techniques, Insight, and Practical Advice on C++

By Danny Kalev

The Informit Reference Guide Series

Cover art: *Shipbu1* by Barry Cronin

Copyright © 2005 by Pearson Education
All rights reserved.

Permission in writing must be obtained from the publisher before any part of this work may be reproduced or transmitted in any form or by any means, electronic or mechanical, including photocopying and recording, or by any information storage or retrieval system.

Printed in the United States of America

10 9 8 7 6 5 4 3 2 1

ISBN 0-536-94146-7

2004200388

EM

Please visit our web site at *www.pearsoncustom.com*

PEARSON CUSTOM PUBLISHING
75 Arlington Street, Suite 300, Boston, MA 02116
A Pearson Education Company

give me understanding, and I shall live
—Psalms 119:144

In memory of my father, Samuel Kalev (1939–2001)

Preface

When I started the C++ Reference Guide in 2003, I decided to organize it as a C++ textbook. Therefore, the decision to produce a printed version seemed natural to me. Yet, this book isn't a facsimile of the online C++ Reference Guide. I updated certain sections and revised others to facilitate navigation. I also reorganized a few chapters to make them more self-contained. However, following Henry Spencer's "Rule of Least Surprise," I tried to preserve the original structure of the online version as much as possible.

The first 15 chapters contain the mandatory C++ knowledge base with which every C++ programmer should be familiar. These topics include the Special Member Functions, Operator Overloading, Memory Management, Templates, Object-Oriented Programming and Design, the Standard Library, etc.

The C++ Reference Guide has always been more than an online C++ tutorial, though. It has enabled me to react on a weekly basis to new developments in the C++ arena, thereby turning it into an ongoing dialog with the latest trends and emerging technologies. Therefore, this book is also a collection of essays, commentaries and excursions about various topics that aren't necessarily confined to pure C++ programming. Chapter 16, "A Tour of C99," presents the recent changes in standard C, (some of which are currently being incorporated into C++ as well). Chapter 17, "Dynamic Linking," discusses the probable standardization of a dynamic linking interface and demonstrates how POSIX and Windows implement this feature. Chapter 18, "Tips and Techniques," the largest chapter in this book, contains dozens of "how do I?" style recipes for solving common programming tasks, plus short essays about miscellaneous topics: migrating to 64-bit platforms, complex arithmetic, the C++ object model, `const` declarations, and many others. Chapter 19, "Design Patterns," is dedicated to classic Patterns such as Singleton and Monostate. It also discusses pattern-related topics: Anti-patterns and Refactoring. Chapter 20, "C++0X: The New Face of Standard C++," presents some of the latest additions to standard C++, including TR1's `<tuple>` library and the reference wrapper family of classes. Finally, chapter 21, "The Reflecting Circle," is the most philosophical chapter in this book. Here you will find a discussion about the future of programming, a brief tutorial on digital sound compression formats, and even an introduction to the latest buzz, namely Aspect-Oriented-Programming.

This book summarizes more than two years of C++ writing. Whether you're a beginner or a seasoned C++ programmer, I hope this convenient and portable format serves you well in your everyday design and programming engagements.

Acknowledgments

I would like to thank my editor, Esther Schindler, for her brilliant suggestions and insights regarding the organization of the C++ Reference Guide, and no less—for her enduring patience. I would also like to thank Jennifer Bortel from Informit for "making it happen."

Daveed Vandevoorde's intriguing comments and Draft Proposals have more than once shed light on topics that were obscure or new to me.

Finally, I would like to thank my family—particularly my mother Rachel—for their endless support and encouragement.

Danny Kalev

About the Author

Danny Kalev is a certified system analyst and software engineer specializing in C++ and theoretical aspects of formal languages. He recently finished his MA in general linguistics summa cum laude. His MA thesis defies the widely-accepted assumptions regarding the genetic and typological classification of Modern Hebrew. He's now pursuing a PhD degree at Tel Aviv University.

Danny was a member of the C++ standards committee between 1997 and 2000. He is the author of *ANSI/ISO Professional Programmer's Handbook* (1999, ISBN 0789720221) and a co-author of the Waite's Group *C++ How To* (1998, ISBN 1571691596).

Currently, he moderates two C++ forums and contributes regularly to various C++ sites and magazines. He also gives lectures on programming languages and applied linguistics at academic institutes.

In his spare time, Danny likes to listen to classical music, read Victorian literature, explore natural languages (such as Hittite, Basque and Irish Gaelic) and attend a good performance at the West End. Additional interests include archeology, geology, and psychology.

About the Informit Reference Guide Series

The Informit Reference Guides started out as a way to give readers of our Web site a structured tour of key technologies. These online primers provide a basic roadmap to the subject at hand and act as a dynamic document responding to the changing products and technologies that IT professionals (and not-so-professionals) care about deeply. The Guides are hosted by a subject matter expert, who adds a small section to the Guide each week. Over time, this slow and steady augmentation let us take the Guides in some fascinating directions. Some of our Guide hosts focus on tool and techniques; others on case studies or responding to the latest technology news. After several years, we have 15 rich and diverse Reference Guides that say as much about the personalities of the Guide hosts as they do about the technology being discussed.

Now, at the request of our readers, we've decided to take this grand experiment into print, offering a paper-and-ink version of what had previously lived only online. We hope you enjoy this and other books in the print series. And remember, if you can't find a print version, you can always visit us online at *http://www.informit.com/guides/index.asp*

Informit Reference Guide Topics

Adobe® Photoshop®
C++
Digital Lifestyles
IT Management
Java™
Linux® Operating System
Macintosh® Operating System
Macromedia® Flash®
Microsoft® .NET™
Microsoft® Office®
Microsoft® SQL Server™
Microsoft® Windows Server™
Security
Web Design
XML and Web Services

CONTENTS

Chapter 1 What Is C++? 1
   C++ as "Better C" 1
   The Structure of a C++ Program 3
   Overloading 4
   Support for Object-Oriented Programming 6
   Generic Programming 6
      InformIT Articles and Sample Chapters 7
      Books and e-Books 8
      Official Documentation 9

Chapter 2 Special Member Functions: Constructors, Destructors, and the Assignment Operator 11
   Constructors 11
      Trivial Constructors 13
      Pseudo-Constructors of Built-in Types 13
      `explicit` *Constructors* 14
         Constructor Categories 14
      The `explicit` *Keyword* 16
      Advice 16
      Member Initialization Lists 17
      Copy Constructor 20
   Assignment Operator 21
   Destructors 22
      Explicit Destructor Invocation 22
   Summary 23
      InformIT Articles and Sample Chapters 23
      Books and e-Books 24
      Online Resources 24

Chapter 3 Operator Overloading 25
   Operator Overloading Guidelines 26
      Returning Objects by Value 29
      Overloading and User-Defined Types 30
   Conversion Operators 32
   Summary 33
      Books and e-Books 34
      Online Resources 34

Chapter 4 Memory Management 35
   Automatic Storage 35
   Static Storage 36

- The Free Store 36
- POD (Plain Old Data) and Non–POD Objects 37
- `malloc()` and `free()` Versus `new` and `delete` 38
- Support for Object Semantics 38
- Safety 39
- Allocating and Deallocating Arrays Using `new[]` and `delete[]` 39
- Dealing with Exceptions 40
- Placement `new` 41
  - *Allocation Strategies* 42
  - *Using Placement* `new` 42
  - *Explicit Destructor Invocation* 44
  - *Cleanup* 44
  - *Summary* 44
  - *Online Books* 45
  - *Articles* 45
- `nothrow new` 46
  - *A Bit of History* 46
  - *Standard-Compliant* `new` 46
  - `nothrow new`'s *Interface* 47
  - *Putting* `nothrow new` *to Work* 48
  - *Summary* 48
- Member Alignment 49
- Overriding `new` and `delete` 49
  - *Declaring* `new` *and* `delete` *as Class Members* 50
  - *Implementation* 50
  - *Additional Customizations* 51
  - *Usage of* `new` *and* `delete` 51
  - *Overriding* `new` *and* `delete` *Globally* 52
- Using Class `auto_ptr` to Automate Memory Management 53
  - *Exceptions and Dynamic Memory Allocation* 54
  - *Introducing* `std::auto_ptr` 54
  - *Using* `std::auto_ptr` 56
  - `auto_ptr` *Caveats* 56
  - *Summary* 57
- Linkage Types 57
- Guidelines for Effective Memory Management 59
  - *Preferring Automatic Storage to Free Store* 59
  - *Instantiating a Local Object* 61
  - *Zero Initialization* 61
  - *Deleting Pointers* 63
- Summary 64
  - *InformIT Articles and Sample Chapters* 64
  - *Online Resources* 65

Chapter 5 Templates 67
Class Templates 67
Declaring a Class Template 67
Instantiation and Specialization 69
Template Arguments 71
Default Type Arguments 72
Template Specializations 72
Defining a Primary Template 73
Defining a Specialization 74
Partial Specializations 75
Explicit Specialization of a Class Template 75
Function Templates 77
exported Templates 77
The Separate Compilation Model 77
export—How It All Began 78
State of the Art 78
Which Compilers Support export? 78
export and User Expectations 79
Future Directions 80
Conclusions 80
Books 80
Summary 81
InformIT Articles and Sample Chapters 81
Books and e-Books 82
Online Resources 82

Chapter 6 Namespaces 83
Applications of Namespaces 83
Properties of Namespaces 84
Fully Qualified Names 84
using-Declarations and using-Directives 85
Namespace Aliases 86
Argument-Dependent Lookup 86
Using and Extending Namespaces 88
Namespace Members 88
Extending a Namespace 89
Referring to a Namespace Member 91
Interaction with Other Language Features 91
Using the Scope Resolution Operator 91
Using static to Indicate Internal Linkage 92
The Naming Convention of Standard Header Files 92
Summary 93
Online Resources 94

Chapter 7 Time and Date Library 95
    Retrieving the Current Time 95
    Time Differences and Time Zones 97
    Summary 98
        Online Resources 98

Chapter 8 Streams 99
    Standard C++ Stream Objects 99
        Format Flags 101
    Extending `<iostream>` to Support User-Defined Types 102
        Supporting Built-In and Standard Types 102
    Overloading `cout`'s `<<` 103
    Overloading `cin`'s `<<` 105
    Summary 105
    String Streams 106
    File Streams 106
    Summary 107
        Online Resources 108

Chapter 9 Object-Oriented Programming and Design Principles 109
    Abstract Datatyping 110
    Information Hiding 110
    Encapsulation 111
    Inheritance 112
    Polymorphism 114
    Dynamic Binding 115
    Summary 117
    The Rise and Fall of Object Orientation 118
        Traditional Object-Oriented Concepts 118
        Code Reuse 119
        Member Functions 119
        Inheritance 120
    Conclusions 120
        InformIT Articles and Sample Chapters 121
        Online Resources 121

Chapter 10 The Standard Template Library (STL) and Generic Programming 123
    Principles of Generic Programming 123
    Organization of STL Header Files 124
    Containers 125
    The `vector` Container Class 125

`capacity()` *and* `size()`	127
Accessing Elements	128
Front and Back Operations	129
The `queue` *Container Class*	129
Iterators, Part I	130
Pointers as Iterators	130
Iterators in STL	131
Iterator Categories	132
Input Iterators	133
Output Iterators	133
Using Container Iterators	133
Summary	135
Iterators, Part II	135
Bidirectional Iterators	135
Reverse Iterators	137
Random-Access Iterators	137
Iterator Functions	139
Summary	139
The `std::list` Container Class	139
Creating a List Object	139
Dealing with Sequences	140
Choosing the Right Container, Part I	141
`vector`	142
Ayes	142
Nays	142
`list`	142
Ayes	143
Nays	143
`deque`	143
Adaptors	143
`stack`	144
`queue`	144
Summary	144
Choosing the Right Container, Part II	144
Container Reallocation	144
Capacity Versus Size	146
Invalidation of `list` *Iterators*	147
Invalidation of `deque` *Iterators*	147
Summary	148
Choosing the Right Container, Part III	148
Fundamentals of Associative Containers	148
Unique Keys Versus Non-Unique Keys	149
Pairs	149
`map`	149
`multimap`	150

Searching a `multimap`	151
`set`	151
`multiset`	151
Summary	152
Support for User-Defined Types	152
Algorithms	153
`find()`	153
`copy()`	154
`sort()`	154
Function Objects	155
Uses of Function Objects	156
Predicate Objects	157
Adaptors	158
Specialized Containers	158
Associative Containers	159
Class `auto_ptr`	160
Class `string`	160
Constructors	161
Conversion to a C-String	161
Accessing Elements	161
Clearing a `string`	162
`string` *Comparison*	162
String Manipulation	163
Case-Insensitive Comparison	163
Finding a String Within a String	164
Substring Replacement	165
Wonder of Wonders	165
Summary	166
InformIT Articles and Sample Chapters	166
Books and e-Books	167
Online Resources	167

Chapter 11 Exception Handling **169**

Traditional Error-Handling Methods	169
Exception-Handling Constructs	170
Stack Unwinding	171
Passing Exception Objects to a Handler	172
Exception Type Match	172
Exception Objects	173
Exception Specifications	173
The Problem	174
Exception Specifications Basics	174
Exception Specifications and Inheritance	175
Empty Exception Specifications and Missing Exception Specifications	176

Exception Specification Enforcement	176
Exception Specifications Theory and Practice	176
Summary	177
Online Resources	177
Exceptions During Construction and Destruction	178
Global Objects	178
Advanced Exception-Handling Techniques	178
Standard Exceptions	179
Exception Handlers Hierarchy	179
Exceptions and Performance	180
Misuses of Exception Handling	181
Summary	182
InformIT Articles and Sample Chapters	182
Online Resources	183

Chapter 12 Runtime Type Information (RTTI) 185

Getting Along Without RTTI	185
RTTI Constituents	187
`dynamic_cast<>`	190
Crosscasts	191
Downcasting from a Virtual Base	193
Summary	193
InformIT Articles and Sample Chapters	194
Online Resources	194

Chapter 13 The New Cast Operators 195

Presenting the New Cast Operators	195
`static_cast`	196
`const_cast`	197
`reinterpret_cast`	197
`dynamic_cast`	198
Summary	198
Online Resources	198

Chapter 14 Miscellaneous Techniques 201

Lock Files	201
Designing a Locking Policy	201
Implementation	202
Lock File Applications	203
Summary	203
Online Resources	204
Using the `swap()` Algorithm	204
Classic `swap()`	204
Swapping Without a Temporary Object	205

Another Temporary-Free Implementation ... 205
   Summary ... 206
Using Class `stopwatch` for Performance Measurements ... 206
   Design and Implementation ... 207
   Analyzing Performance Using Class `stopwatch` ... 208
   Summary ... 210
Signal Processing ... 210
   Setting a Handler ... 210
   Signaling a Process ... 211
   ANSI `<csignal>` *Limitations* ... 211
   Introducing POSIX Signals ... 212
   Blocking Signals ... 213
   Retrieving Pending Signals ... 213
   Summary ... 213
   Online Resources ... 213
Creating Persistent Objects ... 214
   Serializing Built-In Datatypes ... 214
Serializing Class Objects ... 215
   Performance Optimization ... 216
   Summary ... 217
   Online Resources ... 217
Bit Fields ... 218
   Performance Analysis ... 218
   Bit Field Usage ... 219
   Space Optimization ... 219
   Summary ... 220
   Online Resources ... 221
Environment Variables ... 221
   Defining Environment Variables from the Command Line ... 221
   Reading an Environment Variable Programmatically ... 222
   Setting an Environment Variable ... 223
   Dealing with `wchar_t` *Strings* ... 224
   Uses of Environment Variables ... 224
   Summary ... 225
   Online Resources ... 225
Variadic Functions ... 225
   Uses of Variadic Functions ... 226
   Implementation ... 226
   Object-Oriented Alternatives to Variadic Functions ... 228
   Summary ... 229
   Online Resources ... 229

Chapter 15 Pointers to Functions, Pointers to Members, and Function Objects ... 231

Pointers to Functions ... 231
   Declaring a Function Pointer ... 231
   Passing a Callback Function's Address to Its Caller ... 233
   Calling Conventions ... 233
   Function Pointers and Ordinary Pointers ... 234
   Summary ... 234
Pointers to Members ... 234
   Declaring Pointers to Data Members ... 235
   Manipulating a Data Member Through an Object ... 235
   Manipulating a Data Member Through an Object's Pointer ... 236
   Declaring Pointers to Member Functions ... 236
   The Underlying Representation of Pointers to Members ... 237
   Summary ... 238
   Online Resources ... 238
Function Object ... 238
   Implementing a Function Object ... 239
   Usage of Function Object ... 240
   Template Function Objects ... 240
   Function Objects in the Standard Library ... 241
   Summary ... 242

Chapter 16 A Tour of C99 ... 243

Borrowing from C++ ... 243
   `inline` *Functions* ... 243
   Line Comments ... 244
   Dispersed Statements and Declarations ... 244
   Scope of `for` *Loop Variables* ... 244
Novel Core Features ... 245
   Variable-Length Arrays ... 245
   Designated Initializers ... 245
   Variadic Macros ... 246
   `restrict`-*Qualified Pointers* ... 247
   `long long` *Datatype* ... 247
   The `__func__` *Identifier* ... 247
Obsolete Features ... 248
   Obsolescing K&R Function Declaration Style ... 248
   Implicit `int` ... 248
Summary ... 249

Chapter 17 Dynamic Linking ... 251

Static Linking Versus Dynamic Linking ... 251
Advantages of Dynamic Linking ... 251
   Code Sharing ... 252

- Automatic Updates 252
- Security 252
- Disadvantages of Dynamic Linking 252
  - The "DLL Hell" Problem 253
  - Aliasing 253
  - Code Cracking 253
- Summary 254
- Dynamic Linking by Example 254
  - Building a Shared Library 254
  - The `<dlfcn.h>` Interface 255
  - A `<dlfcn.h>` Example 256
  - Summary 257
  - Books 257

Chapter 18 Tips and Techniques 259
- Using enums as Mnemonic Indexes 259
  - Properties of `enum` Types 259
  - Mnemonic Indexes Requirements 260
  - Mnemonic Indexes in Action 261
  - To `enum` But a Few 263
- POD Initialization 264
  - Built-In Types 264
  - Arrays 265
  - Aggregates 266
  - Unions 267
  - Summary 268
- Object Initialization 268
  - Assignment Versus Initialization 268
  - Member Initialization Lists 269
  - Obligatory Initialization 269
  - Class Constants 270
  - Summary 271
- `const` Declarations 271
  - `const` Objects 271
  - `const` Pointers 272
  - `const` Member Functions 272
  - Complex Declarations 273
  - `const` Pointers of `const` Objects 273
  - operator `const_cast<>` 274
  - Summary 274
  - Sample Chapters 275
  - Books 275
- Project Organization Guidelines 275
  - Units 275

- *Header Files Versus Source Files* 276
- *The "One Entity" Rule* 278
- *File Naming* 278
- *Special Cases* 279
- *Summary* 280
- `inline` Functions 280
  - `inline` *Basics* 280
  - *Usage* 281
  - `inline` *Woes* 282
  - *Summary* 283
  - *Online Resources* 283
  - *Books* 283
- All About `bool` 283
  - *The Pre-`bool` Era* 284
  - *Enter* `bool` 285
  - `bool` *Properties* 286
  - *Summary* 287
  - *Books* 287
- Bitwise Operators, Part I 287
  - *Bitwise and Logical Operators* 288
  - *Bitwise Operators* 288
  - *Bitwise NOT* 288
  - *Bitwise AND* 289
  - *Bitwise OR* 289
  - *Bitwise XOR* 290
  - *Self-Assignment* 290
  - *Bit Shifting* 290
  - *Summary* 292
  - *Books and Online Books* 292
- Bitwise Operators, Part II 292
  - *Resetting a Bit String* 292
  - *Setting a Bit String* 293
  - *Flipping a Bit String* 294
  - *Examining a Single Bit* 294
  - *Summary* 295
- Who's `this`? 295
  - *Analyze* `this` 296
  - *More About* `this` 297
  - *Reanalyze* `this` 299
  - `static` *Member Functions* 299
  - *Summary* 300
  - *Books* 300
- A Reference Guide 300
  - *A Bit of History* 300
  - *Usage* 303

    Advantages of Pass by Reference 303
    Summary 304
    Books 304
The Virtues of Multiple Inheritance 304
    Rationale 305
    MI and the Deadly Diamond of Derivation 305
    Tackling the Ambiguity Problem 306
    Virtual Inheritance and Performance 307
    Summary 308
    Books 308
Interfaces 308
    Interfaces Explained 308
    Abstract Classes 310
    Combining Multiple Interfaces 310
    The DDD Strikes Again 311
    Pure Virtual Functions—Final Refinements 312
    Summary 312
Multiple Inheritance—Construction and Destruction Order 313
    Construction and Destruction of Non-Virtual Bases 313
    Construction and Destruction of Virtual Inheritance 316
    Summary 318
`typedef` Declarations 318
    `typedef` *Basics* 318
    Curbing Convoluted Code 320
    Storage Class Specifiers 320
    Facilitating Code Portability 321
    Summary 321
State of the `union` 322
    What's in a `union`? 322
    `union`*-Based Typecasting* 323
    Anonymous Unions 324
    A `union` *Facelift* 325
    Summary 326
`dynamic_cast` Uses 326
    Limitations of Static Typecasting 326
    Pointer Cast 328
    Reference Cast 328
    Crosscasts 329
    Summary 330
    Books 331
Integrating C and C++ 331
    Does C Still Matter? 331
    Understanding ABI 331
    Problems of Compiler-Specific ABIs 333
    `extern "C"` *Limitations* 334

Summary	334
const Correctness	335
const *Origins*	335
The Meaning of const	335
const *Crash Course*	336
const *Correctness in Practice*	336
const *Parameters*	338
Summary	338
const Correctness—Advanced Issues	338
volatile *Semantics*	338
volatile *Declarations*	339
volatile *Correctness in STL*	340
mutable *Data Members*	340
Summary	341
Books	341
Sprucing Up Legacy Code	342
K&R Style Function Declarations	342
Using char* *instead of* void*	343
Compiled Binaries	343
Defaulting to int	343
Non-Tagged Data Structures	344
Summary	345
Books	345
Virtual Constructors	345
Rationale	345
Virtual Default Constructors	346
Virtual Copy Constructors	347
Memory Management Issues	348
Summary	348
Naming Names	348
The Case for Case-Sensitivity	349
What's in an Identifier?	349
Reserved Identifiers	349
C Reserved Names	350
Keywords	350
Summary	351
Function Calls	352
What's in a Function Call?	352
Function Overhead Scale	352
Thunks	352
Passing Arguments in Registers	353
Intrinsic Functions	353
Calling Conventions	354
Summary	354

Speaking Standardese 354
    Side Effects 354
    Sequence Points 355
    The "Maximal Munch" Rule 356
    Summary 357
    Books 357
Declarations and Definitions 358
    A Source of Confusion 358
    Objects 358
    Types 359
    Functions 361
    Summary 361
`finally` at Last? 362
    Exception Handling in C++ and Java 362
    Destructors Versus `finally()` 362
    Evaluation 364
    Summary 365
Local Classes 365
    A Local What? 365
    Restrictions on Local Classes 366
    Member Functions 367
    Static Members 368
    Summary 369
Complex Arithmetic 369
    Complex Without Complications 369
    Constructors and Initialization 371
    Overloaded Operators 371
    Additional Functions 371
    Implicit Conversions 372
    Summary 373
Floating-Point Woes 373
    The Problem 373
    Relative Operators 374
    Remedies 375
    Summary 375
The Object Model, Part I 376
    Memory Layout of Data Members 376
    Non-Virtual Member Functions 377
    Static Member Functions 378
    Virtual Member functions 378
    Summary 380
The Object Model, Part II 380
    Single Inheritance 380
    Inheritance and Polymorphism 381

  Multiple Inheritance 383
  Virtual Inheritance 383
  Summary 384
The Object Model, Part III 384
  Embedded Objects 384
  Advice 386
  Empty Base Classes 387
  Summary 388
Temporary Objects 388
  Calling All Temps 388
  Temporaries' Anonymity 389
  Temporaries' Lifetime 390
  Summary 391
Temporary Objects—Advanced Techniques 392
  Explicit Instantiation of Temporaries 392
  Syntax Musings 393
  Summary 394
Over-Engineering 394
  Exceptions 395
  Over-Genericity 396
  Excessive Operator Overloading 396
  Summary 397
  Online Resources 398
Migrating to 64-Bit Environments 399
  Compatibility Issues 399
  Built-in Types 399
  Pointers 400
  Member Alignment 400
  ABI 400
  Summary 401
  Online Resources 401
Security Enhancements 402
  C++ and Security 402
  What About C? 402
  `memset()` *and Security* 402
  C-Style String Manipulation 404
  Summary 405
Drop the (Automatic) Pilot 405
  Embedded Literals 405
  Avoid "Unnecessary Journeys" 406
  Multithreading 406
  Internationalization 407
  Summary 407
  Books 408

- Arrays and Pointers 408
  - *When Arrays Behave Like Pointers* 408
  - *. . . and When They Don't* 409
  - `sizeof` *Expressions* 410
  - *Array Wrapping* 410
  - *Summary* 411
- Low-Level File I/O, Part I 412
  - *Back to the Source* 412
  - `open()`, `creat()`, `close()`, *and* `unlink()` 412
  - `read()` *and* `write()` 414
  - *Platform-Specific Issues* 414
- Low-Level File I/O, Part II 415
  - *Buffered I/O and Non-buffered I/O* 415
  - `tell()`, `lseek()` *and* `eof()` 415
  - *Random Access:* `lseek()` 416
  - `eof()` *and Error Handling* 417
  - *Summary* 418
- `static` Declarations, Part I 418
  - *Local* `statics` 418
  - *Initialization* 419
  - *Namespace Scope* `static` *Declarations* 420
- `static` Declarations, Part II 422
  - *Initialization of Non-POD Objects* 422
  - *Static Data Members* 423
  - *Static Member Functions* 423
  - *Static Member Function Implementation* 424
  - *Deprecated—Alas, Unavoidable* 425
  - *Afterthoughts* 426
  - *Online Resources* 426
  - *Books* 426
- Static Initialization Order 427
  - *Initialization Order Dependency* 427
  - *Working Around the Initialization Order Problem* 428
  - *Eliminating Initialization Order Dependency* 429
  - *Final Notes* 430

Chapter 19 Design Patterns 431

- Monostate Pattern 431
  - *Problem Analysis* 432
  - *Enter Monostate* 432
  - *Putting It to Work* 433
  - *Summary* 435
  - *Books* 435
- `Singleton` Pattern 435
  - *Rationale* 436

Implementation	436
Design Considerations	437
Applications	438
Summary	439
Books	439
Anti-Patterns	439
What Is an Anti-Pattern?	440
The History Book on the Shelf . . .	440
. . . Is Almost Repeating Itself	440
Language-Specific Anti-Patterns	440
Analysis and Design Anti-Patterns	441
Organizational Anti-Patterns	441
Summary	442
Online Resources	442
Refactoring	442
What Is Refactoring?	442
Refactoring by Example	443
Refactoring Patterns	444
Summary	445

Chapter 20 C++0X: The New Face of Standard C++ 447

Rationale	447
The `<tuple>` Library	448
Helper Functions	448
Applications	449
Summary	450
Reference Wrapper Class	450
Rationale	450
The `reference_wrapper` Class Template	451
Using `reference_wrapper` with Tuples	452
Summary	453

Chapter 21 The Reflecting Circle 455

The Future of Programming	455
Analysts' Views—Early 1980s	455
Experts' Views—2000–2001	456
Revolution? What Revolution?	457
The Conservative Party	457
Characters and Strings, Part I	458
What's in a Character?	458
Double-Byte Coding	459
Unicode	459
String Representation	460
Recommended Books	460
Characters and Strings, Part II	461

- Seven-Bit Strings 461
- Length-Prefixing 461
- Descriptors 463
- Summary 463
- Online Resources 464
- Sound Bytes 464
  - Overture 464
  - Crescendo 465
  - Recitative 466
  - Diminuendo (Data Compression Versus Data Reduction) 466
    - Finale 467
- Aspect-Oriented Programming 467
  - AOP and ISO C++ 467
  - Another Silver Bullet? 468
  - Join-Points, Point-Cuts, and Advices 468
  - Around the Bend? 470
  - Epilogue 471

Index 473

CHAPTER 1

What Is C++?

C++ is a general-purpose, platform-neutral programming language that supports object-oriented programming and other useful programming paradigms, including procedural programming, object-based programming, generic programming, and functional programming.

C++ is viewed as a superset of C, and thus offers backward compatibility with this language. This reliance on C provides important benefits:

- Reuse of legacy C code in new C++ programs
- Efficiency
- Platform neutrality
- Relatively quick migration from C to C++

Yet it also incurs certain complexities and ailments such as manual memory management, pointers, unchecked array bounds, and a cryptic *declarator* syntax, as described in the following sections.

As opposed to many other programming languages, C++ doesn't have versions. Rather, it has an International ANSI/ISO Standard, ratified in 1998, that defines the core language, its standard libraries, and implementation requirements. The *C++ Standard* is treated as a skeleton on which vendors may add their own platform-specific extensions, mostly by means of code libraries. However, it's possible to develop large-scale applications using pure standard C++, thereby ensuring code portability and easier maintenance.

C++ as "Better C"

The primary reason for selecting C++ is its support of object-oriented programming. Yet even as a procedural programming language, C++ is considered an improvement over ANSI C in several aspects. C programmers who prefer for various reasons not to switch to object-oriented programming can still benefit from the migration to C++ because of its tighter type-safety, strongly typed pointers, improved memory management, and many other features that make a programmer's life easier. Let's look at some of these improvements more closely:

- **Improved memory management**. In C, you have to call library functions to allocate storage dynamically and release it afterward. But C++ treats dynamically allocated objects as first-class citizens: It uses the keywords new and delete to allocate and deallocate objects dynamically.
- **User-defined types are treated as built-in types**. For example, a struct or a union's name can be used directly in declarations and definitions just as a built-in type:

  ```
  struct Date
  {
   int day;
   int month;
   int year;
  };

  Date d; //In C, 'struct' is required before Date
  void func(Date *pdate); //ditto
  ```

- **Pass-by-reference**. C has two types of argument passing: by address and by value. C++ defines a third argument-passing mechanism: passing by reference. When you pass an argument by reference, the callee gets an alias of the original object and can modify it. In fact, references are rather similar to pointers in their semantics; they're efficient because the callee doesn't get a copy of the original variable, but rather a handle that's bound to the original object. Syntactically, however, references look like variables that are passed by value. Here's an example:

  ```
  Date date;
  void func(Date &date_ref); //func takes Date by reference
  func(date); // date is passed by reference, not by value
  ```

- **Default argument values**. C++ allows you to declare functions that take default argument values. When the function call doesn't provide such an argument, the compiler automatically inserts its respective default value into the function call. For example:

  ```
  void authorize(const string & username, bool log=true);
  authorize(user); // equivalent to: authorize(user, true);
  ```

In the function call above, the programmer didn't provide the second argument. Because this argument has a default value, the compiler silently inserted `true` as a second argument.
- **Mandatory function prototypes**. In classic C (this include K&R C, C89, and C95), functions could be called without being previously declared. In C++, you must either declare or define a function before calling it. This way, the compiler can check the type and number of each argument. Without mandatory prototypes, passing arguments by reference or using default argument values wouldn't be possible because the compiler must replace the arguments with their references or add the default values as specified in the prototype.

The Structure of a C++ Program

A well-formed C++ program must contain a `main()` function and a pair of matching braces:

```
int main()
{}
```

Though perfectly valid, this program doesn't really do anything. To get a taste of C++, let's look at a more famous example:

```
#include <iostream>
int main()
{
 std::cout<<"hello world!"<<std::endl;
}
```

If you're a C programmer with little or no prior experience in C++, the code snippet above might shock you. It's entirely different from the equivalent C program:

```
#include <stdio.h>
int main()
{
 printf("hello world!\n");
}
```

Let's take a closer look at the C++ example. The first line is a preprocessor directive that `#includes` the standard `<iostream>` header in the program's source file:

```
#include <iostream>
```

`<iostream>` contains the declarations and definitions of the standard C++ I/O routines and classes. Taking after C, the creators of C++ decided to implement I/O support by means of a code library rather than a built-in keyword. The following line contains the `main()` function. The program's body consists of a single line:

```
std::cout<<"hello world!"<<std::endl;
```

Let's parse it:

- `std::cout` is the *qualified name* of the standard output stream object, `cout`. This object is automatically created whenever you `#include <iostream>`.
- The overloaded *insertion operator* `<<` comes next. It takes an argument and passes it on to `cout`. In this case, the argument is a literal string that we want to print on the screen.
- The second argument, `std::endl`, is a *manipulator* that appends the newline character after the string and forces buffer flushing.

As trivial as this program seems, it exposes some of the most important features of C++. For starters, C++ is an object-oriented language. Therefore, it uses objects rather than functions to perform I/O. Secondly, the standard libraries of C++, including `<iostream>`, are declared in the namespace `std` (std stands for *standard*; an exhaustive discussion about namespaces is available in Chapter 6, "Namespaces"). Thus, instead of declaring standard functions, classes, and objects globally, C++ declares them in a dedicated namespace—thereby reducing the chances of clashing with user code and third-party libraries that happen to use the same names.

Overloading

The operator `<<` is particularly interesting. It behaves as a function that takes an argument, yet it looks like the built-in left-shift operator. In reality, it's an *overloaded operator*. Operator overloading is another fundamental concept of C++. An overloaded operator is a function whose name is an operator rather than a string. You can override almost all the built-in operators of C++ (+, *, >, and so on) this way. Operator overloading may sound revolutionary and even dangerous at first; after all, if programmers are free to override the meaning of built-in operators, what's to stop them from defining operator + as the subtraction operator? Rest assured: C++ imposes certain restrictions on operator overloading. The combination of these restrictions and good object-oriented practices guarantees that this feature makes code uniform and intuitive.

Consider the notion of a string. In C, assigning strings with the = operator is not allowed. By contrast, the C++ `std::string` class overloads this operator and enables you to perform direct assignments of strings. For example:

```
std::string s;
s= "please fasten your seatbelt";
```

Without operator overloading, the snippet would look like this:

```
std::string s;
s.assign("please fasten your seatbelt");
```

When dealing with numeric libraries, the ability to overload operators (such as ==, +, and -) for user-defined types is particularly useful.

Overloading in C++ isn't limited to operators. You can also overload functions by giving two or more functions an identical name. The overloaded functions are distinguished by their parameter list. For example, a function that opens a file may have three different overloaded versions:

```
int file_open(int descriptor); // #1
int file_open(const char *pathname); // #2
int file_open(const string & pathname); // #3
```

The compiler determines which of the three overloaded versions is to be called by examining the function's argument. For example:

```
std::string file="modem.log";
file_open(file); // call file_open() #3
```

The resolution is static, meaning that it takes place at compile-time. There are two advantages in static overloading resolution: The compiler is able to detect incorrect arguments, and there's no performance overhead.

Like C, C++ supports the "separate compilation" model, whereby a program may consist of individual source files that are compiled separately. These files are translated into object files that are later linked to produce a single executable file. Unlike several modern programming languages, however, a C++ source file is compiled into native machine code, not bytecodes or any other form of intermediary code that needs to be translated further at runtime. The advantage is efficiency—the compiled code is optimized for the target hardware. The tradeoff is the lack of binary compatibility—the compiled code is platform dependent.

Support for Object-Oriented Programming

Although C++ didn't define object-oriented programming, it was the first widely used programming language that supported this paradigm. Undoubtedly, you've heard of object-oriented programming before. But what does it really mean? An object-oriented programming language must support these features:

- Abstract datatyping
- Information hiding
- Encapsulation
- Dynamic binding
- Polymorphism
- Inheritance

Chapter 9, "Object-Oriented Programming and Design Principles," discusses these concepts in detail. However, suffice it to say that C++ supports all of these criteria as well as many others.

Generic Programming

As stated previously, C++ supports many useful programming paradigms in addition to object orientation—such as *generic programming*. Generic programming enables programmers to write algorithms and classes that are type-independent. The programmer writes a single code mold called a *template*, from which the compiler synthesizes type-specific instances. For example, a generic swap algorithm may be defined as follows:

```
template <typename T> void swap( T & t1, T & t2)
{
 T temp=t1;
 t1=t2;
 t2=temp;
}
int n=5, m=10;
swap(n,m);
```

The compiler treats the template function above as a mold from which it generates an instance of `swap()` that applies to type `int`. In other words, it replaces the symbol `T` with the concrete type `int`. This is quite similar to the way macros work, except that in this case the compiler rather than the preprocessor expands the template. Consequently, it's able to detect type mismatches and other violations of syntax rules. Not very surprisingly, the Standard Library has a `swap()` algorithm, so you don't have to implement it by yourself. In fact, the Standard Library contains dozens of useful generic algorithms that count, sort, merge, replace, splice, and do many other useful operations.

In addition to function templates, C++ supports *class templates*. A class template serves as a mold from which other classes are instantiated. Class templates are widely used in the Standard Library as generic containers—`list`, `vector`, `stack`, and so on. A rich set of generic algorithms that operate on generic containers is one of the main strengths of C++.

InformIT Articles and Sample Chapters

"A Tour of C++" (*http://www.informit.com/articles/article.asp?p=25003*) is a sample chapter from *The C++ Programming Language, Special Edition* (Addison-Wesley, 2000, 0201700735), by Bjarne Stroustrup. This article is an excellent introduction to C++, its standard library, and the various programming paradigms it supports. Stroustrup uses real-world examples to demonstrate the differences between the design and implementation techniques used in each paradigm while exhibiting all the niceties of C++: its core features as well as its rich Standard Library. (For more on this book, visit *http://www.informit.com/bookstore/product.asp?isbn=0201700735*.)

"Generic Programming and the C++ Standard Library" (*http://www.informit.com/articles/article.asp?p=25142*) is a sample chapter from *More Exceptional C++: 40 New Engineering Puzzles, Programming Problems, and Solutions* (Addison-Wesley, 2001, ISBN 020170434X), by Herb Sutter.

This article shows some of the power and flexibility of the C++ standard library. Prior experience with the language is assumed, so this article is ideal for the C++ programmer who want to learn how to use STL (short for *Standard Template Library*) and understand its design concepts. (For more on this book, visit *http://www.informit.com/bookstore/product.asp?isbn=020170434X*.)

"Programming Languages: The Early Years" (*http://www.informit.com/articles/article.asp?p=31670*), by Greg Perry, is a short and nice overview of the evolution of the early programming languages. While most novices are keen to learn the newest buzzwords, familiarity with the breakthroughs as well as the flops of the previous programming languages may help them understand some of the design decisions of C++ creators.

Books and e-Books

The C++ Programming Language, Special Edition (Addison-Wesley, 2000, 0201700735), by Bjarne Stroustrup, is undoubtedly the best C++ book you can find today. Written by the creator of the language, the book covers in detail every aspect of the language. Stroustrup has always used real-world examples and his numerous years of experience in the software development field are well-reflected in every paragraph. Unlike most other C++ books, which merely teach programming techniques, this book contains dozens of tips and practical pieces of advice from a world-renowned authority. Certainly, a must-have for every serious C++ programmer. (For more on this book, visit *http://www.informit.com/bookstore/product.asp?isbn=0201700735*.)

C++ Primer, Third Edition (Addison-Wesley, 1998, ISBN 0201824701), by Stanley B. Lippman and Josée LaJoie, is a well-written C++ primer. Both authors are renowned C++ experts (LaJoie was IBM's representative to the ANSI standardization committee). The book excels in its coverage of C++. The authors carefully explain not just *how*, but *why* things are the way they are in C++. (For more on this book, visit *http://www.informit.com/bookstore/product.asp?isbn=0201824701*.)

The ANSI/ISO Professional Programmer's Handbook (Que, 1999, ISBN 0789720221), by Danny Kalev, discusses the changes that were introduced to the C++ standard in the late 1990s, explains the rationale behind them, and contrasts them with the pre-standard conventions and specifications. This book is primarily aimed at intermediate-to-advanced programmers who aren't fully aware of the latest changes in the language's specifications, including namespaces, RTTI, new cast operators, `bool`, covariant return, standard header names, and many other tidbits. The book contains extensive code samples, all of which are fully ANSI/ISO–compliant. (For more on this book, visit *http://www.informit.com/bookstore/product.asp?isbn=0789720221.*)

Official Documentation

A slightly outdated copy of the C++ standard is available via FTP at the AT&T Labs Research site (visit *ftp://ftp.research.att.com/dist/c++std/WP/CD2*). Note, however, that the standard itself isn't a C++ tutorial, and it's written in "Standardese," so it's mostly useful for checking the validity of certain constructs and expressions.

CHAPTER 2

Special Member Functions: Constructors, Destructors, and the Assignment Operator

Objects are the fundamental unit of abstraction in object-oriented programming. In a broad sense, an *object* is a region of memory storage. Class objects have properties that are determined when the object is initialized. Conceptually, every class object has four *special member functions*: default constructor, copy constructor, assignment operator, and destructor. If these members are not explicitly declared by the programmer, the implementation implicitly declares them. This chapter surveys the semantics of the special member functions and their roles in class design and implementation.

Constructors

A *constructor* initializes an object. A *default constructor* is one that can be invoked without any arguments. If there is no user-declared constructor for a class, and if the class doesn't contain const or reference data members, C++ implicitly declares a default constructor for it. Such an implicitly declared default constructor performs the initialization operations needed to create an object of this type. Note, however, that these operations don't involve initialization of user-declared data members. For example:

```
class C
{
private:
  int n;
```

```
  char *p;
public:
  virtual ~C() {}
};

void f()
{
  C obj;   // 1 implicitly-defined constructor is invoked
}
```

C++ synthesized a constructor for class C because it contains a virtual member function. Upon construction, C++ initializes a hidden data member called the *virtual pointer*, which every polymorphic class has. This pointer holds the address of a dispatch table that contains all the virtual member functions' addresses for that class. The synthesized constructor doesn't initialize the data members n and p, nor does it allocate memory for the data pointed to by the latter. These data members have an indeterminate value after the initialization of obj. This is because the synthesized default constructor performs only the initialization operations that are required by the implementation—not the programmer—to construct an object.

Other implementation-required operations that are performed by implicitly defined constructors are the invocation of a base class constructor and the invocation of embedded object's constructor. However, C++ doesn't declare a constructor for a class if the programmer has defined one. For example:

```
class C
{
private:
  int n;
  char *p;
public:
  C() : n(0), p(0) {}
  virtual ~C() {}
};
C obj;   // 1 user-defined constructor is invoked
```

Now the data members of the object obj are initialized because the user-defined constructor was invoked to create it. This still leaves us with a mystery: The user-defined constructor only initializes the data members n and p. When did the initialization of the virtual pointer take place? Here's the answer: The compiler augments the user-defined constructor with additional code, which is inserted into the constructor's body before any user-written code, and performs the necessary initialization of the virtual pointer.

Trivial Constructors

As noted previously, compilers synthesize a default constructor for every class or `struct`, unless a constructor was already defined by the user. However, in certain conditions, such a synthesized constructor is redundant:

```
class Empty {};
struct Person
{
  char name[20];
  double salary;
  int age;
};
int main()
{
  Empty e;
  Person p;
  p.age = 30;   // public access allowed, no constructor needed
  return 0;
}
```

C++ can instantiate `Empty` and `Person` objects without a constructor. In such cases, the implicitly declared constructor is said to be *trivial*. The fact that a constructor is considered trivial means that neither the programmer nor the compiler generates code for it. We'll discuss this in greater detail shortly.

Pseudo-Constructors of Built-in Types

You might be surprised to hear this: Built-in types such as `char`, `int`, and `float` also have constructors—at least syntactically they appear to have them. You can initialize a variable by explicitly invoking its default constructor:

```
char c = char();
int n = int ();
return 0;
```

This expression:

```
char c = char();
```

is equivalent to this one:

```
char c = char(0);
```

Of course, it's possible to initialize a fundamental type with values other than 0:

```
float f = float (0.333);
char c = char ('a');
int *pi= new int (10);
float *pf = new float (0.333);
```

Note that this form is just "syntactic sugar." It's interchangeable with the more widely used form:

```
char c = 'a';
float f = 0.333;
```

explicit Constructors

Constructors have many peculiar characteristics: they don't have a name (and therefore can't be called directly, as opposed to ordinary member functions), they don't have a return value and their address cannot be taken. Non-default constructors are even peculiar. A constructor that takes a single argument operates as an implicit conversion operator by default. (For details, see Chapter 3, "Operator Overloading.")

Next, I will explore this phenomenon in further detail and explain how to use the `explicit` qualifier to restrain constructors' behavior.

Constructor Categories

In essence, constructors are what differentiates between a POD struct and a real object, as they automatically shape a raw chunk of memory into an object with a determinate state. A class may have several constructors (I'm referring to "plain constructors" in this discussion, not to copy constructors), each of which takes a different number of arguments. A constructor that can be called without any arguments is a *default constructor*. A non-default constructor is one that takes one or more arguments; there's no special name for this type of constructors in the C++ literature, so I'm referring to it as a "non-default constructor." Non-default constructors are further divided into two subcategories: those that take a single argument and thus operate as implicit conversion operators, and those that take multiple arguments. For example,

```
class Date
{
public:
```

```
  Date(); // default ctor; no arguments required
//non-default ctors:
Date(time_t t); // extracts date from a time_t value
Date(int d, int m, int y);
};
```

NOTE: For more on POD structs, see Chapter 4, "Memory Management."

class `Date` has three constructors. The first one is a default constructor. The second one, which takes a single argument, operates as an implicit `time_t` to D conversion operator. As such, it will be invoked automatically in a context that requires a `long` to `Date` conversion. For example,

```
Date d=std::time(0);// invokes ctor # 2 to create d
```

NOTE: Remember that `time_t` is a synonym for `long` or a similar integral type. See Chapter 7, "Time and Date Library," for more on `time_t`.

You're probably wondering how it works. Under the hood, the compiler transforms this code into something like this:

```
//pseudo C++ code
time_t __value;
__value = std::time(0);
Date __temp(__value);//create a temporary Date object
Date d = __temp;
temp.C::~C(); //destroy temp
```

In this example, the automatic conversion is intentional and useful. Yet there are many cases in which an implicit conversion is undesirable, for example:

```
Date p=NULL; //actually meant 'Date *p=NULL'; compiles OK
```

Can you see what's happening here? `NULL` is defined as `0` or `0L` in C++. The compiler silently transformed the code above into this:

```
//pseudo C++ code
Date temp(0L);//create a temporary Date object
Date d = temp; //assigned using operator =
temp.C::~C(); //destroy temp
```

The `explicit` Keyword

The problem here is that the implicit conversion taking place behind the programmer's back switches off the compiler's static type checking. Without this implicit conversion the compiler would have complained about a type mismatch. C++ creators perceived this problem long ago. They decided to add a "patch" to the language in the form of the keyword `explicit`. Constructors declared `explicit` will refuse to perform such implicit conversions:

```
class Date
{
//...
 explicit Date(time_t t); // no implicit conversions
};
```

Now, the previous examples will not compile:

```
Date d =std::time(0); //error, can't convert 'long' to 'Date'
Date p=NULL; //also an error
```

If you want to convert a `time_t` or any other integral value to a `Date` object, you need to use an explicit conversion now:

```
Date d(std::time(0)); //OK
Date d2= Date(std::time(0)); //same meaning as above
```

Advice

If you examine a code corpus, say the Standard Library, you will see that most of the constructors taking one argument are `explicit`. You could argue that this should have been the default behavior of constructors, whereas constructors that permit implicit conversions should have been the exception. Put differently, instead of `explicit`, C++ creators should have introduced the keyword `implicit` and changed the semantics of constructors so that they didn't function as implicit conversion operators. However, this approach would have caused existing code to break. In some classes, for example `std::complex` and other mathematical classes, implicit conversions are rather useful. C++ creators therefore decided to leave the original semantics constructors intact, while introducing a mechanism for disabling implicit conversions, when necessary.

NOTE: For more on the STL, see Chapter 10, "The Standard Template Library (STL) and Generic Programming."

As a rule, every constructor that takes a single argument, including constructors that take multiple arguments with default values such as the following, should be `explicit`, unless you have a good reason to allow implicit conversions:

```
class File
{
public:
  //this ctor may be called with a single argument
  //it's therefore declared explicit:
  explicit File(const char *name,
            ios_base::openmode mode=ios_base::out,
            long protection = 0666);
};
```

Member Initialization Lists

A constructor may include a member initialization (mem-initialization for short) list that initializes the object's data members. For example:

```
class Cellphone //1: initialization by mem-init
{
private:
  long number;
  bool on;
public:
  Cellphone (long n, bool ison) : number(n), on(ison) {}
};
```

The constructor of `Cellphone` can also be written as follows:

```
Cellphone (long n, bool ison) //2: initialization within ctor's body
{
  number = n;
  on = ison;
}
```

There is no substantial difference between the two forms in this case because the compiler scans the mem-initialization list and inserts its code into the constructor's body before any user-written code. Thus, the constructor in the first example is expanded by the compiler into the constructor in the second example. Nonetheless, the choice between using a mem-initialization list and initialization inside the constructor's body is significant in the following four cases:

- Initialization of `const` members. For example:

```
class Allocator
{
private:
  const int chunk_size;
public:
  Allocator(int size) : chunk_size(size) {}
};
```

- Initialization of reference members. For example:

```
class Phone;
class Modem
{
private:
  Phone & line;
public:
  Modem(Phone & ln) : line(ln) {}
};
```

- Passing arguments to a constructor of a base class or an embedded object. For example:

```
class base
{
//...
public:
  //no default ctor
  base(int n1, char * t) {num1 = n1; text = t; }
};
class derived : public base
{
private:
  char *buf;
public:
  //pass arguments to base constructor
  derived (int n, char * t) : base(n, t) { buf = (new char[100]);}
};
```

- Initialization of member objects. For example:

```
#include<string>
using std::string;
```

```
class Website
{
private:
  string URL;
  unsigned int IP;
public:
  Website()
  {
  URL = "";
  IP = 0;
  }
};
```

In the first three cases, a mem-initialization list is mandatory because these initializations must be completed before the constructor's execution. Conceptually, initializations listed in a member-initialization list take place before the constructor executes. In the fourth case, the use of a mem-init list is optional. However, it can improve performance in certain cases because it eliminates unnecessary creation and subsequent destruction of objects that would occur if the initialization were performed inside the constructor's body.

Due to the performance difference between the two forms of initializing embedded objects, some programmers use mem-initialization exclusively. Note, however, that the order of the initialization list has to match the order of declarations within the class. This is because the compiler transforms the list so that it coincides with the order of the declaration of the class members, regardless of the order specified by the programmer. For example:

```
class Website
{
private:
  string URL; //1
  unsigned int IP; //2
public:
  Website() : IP(0), URL("") {} // initialized in reverse order
};
```

In the mem-initialization list, the programmer first initializes the member IP and then URL, even though IP is declared after URL. The compiler transforms the initialization list to the order of the member declarations within the class. In this case, the reverse order is harmless. When there are dependencies in the order of initialization list, however, this transformation can cause surprises. For example:

```
class Mystring
{
private:
  char *buff;
  int capacity;
public:
  explicit Mystring(int size) :
  capacity(size), buff (new char [capacity]) {} undefined behavior
};
```

The mem-initialization list in the constructor of `Mystring` doesn't follow the order of declaration of `Mystring`'s members. Consequently, the compiler transforms the list like this:

```
explicit Mystring(int size) :
buff  (new char [capacity]), capacity(size) {}
```

The member `capacity` specifies the number of bytes that `new` has to allocate, but it hasn't been initialized. The results in this case are undefined. There are two ways to avert this pitfall: Change the order of member declarations so that `capacity` is declared before `buff`, or move the initialization of `buff` into the constructor's body.

Copy Constructor

A *copy constructor* initializes its object with another object. If there is no user-defined copy constructor for a class, C++ implicitly declares one. A copy constructor is said to be *trivial* if it's implicitly declared, if its class has no virtual member functions and no virtual base classes, and if its entire direct base classes and embedded objects have trivial copy constructors. The implicitly defined copy constructor performs a memberwise copy of its sub-objects, as in the following example:

```
#include[string]
using std::string;
class Website //no user-defined copy constructor
{
private:
  string URL;
  unsigned int IP;
public:
  Website() : IP(0), URL("") {}
};
```

```
int main ()
{
  Website site1;
  Website site2(site1); //invoke implicitly defined copy constructor
}
```

The programmer didn't declare a copy constructor for class `Website`. Because `Website` has an embedded object of type `std::string`, which happens to have a user-defined copy constructor, the implementation implicitly defines a copy constructor for class `Website` and uses it to copy-construct the object `site2` from `site1`. The synthesized copy constructor first invokes the copy constructor of `std::string`, and then performs a bitwise copying of the data members of `site1` into `site2`.

Novices are sometimes encouraged to define the four special member functions for every class they write. As can be seen in the case of the `Website` class, not only is this unnecessary, but it's even undesirable under some conditions. The synthesized copy constructor (and the assignment operator, described in the next section) already "do the right thing." They automatically invoke the constructors of base and member sub-objects, they initialize the virtual pointer (if one exists), and they perform a bitwise copying of fundamental types. In many cases, this is exactly the programmer's intention anyway. Furthermore, the synthesized constructor and copy constructor enable the implementation to create code that's more efficient than user-written code, because it can apply optimizations that aren't always possible otherwise.

Assignment Operator

An *assignment operator* assigns to its object another object. For example:

```
std::string s1="hello";
std::string s2;
s2=s1;
```

If there's no user-defined assignment operator for a class, C++ implicitly declares one. An implicitly declared assignment operator has the following form:

```
C& C::operator=(const C&);
```

An assignment operator is said to be *trivial* if it's implicitly declared, if its class has no virtual member functions or virtual base classes, and if its direct base classes and embedded objects have a trivial assignment operator.

Destructors

A *destructor* destroys an object of its class type. It takes no arguments and has no return type (not even `void`). `const` and `volatile` qualities are not applied on an object under destruction; therefore, `const`, `volatile`, or `const volatile` objects may have a destructor. If no user-defined destructor exists for a class, the implementation implicitly declares one. A destructor is trivial if it's implicitly declared and if its direct-base classes and embedded objects have trivial destructors. Otherwise, the destructor is nontrivial. A destructor invokes the destructors of the direct base classes and member objects of its class. The invocation occurs in the reverse order of their construction.

Explicit Destructor Invocation

C++ automatically invokes destructors in the following cases:

- For static objects at program termination
- For an automatic object when the block in which the object is created exits
- For a temporary object when the lifetime of the temporary object ends
- For objects allocated on the free store using `new`, through the use of `delete`
- During stack unwinding that results from an exception

You can also call a destructor explicitly. For example:

```
class C
{
public:
~C() {}
};

void destroy(C& c)
{
   c.C::~C(); //explicit destructor activation
}
```

A destructor can also be explicitly invoked from within a member function of its object:

```
void C::destroy()
{
  this->C::~C();
}
```

In particular, explicit destructor invocation is necessary for objects that were created by the placement `new`. (placement `new` is discussed in Chapter 4, "Memory Management.")

Summary

The constructor, copy constructor, assignment operator, and destructor automate most of the tedium associated with creating, copying, and destroying objects. The symmetry between a constructor and a destructor in C++ is rare among object-oriented programming languages, and it serves as the basis for advanced design idioms.

Each C++ object possesses the four member functions; they're either declared by the programmer or implicitly declared. An implicitly declared special member function can be trivial, which means that C++ doesn't define it. The synthesized special member functions perform only operations that are required by the implementation. User-written special member functions are automatically augmented by the compiler to ensure the proper initialization of base and embedded sub-objects and the virtual pointer.

A mem-initialization list is necessary for the initialization of `const` and reference data members, as well as to pass arguments to a base or embedded sub-object. In all other cases, a mem-initialization list is optional but can enhance performance.

InformIT Articles and Sample Chapters

"Implementing a Stopwatch Class for Performance Measurements" (*http://gethelp.devx.com/techtips/cpp_pro/10min/10min0500.asp*), by Danny Kalev, shows how to implement a stopwatch class that relies on the "resource acquisition is initialization" idiom. In essence, the technique shown here relies on the symmetry between constructors and destructors.

Books and e-Books

The Design and Evolution of C++ (Addison-Wesley, 1994, ISBN 0201543303), by Bjarne Stroustrup, is an exhaustive historical account of the evolution of C++ and the design decisions that its creators made during its standardization process. This book is useful for those of you who wonder why C++ features are implemented the way they are, as well as for compiler writers who want to know the gory details of how high-level C++ features are implemented under the hood. (For more on this book, visit *http://www.informit.com/bookstore/product.asp?isbn=0201543303*.)

C++ Primer, Third Edition (Addison-Wesley, 1998, ISBN 0201824701), by Stanley B. Lippman and Josée LaJoie, is a well-written C++ primer. Both authors are renowned C++ experts (LaJoie was IBM's representative to the ANSI standardization committee). The book excels in its coverage of C++. The authors carefully explain not just *how*, but *why* things are the way they are in C++. (For more on this book, visit *http://www.informit.com/bookstore/product.asp?isbn=0201824701*.)

Online Resources

Bjarne Stroustrup's page of Frequently Asked Questions (*http://www.research.att.com/~bs/bs_faq2.html*) addresses, among other things, the special member functions. Examples of questions that you'll find here: "Why don't we have virtual constructors?" "Why are destructors not virtual by default?"

CHAPTER 3

Operator Overloading

Object-oriented (OO) programming languages treat user-defined types as first-class citizens. One of the manifestations of this principle is that programmers can extend the semantics of built-in operators to support user-defined types as if they were built-in types. Such an extension *overloads* rather than overrides the predefined meaning of an operator.

NOTE: C++ requires at least one of the operands of an overloaded operator to be a user-defined type.

Although you can use ordinary functions for the same purpose, operator overloading provides a uniform notational convention that's clearer than the ordinary function call syntax. Consider the following example:

```
Monday < Tuesday; //overloaded <

Greater_than(Monday, Tuesday);
```

Clearly, the use of an overloaded < operator is a better choice.

The capacity to redefine the meaning of a built-in operator in C++ was a source of criticism. People (mostly C programmers making the migration to C++) felt that overloading an operator was as dangerous as enabling the programmer to add, remove, or change keywords of the language. Still, notwithstanding the potential Tower of Babel that might arise as a result, operator overloading is one of the most fundamental features of C++ and is mandatory in generic programming, as the following sections will show. Today, even languages that tried to do without operator overloading are in the process of adding this feature.

An overloaded operator is merely a function whose name is an operator preceded by the keyword `operator`. The following code listing defines an overloaded version of `operator <` that compares two `Book` objects and returns the one with the lower ISBN (for example, to sort a book collection by ISBN):

```
class Book
{
private:
  long ISBN;
public:
//...
  long get_ISBN() const { return ISBN;}
};

//overloaded  version of <
bool operator < (const Book& b1, const Book& b2)
{
  return b1.get_ISBN() < b2.get_ISBN();
}
```

Operator Overloading Guidelines

When you're overloading an operator to support a user-defined type, it's recommended that you adhere to the basic semantics of the corresponding built-in operator. In other words, an overloaded operator has the same side effects on its operands and manifests the same interface as does the corresponding built-in operator.

Most of the overloaded operators can be declared either as class member functions or as external functions. In the following example, the operator == is overloaded as a non-static class member:

```
class Date
{
private:
  int day;
  int month;
  int year;
public:
  bool operator == (const Date & d ); // 1: member function
};
```

Alternatively, it can be declared as a `friend` function:

```
// overloading == as an external function
class Date;
bool operator ==( const Date & d1, const Date& d2);
class Date
```

```
{
private:
  int day;
  int month;
  int year;
public:
  friend bool operator ==( const Date & d1, const Date& d2);
};
```

However, the operators [], (), =, and -> can only be declared as non-static member functions; this ensures that their first operand is an *lvalue*.

When you overload an operator, adhere to the interface of its built-in counterpart. The interface of an operator consists of the number of operands to which it applies, whether any of these operands can be altered by the operator, and the return value of that operator. For example, consider operator ==. Its built-in version is applicable to a wide variety of fundamental types, including `int`, `bool`, `float`, and `char`, and to pointers. In all these cases, the built-in == operator tests its left and right operands for equality and returns a result of type `bool`. Note that == doesn't modify any of its operands and that their order is immaterial. To implement all these features in an overloaded ==, define it as a `friend` function rather than a member function. The following example shows the difference between these two options:

```
class Date
{
private:
  int day;
  int month;
  int year;
public:
  Date();
  bool  operator == (const Date & d) const;   // 1 asymmetrical
  //2 symmetrical
  friend bool operator ==(const Date& d1, const Date& d2);
};

bool operator ==(const Date& d1, const Date& d2);
```

The member overloaded operator == (1) is inconsistent with the built-in operator == because its arguments have different types. The compiler transforms the member operator == into the following:

```
bool  Date::operator == (const Date *const,  const Date&) const;
```

The first argument is the implicit `this` pointer. The second argument is a reference to `const Date`. By contrast, the `friend` version takes two arguments of the same type. There are practical implications to favoring the `friend` version over the member function. STL algorithms rely on a symmetrical version of the overloaded operator ==. For example, containers that store objects that don't have symmetrical operator == cannot be sorted.

Another example, built-in operator +=, which also takes two operands, modifies its left operand but leaves the right operand unchanged. The interface of an overloaded += needs to reflect the fact that it modifies its object but not its right operand. This is reflected by the declaration of the function parameter as `const`, whereas the function itself is a non-`const` member function:

```
class Date
{
...
public:
  Date();
  //built-in += changes its left operand but not its right one
  //the same behavior is maintained here
  Date & operator += (const Date & d);
};
```

To conclude, it can be said that every overloaded operator must implement the same interface of its built-in counterpart.

As previously noted, an overloaded operator is a function that's declared with the `operator` keyword, immediately followed by an *operator ID*. An operator ID can be one of the following:

```
new   delete   new[]   delete[]
+     -    *    /    %    ^    &    |    ~
!     =    <    >    +=   -=   *=   /=   %=
^=    &=   |=   <<   >>   >>=  <<=  ==   !=
<=    >=   &&   ||   ++   --   ,    ->*  ->
()    []
```

In addition, the following operators can be overloaded both in their unary and binary forms:

```
+    -    *    &
```

Derived classes inherit the overloaded operators of their base classes in the same manner as ordinary member functions are inherited (the assignment operator is an exception).

An overloaded operator must take at least one argument of a user-defined type. This rule ensures that users cannot alter the meaning of expressions that contain only fundamental types. For example:

```
int i,j,k;
k = i + j; //always uses built-in = and +
```

An overloaded operator extends a built-in one, so you cannot introduce new operators into the language.

Neither the precedence nor the number of arguments of an operator can be altered. For example, an overloaded && must have exactly two arguments, as does the built-in && operator. In addition, you can't change the precedence of an operator. A sequence of two or more overloaded operators, t2<t1/t2, is evaluated according to the precedence rules of the built-in operators. Because the division (/) operator ranks higher than the less-than (<) operator, the expression is always interpreted as t2<(t1/t2), whether < is an overloaded version or not.

Unlike ordinary functions, overloaded operators cannot declare a parameter with a default value, although operator () is the exception to this rule.

Several operators cannot be overloaded. These operators take a name, rather than an object, as their right operand:

- Direct member access (.)
- Deference pointer to class member (.*)
- Scope resolution (::)
- Size of (sizeof)

The conditional operator (?:) also cannot be overloaded.

Additionally, the new typecast operators—static_cast<>, dynamic_cast<>, reinterpret_cast<>, and const_cast<>—and the # and ## preprocessor tokens cannot be overloaded.

Returning Objects by Value

Large objects are usually passed to or returned from a function by reference or by their addresses. In a few circumstances, however, the best choice is to return an object by value. Operator + is an example of this situation. It has to return a result object, but it cannot modify any of its operands. The seemingly natural choice is to allocate the result object dynamically and return its address. But this is not such a good idea. Dynamic memory allocation is significantly slower than local storage. It also might fail and throw an exception. Worse yet, this solution is error-prone because it's unclear who is responsible for deleting this object.

Returning a reference to a static object might seem tempting:

```
class Year
{
private:
  int year;
public:
  Year(int y = 0) : year(y) {}
  Year& operator + (const Year& other) const; //returns a reference to
                                              //a local static Year
  int getYear() const;
  void setYear(int y);
};

Year& Year::operator + (const Year& other) const
{
  static Year result;
  result = Year(this->getYear() + other.getYear() );
  return result;
}
```

Alas, on each invocation of the overloaded operator, the *same object* is being modified and returned to the caller. Therefore, the safest and most efficient solution is to return the result object by value:

```
class Year
{
private:
  int year;
public:
  Year(int y = 0) : year(y) {}
  //return Year object by value
  Year operator + (const Year& other) const; int getYear() const;
  void setYear(int y);
};

Year Year::operator + (const Year& other) const
{
  return Year(this->getYear() + other.getYear() );
}
```

Overloading and User-Defined Types

Overloading isn't limited to classes. You can overload an operator for enum types as well. Here's an example:

```cpp
#include <iostream>
using namespace std;

enum Days
{
  Monday,
  Tuesday,
  Wednesday,
  Thursday,
  Friday,
  Saturday,
  Sunday
};

Days& operator++(Days& d, int)   // postfix ++
{
  if (d == Sunday)
     return d = Monday; //rollover
  int temp = d; //convert to an int
  return d = static_cast<Days> (++temp);
}

int main()
{
 Days day = Monday;
 for (;;) //display days as integers
  {
   cout<< day <<endl;
   day++; // overloaded ++
   if (day == Sunday)
      break;
  }
  return 0;
}
```

If you prefer to view the enumerators in their symbolic representation rather than as integers, you can overload the operator << as well:

```cpp
//display Days in symbolic form
ostream& operator<<(ostream& os, Days d)
{
   switch(d)
   {
   case Monday:
```

```
      return os<<"Monday";
   case Tuesday:
      return os<<"Tuesday";
   case Wednesday:
      return os<<"Wednesday";
   case Thursday:
      return os<<"Thursday";
   case Friday:
      return os<<"Friday";
   case Saturday:
      return os<<"Saturday";
   case Sunday:
      return os<<"Sunday";
   default:
      return os<<"Unknown";
   }
}
```

Conversion Operators

A *conversion operator* can be thought of as a user-defined typecasting operator; it converts its object to a different type in contexts that require that specific type. The conversion is done automatically. For example:

```
class Mystring
{
private:
  char *s;
  int size;
public:
  Mystring();
  //convert Mystring  to a C-string
  operator const char * () {return s; } //...
};

int n = strcmp(str, "Hello"); //OK, automatic conversion of str
                              //to const char *
```

Conversion operators differ from ordinary overloaded operators in two ways. First, a conversion operator has no return value (not even `void`). The return value is inferred from the operator's name. Secondly, a conversion operator takes no arguments. Conversion operators can convert their objects to any given type, fundamental and user-defined alike:

```
struct DateRep   //legacy C code
{
  char day;
  char month;
  short year;
};

class Date // object-oriented wrapper
{
private:
  DateRep dr;
public:
  // automatic conversion to DateRep
  operator DateRep () const { return dr;} };

// C-based communication API function
extern "C" int transmit_date(DateRep);

int main()
{
  Date d;
  //...use d

  //transmit date object as a binary stream to a remote client
  int ret_stat = transmit_date(d); //using legacy communication API
  return 0;
}
```

Summary

Operator overloading is one of the most fundamental facilities for implementing abstract datatypes. Overloaded operators in C++ behave like ordinary member functions in many aspects: They are inherited, they can be overloaded more than once, and they can be declared either as non-static members or as non-member functions. However, several restrictions apply to overloaded operators. An overloaded operator has a fixed number of parameters, and it cannot have default arguments. In addition, the associativity and the precedence of an operator cannot be altered. Built-in operators have an interface consisting of the number of operands to which the operator can be applied, whether the operator modifies any of its operands, and the result that's returned by the operator. When you're overloading an operator, it's recommended that you conform to its built-in interface.

Unlike ordinary overloaded operators, conversion operators have neither a return value nor parameters.

Books and e-Books

Inside the C++ Object Model (Addison-Wesley, 1996, ISBN 0201834545), by Stanley B. Lippman, is one of my all-time favorites. Although it isn't dedicated to operator overloading exclusively, it does explain in detail the inner workings of C++ compilers and how they support this feature. (For more on this book, visit *http://www.informit.com/bookstore/product.asp?isbn=0201834545*.)

Online Resources

"Overloading Operator + the Right Way" (*http://gethelp.devx.com/techtips/cpp_pro/10min/2001/august/10min0801.asp*), by Danny Kalev, explains the principles of operator overloading in general and focuses on operator + as an example of a symmetrical, binary operator.

The "Operator Overloading" section of C++ FAQ Lite (*http://www.parashift.com/c++-faq-lite/operator-overloading.html*) provides many useful tips and guidelines. Some of the questions are rather intriguing; for example, is it allowed to define an overloaded version of operator **?

CHAPTER 4
Memory Management

C++ has three types of storage (memory): *automatic storage*, *static storage*, and the *free store*. Each of these storage types has different semantics of object initialization and lifetime. The following sections explain the differences between these storage types and show how to use them effectively and safely.

Automatic Storage

Local objects that are not explicitly declared `static` or `extern`, local objects that are declared `auto` or `register`, and function arguments have *automatic storage*. This type of storage is also called *stack memory*. The following example contains various declarations, objects, and variables with an automatic storage type:

```
void f(const std::string & s); //s' storage type is
                               //determined by the caller
void g(register int n); //arguments passed by value are automatic
int main()
{
  int n;            // automatic because local, non-static, non-extern
  register int i;   // register implies automatic
  auto double d;    //
  g(n); //passing a copy of n; the copy is automatic
  std::string s; // automatic because local, non-static, non-extern
  f(std::string temp()); // a temp object is automatic
}
```

Automatic objects are created automatically upon entering a function or a block. They are destroyed when the function or block exits. Thus, on each entry into a function or a block, a fresh set of its automatic objects is created. The default value of automatic variables and non-class objects is indeterminate.

Static Storage

Global objects, static data members of a class, namespace variables, and static variables in functions reside in *static memory*. A static object resides in the same memory address throughout the program's execution. Every static object is constructed only once during the lifetime of the program. By default, static data is initialized to binary zeros. Static objects with a *nontrivial constructor*—that is, a constructor that's implemented either by the programmer or by C++ (see Chapter 2 "Special Member Functions: Constructors, Destructors, and the Assignment Operator")—are subsequently initialized by their constructors. The scope of an object that's declared static within a function is restricted to that function. Objects with static storage are included in the following examples:

```
int num; //global variables have static storage
int func()
{
  static int calls; //initialized to 0 by default
  return ++calls;
}

class C
{
private:
  static bool b;
};

namespace NS
{
  std::string str; //str has static storage
}
```

The Free Store

Free store memory, also called *heap memory* (this term is used in C) or *dynamic memory*, contains objects and variables created by the operator new. Objects and variables that are allocated on the free store persist until they're explicitly released by a subsequent call to the operator `delete`. Failing to call `delete` results in memory leaks; in the case of objects with a destructor, the result is undefined behavior. Unlike with static objects, the address of an object allocated on the free store is determined at runtime. (Auto objects are allocated when the function or block using them is called.) The initial value of raw memory (a char array, as opposed to a class object) allocated by new is unspecified. C++ distinguishes between plain, or scalar, new and delete, which allocate and deallocate a single object, respectively; and new[] and delete[], which operate on arrays. For example:

```
void f(const std::string & s); //s' storage type is
                               //determined by the caller
int *p = new int;
char *s = new char[1024];
Shape *ps=new Triangle;
std::string *pstr=new std::string;
f(pstr);
delete p;
delete[] s; //s is an array
delete  ps; //invokes the destructor
delete pstr; //ditto
```

POD (Plain Old Data) and Non–POD Objects

C++ distinguishes between two types of objects: POD (plain old data) and non–POD objects. A *POD object* has one of the following datatypes: a built-in type, pointer, union, struct, array, or class with a trivial constructor. For example:

```
int n;
class C
{
public:
 int j,k;
};
C c; // c is a POD object
struct S
{
 int j,k;
};
S s;
char *pc;
bool barr[10];
```

Conversely, a non–POD object is one for which a nontrivial constructor exists. Note that this distinction between POD and non–POD doesn't exist in pure object-oriented languages; it's an artifact of the hybrid nature of C++. It's used to differentiate between traditional C datatypes and real C++ objects. A POD object begins its lifetime when it obtains storage with the proper alignment and size for its type, and its lifetime ends when the storage for the object is either reused or deallocated. A non–POD object begins its lifetime after its constructor has executed; its lifetime ends when its destructor has started.

`malloc()` and `free()` Versus `new` and `delete`

C++ still supports the C library functions `malloc()` and `free()`. This backward compatibility with C is useful in three cases:

- Combining legacy C code with C++ programs
- Writing C++ code that's meant to be supported in C environments
- Implementing or overriding `new` and `delete` by calling `malloc()` and `free()`

Otherwise, `malloc()` and `free()` are not to be used in C++ code because they don't support object semantics. Furthermore, the results of calling `free()` to release an object that was allocated by `new`, or of using `delete` to release memory that was allocated by `malloc()`, are undefined. The C++ standard doesn't guarantee that the underlying implementation of operator `new` uses `malloc()`; in fact, on some implementations `malloc()` and `new` use different heaps.

Support for Object Semantics

`new` and `delete` automatically construct and destroy objects. `malloc()` and `free()`, on the other hand, merely allocate and deallocate raw memory from the heap. In particular, using `malloc()` to create a non–POD object causes undefined behavior:

```
//disastrous!
std::string  *pstr =(std::string*)malloc(sizeof(std::string));
```

Safety

Operator new automatically calculates the size of the object that it constructs. Conversely, with malloc(), the programmer has to specify explicitly the number of bytes that have to be allocated. In addition, malloc() returns void *, which has to be explicitly cast to the desired type. This is both tedious and dangerous. Operator new returns a pointer to the desired type, so no explicit typecast is required. For example:

```
void func()
{
  int * p = static_cast<int *> malloc(sizeof(int));//fine but tedious
  int * p2 = new int;
}
```

Allocating and Deallocating Arrays Using new[] and delete[]

new[] allocates an array of objects of a specified type. The return value of new[] is the address of the first element in the allocated array. For example:

```
int main()
{
  int *p = new int[10];
  bool equal = (p == &p[0]); //true
  delete[] p;
  return 0;
}
```

To release objects allocated by new[], you must call delete[]. Using delete instead of delete[] or vice versa will cause undefined behavior. This is because when new[] executes, C++ caches the number of elements in the allocated array somewhere. delete[] retrieves this cached value, thereby destroying the correct number of elements.

Contrary to popular belief, the same rules apply to arrays of built-in types, not just to arrays of objects. Although delete[] doesn't invoke destructors in this case, it still has to retrieve the number of elements in the array to calculate the complete size of the memory block.

Dealing with Exceptions

In pre–Standard C++, new returned a null pointer when it failed to allocate the requested amount of memory. In this regard, new behaved like malloc() in C. Programmers had to check the return value of new to make sure that it was not NULL. For example:

```
void f(int size) //anachronistic usage of new
{
  char *p = new char [size];
  if (p)   //this was fine until 1994
  {
    //...use p safely
    delete [] p;
  }
  else
  {
  //...handle allocation failure
  }
}

const int BUF_SIZE = 1048576L;

int main()
{
  f(BUF_SIZE);
  return 0;
}
```

Returning a null pointer upon failure was problematic. It forced programmers to test the return value every time they called new. This is a recipe for human error and code bloat. Failures in dynamic memory allocation are rather rare and generally indicate an unstable system state. This is exactly the kind of runtime errors that exception handling was designed to cope with. For these reasons, the C++ standardization committee changed the specification of new nearly a decade ago. The C++ standard now states that the operator new should throw an exception of type std::bad alloc when it fails, rather than returning a null pointer. A program that calls new either directly or indirectly (for example, if it uses STL containers that in turn allocate memory using new) must contain an appropriate handler to catch a std::bad alloc exception. Otherwise, whenever new fails, the program will abort due to an uncaught exception. The exception-throwing policy also implies that testing the result of new is completely useless. If new is successful, the redundant test wastes system resources. On the other hand, in the event of an allocation failure, the thrown exception will abort the current execution flow, so the test won't execute anyway. The revised, standard-conforming form of the previously presented program looks similar to the following:

```cpp
void f(int size) //standard-conforming usage of new
{
  char *p = new char [size];
  //...use p safely
  delete [] p;
  return;
}
#include <stdexcept>
#include <iostream>
using namespace std;

const int BUF_SIZE = 1048576L;

int main()
{
  try
  {
    f(BUF_SIZE);
  }
  catch(bad_alloc& ex)   //handle exception thrown from f()
  {
    cout<<ex.what()<<endl;
    //...other diagnostics and remedies
  }
  return -1;
}
```

Placement new

An additional version of operator new enables you to construct an object or an array of objects at a predetermined memory position. This version is called *placement new* and has many useful applications, including building a custom-made memory pool or a garbage collector. Additionally, it can be used in mission-critical applications because there's no danger of allocation failure; the memory that's used by placement new has already been allocated. Placement new is also faster because the construction of an object on a preallocated buffer takes less time.

Allocation Strategies

The most common forms of new are scalar new and array new as shown in the following example:

```
string * s = new string;
char *line = new char[81];
```

These versions of new (to which I will refer as *ordinary new* henceforth) allocate storage from the free store at runtime. (See the section "The Free Store" for details.)

For most purposes, this allocation policy is plausible and rather efficient. In certain applications, however, determinacy is paramount. Not only must the program ensure that object allocation succeeds, but the allocation should be completed within a predictable amount of time. Preallocating a large chunk of memory in advance and using it during the application's lifetime is a common strategy. To facilitate this task, C++ defines a special version of operator new called *placement new*.

Using Placement new

Unlike ordinary new, placement new takes an additional argument: the memory address on which the object will be constructed. Since placement new doesn't really allocate storage, it's faster and safer than ordinary new. Of course, the programmer must guarantee that the preallocated storage is sufficiently large and that it meets the system's alignment requirements.

NOTE: See the DevX.com tip "Placement New Requires Heap-Allocated Buffers" (*http://www.devx.com/tips/Tip/12756*).

To meet these criteria, use ordinary new to allocate raw storage. Then use placement new to construct the desired object on the previously allocated storage. Let's look at a concrete example.

Suppose you have the following class:

```
class Timer
{
public:
  int sleep(long msec);
  int reset();
  Timer(char * name="");
  ~Timer();
//...
```

```
private:
  int timer_id;
  int thread_id;
//...
};
```

You're developing an application that uses a timer to invoke a screensaver after 10 minutes of inactivity. This application must run for weeks and even months without interruption. Repeatedly allocating objects using ordinary `new` is ruled out because it might fragment the heap until the application crashes. Instead, you decide to preallocate sufficient storage from the free store at program startup and then recycle it to construct new objects as needed. Your first step is to preallocate raw storage like this:

```
char * raw_mem = new char [sizeof (Timer)];
```

C++ guarantees that the memory returned from `new` meets the strictest alignment requirements for every type of object. Therefore, you can use a dynamically allocated `char` array as the basis for constructing any other type of object. However, don't be tempted to use stack memory for this purpose (see the section "Automatic Storage"):

```
char buff [sizeof (Timer)]; //bad idea
```

A `char` array allocated in this way might not be properly aligned for objects of any other type but `char`.

Next, construct an object on the preallocated storage like this (remember to `#include` the standard header `<new>` when using placement `new`):

```
#include <new>
Timer * ptimer = new (raw_mem) Timer; // #1
```

In the statement numbered #1 placement `new` constructs a `Timer` object on `raw_mem` and returns its address. The argument `raw_mem` is enclosed between a pair of parentheses after the keyword `new`. It's the address on which the object will be constructed. Placement `new` is exception-safe; unlike ordinary `new`, it doesn't throw. (See Chapter 11, "Exception Handling.")

You can now use `ptimer`:

```
ptimer->sleep(60000*15); //sleep for 15 minutes
```

Explicit Destructor Invocation

Objects allocated by placement new require an *explicit destructor invocation* once they aren't needed. (See Chapter 2, "Special Member Functions: Constructors, Destructors, and the Assignment Operator.") Don't use `delete` or `delete[]` to destroy them, as this would cause undefined behavior:

```
delete ptimer; // bad idea
```

The problem is that `delete` knows which object new allocated *originally*, namely a `char` array. It doesn't know that a different object was later constructed on that array. Therefore, it won't invoke `Timer`'s destructor. Worse yet, because the original buffer was allocated using `new[]`, you must use `delete[]` to release it. Here's how you invoke `Timer`'s destructor:

```
ptimer->~Timer(); //explicit destructor invocation
```

At this point, you can recycle `raw_mem` and construct a new object on it:

```
Timer * ptimer2 = new (raw_mem) Timer("2nd timer");
ptimer2->sleep(60000); //sleep for 1 minutes
```

You can repeat the construction and destruction steps indefinitely. This way, you both avoid the memory fragmentation incurred by dynamic allocations and ensure determinacy.

Cleanup

An explicit destructor invocation only destroys the `Timer` object. To release `raw_mem`, you still need to use `delete[]` thereafter:

```
delete[] raw_mem;
```

Summary

Placement `new` is a powerful but dangerous feature. Although the example shown here uses a simple class, in real-world applications you would use it to allocate large objects, say images, files and so on. Note also that while placement `new` doesn't support arrays, you can easily build multiple objects on the same preallocated storage by calculating the offset of each object. When using placement `new`, follow these guidelines to prevent bugs, memory leaks and inefficiencies:

- Preallocate storage using `new` to meet the strictest alignment requirements.
- Use `sizeof()` to determine the size of the object to be allocated.
- Invoke the object's destructor explicitly when it's no longer needed. You can then recycle the raw storage to construct more objects.
- Before the program terminates, remember to release the storage by calling `delete[]`.

Online Books

Applied C++: Practical Techniques for Building Better Software (Addison-Wesley, 2003, ISBN 0321108949), by Philip Romanik and Amy Muntz, discusses various software engineering issues, including memory management. The authors teach how to develop a toolkit to solve the complex problem of digital image manipulation. Along the way, they address software engineering issues such as performance, memory management and allocation policies, reuse, and advanced template programming.(For more on this book, visit *http://www.informit.com/title/0321108949*.)

Interprocess Communications in Linux: The Nooks and Crannies (Prentice Hall, 2003, ISBN 0130460427), by John Shapley Gray, is an excellent guide to system programming. The book doesn't cover memory management directly. However, it explains key concepts such as system memory, process memory, address spaces, shared memory, and threads that serve as the foundation of higher-level memory management tasks. (For more on this book, visit *http://www.informit.com/title/0130460427*.)

Articles

"C++ Memory and Resource Management" (*http://www.informit.com/articles/article.asp?p=30642*), by Stephen Dewhurst, surveys most of the memory management facilities of standard C++. Although it doesn't cover placement `new`, it can be a useful guide for beginners and intermediate level programmers who want to master the major memory management concepts of C++.

The section "Using Class `auto_ptr` to Automate Memory Management" teaches another advanced memory management technique that relies on the Standard Library's `auto_ptr` template to smooth the interaction between exceptions and dynamic memory.

nothrow new

Previously I discussed several flavors of operator new, including the ordinary versions of new and placement new. Standard C++ has another version of this operator, called *nothrow new*. In the following sections, I will describe its raison d'être and usage.

A Bit of History

Until the early 1990s, operator new behaved very much like standard C's `malloc()` as far as allocation failures were concerned. When it failed to allocate a memory block of the requested size, it would return a null pointer. In those days, a typical new expression would look like this:

```
//pre-standard C++
CWindow * p;
p = new DerivedWind;
if (!p) //NULL indicates a failure
{
 cout<<"allocation failure!"
 exit(1);
}
//...continue normally
```

Programs had to check the pointer returned from new to verify that the allocation was successful; a pointer with a nonzero value indicated success. This behavior was changed in the early 1990s. Instead of returning a null pointer, new throws an exception to indicate a failure. Because exceptions were rather new at that time, and because legacy code that relied on the original behavior of new was still widely used, vendors were rather slow in adopting this change. Today, however, most existing compilers implement new in a standard-compliant manner.

Standard-Compliant new

Let's examine the behavior of standard-compliant new more carefully. As previously said, it throws an exception of type `std::bad_alloc` in case of failure. This means that testing the return value like this is utterly wrong:

```
p = new DerivedWind;
if (!p) //not to be used under ISO compliant compilers
{
```

```
cout<<"allocation failure!"
exit(1);
}
```

There are several problems with this code. The `if` condition is never evaluated in the event of an allocation failure because the exception thrown by `new` has already transferred control to a matching `catch()` clause, if one exists. If no matching handler is found, C++ automatically calls function `terminate()`, which terminates the program unconditionally. Unfortunately, quite a few programmers still use this coding practice even today, not knowing how dangerous and erroneous it is. A standard-compliant version of this code should look like this:

```
try
{
 p = new DerivedWind;
}
catch (std::bad_alloc &ba)
{
 cout<<"allocation failure!"
 //...additional cleanup
}
```

There are, however, certain cases in which the pre-standard behavior of `new` is needed. Embedded systems for example don't always support exceptions. In such environments, `nothrow new` can be rather useful.

nothrow new's Interface

The standard header file `<new>` defines a struct called `std::nothrow_t` like this:

```
struct nothrow_t {}; //defined in namespace std
```

This empty struct merely serves as a policy-enforcing parameter in the following overloaded versions of `new`:

```
//declarations appear in <new>
void* operator new (size_t size, const std::nothrow_t &);
void* operator new[] (void *v, const std::nothrow_t &nt);
```

`<new>` also defines a global object of type `std::notrow_t`:

```
extern const std:: nothrow_t nothrow;
```

The existence of a global object enables all C++ programs to use `nothrow new` uniformly by using that object as the argument name.

Putting `nothrow new` to Work

By using `nothrow new` one can easily make the previous code listing standard-compliant while retaining its original structure and semantics:

```
//standard C++ code
#include <new> //required for nothrow new

CWindow p;
p = new(std::nothrow) DerivedWind;
if (!p) //fine now
{
 cout<<"allocation failure!"
 exit(1);
}
//...continue normally
```

Notice that no changes were made to the original code save the `new(nothrow)` expression. If you want to test the behavior of this code fragment in case of an allocation failure, try to allocate a huge amount of memory:

```
//force an allocation failure to test
//the behavior of nothrow new
p = new(std:::nothrow) DerivedWind[1000000000];
if (!p)
{
 cout<<"allocation failure!"
 exit(1);
}
```

Summary

The existence of `nothrow new` exemplifies the constant conflicts that C++ creators have faced during more than 20 years of existence. On the one hand, they've attempted to ensure that existing code wouldn't break due to changes in the core language. On the other hand, they haven't avoided necessary extensions and modifications. That said, `nothrow new` isn't necessarily a transitory feature. As stated previously, C++ is used in resource-constrained environments in which exceptions aren't supported. Such environments necessitate the use of `nothrow new` in new code as well.

Member Alignment

The size of a class or a `struct` might be larger than the sum of its members' sizes. This is because the compiler is allowed to insert *padding bytes* between members whose size doesn't fit exactly into a machine word. For example:

```
#include <cstring>
using namespace std;

struct Person
{
  char firstName[5];
  int age; // int occupies 4 bytes
  char lastName[8];
}; //the actual size of Person is most likely larger than 17 bytes
```

On a 32-bit architecture, the compiler may insert three padding bytes between the first and the second members of `Person`, increasing its size to 20 bytes. Therefore, always use `sizeof()` to obtain the correct size of an object:

```
memset(&p, 0, sizeof(Person));
```

Overriding `new` and `delete`

For most programming tasks, the default implementation of `new` and `delete` is sufficient. In fact, many C++ programmers get along without even *knowing* that they can override these operators. However, in certain advanced programming tasks, redefining these operators for a given class is essential: for example, when you want to ensure that all instances of that class are allocated from a custom memory pool instead of the free store.

> **TIP:** You can achieve a similar effect by using placement `new`. However, it doesn't block users from using global `new`.

There are other useful applications of overriding `new` and `delete`: implementing a garbage collector or ensuring that objects are allocated on a specific memory address (e.g., a video card's internal memory buffer). In this section I will show how to override these operators, first on a per-class basis, and then globally.

Declaring new and delete as Class Members

Suppose you want to override `new` and `delete` for class A. Your first step is to declare these operators as member functions of this class:

```
#include <new> // for size_t
class A
{
public:
 A();
 ~A();
 static void* operator new (size_t size);
 static void operator delete (void *p);
};
```

When you declare `new` and `delete` as class members, they are implicitly declared `static`. Still, it's advisable to add the keyword `static` to their declarations to document this property explicitly.

Implementation

The implementation of `new` is straightforward: it calls a custom allocation function, say, `allocate_from_pool()`, and returns the resulting pointer. You can use any other memory allocation function that suits your needs—e.g., `malloc()`, `GlobalAlloc()`, etc.—so long as that function meets the memory alignment requirement of your objects. Here's a typical implementation of `new`:

```
void* A::operator new (size_t  size)
{
 void *p=allocate_from_pool(size);
 return p;
} // A's default ctor implicitly called here
```

Note that when this function exits, the class's default constructor executes automatically and constructs an object of type A. The matching version of `delete` looks as follows:

```
void A::operator delete (void *p)
{
 release(p); // return memory to pool
} // A's dtor implicitly called at this point
```

C++ guarantees that an object's destructor is automatically called just before `delete` executes. Therefore, you shouldn't invoke A's destructor explicitly (doing so would cause undefined behavior as the destructor will actually run twice).

Additional Customizations

Overriding `new` enables you to customize its functionality in various ways. For instance, you can add an error-handling mechanism to the existing implementation by defining a special exception class, `mem_exception`. An object of this class will be thrown in case of an allocation failure:

```
class mem_exception {};
void* A::operator new (size_t  size)
{
 void *p=allocate_from_pool(size);
 if (p==0)
   throw mem_exception();
 return p;
}
```

In a similar vein, you can extend `delete`'s functionality to report the amount of available memory, write a message to a log file, and so on:

```
#include <ctime> // for time()
void A::operator delete (void *p)
{
 release(p);
 cout << "available pool size: " << get_pool_size();
 write_to_log("deletion occurred at: ", time(0));
}
```

Usage of `new` and `delete`

You use the overriding `new` and `delete` as you would use the built-in version of these operators; C++ automatically selects the overriding versions if they have been overridden in a specific class. Classes for which no overriding versions exist continue to use the built-in versions. For example:

```
int main()
{
 A *p=new A; // A::new
 delete p; // A::delete
```

```
 B *q=new B; // global built-in new
 delete q; // global built-in delete
}
```

Overriding new and `delete` Globally

Up until now, I've focused on a class-based override. What if you want override new and `delete` not just for one class, but for the entire application? C++ allows you to do that by defining global versions of these operators. Unlike a class-based override, the global new and `delete` are declared in the global namespace (remember that you cannot declare these operators in any other namespace). This technique may be useful for users of older versions of Visual C++ (versions 6.0 and below) and other slightly outdated compilers. The implementation of new in Visual C++ 6.0 isn't standard-compliant; new returns NULL upon failure instead of throwing a `std::bad_alloc` exception, as required by the C++ ANSI/ISO standard.

> **TIP:** For more on new and standards compliance, see the Microsoft article "PRB: Operator New Doesn't Throw bad_alloc Exception on Failure," *http://support.microsoft.com/kb/q167733/*.

The following example overrides global new and `delete` to force standard-compliant behavior:

```
#include <exception> // for std::bad_alloc
#include <new>
#include <cstdlib> // for malloc() and free()


// Visual C++ fix of operator new

void* operator new (size_t size)
{
 void *p=malloc(size);
 if (p==0) // did malloc succeed?
   throw std::bad_alloc(); // ANSI/ISO compliant behavior
 return p;
}
```

The matching `delete` looks as follows:

```
void operator delete (void *p)
{
 free(p);
}
```

Now you can use `try` and `catch` blocks to handle potential allocation exceptions properly, even if your compiler isn't yet fully compliant in this regard:

```
int main()
{
 try
 {
  int *p=new int[10000000]; // user-defined new
  //..use p
  delete p; // user-defined delete
 }
 catch (std::bad_alloc & x)
 {
  std::cout << x.what(); // display exception
 }
}
```

Very few programming languages allow you to access and modify their inner workings as does C++. Indeed, overriding `new` and `delete` is a very powerful feature: it gives you tighter control over the language's memory management policy and enables you to extend its functionality in various ways. However, the built-in implementation of `new` and `delete` is suitable for most purposes; don't override these operators unless you have compelling reasons to do so, and when doing so, remember always to override *both* of them.

Using Class `auto_ptr` to Automate Memory Management

A C++ program should contain a matching `delete` for every `new` expression as well as a matching `delete[]` for every `new[]` expression. In practice, however, it is easy to lose track of previously allocated memory if the execution flow is complex or if the program uses exceptions. In the following sections I will show a technique based on class `std::auto_ptr` for eliminating the risk of memory leaks in the event of an exception.

Exceptions and Dynamic Memory Allocation

Throwing an exception breaks the program's normal flow of control, thus causing a risk of potential memory leaks. The following example demonstrates this:

```
void func(string *pstr) //might throw
{
  bool success;
  //..
  if (!success)
    throw Y();
}
void h()
{
  string * p = new string;
  func(p); //memory leak if func throws
  delete p; //unreachable code if g() throws
}
int main()
{
  try
  {
    h();
  }
  catch(...)
  {}
}
```

If `func()` throws an exception, C++ performs *stack unwinding*, meaning `h()` exits and control is transferred to the `catch(...)` handler in `main()`. The transfer of control causes the `delete` statement in `h()` to be skipped. Consequently, the memory bound to p will leak. Indeed, you could avoid this bug easily by using a local automatic `string` instead of allocating it dynamically:

```
void h()
{
  string   s;
  func(&s); //no memory leaks
}
```

Introducing `std::auto_ptr`

For simple cases like this, the use of a local automatic object neatly solves the problem of memory leaks. However, frameworks such as STL, infrastructure code and other real-world applications such as database engines still must use dynamically allocated memory. For such applications, you can use the Standard Library's `std::auto_ptr` class template (for the sake of brevity, I will refer to it as `auto_ptr` henceforth). This template is primarily meant to simplify the interaction between dynamic memory and exceptions by ensuring that objects allocated on the free store are automatically destroyed and their memory is released when an exception occurs.

> **NOTE:** For more on dynamic memory, see the section "The Free Store." For details on exceptions, see Chapter 11, "Exception Handling."

The following sections focus on using `auto_ptr` for memory management purposes; with minimal adjustments you can use it to manage other resources that need to be released automatically such as file locks, threads, and so on.

Class `auto_ptr` is defined in the standard header `<memory>`. Creating an `auto_ptr` object is peculiar because you need to initialize it with a pointer to a dynamically allocated object in a certain way. The following example demonstrates this principle:

```
#include <memory>
#include <string>
using namespace std;
void func()
{
   auto_ptr<string> p (new string); //#1
}
```

I'll explain the statement in line 1 in detail. Since `auto_ptr` is a template, you need to create a specialization thereof by specifying a type in the angle brackets. (See Chapter 5, "Templates.") The specialization in this case is `auto_ptr<string>`. Next comes the name of the `auto_ptr` object, `p` in this example. Finally, you initialize `p` with a pointer to a dynamically allocated object (the *bound object*). Note that using the assignment operator for initialization isn't allowed:

```
auto_ptr<string> p = new string; //compilation error
```

The beauty of `auto_ptr` is that it's completely generic. (See "The Rise and Fall of Object Orientation" at *http://www.informit.com/guides/content.asp?g=cplusplus&seqNum=84*.) Therefore, you can bind to it any type of object, including built-in types. For example:

```
auto_ptr<long> pl (new long);
```

Once you have instantiated and initialized an `auto_ptr` object, you use it as if it were an ordinary pointer:

```
*p = "hello world"; //*p is a string
p->size(); //call string::size()
```

How does this magic work? Operator overloading is the answer. `auto_ptr` overloads the operators &, *, and -> so that you can use it as you would use a pointer. However, don't let the syntax mislead you: p is an object, not a pointer.

NOTE: For details about operator overloading, see Chapter 3, "Operator Overloading."

Using `std::auto_ptr`

You're probably wondering how `auto_ptr` solves the potential memory leak previously discussed. The answer lies in `auto_ptr`'s destructor. When it executes, it destroys its bound object—the string that was allocated when p was created. You should never delete an `auto_ptr` because it's an automatic object that *owns* a resource. Ownership means responsibility for releasing its bound resource.

To show how `auto_ptr` averts the potential memory leak problem, look at a modified version of h(), this time using `auto_ptr`:

```
void h()
{
  auto_ptr<string> p (new string);
  func(); //p is destroyed automatically if g() throws
}
```

C++ guarantees that automatic objects are properly destroyed during stack unwinding. Therefore, if h() throws an exception after being called from h(), the destructor of p will execute before control is transferred to the catch(...) handler in main(). p's destructor deletes the bound object unconditionally, thereby eliminating the risk of a memory leak.

`auto_ptr` Caveats

Bear in mind that `auto_ptr` neatly solves a specific type of memory management problem but not all of them. Programmers who are new to `auto_ptr` tend to overuse it in contexts in which it shouldn't be used at all.

A common mistake is trying to store `auto_ptr` objects in STL containers. The C++ Standard explicitly forbids this because STL containers may only contain objects that are *copy-constructible* and *assignable*. Without delving into long-winded definitions, these terms basically mean that copying or assigning a source object to a destination object doesn't alter the state of the source. `auto_ptr` doesn't meet this criterion; when you assign it to another object, the assignment operation changes *both* operands.

Another common mistake is using an `auto_ptr` to bind an array:

```
auto_ptr<char>  p (new char[10] );  //bad idea
```

Can you see the problem here? As previously said, whenever you're using `new[]`, you need a matching `delete[]` to properly destroy the array. However, `auto_ptr`'s destructor uses only scalar `delete`. The result of binding an array to an `auto_ptr` is therefore undefined because the array isn't deleted properly.

Summary

Smart pointers are objects that simulate pointer syntax by overloading operators `->` and `*` while performing useful tasks under the hood such as allocating and deallocating storage automatically. In this regard, `auto_ptr` is an example of a smart pointer, although the restrictions on its usage usually drive programmers to either roll their own smart pointers or use third-party class libraries that offer more functionality. That said, `auto_ptr` excels at what it was originally designed for, namely simplifying the interaction of dynamic memory management and exception handling. When used properly, it can save you a great number of bugs and code maintenance problems.

TIP: For a good introduction to smart pointers, see "Smart Pointers in C++" by Andrei Alexandrescu (*http://www.informit.com/articles/article.asp?p=31529*). This article introduces the basic concepts of smart pointers and then moves to the most advanced design and implementation techniques.

Linkage Types

Objects, references, functions, types, templates, and namespaces are all considered *names*. A name can have one of three linkage types: external linkage, internal linkage, or no linkage. The linkage type of a name specifies its visibility from other scopes and translation units. A name with external linkage can be referred to from every translation unit of the program. Examples of such names include ordinary functions that aren't explicitly declared as `static`, global objects, `const` objects explicitly declared `extern`, classes, enumerations and their enumerators, templates, namespaces, and so on. Here are a few examples of names with external linkage:

```
int n; //global non-static, hence external linkage
class C
{
 void f(); // member functions
 static int n;// static data members
};
extern const K; //defined in a different translation unit
void func ();
namespace NS
{
 class D{}; // qualified name NS::D has external linkage
}
enum DIR
{
 Up,
 Down
} // DIR, Up, and Down have external linkage
```

A name with internal linkage is visible only from within the translation unit in which it was declared. A name declared in a namespace scope (that is, declared globally or within a namespace) has internal linkage if it's the name of a static object, a static function, a member of an anonymous union, a member of an anonymous namespace, a typedef name, or a `const` object not declared `extern`. Here are some examples of names with internal linkage:

```
static void f(); //a static function
static int q; //a static object declared in global scope
namespace //members of anonymous namespace
{
 class C{};
 int x;
}
const M=1000; //const object not declared extern
union{ //members of an anonymous union
 int x;
 float y;
};
typedef int I; // typedef names
```

Names with no linkage are visible only in the scope in which they're declared. Such names include local objects, local classes, and other local types. Put differently, any name that has neither external linkage nor internal linkage has no linkage. Here are some examples of such names:

```
int main()
{
 class C{}; // C is a local class; has no linkage
 int j; // local object not declared extern has no linkage
 C c;  // the object c has no linkage
 enum Parity  // local enum and enumerators
 {
  Even,
  Odd
 };
}
```

Guidelines for Effective Memory Management

Choosing the correct type of storage for an object is a critical implementation decision because each type of storage has different implications for the program's performance, reliability, and maintenance. Choosing the correct type of storage will help you avoid common pitfalls and performance penalties, as I'll show momentarily. In addition, the following sections discuss general topics that are associated with the unique memory model of C++, and compare C++ to other languages.

Preferring Automatic Storage to Free Store

When compared to automatic storage, creating objects on the free store is more expensive in terms of performance for several reasons:

- **Runtime overhead**. Allocating memory from the free store involves negotiations with the operating system. When the free store is fragmented, finding a contiguous block of memory can take even longer. In addition, the exception-handling support in the case of allocation failures adds runtime overhead.
- **Maintenance**. Dynamic allocation might fail; additional code is required to handle such exceptions.

- **Safety**. An object might be accidentally deleted more than once, or it might not be deleted at all. Both of these are a fertile source of bugs and runtime crashes in many applications.

The following code sample demonstrates two common bugs that are associated with allocating objects on the free store:

```
#include <string>
using namespace std;
void f()
{
  string *p = new string;
  //...use p
  if (p->empty()== false)
  {
    //...do something
    return; //OOPS! memory leak: p was not deleted
  }
  else //string is empty
  {
    delete p;
    //..do other stuff
  }
  delete p; //OOPS! p is deleted twice if isEmpty == true
}
```

Such bugs are quite common in large programs that frequently allocate objects on the free store. Often, it's possible to create objects on the stack, thereby simplifying the structure of the program and eliminating such potential bugs. Consider how the use of a local `string` object simplifies this function:

```
#include <string>
using namespace std;
void f()
{
  string s;
  //...use s
  if (s.empty()!= false)
  {
    //...do something
    return;
  }
  else
```

```
{
   //..do other stuff
  }
}
```

As a rule, automatic and static storage types are always preferable to free store.

Instantiating a Local Object

This is the correct form of instantiating a local object:

```
string str;    //no parentheses
```

Empty parentheses are allowed after the class name

```
string str();    //entirely different meaning
```

but this statement has an entirely different meaning. It's parsed as a declaration of a function named `str`, which takes no arguments and returns a `string` by value.

Zero Initialization

The literal 0 is of type `int`. However, it can be used as a universal initializer for every fundamental datatype. Zero is a special case in this respect because the compiler examines its context and automatically casts accordingly. For example:

```
void *p = 0;    //zero is implicitly converted to 'void *'
float salary = 0;  // 0 is cast to a float
char name[10] = {0};  // 0 cast to a '\0'
bool b = 0; // 0 cast to 'false'
void (*pf)(int) = 0;  // pointer to a function
int (C::*pm) ()  = 0; //pointer to a class member
```

An uninitialized pointer has an indeterminate value. Such a pointer is often called a *wild pointer*. It's almost impossible to test whether a wild pointer is valid, especially if it's passed as an argument to a function. For example:

```
void func(char *p );

int main()
{
```

```
   char * p; //dangerous: uninitialized
       //...many lines of code; p left uninitialized by mistake
if (p) //erroneously assuming that a non-null value indicates
        //a valid address
{
    func(p);  // func has no way of knowing whether p
              //has a valid address
}
   return 0;
}
```

Even if your compiler initializes pointers automatically, it's best to initialize them explicitly to ensure code readability and portability.

As noted previously, POD objects with automatic storage have an indeterminate value by default. However, you can initialize automatic POD objects explicitly when necessary. One way to initialize automatic POD objects is by calling `memset()`. However, there's a much simpler way to do it:

```
struct  Person
{
  long ID;
  int bankAccount;
  bool retired;
};

int main()
{

  Person person ={0}; //ensures that all members of
                      //person are initialized to binary zeros
   return 0;
}
```

This technique is applicable to every POD `struct`. It relies on the fact that the first member is a built-in datatype. The initializer zero is automatically cast to the appropriate built-in type. C++ guarantees that whenever the initialization list contains fewer initializers than the number of members, the rest of the members are initialized to binary zeros as well. Note that even if the definition of `Person` changes and members are added, all its members are still initialized. The same initialization technique is also applicable to local automatic arrays of fundamental type:

```
void f()
{
  char  name[100] = {0}; //all array elements are initialized to '\0'
  float farr[100] = {0}; //all array elements are initialized to 0.0
  int   iarr[100] = {0}; //all array elements are initialized to 0
  void *pvarr[100] = {0};//array of void *; all elements
                         //are initialized to 0
  //...use the arrays
}
```

This technique works for any combination of `structs` and arrays:

```
struct A
{
  char name[20];
  int age;
  long ID;
};
void f()
{
  A a[100] = {0};
}
```

Deleting Pointers

The result of applying `delete` to the same pointer after it has been deleted is undefined. Clearly, this bug should never happen. However, it can be prevented by assigning a null value to a pointer immediately after it has been deleted. Deleting a null pointer is harmless:

```
#include <string>
using namespace std;
void func
{
  string * ps = new string;
  //...use ps
  if ( ps->empty() )
  {
    delete ps;
    ps = 0; //safety measure
  }
  //...many lines of code
  delete ps; // harmless
}
```

Summary

Effective and bug-free use of the diversity of C++ memory-handling constructs and concepts requires a high level of expertise and experience. It isn't an exaggeration to say that most of the bugs in C/C++ programs are related to memory management. However, this diversity also renders C++ a multipurpose, no-compromise programming language.

The complex memory model of C++ enables maximum flexibility. The three types of data storage—automatic, static, and free store—provide a level of control that no other language offers. The fundamental constructs of dynamic memory allocation are the operators `new` and `delete`. Each of these has no fewer than six different versions: scalar and array variants, each of which comes in three flavors (exception throwing, exception free, and placement).

Many object-oriented programming languages have a built-in *garbage collector*, which is an automatic memory manager that detects unreferenced objects and reclaims their storage. The reclaimed storage can then be used to create new objects, thereby freeing the programmer from having to explicitly release dynamically allocated memory. Having an automatic garbage collector is handy because it eliminates a major source of bugs, runtime crashes, and memory leaks. However, garbage collection is not a panacea. It incurs additional runtime overhead due to repeated compaction, reference counting, and memory-initialization operations. The overhead of these operations may be unacceptable in time-critical applications. Furthermore, when garbage collection is used, destructors are not necessarily invoked immediately when you destroy an object, but at an indeterminate time afterward. For these reasons, C++ doesn't provide a garbage collector. Nonetheless, there are techniques to minimize the perils and drudgery of manual memory management, without the associated disadvantages of garbage collection. The easiest way to ensure automatic memory allocation and deallocation is to use automatic storage. For objects that have to grow and shrink dynamically, you can use STL containers that automatically adjust their size. Finally, in order to create an object that exists throughout the execution of a program, you can declare it `static`.

InformIT Articles and Sample Chapters

"Smart Pointers in C++" (*http://www.informit.com/articles/article.asp?p=31529*), by Andrei Alexandrescu, introduces the basic concepts of smart pointers and then moves on to the most advanced design and implementation techniques.

Online Resources

The DevX.com tip "Understanding What Memory Alignment Means" (*http://www.devx.com/tips/Tip/13265*), by Danny Kalev, explains the notion of memory alignment and why it's important to use allocation functions that meet this criterion.

"Using the `auto_ptr` Class Template to Facilitate Dynamic Memory Management" (*http://gethelp.devx.com/techtips/cpp_pro/10min/10min1199.asp*), by Danny Kalev, discusses the standard class template `auto_ptr` and explains how to use it to simplify dynamic memory allocation. `auto_ptr`'s behavior is rather peculiar in terms of its "strict ownership semantics." Therefore, many programmers aren't aware of the dangers and pitfalls that it might incur. Still, it's a useful tool that professional programmers should know how to use properly.

"Constructing an Object at a Predetermined Memory Position" (*http://gethelp.devx.com/techtips/cpp_pro/10min/10min0999.asp*), by Danny Kalev, discusses placement `new` in detail and provides guidelines for using it correctly and efficiently.

"Forcing Object Allocation on the Free Store" (*http://gethelp.devx.com/techtips/cpp_pro/10min/2002/January/10min0102.asp*), by Danny Kalev, is another article that discusses free store–related programming techniques. In certain cases, it's necessary to force the creation of certain objects on the free store. This article shows how it can be done.

CHAPTER 5

Templates

A *template* is a mold from which the compiler generates a family of classes or functions. C++ programming styles and concepts have changed considerably since the introduction of templates in 1991. Initially, templates were viewed as a support for generic container classes such as `Array` and `List`. In recent years, the experience of using templates has shown that this feature is most useful in designing and implementing general-purpose libraries such as the Standard Template Library (STL), which is discussed in Chapter 10, "The Standard Template Library (STL) and Generic Programming." With the widespread use of templates, C++ added more sophisticated constructs to control template behavior and performance. Such constructs include partial specializations, explicit specializations, template members, default type arguments, and so on. The following sections discuss all of this and more.

Class Templates

Many algorithms and data structures can be defined independently of the concrete datatypes that they manipulate. The concept of a complex number, for instance, is not exclusively limited to `double`. Rather, it's applicable to every floating-point type. Designing a type-independent class that abstracts the concept of a complex number enables users to choose the desired level of precision for a specific application without having to duplicate code manually. In addition, type-independent classes are portable among different platforms and locales.

Declaring a Class Template

A class template is declared using the keyword `template`, followed by a *template parameter list* enclosed in angle brackets (<>) and a declaration or a definition of the class. For example, consider the following template declaration:

```
template <class T> class Vector; //declaration
template <class T> class Vector  //definition
{
private:
  size_t sz;
  T * buff;
public:
  explicit Vector<T>(size_t s = 100);
  Vector<T> (const Vector <T> & v); //copy constructor
  Vector<T>& operator= (const Vector<T>& v); //assignment operator
  ~Vector<T>(); //destructor
  //other member functions
  T& operator [] (unsigned int index);
  const T& operator [] (unsigned int index) const;
  size_t size() const;
};
```

Member functions can be defined outside the class body. The following code sample contains out-of-class definitions of four member functions:

```
//definitions of Vector's member functions
//follow the class declaration

//constructor definition
template <class T> Vector<T>::Vector<T> (size_t s)
: sz(s),
buff (new T[s])
{}
template <class T> //copy ctor
Vector<T>::Vector<T> (const Vector <T> & v)
{
  sz = 0;
  buff = 0;
  *this = v; //use overloaded assignment operator
}

template <class T> inline size_t Vector<T>::size () const
{
  return sz;
}

template <class T> Vector<T>::~Vector<T> () //destructor
{
  delete [] buff;
}
```

The prefix `template <class T>` indicates that T is a *template parameter*, which is a placeholder for a yet-unspecified type. The keyword `class` is of particular interest because the corresponding argument for the parameter T is not necessarily a user-defined type; it can also be a built-in type, such as `char` or `int`. If you prefer a more neutral term, you can use the `typename` keyword instead:

```
//typename instead of class
//no semantic difference between the two forms
template <typename T> class Vector
{/**/};
template <typename T> Vector<T>::Vector<T> (size_t s)
: sz(s), buff (new T[s]) {}
```

Within the scope of Vector, qualification with the parameter T is redundant, so the member functions can be declared and defined without it. The constructor, for example, can be defined as follows:

```
template <class T> class Vector
{
public:
 Vector (size_t s = 100);
   // equivalent to Vector <T>(size_t s = 100);
};
// equivalent to template <class T> Vector<T>::Vector<T>(size_t s)
template <class T> Vector<T>::Vector
 (size_t s) : buff (new T[s]), sz(s)
{}
```

Instantiation and Specialization

A class template is not a "real" class. The process of instantiating a "real" class from a template is called *template instantiation*. A specialization consists of a template name followed by a list of arguments in angle brackets (for example, `Vector<int>`). A specialization can be used exactly like any other class. Here are a few examples:

```
void func (Vector <float> &); //function parameter
size_t n = sizeof( Vector <char>); //sizeof expression
class myStringVector: private Vector<std::string> //base class
{/*...*/};
cout<<typeid(Vector< string>).name(); //typeid expression
Vector<int> vi; // creating an object
```

The compiler instantiates only the necessary member functions of a given specialization. In the following example, points of member instantiation are numbered:

```
int main()
{
  Vector<int> vi(5);  // 1
  for (int i = 0; i<5; i++)
  {
    vi[i] = i; //fill vi   // 2
    cout<<vi[i]<<endl;
  }
} //3
```

The compiler generates code only for the following `Vector` member functions, which are used either explicitly or implicitly in the program:

```
Vector<int>::Vector<int> (size_t s) //1: constructor
: sz(s), buff (new int[s]) {}

inline int&   //2: operator []
Vector<int>::operator [] (unsigned int idx)
{
  return buff[idx];
}

Vector<int>::~Vector<int> () //3: destructor
{
  delete [] buff;
}
```

In contrast, code for the member function `size_t Vector<int>::size() const` is not generated, as it's not required in this program. The "generate on demand" policy is required by the Standard, and has two functions:

- **Efficiency.** It's not uncommon for certain class templates to define hundreds of member functions (STL containers, for example); normally, however, fewer than a dozen of these are actually used in a program.
- **Flexibility.** In some cases, not every function defined in a class template is supported in the target platform or program. For example, a container class can use `ostream`'s operator << to display objects for which an overloaded << is defined. However, a POD (plain old data) `struct` for

which no overloaded version of << exists can still be stored in such a container, as long as the program doesn't call the << operator.

Template Arguments

A template can take one or more *type parameters*: that is, symbols that represent an as-yet-unspecified type. For example:

```
template <class T > class Vector {/*...*/};
```

A template can also take ordinary types such as `int` and `long` as parameters:

```
template <class T, int n> class Array
{/*...*/};
```

Note, however, that when a non-type is used as a template argument, it must be a constant or a constant expression of an integral type. For example:

```
const int cn = 5;
int num = 10;
Array<char, 5> ac;   // OK, 5 is a const
Array<float, cn> af;  // OK, cn is a const
Array<unsigned char, sizeof(float)>
   auc;  // OK, constant expression used
Array<bool, num> ab;  // error, num is not a constant
```

Besides constant expressions, the only other arguments allowed are a pointer to a non-overloaded member, and the address of an object or a function with external linkage. This also implies that a string literal cannot be used as a template argument because it has a static storage type (see Chapter 4, "Memory Management").

A template can take a template as an argument:

```
int send(const Vector<char*>& );
int main()
{
  //a template used as an argument
 Vector <Vector<char*> > msg_que(10);
  //...fill msg_que
 for (int i =0; i < 10; i++) //transmit messages
    send(msg_que[i]);
```

```
    return 0;
}
```

Note that when a template is used as an argument, the space between the right two angle brackets is mandatory:

```
Vector <Vector<char*> > msg_que(10);
```

Otherwise, the >> sequence would be parsed as the right-shift operator.

Default Type Arguments

Class templates can have default type arguments.

As with default argument values of a function, the default type of a template gives the programmer more flexibility in choosing the optimal type for a particular application. For instance, the `Vector` template can be optimized for special memory management tasks. Instead of using the hard-coded `size_t` type for storing the size of a `Vector`, it can have a size type as a parameter. For most purposes, the default type `size_t` is used. However, for managing extremely large memory buffers (or very small ones), the programmer is free to choose other suitable datatypes instead. For example:

```
template <class T, class S = size_t > class Vector
{/*..*/};
Vector <int> ordinary; //second argument is size_t
Vector <int, unsigned char> tiny(5);
```

Template Specializations

The generic nature of templates enables you to define molds of classes and functions from which compilers generate concrete instances, or *specializations*. For example, the *primary template* `std::vector` may produce the following specializations:

```
vector <int> vi;
vector <string> vs;
vector <Date> vd;
//...and so on.
```

Likewise, function templates such as `std::random_shuffle()` can generate a sequence of integers, string, files, etc. The type-unawareness of templates is what makes them so useful. Yet there are times when type-unawareness becomes a problem. The solution is using *template specializations* and *partial specializations* to override the default behavior of a primary template in special cases.

Defining a Primary Template

Suppose we want to define a generic max() function that returns the highest of two values. To avoid a potential name conflict, I'll call it mymax():

```cpp
template <class T> inline T mymax(const T& t1, const T& t2)
{
 return  t1 < t2 ? t2 : t1;
}
```

In fact, this is exactly how the std::max() template is defined in <algorithm>. Let's test it:

```cpp
int main()
{
 int highest = mymax(5,10);
 char c = mymax ('a', 'z');
 string s1= "hello", s2 = "world";
 string maxstr = mymax(s1, s2); // lexicographic comparison
}
```

As expected, the first two mymax() calls return the correct result. In the third example we also get the correct result because std::string overloads operator <. This is all well and good. Now consider the following:

```cpp
const char * arr1 = "hello";
const char * arr2 = "world";
const char * p = mymax (arr1, arr2); // oops!
```

This time, mymax() returns an incorrect result. The problem is that it merely compares the pointers arr1 and arr2 instead of comparing the strings stored in these addresses. Instead, you would like to have mymax() distinguish between two sets of types: all types except const char * on the one hand, and const char * on the other hand, which should be handled differently. For this purpose, define a specialization that the compiler will use whenever the argument of mymax() is of type const char *.

Defining a Specialization

A *user-defined specialization* looks like an ordinary template definition except that it must appear after its primary template. The first step in creating such a specialization is to replace every occurrence of T in the specialization with `const char *`. In addition, the *template parameter list* should now be empty. The specialization calls `strcmp()` to compare the strings lexicographically:

```
template <> // specialization, hence empty parameter list
const char * mymax(const char * t1, const char * t2)
{
 return (strcmp(t1, t2) > 0) ? t1 : t2;
}
```

Let's test it again:

```
#include <string>
#include <cstring> // for strcmp
using std::string;

template <class T> // primary template
T mymax(const T t1, const T t2)
{
 return  t1 < t2 ? t2 : t1;
}
template <> // specialization
const char * mymax(const char * t1, const char * t2)
{
 return (strcmp(t1, t2) < 0) ? t2 : t1;
}

int main()
{
 int highest=mymax(5,10); // #1 calls primary
 char c=mymax ('a', 'z'); // #2 calls primary
 string s1="hello", s2="world";
 string maxstr=mymax(s1,s2); // #3 calls primary
 const char *arr1="hello";
 const char *arr2="world";
 const char * p=
  mymax (arr1, arr2);  // #4  calls specialization
}
```

This time, p is now pointing to "world," as it should.

Partial Specializations

Many C++ implementations use user-defined specializations internally. Specializations of template function objects such as less<> are particularly useful because they are used internally in many STL algorithms and containers.

You can define a *partial specialization*, which applies to a subset of types. For example, you can define a general template called f<T>, a partial specialization thereof called f<T*> that applies to pointers, and a specialization f<const char*> that applies to const char * exclusively:

```
template <class T> void f(T & t1) // general version
{
//...
}
template <class T> void f(T * t1) // partial specialization
{
//...
}
template <> void f(const char * t1) // specialization
{
//...
}
int main()
{
 int n;
 f(n,n); // calls f<T>
 f(&n,&n); // calls f<T*>
 f("A", "C"); // calls f<const char *>
}
```

The number of specializations and partial specializations that you can define is unlimited. However, they must be ordered in a top-down hierarchy where the least specialized versions come first. In other words, the definition of f<T*> must come after f<T> because T* is more specialized than T. In a similar vein, f<const char *> must come after f<T*> because const char * is more specialized than T *.

Explicit Specialization of a Class Template

An *explicit specialization* of a class template provides an alternative definition of the primary template. It's used instead of the primary definition if the arguments in a particular specialization match those that are given in the explicit specialization. When is it useful? Consider the `Vector` template: The code generated by the compiler for the specialization `Vector<bool>` is very inefficient. Instead of storing every Boolean value in a single bit, it occupies at least an entire byte. Following is an example of an explicit specialization, `Vector<bool>`, that manipulates bits rather than bytes:

```
template <> class Vector <bool> //explicit specialization
{
private:
  size_t sz;
  unsigned char * buff;
public:
  explicit Vector(size_t s = 1) : sz(s),
    buff (new unsigned char [(sz+7U)/8U] ) {}
  Vector<bool> (const Vector <bool> & v);
  Vector<bool>& operator= (const Vector<bool>& v);
  ~Vector<bool>();
  //...other member functions
};
Vector< bool> bits(8);
bits[0] = true; //assign
bool seventh = bits[7];
```

The `template<>` prefix indicates an explicit specialization of a primary template. The template arguments for a specialization are specified in the angle brackets that immediately follow the class name. The specialization hierarchy of `Vector` that has been defined thus far is as follows:

```
template <class T> class Vector //primary template
{};
template <class T> class Vector <T*> //partial specialization
{};
template <> class Vector <bool> //explicit specialization
{};
```

As a side note, it's worth mentioning that the Standard Template Library already defines a specialization of `std::vector<bool>` for manipulating bits optimally. Alas, during the past five years, `std::vector<bool>` has fallen from grace in the eyes of the C++ standardization committee as well as other people for various reasons that I discuss in Chapter 10, "The Standard Template Library (STL) and Generic Programming." The bottom line, however, is this: Stay away from `std::vector<bool>`.

Function Templates

A *function template* declaration contains the keyword `template`, followed by a list of template parameters and a function declaration. As opposed to ordinary functions, which are usually declared in one translation unit and defined in another, the definition of a function template follows its declaration. For example:

```
template <class T> T max( T t1, T t2)
{
  return (t1 > t2) ? t1 : t2;
}
```

Function template parameters are implicitly deduced from the types of their arguments. In the following example, the compiler instantiates three distinct specializations of `max`, according to the types of arguments used in each invocation:

```
int i = 0, j = 8;
char c = 'a', d = 'z';
string s1 = "first", s2 = "second";
int nmax = max(i, j);      // int max (int, int);
char cmax = max(c, d);     // char max (char, char);
string smax = max(s1, s2); // string max (string, string);
```

`export`ed Templates Revisited

Several sections back, I discussed `exported` templates. This topic elicited many comments from readers. Therefore, I decided to dedicate another section to this feature and fill in the missing bits.

The Separate Compilation Model

The separate compilation model (see the section "Initialization Order Dependency" in Chapter 18, "Tips and Techniques") enables us to define functions, types, and objects in one translation unit and refer to them from other translation units. (See the section "Naming Names", also in Chapter 18.) After compiling all the translation units of a program, the linker subsequently resolves all the references to `extern` symbols, producing a single executable file.

When dealing with ordinary functions and classes, the separate compilation model works neatly. Templates, however, are a different beast. When you instantiate a template, the compiler must see its definition. This is an explicit requirement in the C++ standard, which states that *dependent names* (names that depend on the type of a template parameter) shall be looked up in both the current context (i.e., the place of instantiation) and the context of the template's definition. The compiler cannot generate the code of a specialization without looking at the template's definition—even if the definition appears in a separate translation unit.

If the template is defined in several source files, all the definitions must comply with the One Definition Rule. (See the section "Speaking Standardese," p. 354.) As I explained elsewhere (see the section "Project Organization Guidelines," p. 275), the common approach is to define the template in a header file and `#include` it in every source file that uses that template. If you have used templates before, you already know that. However, standard C++ defines another compilation model for templates, known as the *separation model*.

export—How It All Began

Right from the start, C++ creators called for separate compilation of templates. However, they didn't specify how this could be accomplished. Unlike most other C++ features, which were standardized only after being implemented by one vendor at least, `exported` templates were added to C++ in 1996 with no existing implementation whatsoever. In 1996, many compilers hardly supported ordinary templates and the C++ community had gained little experience with advanced template techniques such as meta-programming. Therefore, the implications of implementing `export` weren't fully recognized. The very few people who have implemented `exported` templates agree that this is an arduous task indeed.

State of the Art

The most popular C++ compilers—e.g., Microsoft's Visual C++ .Net, Borland's C++ BuilderX, GNU's GCC and others— don't support `export`. Even vendors who have expressed their commitment to "100% ISO compliance" exclude `export` from their checklist. The frequently cited reason for this is "lack of demand." Could it be that users don't demand this feature because they've never had a chance to use it?

Which Compilers Support `export`?

In addition to Comeau C/C++, Intel's 7.x compiler also supports `export`, although by default it's disabled and "currently undocumented and unsupported." Other EDG-derived implementations may also support this feature.

> **TIP:** For details on Comeau C/C++, see the "Comeau C++ Export Overview" at *http://www.comeaucomputing.com/4.0/docs/userman/export.html*. Also see Greg Comeau's article "Serious Promises and Standard C++" at *http://www.comeaucomputing.com/iso/promises.html*.

export **and User Expectations**

If judged by the amount of questions pertaining to linkage errors due to the use of templates, C++ programmers indeed expect compilers to support separate template compilation. However, my impression is that they are looking for something quite different from what export actually does. One might naively assume that by declaring a template export in a header file, it would be possible to define it in a .cpp file that gets compiled only once, and then #include only the header file in other translation units:

```
//func.h
export template <class T> void func(T t); //only a declaration
//func.cpp
 template <class T> void func(T t) {//implementation
//...
}
//main.cpp
#include "func.h"
int main()
{
 func(5); //instantiate void func(int) here
}
```

Indeed, compilers that support exported templates allow this. However, when the compiler sees the call to func(), it has to look at the template's definition, not just its declaration. How do export-enabled compilers accomplish this? When a file containing definitions of exported templates is compiled, Comeau C/C++ for instance creates a file with an .et suffix. Then, when the template in question is instantiated, the compiler uses the .et files to find the translation unit that defines a given exported template. The sources containing the exported template definitions must therefore be made available at the time of instantiation. *The export facility is not a mechanism for avoiding the publication of template definitions in source form.*

In my opinion, this is the most crucial point in the debate about the usefulness of export. Many users mistakenly believe that export enables them to ship compiled .obj, .lib, or .dll files without having to provide the templates' definitions. This isn't the case.

Future Directions

Considering the strict requirements of the Standard, would it be possible, at least theoretically, to avoid shipping the template definitions in source form? Vendors may come up with a technology for compiling a template's definition into a pseudocode or some other intermediary language. However, such a compiler must be able to reconstruct the original template's definition from the intermediary code. .Net and Java already offer such a technology with the obvious advantage of portability. In C++, I can't think of a compelling reason to adopt this approach. For developers who want to protect their intellectual property by hiding templates' definitions, this solution is pretty useless since customers would be able to reconstruct the definitions from the intermediary code. Worse yet, compiling a template's definition into intermediary code and then decompiling it back during instantiation will increase build time considerably.

Conclusions

Considering its inherent complexities (both from an implementer's point of view and a user's point of view), `export` is expensive. Yet it doesn't offer any breathtaking advantages. Worse, it incurs a few undesirable side effects such as delayed compilation errors, and semantic differences from the inclusion model with respect to overload resolution and the "externalization" of file-scope identifiers. Then again, `export` is in the Standard.

NOTE: A proposal to remove `export` was recently rejected; see "Why We Can't Afford Export" at *http://www.open-std.org/jtc1/sc22/wg21/docs/papers/2003/n1426.pdf* (PDF).

Will this feature ever become widely used? My impression is that vendors will continue to ignore it as they have been doing in the past eight years.

Books

C++ Templates: The Complete Guide (Addison-Wesley, 2002, ISBN 0201734842), by David Vandevoorde and Nicolai M. Josuttis, is in my opinion the best template guide yet. In addition to covering state-of-the-art template programming techniques (which is why you should read this book in the first place), the authors also dedicate a few pages to the somewhat confusing template terminology: e.g., explaining the difference between a specialization and instantiation, or the difference between a template parameter and a template argument. Even `export` gets its share in Chapter 6, where the authors discuss its semantics and usage. (For more on this book, visit *http://www.informit.com/bookstore/product.asp?isbn=0201734842*.)

Summary

Templates automate the implementation of generic containers and functions. The two main template categories in C++ are class templates and function templates. A class template encapsulates parameterized data members and function members. Function templates are a means of implementing generic algorithms. Explicit specializations of a class template are always required. For function templates, the compiler usually deduces the specialization from the types of the arguments.

It's possible to define partial specialization of a class template that overrides the primary class template for a set of types. A partial specialization is indicated by a secondary list of parameters following the name of the template. An explicit specialization enables the programmer to override the automatic instantiation of a class template for a certain type.

Templates and operator overloading are the building blocks of generic programming. The Standard Template Library is an exemplary framework of generic programming, as you'll see in Chapter 10.

InformIT Articles and Sample Chapters

"C++ Templates: Metaprograms" (*http://www.informit.com/articles/article.asp?p=30667*) is a sample chapter from *C++ Templates: The Complete Guide* (Addison-Wesley, 2002, ISBN 0201734842), by David Vandevoorde and Nicolai M. Josuttis. This chapter provides excellent examples of the sophisticated programming techniques that can be implemented with templates. Although some of the examples aren't exactly practical for real-world applications, they teach advanced programmers how to push templates to their limits. (For more on this book, visit *http://www.informit.com/bookstore/product.asp?isbn=0201734842*.)

"Templates and Inheritance Interacting in C++" (*http://www.informit.com/articles/article.asp?p=31473*) is a sample chapter from *C++ Templates: The Complete Guide* (Addison-Wesley, 2002, ISBN 0201734842), by David Vandevoorde and Nicolai M. Josuttis. This chapter discusses some interesting aspects of the interaction between templates and inheritance such as the relationship between a base class template and its derived classes, virtual inheritance and multiple inheritance, the empty base class optimization and other template wizardry. (For more on this book, visit *http://www.informit.com/bookstore/product.asp?isbn=0201734842*.)

Books and e-Books

C++ Templates: The Complete Guide (Addison-Wesley, 2002, ISBN 0201734842), by David Vandevoorde and Nicolai M. Josuttis, is an exhaustive and authoritative guide to C++ templates. Unlike other C++ books, which dedicate a chapter or two to this issue, this book focuses almost exclusively on templates, starting with the basic and proceeding to state-of-the-art template wizardry. (For more on this book, visit *http://www.informit.com/bookstore/product.asp?isbn=0201734842*.)

Online Resources

"Optimize Abstract Operations with Function Templates" (*http://gethelp.devx.com/techtips/cpp_pro/10min/2001/march/10min0301.asp*), by Danny Kalev, teaches how to use templates to define generic functions. It's written especially for C++ programmers who have little or no experience in template-based programming, so it can serve as a good starting point.

"Template Specializations" (*http://gethelp.devx.com/techtips/cpp_pro/10min/2002/May/10min0502.asp*), by Danny Kalev, discusses partial and explicit specializations of templates. The article assumes prior experience in templates but teaches these more advanced techniques from the beginning, along with providing extensive code samples.

CHAPTER 6

Namespaces

Namespaces are a mechanism that enables programmers to declare classes, functions, constants and other declarations collectively known as names in separate scopes called namespaces. To understand why they are necessary, I'll use an analogy. Imagine that the file system on your computer did not have directories and subdirectories. All files would be stored in a flat repository, visible all the time to every user and application. Consequently, extreme difficulties would arise: Filenames would clash and simple operations such as listing, copying or searching files would be much more difficult. Namespaces are similar to directories. They enable you to restrict the visibility of names to certain scopes while keeping them hidden from other scopes. This way, they protect your code from name clashes and provide a higher level of encapsulation.

Applications of Namespaces

In large-scale software projects, short and elegant names for classes, functions and constants can also cause name conflicts because the same name might be used more than once to indicate different entities by different developers. In the pre-namespace era, the only workaround was to use various affixes in identifiers' names. This practice, however, is laborious and error-prone:

```
class string  // short but dangerous
{
    // ...
};

// safer but tedious
class excelSoftCompany_string
{
  //...
};
```

Namespaces enable you to use convenient, short, and intelligible names safely. Instead of repeating the unwieldy affixes, you group your declarations in a namespace and factor out the recurring affix like this:

```
//file excelSoftCompany.h
namespace excelSoftCompany   // a namespace definition
{
  class string {/*..*/};
  class vector {/*..*/};
}
```

You can separate the definition from the declaration of a namespace member as follows:

```
#include <iostream>
using namespace std;
namespace A
{
  void f(); //declaration
}
void A::f() //in a separate file, definition
{
  cout<<"in f"<<endl;
}
int main()
{
  A::f();
}
```

Properties of Namespaces

Namespaces are more than just directories or containers of names. In the following passages I will discuss some of the namespaces' features and their use.

Fully Qualified Names

A namespace is a scope in which declarations and definitions are grouped together. In order to refer to any of these from another scope, a *fully qualified name* is required. A fully qualified name has the form: namespace::classname::identifier. Since both namespaces and classes can be nested, the resulting name can be rather long but it ensures uniqueness:

```
unsigned int  maxlen = std::string::npos;
```

If repeating the fully qualified name seems tedious, you can use a using-declaration or a using-directive instead.

using-**Declarations and** using-**Directives**

A using-declaration consists of the keyword using followed by a *namespace::member*. It instructs the compiler to locate every occurrence of a certain namespace member (type, operator, function, constant, etc.) in the specified namespace, as if the fully qualified name were used. For example:

```
#include <vector>  //STL vector; defined in namespace std
int main()
{
  // the following is a using declaration; every
  //occurrence of vector is looked up in std
  using std::vector;
  vector <int> vi;
}
```

A using-directive, on the other hand, renders all the names of a certain namespace accessible in the directive's scope. For example:

```
#include <vector> // belongs to namespace std
#include <iostream> // also in namespace std
int main()
{
  using namespace std; // a using directive
 //all <iostream> and <vector> declarations
 //can now be accessed without
 //fully qualified names
  vector <int> vi;
  vi.push_back(10);
  cout<<vi[0];
}
```

Let's look back at our string class example:

```
//file excelSoftCompany.h
namespace excelSoftCompany
{
  class string {/*..*/};
```

```
  class vector {/*..*/};
}
```

You can access your own string class as well as the standard string class in the same program without risking name clashes like this:

```
#include <string> // std::string
#include "excelSoftCompany.h"

int main()
{
  using namespace excelSoftCompany;
  string s; // referring to class excelSoftCompany::string
  std::string standardstr; // ANSI string
}
```

Namespace Aliases

Choosing a short name for a namespace can eventually lead to a name clash—the very same problem we wanted to avoid in the first place. However, very long namespaces are tiresome. For this purpose, you can use a namespace alias. In the following example, I define an alias called ESC for the unwieldy `Excel_Software_Company` namespace:

```
//file decl.h
namespace Excel_Software_Company
{
  class Date {/*..*/};
  class Time {/*..*/};
}

//file calendar.cpp
#include "decl.h"
int main()
{
  namespace ESC = Excel_Software_Company; //alias
  ESC::Date date;
  ESC::Time time;
}
```

Argument-Dependent Lookup

Andrew Koenig devised an algorithm formerly known as *Koenig lookup* and later named *argument-dependent lookup (ADL)* for resolving namespace members. This algorithm is used in all standard-conforming compilers to handle cases like the following:

```
namespace MYNS
{
  class C {};
  void func(C);
}

MYNS::C c; // global object of type MYNS::C

int main()
{
  func(c); // OK, MYNS::f called
}
```

Neither a using-declaration nor a using-directive appears in the program. And yet, the compiler did the right thing—it correctly identified the unqualified name `func` as the function declared in namespace MYNS by applying ADL. How does it work? ADL causes the compiler to look at not just the usual places such as the local scope, but also the namespace that contains the argument's type. Thus, in the following source line, the compiler detects that the object `c`, which is the argument of the function `func`, belongs to namespace MYNS. Consequently, it looks at namespace MYNS to locate the declaration of `func`, "guessing" the programmer's intent.

```
func(c); // OK, MYNS::f called
```

Without ADL, namespaces would impose an unacceptable burden on the programmer, who would have to repeatedly specify the fully qualified names, or instead use numerous *using*-declarations. To push the argument in favor of ADL even further, consider the following example:

```
#include<iostream>
using std::cout;

int main()
{
 cout<< "hi"; //OK, operator <<
              //was brought into scope
              //by ADL
}
```

The `using`-declaration injects `std::cout` into the scope of `main()`, thereby enabling the programmer to use the non-qualified name `cout`. However, the overloaded `<<` operator, as you may recall, is not a member of `std::cout`. Rather, it's declared in namespace `std` as an external function that takes a `std::ostream` object as its argument. Without ADL, the programmer would have to write something like this:

```
std::operator<<(cout, "hi");
```

Fortunately, ADL "does the right thing" and saves the programmer from this tedium in an elegant way.

Using and Extending Namespaces

Most C++ programmers are familiar with the basic concepts of namespaces. And yet, they tend to use namespaces passively, e.g., by yanking code and data from namespaces defined by a third party. They rarely declare their own classes and functions in namespaces, though. In the following passage I will show that the task of declaring your classes and functions in a namespace isn't as intimidating as it might seem at first.

Namespace Members

As previously said, a namespace is a scope that contains declarations of classes, functions, constants, templates, etc. These are called *namespace members*. For example:

```
namespace proj_alpha
{
  //the following are members of namespace proj_alpha
  class Spy {/*..*/};
  void encrypt (char *msg);
  const int MAX_AGENTS = 8;
}
```

In this example, class `Spy` is implemented in a single source file. Normally, you declare a class in a header file and define its member functions separately, in a separate source file. How do you split a class that is declared as a namespace member into two or more source files?

In the following header file, Foo.hpp, I defined a namespace called `NS` that contains a declaration of class `Foo`:

```
//Foo.hpp
namespace NS
{
  class Foo
  {
  public:
    void f();
    void g();
  };
}//close NS
```

Then, in a separate source file called Foo.cpp, I first #include the header file Foo.hpp and define Foo's member functions f() and g():

```
//Foo.cpp
#include "Foo.hpp"
void NS::Foo::f()
{ /*..*/ }

void NS::Foo::g()
{ /*..*/ }
```

To refer to a namespace member, you need to use the member's fully qualified name. The fully qualified name of class Foo is NS::Foo. So that the compiler knows that NS is a namespace name, the header file Foo.hpp must be #included before any reference to it is made.

Extending a Namespace

Namespaces are extendable . You can add more members to the same namespace in other .hpp files, as in the following example:

```
//Bar.hpp
namespace NS //extends NS
{
  class Bar
  {
  public:
    void a();
    void b();
  };
}
```

Alternatively, you can forward declare the class in the namespace and then define it in a separate file:

```
namespace NS //extends NS
{
 class Bar; //fwd declaration
}

class NS::Bar //definition of
           //previously declared class
{
public:
 void a();
 void b();
};
```

Then, in the file Bar.cpp you define the newly added class's member functions as follows:

```
#include "Bar.hpp"
void NS::Bar::a()
{/*..*/}

void NS::Bar::b()
{/*..*/}
```

Now both Foo and Bar are members of namespace NS. The compiler and the linker are able to identify these classes as members of the same namespace, although they appear in separate headers. Note that you cannot extend a namespace simply by using a fully qualified name of a new member of an existing namespace. In other words, even if namespace NS has been declared elsewhere and its declaration is visible to the compiler (e.g., because its header file was #included), the following code is ill-formed:

```
#include "Bar.hpp" //namespace NS is now visible
class NS::C //Error, C hasn't been declared
         // explicitly as a member of NS
{
public:
 void a();
 void b();
};
```

To fix this code, you have to explicitly declare C as a member of namespace NS before defining it.

Now the question is: how do you use these classes in an application?

Referring to a Namespace Member

Inside the main.cpp file, you first have to `#include` the header files that declare `Foo` and `Bar`. Then, add an appropriate `using` declaration:

```
#include "Bar.hpp"
#include "Foo.hpp"
int main()
{
  using NS::Bar; //a using declaration
  using NS::Foo; //ditto
  Bar b;
  Foo f;
  f.f();
  //...
}
```

Interaction with Other Language Features

Namespaces interact with other features of the language and affect programming techniques. They make some features in C++ superfluous or undesirable, as I will show below.

Using the Scope Resolution Operator

In some frameworks, it's customary to add operator :: before a function's name to mark it explicitly as a function that is not a class member. For example:

```
void C::fill (const char * source)
{
  ::strcpy (this->pbuf, source);
}
```

This practice is not recommended, though. Many of the standard functions that used to be global are now declared in namespaces. For example, `strcpy` now belongs to namespace `std`, as do most of the Standard Library's functions.

Preceding a :: to these functions might confuse the compiler's lookup algorithm and mislead human readers. Therefore, either use the function's fully qualified name or use an appropriate using-declaration to refer to such a function.

Using static to Indicate Internal Linkage

In standard C, a nonlocal identifier declared static has internal linkage, which means that it's accessible only from the translation unit in which it is declared (linkage types are discussed in Chapter 4, "Memory Management"). This technique is used to support information hiding as in the following sample:

```
//File hidden.c
//invisible from other files */
static void decipher(FILE *f);

decipher ("passwords.bin");

//end of file
```

Although this convention is still supported in C++, it's now considered deprecated. This means that future releases of your compiler might issue a warning message if you declare a nonlocal variable `static`. In order to make a function accessible only from within its translation unit, use an unnamed namespace instead. You should do that, for instance, when you migrate from C. For example:

```
//File hidden.cpp

namespace //anonymous
{
  void decipher(FILE *f);
}
// now use the function in hidden.cpp.
//No using declarations or directives are needed
decipher ("passwords.bin");
```

Members of an anonymous namespace can never be seen from any other translation unit, so the net effect is as if they had static linkage. If you declare another function with the same name in an unnamed namespace in another file, the two functions will not clash.

The Naming Convention of Standard Header Files

All Standard C++ header files now have to be `#included` in the following way:

```
#include <iostream> //note: no ".h" extension
```

The former .h extension was omitted from the headers' names. This convention also applies to the standard C header files, with the addition of the letter *c* affixed to their name. Thus, a C standard header formerly named <xxx.h> is now <cxxx>. For example:

```
#include <cassert> //formerly: <assert.h>
```

Although the older convention for C headers; i.e., <xxx.h>, is still supported, it's now considered a deprecated feature and should not be used in new C++ code. The problem is that C <xxx.h> headers inject their declarations into the global namespace. In C++, on the other hand, most standard declarations are declared in namespace std and so are the <cxxx> standard C headers. Recall that you need a using-declaration, a using-directive, or a fully qualified name in order to access the declarations in the new-style standard headers:

```
#include <cstdio>
using std::printf;

void f()
{
  printf("Hello World");
}
```

Summary

Namespaces are an efficient and rather intuitive means of avoiding name conflicts. C++ offers three methods for injecting a namespace constituent into the current scope. The first is a using-directive, which renders all of the members of a namespace visible in the current scope. The second is a using-declaration, which is more selective and enables the injection of a single component from a namespace. Finally, a fully qualified name uniquely identifies a namespace member.

While most programmers are familiar with the constructs of bringing an existing namespace member into scope, it's important to know how to define your own namespaces and how to declare their members correctly. You can always extend an existing namespace by adding new members to it. The new members needn't be declared within the pair of { and } of the original namespace declaration. However, it's advisable to group all namespace members' declarations within the same physical file for maintenance and documentation purposes.

The argument-dependent lookup captures the programmer's intention without forcing him or her to use wearying references to a namespace.

Online Resources

"Declaring Classes and Member Functions in a Namespace" (*http://gethelp.devx.com/techtips/cpp_pro/10min/10min1099.asp*), by Danny Kalev, is a short article that teaches how to use namespaces effectively in projects while avoiding common pitfalls.

CHAPTER 7

Time and Date Library

All the time and date functions and data structures are declared in the standard header `<ctime>` (`<time.h>` in C). Time is represented as a positive integer of type `time_t` that contains the number of seconds elapsed since *the epoch*, or January 1st, 1970, 00:00 GMT. `time_t` is a platform-defined signed integral type containing at least 32 bits. As large as this type may seem, on 32-bit architectures `time_t` will roll over on January 18, 2038. Fortunately, hardware architectures are gradually switching to a 64-bit `time_t`, which can represent billions of years.

Retrieving the Current Time

The function `time()` retrieves the current calendar time from the system's clock. It has the following prototype:

```
time_t time(time_t * tp);
```

In systems in which no clock is available, the function returns -1. If `tp` is not null, the value is also written to `*tp`. The following program retrieves the current time and displays it in its raw format:

```
#include <ctime>
using namespace std;
int main()
{
 time_t curr=time(0);
 cout << "current time is: " << curr <<endl;
}
```

The output is a number such as 980898685. This is the number of seconds that have elapsed since the epoch. As you can see, `time_t` isn't a human-readable format. To present the current time and date in a human-readable format you have to convert it to a string using the `ctime()` function, which is declared as follows:

```
char * ctime(const time_t * tp);
```

This function returns a null-terminated string of the form:

```
Wed Jan 31 01:51:25 2001\n\0
```

To break the time into individual constituents such as year, month, and day of the week, use the `tm` struct:

```
struct tm
{
  int tm_sec; //seconds after the minute (0-61)
  int tm_min; //minutes after the hour (0-59)
  int tm_hour; //hours since midnight (0-23)
  int tm_mday; //day of the month (1-31)
  int tm_mon; // months since January  (0-11)
  int tm_year; // elapsed years since 1900
  int tm_wday; // days since Sunday (0-6)
  int tm_yday; //days since January 1st  (0-365)
  int tm_isdst; //1 if daylight savings is on, zero if not,
                //-1 if unknown
};
```

Remember: The key to manipulating date and time is knowing how to convert `time_t` to `tm` and vice versa. To fill a `tm` struct with the local time, use the function `localtime()`:

```
struct tm* localtime (const time_t *pt);
```

`localtime()` takes a pointer to a valid `time_t` object, converts it to a local static `tm` struct and returns its address. Note that subsequent invocations of `localtime()` override the previous value of its local static `tm` object. Therefore, you should copy the result immediately to your own `tm` object. The following program fills a `tm` object with the current local time:

```
#include <ctime>
using namespace std;
int main()
{
 time_t curr;
 tm local;
 time(&curr); // get current time_t value
```

```
local=*(localtime(&curr)); // dereference and assign
}
```

To convert a `tm` struct to `time_t`, use the `mktime()` function:

```
time_t curr;
tm local;
time(&curr); // get current time_t value
local=*(localtime(&curr)); // dereference and assign
time_t temp=mktime(&local); // temp and curr are equal
```

Time Differences and Time Zones

To compute the time difference between two dates, use the standard function `difftime()`:

```
double difftime (time_t t1, time_t t2);
```

This function takes two variables of type `time_t` and returns `t2-t1` expressed in seconds. For example:

```
time_t now=time(0);
time_t last_week=now-(60*60*24*7); // a week ago
double seconds=difftime(now, last_week);
```

To calculate time zone differences, use the `gmtime()` function:

```
struct tm * gmtime(const time_t * tp);
```

`gmtime()` converts the calendar time into its GMT equivalent. The following code calculates the difference between your local time zone and GMT:

```
time_t curr=time(0);// current local time
tm local=*gmtime(&curr);// convert curr to GMT, store as tm
time_t utc=(mktime(&local));// convert GMT tm to GMT time_t
double diff=difftime(utc,curr)/3600; //difference in hours
```

NOTE: The term *Greenwich Mean Time* (GMT) was changed to *Universal Time Coordinated* (UTC) several years ago but GMT is still widely used in the literature and, more importantly, it's used in the Standard Library's function names.

Summary

The <ctime> library provides the building bricks of time retrieval, processing and formatting. Using this library instead of any other proprietary library offers three major benefits: portability, efficiency and minimal memory and speed overhead. For more advanced uses, you can find useful open source utilities that implement timers and progress bars that are based on the <ctime> library, such as the Boost time and date library.

Online Resources

"C++ Boost Timer Library" (*http://www.boost.org/libs/timer/*) supplies a timer class for measuring elapsed time, a progress_timer class for reporting elapsed time, and a progress_display class for displaying an indication of progress toward a goal. The source code includes extensive documentation about the library, its applications, and rationale.

Time and Date.com (*http://www.timeanddate.com/*) is a very informative site that discusses time and date conventions, calculations and abbreviations. In addition, it includes time calculators that calculate the duration between two dates, the date in n days, and a full world clock that shows the current time in every major capital of the world.

CHAPTER 8

Streams

C traditionally associates three *file descriptors*—small positive integers—with each program: `stdin`, `stdout`, and `stderr`, which represent the standard input, standard output, and standard error, respectively. Although these descriptors are typically mapped to I/O devices such as a keyboard and a monitor, they're treated as files. This convention stems from the fact that C was originally developed on UNIX. UNIX treats every I/O source as a file, even when referring to physical devices such as a keyboard or a screen. C++ replaced the vintage `<stdio.h>` library of standard C with an object-oriented stream library called `<iostream>`. In addition, the Standard Library provides the `<sstream>` library for string-based I/O and the `<fstream>` library for file I/O.

Standard C++ Stream Objects

The notion of *streams* refers to any form of data represented as a sequence of bytes that come from a certain source, such as a keyboard, a file, or a network connection. The most common stream objects are `cin` and `cout`, which represent the standard input and standard output, respectively. In addition, C++ defines two more stream objects: `cerr` and `clog`. `cerr` is an object that directs output to the standard error device. In most cases this is the user's screen, although certain systems use a dedicated console or a log file. `clog` is pretty similar to `cerr` except that it can use *buffered I/O*, whereas `cerr` doesn't. (I'll discuss buffered I/O shortly.)

Note that all these streams are real objects, not classes. However, unlike with other user-defined classes, you don't have to instantiate them manually. C++ automatically creates these objects in the program's startup code so you can use them directly if your program `#include`s the `<iostream>` header. For example:

```
#include <iostream>
int main()
{
std::cout<<"hello world!"<<std::endl;
}
```

This program prints the greeting `hello world!` on the standard output. Notice that like all standard components, the `<iostream>` objects are declared in `std` namespaces. (For further information on namespaces, see Chapter 6, "Namespaces.")

NOTE: The four stream objects—`cin`, `cout`, `cerr`, and `clog`— also have wide-char equivalents: `wcin`, `wcout`, `wcerr`, and `wclog`.

The `std::endl` part of the code above is of special interest. (By the way, it's pronounced *end ell*; the last character is the lowercase letter *L*, not the number 1.) It's a *manipulator*—that is, an argument that affects the I/O operation is a certain way. The `endl` manipulator, for example, has two effects:

- It forces output *flushing*, meaning that it causes `cout` to output its buffered contents immediately.
- It appends a line break after the output operation.

Thus, the next `cout` statement will display its content on the next line.

As previously mentioned, some `iostream` objects use buffered I/O. This means that they're allowed to lump several I/O operations and perform them at once. For example, the following statements may not be performed as three consecutive operations:

```
std::cout<<"hello";
std::cout<<" ";
std::cout<<"world!";
```

Instead, the implementation may delay the output to the screen for efficiency reasons, and display the three strings in one shot. This buffering isn't always desirable. For example, if you're designing an interactive application that prompts the user to insert a password, you certainly don't want the user to wait indefinitely until the system decides to flush `cout` and display the prompt onscreen. The `endl` manipulator overrides this behavior and causes the output to be displayed without a delay:

```
std::cout<<"dear user, ";
std::cout<<"please enter your password: "<<std::endl;
```

Not all stream objects use buffered I/O. `cerr`, for example, doesn't buffer its content. The rationale is that error messages usually require immediate attention from the user and shouldn't be delayed. If the system is running out of memory, there's no point in delaying the error message when any further delay might cause a crash. Therefore, `cerr` automatically flushes its content with each output operation. By contrast, `clog` is intended to be a buffered stream object. As the name suggests, it's used for normal logging operations that don't require immediate attention.

Input streams and output streams are *tied* to each other. This means that when you combine input and output operations, `cout` is flushed before any `cin` operation and vice versa, even when no explicit manipulator is present. The following example demonstrates this principle:

```
std::cout<<"dear user, ";
std::cout<<"please enter password: "; //OK, no endl
std::cin>>pwd; //at this point, cout has been flushed
std::cout<<"your password has been read"<<std::endl;
```

The first two `cout` operations complete before the `cin` statement reads the user's password. Likewise, the `cin` operation completes before the last `cout` statement takes place.

Format Flags

The `<iostream>` library defines a rich set of format flags. These flags enable you to control the width, alignment, precision, and so on for the displayed data. Here's a list of these flags:

Flag	Description	Example
skipws	Skip whitespace on input	
left	Pad before value	" 100"
right	Pad after value	"100 "
internal	Pad between sign and value	"+ 120"
boolalpha	Display `true` and `false` instead of 1 and 0	
dec	Base 10 output	109
hex	Base 16 output	0xfad2
oct	Base 8 output	0766
scientific	Floating-point notation	ddd.ddEdd
fixed	Fixed decimal notation	dd.ddd
showbase	Prefix `oct` with 0 and `hex` with 0x	
showpoint	Print trailing zeros	
showpos	Show + for positive integers	
uppercase	Use E, X instead of e, x	

Extending `<iostream>` to Support User-Defined Types

Legacy applications and diehards still use C's `<stdio.h>` for performing I/O tasks. Yet this library suffers from several imitations that make it unsuitable in object-oriented environments. For instance, you can't extend `<stdio.h>` to support user-defined types. Unlike `<stdio.h>`, `<iostream>` classes and objects are extendable. In the following sections, I will show how to extend `<iostream>` components by overloading operator << so that it can display a user-defined object.

Supporting Built-In and Standard Types

The most widely used objects of the `<iostream>` library are `cin` and `cout`, which perform console-oriented input and output, respectively. Note that `cin` and `cout` are real objects, not classes, that C++ instantiates before the program's outset. These objects define several overloaded versions of operators >> and << for data input and output. The overloaded versions support all of the built-in types of C++ such as `int`, `double`, and `bool`. In addition, they support various types of pointers: `char *` (i.e., C-strings), `void *` (for pointers in general) and some of the Standard Library's classes, including `std::string` and `std::complex`. For this reason, the following program will run smoothly on any standard-compliant C++ implementation:

```
#include <iostream>
#include <string>
#include <complex>
using namespace std;

int main()
{
complex <double> comp(1.0, 0.0);
cout<<comp<<endl;
string s;
const char * msg="enter your name: ";
cout<<msg<<endl;
cin>>s;
bool b= true;
void *p = &b;
cout<<"b's value is: "<<b<<", b's address is: "<<p<<endl;
}
```

The output from this program should look more or less as follows:

```
<1,0>
enter your name:
Danny
b's value is: true, b's address is: 0012ff3b
```

This is all well and good. Not only do `cin` and `cout` support a vast set of datatypes and standard classes such as `std::string`, you're free from the burden of using cumbersome format flags to indicate the type of an argument in a `cout` expression. However, suppose you declared the following class:

```
class student
{
private:
  string name;
  string department;
public:
  student(const string& n, const string& dep)
    : name(n), department(dep) {}
  student() {}

  string get_name() const { return name; }
  string get_department () const { return department; }
  void set_name(const string& n) { name=n; }
  void set_department (const string& d) {department=d;}
};
```

And you want to be able to use it in a `cout` statement as follows:

```
student st("James E.", "Biology");
cout<<st; // display student's details
```

The `cout` expression will cause a compilation error because there's no overloaded version of << that supports `student`.

Overloading `cout`'s <<

To extend `cout`'s support for a user-defined type you need to overload the operator << of class `ostream` (note that `cout` is an instance of `ostream`). The canonical form of such an overloaded << looks as follows:

```
ostream& operator << (ostream& os, const student& s);
```

In other words, an overloaded << returns a reference to an `ostream` object and takes two parameters by reference: an `ostream` object and a user-defined type. The user-defined type is declared `const` because the output operation doesn't modify it.

The body of the overloaded << inserts members of the user-defined object that `cout` does support into the `ostream` object. In this case, the two data members of `student` are of type `std::string`. As previously shown, `cout` natively supports this class:

```
os<<s.get_name()<<'\t'<<s.get_department()<<endl;
```

Make sure that the members inserted are separated by a tab, newline or spaces or else they will appear as if they were concatenated when displayed on the screen. Remember also to place the `endl` manipulator at the end of the insertion chain to force a buffer flush. Finally, the overloaded operator should return the `ostream` object into which the members have been inserted. This will enable you to chain several objects in a single `cout` statement like this:

```
student s1("Bill","CS"),  s2("Jane", "Linguistics");
cout<<s1<<s2;  // chaining multiple objects
```

The complete definition of the overloaded << operator is as follows:

```
ostream& operator << (ostream& os, const student& s)
{
 os<<s.get_name()<<'\t'<<s.get_department()<<endl;
 return os;
}
```

The insertion operations and the return statement can be accomplished in a single statement:

```
ostream& operator << (ostream& os, const student& s)
{
 return os<<s.get_name()<<'\t'<<s.get_department()<<endl;
}
```

Now you can use the overloaded << in your code:

```
int main()
{
student s1("Bill F.","CS"),  s2("Jane E.", "Linguistics");
```

```
cout<<s1<<s2;  // chaining multiple objects
}
```

As expected, this program displays:

```
Bill F.    CS
Jane E.    Linguistics
```

Overloading `cin`'s `<<`

At this point you're probably wondering whether it's possible to extend `cin` as well so that it can read an entire object from the standard input in a single `cin` expression. The answer is "yes." Although this technique is less commonly used, you can define an overloaded version of operator `<<` that reads the values of `student`'s data members from the standard input like this:

```
istream& operator >> (istream& is, student & stu)
{
 string name, dep;
 cout<<"enter name: ";
 cin>>name;
 stu.set_name(name);
 cout<<"enter department: ";
 cin>>dep;
 stu.set_department(dep);
 return is; //enable chaining
}
student s1, s2;
cin>>s1>>s2; //fill the objects
cout<<s1<<s2;
```

Summary

For trivial classes such as `student`, you don't really have to define a specialized version of operator `<<`. Instead, you can access its two data members through `student`'s `get_name()` and `get_department()` or `set_name()` and `set_department()`. However, for more complex classes that have dozens of data members, it's advisable to overloaded `<<` and `>>` and thus spare users the trouble of having to extract or insert every data member individually.

String Streams

The <sstream> library provides a set of classes that perform string-based I/O. These classes enable you to convert between datatypes automatically and safely. The ostringstream, istringstream, and stringstream classes perform output string I/O, input string I/O, and combined input and output I/O, respectively. Each of these classes has a wide-char equivalent: wostringstream, wistringstream, and wstringstream, respectively.

The <sstream> library is meant to replace the traditional sprintf() and scanf() family of functions of standard C. The following program uses a stringstream object to convert an int to a string:

```
#include <sstream>
#include <iotream>
#include <string>
using namespace std;
int main()
{
 stringstream stream; //instantiate a stream object
 int n=10000;
 string result;
 stream<<n; //insert n into the stream
 stream>>result;// extract value from stream into result
 cout<<result<<endl; //result now contains "10000"
}
```

File Streams

The <fstream> library provides a set of classes that perform file I/O. This library is a replacement for the standard C <stdio.h> library. The <fstream> library includes the ifstream, ofstream, and fstream classes for input file operations, output file operations, and combined input and output operations, respectively. Each of these classes also has a wide-char equivalent: wifstream, wofstream, and wfstream, respectively.

The ifstream class supports the overloaded >> operator. Likewise, ofstream supports the << operator. fstream combines input and output operations; it therefore overloads both the >> and << operators. The following program creates an ifstream object called dictionary and prints each word in it onscreen:

```
#include <iostream>
#include <string>
#include <fstream>
#include <cstdlib>
using namespace std;
int main()
{
 string s;
 cout<<"enter dictionary file: ";
 cin>>s;
  //fstream's ctor accepts only char * filenames
 ifstream dictionary (s.c_str());
 if (!dictionary) // were there any errors on opening?
   exit(-1);
 while (dictionary >> s) cout << s <<'\n';
}
```

The call to the `string::c_str()` member function is required because `<fstream>` objects accept only `const char *` filenames. When you pass a filename as an argument, the constructor attempts to open that file. Next, the overloaded `!` operator checks the file's status. If an error has occurred, the operator evaluates as `true`. The last line contains a loop that, on each iteration, reads a word from the file, copies it to `s`, and displays it. Note that the program doesn't check for an EOF character explicitly, because the overloaded `>>` operator handles this condition automatically. Furthermore, it doesn't close the file explicitly; the destructor does that automatically.

Summary

The `<iostream>`, `<sstream>`, and `<fstream>` libraries are closely related. They contain classes derived from a common set of abstract I/O classes that define the basic interface of C++ I/O. Each of these libraries defines a specialized form of I/O: screen I/O, string I/O, and file I/O, respectively. The object-oriented interface of these libraries simplifies their usage immensely. Thus, instead of opening and closing a file manually, you simply pass a filename as an argument to an `ifstream` object and let it take care of the rest.

A common complaint from programmers who are used to the `<stdio.h>` library is that C++ streams don't offer the same level of finely tuned format flags. This claim is incorrect, however. C++ offers a rich set of flags and manipulators that offer the same functionality.

Two of the main advantages of the C++ stream libraries is their type-safety and extensibility. It's easy to extend these classes and define additional overloaded member functions and operators such as <<, >>, etc. to support user-defined types.

Online Resources

"How to Use <fstream> for File I/O" (*http://gethelp.devx.com/techtips/cpp_pro/10min/2001/june/10min0601.asp*), by Danny Kalev, is an introduction to the <fstream>class library. This article is useful for programmers who have prior experience with C-style file I/O and want to migrate to <fstream>.

"Overloading Operator << for a User-Defined Type" (*http://gethelp.devx.com/techtips/cpp_pro/10min/10min0400.asp*), by Danny Kalev, demonstrates how to extend <iostream> objects to support user-defined types.

"Automating Type Conversions with stringstream Objects" (*http://gethelp.devx.com/techtips/cpp_pro/10min/2001/april/10min0401.asp*), by Danny Kalev, provides a detailed account of the <sstream> library components and shows how to use them to facilitate type conversions.

CHAPTER 9

Object-Oriented Programming and Design Principles

Despite a common belief to the contrary, object-oriented programming isn't new. Back in the late 1960s, the Modula programming language already implemented many of the principles of this paradigm. Smalltalk, which appeared in 1972, was the first pure object-oriented language. Unlike other languages, it *enforced*—rather than enabled—strict object-oriented practices. Although Smalltalk never gained much popularity, it inspired many other programming languages such as Eiffel and Java (but not C++), which adopted its object model. The primary data abstraction mechanism in OO programming languages is a *class*. A class is a user-defined type that represents an object or a concept—a file, a hardware device, a database record, a document, an airplane, etc. An *object* is an instance of a class, just as a variable in procedural programming languages is an instance of a type. Before we continue our discussion, let's look at the principles of object-oriented programming and see how they're implemented in C++. The six major criteria are as follows:

- Abstract datatyping
- Information hiding
- Encapsulation
- Inheritance
- Polymorphism
- Dynamic binding

Abstract Datatyping

Programming languages that support *abstract datatyping* (ADT) allow programmers to extend the language's set of built-in types by adding user-defined types that are treated as first-class citizens. In C++, the most prevalent form of this is concrete classes such as `string`, `vector`, `list`, and so on. However, ADT isn't confined to classes. C++ also enables you to declare `struct`s, unions, enum types, and `typedef` names that behave as native types. While it's true that `struct`s, unions, and enum types also exist in C, they're not considered first-class citizens in this language. The following C snippet demonstrates the difference:

```
enum Traffic_light{ red, yellow, green};
int val;
enum Traffic_light t; /* enum must be used in C*/
```

When you create an `enum` variable in C, you must include the keyword `enum` before the enumeration's typename. The same is true for `struct`s and `union`s. Writing something like this:

```
Traffic_light t;
```

is allowed only with typedefs. In C++, this restriction doesn't exist:

```
int val;
Traffic_light t; // allowed in C++
```

Abstract datatyping enables programmers to extend and perfect the limited set of built-in types available in their programming languages. String classes are a good example of this. Although C++ doesn't have a built-in string type, the C++ Standard Library provides a `string` class that remedies this lack.

Information Hiding

Information hiding is manifested by enabling programmers to restrict access to certain data and code. This way, a class can prevent other classes and functions from accessing its data members and some of its member functions, while allowing them to access its non-restricted members. Let's look at a concrete example. Suppose we have a `Time` class that counts the time of day:

```
class Time
{
public:
 void Display();
private:
 int ticks;
};
```

The `Display()` member function prints the current time onscreen. This member function is accessible to all. It's therefore declared `public`. By contrast, the data member `ticks` is declared `private`. Therefore, external users can't access it. Only `Time`'s member functions are allowed to access it. In other words, the type of `ticks`; its current value; and, in fact, its very existence are pieces of information that we want to hide because these are all implementation details. What's so special about implementation details that object-oriented languages strive so hard to hide them? The main problem with exposing such details is that they're likely to change in the future. If these details were indiscriminately accessible to all, the result would be a maintenance nightmare because every change in an implementation detail would propagate to every piece of code that depends on that detail. For example, if we decide to store the current time as the number of CPU cycles rather than the number of the system's clock ticks, every piece of code that relied on the previous representation would break. By contrast, the public members of a class are its *interface*. Interfaces are less likely to change. Regardless of how `Display()` extracts the current timestamp from `ticks`, users can be sure that it will "do the right thing" and display the correct time onscreen.

In addition to `private` and `public`, C++ has a third access-specifier: `protected`. Protected members of a class are accessible to its members as well as to members of classes derived from it. However, they are inaccessible to any other classes or functions. I'll discuss this in further detail in the section "Inheritance."

Encapsulation

Encapsulation is often confused with information hiding. However, these terms are not interchangeable. Encapsulation is the ability to bundle related data and functionality within a single, autonomous entity called a *class*. For example, a class called `LoggerFile` might bundle data members such as the log file's path; a buffer of data waiting to be written to that file; and member functions that open, read, write, and close that file, as in the following code listing:

```cpp
class LogFile
{
public:
 int Open();
 int Read(char *buff);
 int Write(const char *buff);
 int Close();
private:
 FILE *logfile;
  bool _open;
//...additional data members
};
```

In procedural languages such as C, you declare these data members and the associated functions separately. Consequently, a global function that opens a log file may be mistakenly called to open a file that has already been opened. Worse yet, users might delete a log file and then attempt to write to it. By bundling the data and functionality in an autonomous class, it's much easier to avert such human errors, because the class maintains the state of the file and is therefore able to prevent such errors.

Inheritance

Inheritance is the flagship of object-oriented programming. It enables you to derive more specialized classes from another class—a *base class*. Derivation enables a derived class to inherit the functionality of the base class and extend it or alter only specific parts of it. The main advantage of derivation is code reuse. Suppose we want to create a new `LogFile` class that performs periodic backups of data. Instead of writing all the functionality of a log file class from scratch, we can derive the new class from `LogFile` and add the necessary data members and functions to it:

```cpp
class BackupLogFile: public LogFile
{
public:
 int Backup();
private:
 time_t previous_backup;
};
```

Notice that the programmer only had to declare the additional functionality. Inheritance, of course, isn't limited. You can derive another class from `BackupLogFile`, say `NetBackupLogFile`, that enables the system manager to monitor the backup process from a remote web browser.

C++ is one of the few OO programming languages that support multiple inheritance (MI), whereby a class inherits from two or more base classes simultaneously. While many OO critics claim that MI is dangerous and complicates the language unnecessarily, it's hard to ignore its power. Consider a multimedia player class. Usually, such media players consist of two major components: an audio player and a video player. Deriving a multimedia player from these classes seems like a natural choice:

```
class MediaPlayer: public AudioPlayer, public VideoPlayer
{
public:
 int Play();
 //...
};
```

The use of MI in this case reflects the symmetric nature of a multimedia player better than a single inheritance model would. This is all well and good, but MI might incur complexities. In the previous example, we didn't look at the definitions of classes `AudioPlayer` and `VideoPlayer`. In well-designed OO projects, it's likely that these classes are derived from other classes as well. And if both of them happen to derive from the same class, we could get into trouble:

```
class DataCompressor
{
public:
 void CompressStream();
 void DecompressStream();
//...
};
class AudioPlayer :public DataCompressor
{
//...
};
class VideoPlayer :public DataCompressor
{
//...
};
```

Can you see what can go wrong with this? `AudioPlayer` and `VideoPlayer` each contain a distinct copy of `DataCompressor`. `MediaPlayer` inherits from these two classes and consequently gets two copies of `DataCompressor`, one from each base class. This duplication results in ambiguity when `MediaPlayer` objects try to invoke member functions of `DataCompressor`. For example:

```
MediaPlayer player;
//..load a clip
player.DecompressStream();// ambiguous call
```

While it's possible to resolve this ambiguity by using a qualified name of the member function in question, this is still a nuisance. To avoid such ambiguities, you use *virtual inheritance*. Regardless of the derivation lattice, there's always a single instance of a virtual base class in its derived classes. For example:

```
class AudioPlayer : virtual public DataCompressor
{...};
class VideoPlayer : virtual public DataCompressor
{...};
class MediaPlayer: public AudioPlayer, public VideoPlayer
{...};
```

Now `MediaPlayer` has only a single instance of `DataCompressor`. `DecompressStream()` is therefore unambiguous. Virtual inheritance affects the order of the construction of base classes in a derived class. To ensure that only a single instance of a virtual sub-object exists in a derived class, virtual base classes are constructed before non-virtual base classes.

Polymorphism

Polymorphism is another elusive term. Many programmers confuse it with *dynamic binding*, which I'll discuss shortly. However, dynamic binding is only one of three manifestations of polymorphism in C++. The word *polymorphism* is composed of two Greek words that mean "multiple forms." In natural languages such as English, polymorphism is widely used. Consider the verb *to open*. Its exact interpretation depends on the object it takes. For example, opening a book, opening a door, and opening a conversation are three different actions. As a speaker of the language, you can tell the difference between these instances by examining the context and the objects that the verb takes.

In programming languages, polymorphism refers to the object's ability to respond in an individual manner to the same message.

Imagine a program that has a set of shape objects: square, triangle and trapezium. All these objects are derived from a common `Shape` base class, which has a member function called `Draw()`. When you call `Draw()` on a triangle, it reacts by drawing a triangle on the screen; calling `Draw()` on a square object causes it to draw a square on the screen, and so on. As you can see, the `Draw()` function behaves like the verb *to open*: Its exact interpretation depends on the object that it takes. Here again, programming languages separate between the interface (in this case, a member function called `Draw()` that causes a shape object to be drawn onscreen) and the implementation details (how exactly the `Draw()` operation is implemented in every object), which remain hidden from the users.

This form of polymorphism is achieved by means of dynamic binding. However, C++ supports three more flavors of polymorphism: function overloading, operator overloading, and templates. I discuss each of these features in their relevant sections. However, I'll give a few examples here to demonstrate. The use of the `+=` operator with integers or string objects, for example, is interpreted by each of these objects in an individual manner. Obviously, the underlying implementation of `+=` differs for every type. Yet, intuitively, we can predict what the results will be.

Templates are another example of polymorphism. A `vector` of integers and a `vector` of strings implement the `push_back()` member function differently, although the gory implementation details are hidden from the user:

```
vector <int> vi;
vector <string> names;
vi.push_back( 5 );
names.push_back (string("James"));
```

Dynamic Binding

Earlier, I explained how dynamic binding and polymorphism are related. However, I didn't explain how this relationship is implemented. Dynamic binding refers to the mechanism that resolves a *virtual function* call at runtime. This mechanism is activated when you call a virtual member function through a reference or a pointer to a *polymorphic object*. Imagine a class hierarchy in which a class called `Shape` serves as a base class for other classes (`Triangle` and `Square`):

```
class Shape
{
public:
 void virtual Draw() {} //dummy implementation
//..
};
class Square
{
public:
 void Draw(); //overriding Shape::Draw
}
class Triangle
{
public:
 void Draw(); //overriding Shape::Draw
}
```

Draw() is a dummy function in Shape. It's declared virtual in the base class to enable derived classes to override it and provide individual implementations. The beauty in polymorphism is that a pointer or a reference to Shape may actually point to an object of class Square or Triangle:

```
void func(const Shape* s)
{
 s->Draw()
}
int main()
{
 Shape *p1= new Triangle;
 Shape *p2 = new Square;
 func(p1);
 func(p2);
}
```

C++ distinguishes between a *static type* and a *dynamic type* of an object. The static type is determined at compile-time. It's the type specified in the declaration. For example, the static type of both p1 and p2 is Shape *. However, the dynamic types of these pointers are determined by the type of object to which they point: Triangle * and Square *, respectively. When func() calls the member function Draw(), C++ resolves the dynamic type of s and ensures that the appropriate version of Draw() is invoked. Notice how powerful dynamic binding is: You can derive additional classes from Shape that override Draw() even after func() was compiled. When func() invokes Draw(), C++ will still resolve the call according to the dynamic type of s.

As the example shows, dynamic binding isn't confined to the resolution of member function calls at runtime; rather, it applies to the binding of a dynamic type to a pointer or a reference that may differ from its static type. Such a pointer or reference is said to be *polymorphic*. Likewise, the object bound to such a pointer is a *polymorphic object*.

Dynamic binding exacts a toll, though. Resolving the dynamic type of an object takes place at runtime and therefore incurs performance overhead. However, this penalty is negligible in most cases. Another advantage of dynamic binding is reuse. If you decide to introduce additional classes at a later stage, you only have to override `Draw()` instead of writing entire classes from scratch. Furthermore, existing code will still function correctly once you've added new classes. You only have to compile the new code and relink the program.

Summary

Some of the six criteria that I've surveyed may be implementable in procedural programming languages as well, albeit with a significant effort and programmer's ingenuity. C++ automates and simplifies this immensely by means of keywords, strict type-checking, and state-of-the-art compiler technology. Remember that while all object-oriented programming languages adhere to these criteria, they differ radically in their underlying implementation. In Smalltalk, for instance, every type is a class, including characters, integers, and so on. C++, on the other hand, distinguishes between primitive types (also called *built-in types* or *fundamental types*) such as `int` and `bool` on the one hand, and classes on the other hand. This design decision isn't an omission: The creators of C++ attempted to keep it as efficient as C, and therefore needed to make certain compromises.

While critics bemoan the fact that C++ is not a pure object-oriented language, its support of multiple programming paradigms is deliberate and fruitful; without this leeway, generic programming would be nearly impossible. Likewise, if C++ didn't support procedural programming, it wouldn't have become a widely used general-purpose programming language. That said, I believe I've shown here that C++ is even more object-oriented than other programming languages. For example, it's one of the few languages that support multiple inheritance, operator overloading, and templates.

Notice how the term *object-oriented* has been misused throughout the years. From the criteria above, it's obvious that fancy GUI and point-and-click interfaces have little to do with this programming paradigm; in order to qualify as object-oriented, a programming language must meet the design criteria discussed here. In fact, if you carefully examine some of the frameworks, programming languages, and software tools that boast their alleged object-oriented approach, you'll discover that they aren't truly OO, because they don't comply with these design principles.

The Rise and Fall of Object Orientation

Slowly but surely, state-of-the-art C++ programming is becoming less and less object-oriented. No, C++ isn't falling back to procedural programming—quite the contrary. However, if you examine standard C++ libraries such as STL, `<tuple>`, `reference_wrapper`, and just about any other recent addition to the language, you will notice that the traditional concepts of object-oriented programming have fallen from grace, being replaced by more advanced paradigms and techniques. It wouldn't be an exaggeration to say that classic object orientation is now a thing of the past. In this section, I will discuss this paradigm shift and its causes.

Traditional Object-Oriented Concepts

The roots of object orientation date back to the late 1960s, when languages such as Modula-2 implemented these features:

- Dynamic binding (see the section "Dynamic Binding")
- Encapsulation (see the section "Encapsulation")
- Inheritance (see the section "Inheritance")

Later programming languages (particularly Smalltalk 72) refined these concepts, forming a new paradigm called *object-oriented programming* (OOP). If anything, OOP focused on the ability to define autonomous units that bundle data and related operations as an object. Many of the early OO languages relied on dynamic typing: virtual functions, inheritance and the ability to pick and mix properties of multiple objects at runtime. As always, proponents of the new paradigm promised a higher level of code reuse, resilience to design changes, safety, reliability and portability. Indeed, if you compare antiquated programming languages such as Fortran and COBOL to Smalltalk, OO has fulfilled these promises to some extent. And yet today, more than a decade after the revolution that made OO a predominant programming paradigm, we realize that traditional OO programming is a disappointment. Diplomatic understatements and lip service won't change this fact. Let's see why OO programming has lost its luster in C++.

Code Reuse

Code reuse was the biggest promise of OOP. Pundits claimed that by using virtual member functions and inheritance, you could get the ultimate level of code reuse while still benefiting from resilience to design changes. In practice, though, this software design model has resulted in a large number of extremely inefficient frameworks and libraries. Take MFC for example. Its set of collection classes is light years behind STL. The problem isn't with MFC, though. Similar frameworks, say OWL and National Institute of Health Class Library (NIHCL), repeated exactly the same design mistakes: deriving every collection class from an abstract collection class and relying on virtual member functions and dynamic typing. This suggests that OO itself is the culprit, not the designers.

Member Functions

Member functions, or methods as they are called in other programming languages, are a fundamental aspect of OOP. Think for minute: What could be more logical and properly designed than a member function that is familiar with the intimate details of its object? Obvious advantages notwithstanding, member functions are disfavored in state-of-the-art C++ libraries. The problem is that a member function is useful only for a single class. This is the bane of code reuse. Think for example of a library of containers. If each container class defines its own `size()` member function, you will end up writing numerous `size()` functions that basically do the same thing. The alternative is to define a generic function (let's call it an *algorithm* to make it more palatable for hardcore OO aficionados) that works for every container type. Isn't this a step backward into the good old days of procedural programming, when data structures and functions that manipulated them were kept apart? Syntactically speaking, yes. Generic programming looks like procedural programming more than object-oriented programming does. Yet under the hood, things work very differently. A generic algorithm, unlike a typical function in a procedural language, knows very little about the data structure it manipulates. Furthermore, it doesn't peek into the data structure directly but uses iterators for this purpose. So the syntactic similarity is misleading.

Should member functions be thrown out the window? Not quite. They are useful under the following conditions: when the language forces you to use a member function (constructors, destructors and conversion operators for example), or when the member function implements a service that is meaningful only in the context of a certain class. An example of this is a `connect()` member function of a socket class. In most other cases, experience has shown that common operations such as `insert()`, `assign()`, `replace()`, `sort()`, and `copy()`, which are applicable to a very wide set of objects, are best implemented as freestanding algorithms rather than being replicated as a member function in every class.

Inheritance

Another sacred cow of traditional OO design is inheritance. STL hardly uses inheritance; it seems that the newer a C++ library is, the less it uses inheritance. Why is this? In theory at least, inheritance is the primary means of reuse. However, it incurs a lot of complications and overhead. First, every class hierarchy that relies on inheritance must have a virtual destructor and virtual functions. For certain abstractions such as C++ streams (see Chapter 8, "Streams"), this model is used effectively. Yet in other abstractions such as containers, there's little motivation to derive container classes from a common base class. Inheritance incurs another onerous problem: it propagates bugs. A faulty member function in a base class contaminates every derived class. Even if the base class's functions are bug-free, derived classes often carry the excess baggage inherited from their base classes. Look at `cout` and for example. How many programmers ever bother to use the numerous member functions that the `ios_base` and `basic_ios` base classes pass on to them?

By forgoing inheritance, STL containers don't carry such excess baggage. Furthermore, the fact that every container class is independent enables implementers to optimize each of them.

Conclusions

One of the tricks that OO diehards use is to broaden its definition. They claim that a through-and-through OO language should provide facilities for generic programming and functional programming in addition to the traditional OO concepts. Under this broad definition, the recent additions to the Standard Library still follow the OO model. However, this is just a verbal maneuver that is meant to camouflage the facts: OO in its classic sense is a thing of the past, at least in C++. Experience has shown that generic programming and, to a smaller extent, functional programming achieve a high level of code reuse, portability and efficiency.

TIP: For more on traditional OO concepts, see the section "Object-Oriented Programming and Design Principles."

InformIT Articles and Sample Chapters

"Generic Programming and the C++ Standard Library" (*http://www.informit.com/articles/article.asp?p=25142*) is a sample chapter from *More Exceptional C++: 40 New Engineering Puzzles, Programming Problems, and Solutions* (Addison-Wesley, 2001, ISBN 020170434X), by Herb Sutter. This article shows some of the power and flexibility of the C++ standard library. Prior experience with the language is assumed, so this article is ideal for the C++ programmer who want to learn how to use STL (short for *Standard Template Library*) and understand its design concepts. (For more on this book, visit *http://www.informit.com/bookstore/product.asp?isbn=020170434X*.)

"Object Orientation: C++ Specifics" (*http://www.informit.com/articles/article.asp?p=14745*) is a sample chapter from *The Waite Group's C++ How-To* (Sams, 1999, ISBN 1571691596), by Danny Kalev and Paul Snaith. This article presents OO design and implementation techniques using the C++ language. Primarily aimed at beginners, it isn't an exhaustive account of OO design principles, but it contains extensive code samples. (For more on this book, visit *http://www.informit.com/bookstore/product.asp?isbn=1571691596*.)

"Deitel Introduces Polymorphism in C++" (*http://www.informit.com/articles/article.asp?p=29448*), by Deitel & Associates, discusses certain aspects of object-oriented programming, namely implementing polymorphism by means of virtual functions and dynamic binding. This article does a nice job of explaining all the details while providing easy-to-follow code samples and dispelling some of the myths concerning virtual functions.

Online Resources

"The Ada 95 Reference Manual" (*http://www.adahome.com/rm95/*) describes Ada 95, a fully object-oriented programming language based on the original Ada 83 language. If you're interested in object-oriented theory, one of the things you'd certainly want to do is contrast C++ with other object-oriented languages and assess the differences between them. I picked Ada because it's less popular and hyped than Java or Smalltalk, and it shares the same evolution path of C++: a non-object-oriented language that was extended into a multi-paradigm programming language. Ada is of special interest to C++ programmers for another reason: It was the first language to support generic programming.

CHAPTER 10

The Standard Template Library (STL) and Generic Programming

The generic programming paradigm is meant to enable a higher level of code reuse than traditional object-oriented programming does. Instead of relying on inheritance and polymorphism, it relies on type independence. C++ has two features that support this paradigm: templates and operator overloading. A combination of these features allows a generic algorithm to assume very little about the actual object to which it's applied, whether it's a fundamental type or a user-defined type. Consequently, such an algorithm offers a higher reusability potential than does a type-dependent algorithm.

The *Standard Template Library* (STL) is an exemplary framework built on the foundations of generic programming. STL is a collection of generic algorithms and containers that communicate through *iterators*, which are pointers or pointer-like constructs. A complete account of every STL container and algorithm can fill a book of its own. (Several excellent books on the topic have been published in recent years; see the recommendations in the resources sections.) Therefore, this section only discusses the basic concepts of generic programming, starting with an overview of STL header files, and then moving on to containers, iterators, algorithms, function objects, adaptors, and allocators. Finally, I describe the class `std::string`.

Principles of Generic Programming

Reusability is characterized by two key features: adaptability and efficiency. It's not difficult to imagine highly adaptive software components that are too inefficient to become widely used. (These are usually implemented by complex inheritance hierarchies, virtual functions, and extensive use of runtime-type information.) Conversely, efficient components are generally written in low-level, compiler-dependent code that's both non-portable and hard to maintain. Templates overcome these difficulties because they're high level and use static type-checking. The most useful generic components are containers and algorithms.

In the latest phases of the standardization of C++, Alex Stepanov suggested adding a generic library of containers and algorithms to C++. He based his proposal on a similar generic library that he had previously designed for Ada. The proposed generic library was a collection of containers based on mathematical data models such as vectors, queues, lists, and stacks. It also contained a set of generic algorithms such as `sort`, `merge`, `find`, `replace`, and so on. These library constituents were implemented with templates. It's time to examine these components in greater detail.

Organization of STL Header Files

STL components are defined in the following header files:

- **Containers**. Container classes are defined in the header files shown in the following table. The associative containers `multimap` and `multiset` are defined in <map> and <set>, respectively. Similarly, `priority_queue` and `deque` are defined in <queue>.

STL Containers

Header	Contents
<vector>	An array of T
<list>	A doubly linked list of T
<deque>	A double-ended queue of T
<queue>	A queue of T
<stack>	A stack of T
<map>	An associative array of T
<set>	A set of T
<bitset>	A set of Boolean values

- **Algorithms**. The Standard Template Library's algorithms are all defined in the header file <algorithm>.
- **Iterators**. Iterators are defined in the header file <iterator>.

- **Numeric library.** STL provides several classes and algorithms that are specifically designed for numeric computations. They're defined in the headers shown in the following table.

Numeric Containers and Algorithms

Header	Contents
`<complex>`	Complex numbers and their associated operations
`<valarray>`	Mathematical vectors and their associated operations
`<numerics>`	Generalized numeric operations

- **Utilities.** The headers in the following table define auxiliary components that are used in STL containers and algorithms. These include function adaptors, pairs, and the class `auto_ptr` (discussed later).

General Utilities

Header	Contents
`<utility>`	Operators and pairs
`<functional>`	Function objects
`<memory>`	Allocators and auto_ptr

Containers

A *container* is an object that stores other objects as its elements. A *generic container* can store objects of any kind. A *sequence container* organizes a collection of objects of the same type T into a strictly linear arrangement. Examples of sequence containers include a built-in array (which means that all STL algorithms that apply to sequences are applicable to built-in arrays as well), `std::vector`, `std::deque`, and `std::list`.

The `vector` Container Class

STL containers automatically grow as necessary, freeing the programmer from the burden of manual memory management. For example, a `vector` can be used to read an unknown number of elements from the keyboard, like this:

```cpp
#include <vector>
#include <iostream>
using namespace std;
int main()
{
  vector <int> vi;
  for (;;) //read numbers from keyboard until 0 is input
  {
    int temp;
    cout<<"enter a number; press 0 to terminate" <<endl;
    cin>>temp;
    if (temp == 0 )
      break;
    vi.push_back(temp); //insert int into the buffer
  }
  cout<< "you entered "<< vi.size() <<" elements" <<endl;
}
```

The memory allocation scheme of STL containers must address two conflicting demands:

- A container shouldn't preallocate large amounts of memory because it can impair the system's performance.
- Letting a container reallocate memory with every new element insertion is rather inefficient.

Many implementations use this approach as a compromise between these two conflicting demands: The container initially allocates a small memory buffer, which grows exponentially with every reallocation. For example, a vector object may start with 16 free slots; then it reallocates to 32, 64, and so on. The reallocation process consists of four steps:

1. Allocate a new memory buffer that's large enough to store the container.
2. Copy the existing elements to the new memory location.
3. Successively invoke the destructors of the elements in their previous location.
4. Release the original memory buffer.

Obviously, reallocation is a costly operation. Sometimes, however, it's possible to estimate in advance how many elements the container will have to store. In this case, you can preallocate a sufficient amount of memory to avoid recurrent reallocations. You do this by calling the member function `reserve()`. `reserve(n)` ensures that the container reserves sufficient memory for at least *n* elements in advance, as in the following example:

```
vector <Message> msgs;
 // make room for 1000 Messages
msgs.reserve(1000);
//no reallocation should occur before 1,000 objects have been stored
FillWithMessages(msgs);
```

`capacity()` and `size()`

The member function `capacity()` returns the total number of elements that the container can hold without requiring reallocation. `size()` returns the number of elements that are currently stored in the container. In other words, `capacity() - size()` is the number of available "free slots" that can be filled with additional elements without reallocating.

The capacity of a container can be controlled by calling either `reserve()` or `resize()`. These member functions differ in two respects. `resize(n)` allocates memory for *n* objects and default-initializes them. `reserve()` allocates raw memory without initializing it. In addition, `reserve()` doesn't change the value returned from `size()`—it only changes the value returned from `capacity()`. `resize()` changes both these values. For example:

```
using namespace std;
vector <string> vs;
vs.reserve(10);   //make room for at least 10 more strings
vs.push_back(string()); //insert an element
cout<<"size: "<< vs.size()<<endl; //output: 1
cout<<"capacity: "<<vs.capacity()<<endl; //output: 10
cout<<"there's room for "<<vs.capacity() - vs.size()
    <<" elements before reallocation"<<endl;
  //allocate 10 more elements, initializing each with string::string()
vs.resize(20);
cout<<"size: "<< vs.size()<<endl; //output 20
cout<<"capacity: "<<vs.capacity()<<endl; //output 20;
```

It's possible to specify the requested storage size during construction, like this:

```
vector<int>  vi(1000); //initial storage for 1000 int's
//vi contains 1000 elements initialized by int::int()
```

The constructor initializes the allocated elements by invoking their default constructor. In the case of built-in types, this simply means zero-initializing these elements. You can specify a different initializer value, though:

```
vector<int>  vi(1000, 4); //initialize all 1000 int's with 4
```

Accessing Elements

The overloaded operator [ ] and the member function at() enable direct access to a vector's element. Both have a const and a non-const version, so they can be used to access an element of a const and a non-const vector, respectively. The overloaded [ ] operator was designed to be as efficient as its built-in counterpart. Therefore, [ ] doesn't perform range checking. The lack of runtime checks ensures the fastest access time (an operator [ ] call is usually inlined). However, using operator [ ] with an illegal subscript yields undefined behavior. When performance is paramount, and when the code is written carefully so that only legal subscripts are accessed, use the [ ] operator. The [ ] notation is also more readable and intuitive. However, runtime checks are unavoidable in some circumstances. In such cases, use the member function at(). at() performs range checking and, in case of an attempt to access an out-of-range member, it throws an exception of type std::out_of_range. Here's an example:

```
#include <vector>
#include <iostream>
#include <string>
#include <stdexcept>
using namespace std;
int main()
{
  vector<string> vs; // vs has no elements currently
  vs.push_back("bustopher"); //add first element
  vs[0] = "macavity"; //override it using []
  try
  {
    cout<< vs.at(10) <<endl; //out of range element, exception thrown
  }
  catch(out_of_range & except)
  {
    // handle out-of-range subscript
  }
}
```

Front and Back Operations

The terms *front operation* and *back operation* refer to the beginning and the end of a container, respectively. The member function `push_back()` appends an element to the end of the container. When the container has exhausted its free storage, it reallocates additional storage, and then appends the element. The member function `pop_back()` removes the last element from the container. The member functions `front()` and `back()` access a single element at the container's beginning and end, respectively. They both have a `const` and a `non-const` version. For example:

```
vector <short> v;
v.push_back(5);
v.push_back(10);
cout<<"front: " << v.front() << endl; //5
cout<<"back: " << v.back() << endl; //10
v.pop_back(); //remove v[1]
cout<<"back: " << v.back() << endl; //now 5
```

The `queue` Container Class

In a queue data model, the first element that's inserted is located at the topmost position, and any subsequent elements are located at lower positions. (A queue is also called *FIFO*—short for "First in, first out.") The two basic operations in a queue are `pop()` and `push()`. A `push()` operation inserts an element into the bottom of the queue. A `pop()` operation removes the element at the topmost position, which was the first to be inserted; consequently, the element that's located one position lower becomes the topmost element. The STL `queue` container can be used as follows:

```
#include <iostream>
#include <queue>
using namespace std;
queue <int> iq;
iq.push(93); //insert the first element; it's the topmost one
iq.push(250);
iq.push(10); //last element inserted is located at the bottom
cout<<"currently there are "<< iq.size() << " elements" << endl;
while (!iq.empty() )
{
    cout <<"the last element is: "<<  iq.front()
  << endl; //front() returns the topmost element
 iq.pop(); //remove the topmost element
}
```

STL also defines a double-ended queue, or *deque* (pronounced *deck*), container. A `deque` is a queue optimized to support operations at both ends efficiently. Another type of queue is the `priority_queue`, whose elements are sorted internally according to their priority. The element with the highest priority is located at the top. To qualify as an element of `priority_queue`, an object has to define the < operator.

Iterators, Part I

Iterators are a key concept in STL and generic programming. In many ways, they behave like pointers although they needn't do so. In this section I will present the fundamental concepts of iterators and their usage in STL.

Pointers as Iterators

Iterators enable you to traverse a container, read an individual element, assign it a new value and so on. The simplest form of a container is the built-array. Arrays may contain different types of objects: characters, integers, pointers and user-defined types (UDT). However, each array contains only one type of objects. For example:

```
char message[]="hello world";
```

Suppose you want to find the number of characters in `message` without calling `strlen()`. You can write something like this:

```
int mystrlen(const char * str)
{
 int length=0;
 while(*str++)
  length++;
 return length;
}
```

Even in such a simple function you need an iterator to traverse the array. In this case, the pointer `str` serves as an iterator. The nice thing about iterators in general is that they "remember" their position in the container. Thus, every `str++` statement advances `str` to the next position in the array. In addition, an iterator enables you to view the content of the current position by means of dereferencing it:

```
char c=*str; //dereference str
str++; //advance to the next char
```

Dereferencing and moving to the next element in a container are the two basic operations that every iterator must support. Iterators may support additional operations as well: You can test them for equality, assign a new value to them or add an integer to them:

```
char *p = "Hello";
if(str==p) //equality test
str=p; //assignment
str=p+4; //addition, p now points to 'o\0'
```

C++ programmers often find it surprising that all these high-level operations on pointers date back to K&R C! However, pointers confine you to a specific type. You can't use `mystrlen()` to compute the length of an array of `int` for example. And this is why STL designers designed a more abstract concept of iterators.

Iterators in STL

Instead of relying on specific pointer types, STL defines iterators by means of operations that they must support. The underlying representation of an iterator is usually implementation dependent. Thus, an iterator can be a real pointer, an integer or a class object so long as it supports the operations *, ++, =, and ==.

As we saw previously, pointers support additional operations. These can be summarized for iterators x and y and an integer n as follows:

x++	x+n	x-y	x>y	*x
++x	x-n	x==y	x<=y	x=y
x--	x+=n	x!=y	x>=y	
--x	x-=n	x<y	x[n]	

Implementing an iterator that supports all these operations regardless of its underlying type makes it indistinguishable from an ordinary pointer. This exactly what STL designers intended to achieve—define an iterator that offers the interface of a pointer without being forced to use pointers. Notice that this abstraction makes ordinary pointers valid iterators in STL algorithms. Take for example the `std::reverse()` algorithm. You can use it to reverse a container object as well as a built-in array:

```
#include <vector>
#include <algorithm>
```

```cpp
std::vector<int> vi;
vi.push_back(1);
vi.push_back(2);
std::reverse(vi.begin(), vi.end());//using vector<int>::iterator
int arr[2]={1,2};
std::reverse(arr, arr+2);//using pointers as iterators
```

Iterator Categories

It would be inefficient to have all iterators support all these operations. Take a singly linked list as an example. While certain operations such as operator ++ are easily implemented by following a link to the next element, an operation such as operator -- is much more complicated. In order to move back to the previous element you would have to return to the head of the list and then traverse the list until the sought-after element has been found. This is terribly inefficient. Naive users who aren't aware of this crucial difference between ++ and -- might use operator -- frequently, e.g., in a tight loop that decrements an iterator numerous times. STL designers were aware of this potential problem. Therefore, they decided to omit certain operations that are extremely inefficient for a certain data structure, thereby encouraging the users to look for a suitable container that supports the requested operation. More importantly, they defined a set of iterator categories, each of which supports a different set of operations. These categories are:

- **Forward iterators**. Iterators that can be advanced a single element at a time only in the forward direction.
- **Bidirectional iterators**. Iterators that can be advanced a single element at a time in either the forward or reverse directions.
- **Random-access iterators**. Iterators that can be advanced either forward or backward and can move more than a single element at once.

As you may have noticed, each category is a subset of its successive category; a bidirectional iterator is also a forward iterator and a random-access iterator supports all the operations of a bidirectional iterator. By classifying iterators into these categories, containers disable inefficient operations. A singly linked list container class uses only forward iterators and thus disables operator --. By contrast, a doubly linked list uses a bidirectional iterator and thus supports operator -- as well.

In addition to these three categories, STL also distinguishes between *input iterators* and *output iterators*.

Chapter 10 The Standard Template Library (STL) and Generic Programming

Input Iterators

Input iterators can be moved one position at a time in the forward direction and allow dereferencing only when used as an r-value. In other words, for an iterator `ix` you can do the following:

```
val=*ix;
```

but not this:

```
*ix=val; //error, *ix can only be read
```

You can think of input iterators as read-only forward iterators.

Output Iterators

Output iterators can be moved one position at a time in the forward directions and allow dereferencing only when used as an l-value. In other words, for an iterator `ox` you can do the following:

```
*ox=val;
```

but not this:

```
val=*ox; //error, *ox can only be written to
```

You can think of output iterators as write-only forward iterators.

Using Container Iterators

Each container class defines an iterator type suitable to that particular container design. To create an iterator suitable for `vector<int>`, you can do this:

```
vector<int>::iterator p;
```

Here, `vector<int>::iterator` is a `typedef` for the underlying type used as an iterator. You then can use `p` to point to an element in a `vector<int>` object, `*p` to read an element or write to it, `p++` to advance to the next element, `p[n]` to access the *n*th element of the vector, and so on.

If you need a "read-only" iterator, i.e., an iterator through which elements can be read but not modified, create a `const_iterator` like this:

```
vector<int>::const_terator cp;
```

All STL containers provide the `begin()` and `end()` member functions. `begin()` returns an iterator that points to the first element of the container. For example:

```
std::vector <int> v();
v.push_back(10);
// make p point to the first element of v
std::vector<int>::iterator p  = v.begin();
*p = 11; //assign a new value to v[0] through p
std::cout << *p<<std::endl; //output 11
```

The member function `end()` returns an iterator that points *one position past* the last valid element of the container. This may seem surprising at first, but if you consider how C-strings are represented—with an additional '\0' character automatically appended one position past the final character—it shouldn't sound so unusual. The additional element in STL has a similar role: namely, indicating the end of the container. This is particularly useful in `for` and `while` loops:

```
using std::vector;
vector <int> v(10);
int n=0;
for (vector<int>::iterator p = v.begin(); p!=v.end(); p++)
  *p = n++;
```

The member functions `rbegin()` and `rend()` (reverse `begin()` and reverse `end()`) are similar to `begin()` and `end()`, except that they return *reverse iterators*, which apply to reverse sequences. Reverse iterators are ordinary iterators, except that they invert the semantics of the overloaded ++ and -- operators. They're useful for accessing container elements in a reverse order:

```
void descending_order()
{
  vector <double> v(10);
  double d = 0.1;
  for (vector<double>::iterator p=v.begin();p<v.end(); p++)
  {
    *p = d;
    d+= 0.1;
  }
   //display elements of v in descending order
  for (vector<double>::reverse_iterator rp
```

```
    =v.rbegin(); rp!=v.rend(); rp++)
      std::cout<< *rp<<std::endl;
}
```

Summary

At the heart of every STL container and algorithm lies one or more iterators. If you look at the standard `<algorithm>` header you will see for example the following declaration:

```
template <class BidirectionalIterator> void
  reverse (BidirectionalIterator first,
           BidirectionalIterator last);
```

You can conclude that this algorithm can apply both `--` and `++` to `first` and `last`. In a similar vein,

```
template <class ForwardIterator>
  ForwardIterator adjacent_find (ForwardIterator first,
                                 ForwardIterator last);
```

`adjacent_find()` applies only operator `++` to `first` and `last`.

Understanding the iterators and their categories is essential for using STL effectively.

Iterators, Part II

Now that I've introduced the basic concepts of iterators, let's focus on the semantic differences among iterator categories, such as bidirectional iterators, reverse iterators, and random-access iterators.

Bidirectional Iterators

Bidirectional iterators have all the properties of forward iterators plus the ability to move backward when decremented. This can be useful in algorithms that require multiple passes through their data or in algorithms that process data in reverse order. STL defines two types of bidirectional iterators: `bidirectional_iterator` and `reverse_bidirectional_iterator`. The latter is created by means of applying an *adaptor*—i.e., a component that modifies the interface of a certain construct—to an ordinary `bidirectional_iterator`.

> **NOTE:** For more on adaptors, see the section "Choosing the Right Container, Part I."

All STL containers support the `begin()` and `end()` member functions. These functions return bidirectional iterators. In addition, the `rbegin()` and `rend()` member functions return reverse bidirectional iterators for processing data in the reverse direction. The differences between these two iterator types are manifested in their initialization form and in the way they determine a sequence's end.

If you want to process a sequence in the forward direction, you normally use the `begin()` and `end()` member functions to obtain an iterator pointing to the first element of a sequence and one that points to one-element-past-the-end of a sequence, respectively:

```
int arr[]={0,1,2};
int *pbeg=&arr[0];
```

The iterator `pbeg` points to the first element in the array. If you copy the elements of this array to a vector:

```
vector<int> vi(&arr[0], &arr[3]); //initialize vi with arr
```

`vi` has three data members: `vi[0]`, `vi[1]` and `vi[2]`.

However, the `end()` member function returns the address of an invalid member, namely `vi[3]`. This might look surprising at first but all algorithms and containers in STL are aware of this. They never access this element but use the range:

```
begin()<=iter ... iter<end()
```

Notice that the same idiom is applied in the initializer of `vi`. The second argument `&arr[3]` is an address of one element past `arr`'s boundaries. Here again, `vector`'s constructor knows to read all the elements within the valid range.

In the following example, the iterator `iter` is both incremented and decremented:

```
vector<int>::iterator iter = vi.begin();
int first= *iter++; //copy vi[0] and move to the next
int second=*iter--;//copy vi[1] and return to the previous
cout<<*iter<<endl; //display vi[0]
```

Reverse Iterators

Reverse iterators are bidirectional iterators that invert the meaning of operators +, -, ++, and --. Thus, incrementing a reverse iterator moves it one position *backward*, whereas decrementing it causes it to move to the *next* element. The rbegin() and rend() member functions return reverse iterators:

```
void print_backward(vector<int> &vi)
{
 vector<int>::reverse_iterator rit=vi.rbegin();
 while (rit<vi.rend())
 {
  cout<<*rit<<endl;
  ++rit; //move one position backward
 }
}
```

Here's the output from this function:

```
2
1
0
```

Accidentally initializing a reverse iterator with begin() instead of rbegin() would cause unpredictable results because neither the logical end of a container nor its beginning is properly defined. To avoid such mishaps, iterators in STL are strongly typed:

```
vector<int>::iterator rit=vi.rbegin();//compilation error
```

Random-Access Iterators

Random-access iterators have the ability to be moved in increments greater than one as well as the ability to be subscripted. The following example demonstrates the operations that random-access iterators support:

```
vector<int>::iterator iter = vi.begin();
int n=
   *(iter+2); //access v[2] without changing iter's value
iter+=2; //make iter point to vi[2]
n=*iter;// n=2
iter-=2; //point to vi[0] again
```

```
for (int i=0; i<3; i++)
  cout << iter[i] << endl; //subscripting iter
```

Let's analyze this example. The expression

```
iter+2;
```

advances an iterator two positions ahead, making it point to the third element of vi. To make the assignment to iter permanent, use the self-assignment operator:

```
iter+=2;
```

Because random-access iterators offer all the features of bidirectional iterators, you can decrement them as well:

```
iter-=2;
```

Finally, random-access iterators support subscripting. This means that you can access elements of a container through an iterator by using the [ ] notation:

```
vector<int>::iterator iter = vi.begin();
for (int i=0; i<3; i++)
  cout << iter[i] << endl; //subscripting iter
```

This is the output from this for loop:

```
2
1
0
```

Random-access iterators can be compared to determine if the position of one iterator is before or after another:

```
vector<int>::iterator iter=vi.begin();
vector<int>::iterator iter2=iter;
bool eq=(iter==iter2); //true
iter2+=2;
ptrdiff_t diff=iter2-iter; //2
diff=iter-iter2; //-2
```

Iterator Functions

You can also use the `distance()` function to calculate the difference between two random-access iterators:

```
distance(iter, iter2, diff); //2
```

Another function is `advance()`, which takes two arguments: an iterator and the distance it should move. The distance can be negative only if the first argument is a bidirectional or random-access iterator:

```
advance(iter, 2); //effect: iter+=2
```

Summary

The semantic differences between iterator categories affect the operations that they support and the algorithms that operate on them. Random-access iterators offer all the operations that ordinary pointers support. Reverse iterators are special iterators that invert the semantics of increment and decrement operations. Finally, STL includes the `distance()` and `advance()` functions for iterator manipulation.

The `std::list` Container Class

Linked lists are another widely used data structure. Yet writing a linked list from scratch is an arduous, frustrating and time-consuming task. Instead of reinventing the wheel every time, use the STL `std::list` container class. Its uniform interface, generic nature and seamless integration with other STL constructs make it a superior choice to any homemade list class, as I will show in the following sections.

Creating a List Object

The header `<list>` contains the declaration of `std::list` and its specialized algorithms. Our first step is to create an empty list of integers called `li`:

```
#include <list>
using std::list;
int main()
```

```
{
 list <int> li;
}
```

To insert a single element, use the `push_back()` member function:

```
li.push_back(1);
```

To remove the last element of a list, use the `pop_back()` member function

```
li.pop_back();
```

As opposed to `push_back()`, `push_front()` inserts an element before the list's beginning:

```
li.push_front(0); // the first element is now 0, not 1
```

Similarly, `pop_front()` removes the first element of a list:

```
li.pop_front();
```

To remove a certain value from the list without indicating its exact position, use `remove()`. `remove(n)` removes all the elements that equal to n from the list:

```
li.remove(0); // li doesn't contain
              //any zeros anymore
```

Dealing with Sequences

Up until now I have exemplified list operations that operate on a single element at a time. `std::list` supports *sequence operations* as well. These operations enable you to traverse, fill, sort and reverse multiple elements at once.

Iteration is easy. The `begin()` and `end()` member functions return iterators pointing at the list's beginning and end, respectively. Use them to access all the list's elements sequentially. Note that we're using a `const_iterator` instead of an ordinary `iterator` object because the iteration process in this case doesn't modify the list's state:

```
list<int>::const_iterator it;
for(it=li.begin(); it!=li.end(); ++it)
{
 cout << *it << endl; // each element on a separate line
}
```

The `assign()` member function fills a list with the contents of another sequence such as a vector or an array. It takes two *input iterators* (for further information on iterator categories, see the resources below) that mark the sequence's beginning and end, respectively. In the following example, we fill a list with the elements of an array:

```
int arr[3] = {10,20,30};
li.assign( &arr[0], &arr[3]);
```

You can merge two lists into one. The `merge()` member function takes a reference to another list object:

```
list <int> x;
//..fill x
li.merge(x); // merge the elements of x into li
```

`merge()` merges x into li. x becomes empty after the merge operations. To erase one or more elements, use the `erase()` member function. This function has two overloaded versions; the first of which takes an iterator and erases the element to which it points. The second version takes two iterators that mark the beginning and the end of the sequence to be erased. Suppose you have a list of 10 elements and you want to remove all the elements but the first two. Use `erase()` as follows:

```
list<int>::it=li.begin();
++it; ++it; // advance to third element
li.erase(it, li.end()); // erase elements 3-10
```

Choosing the Right Container, Part I

In many ways, STL has reshaped software engineering not only for C++ programmers but for users of other languages as well. And yet, the tricky part is choosing the right container for a specific task. In this section, I will characterize some of the widely used containers and container adaptors (e.g., `stack` and `queue`) and suggest guidelines for selecting each container—without a single word about the Big-Oh notation!

vector

`vector` (declared in `<vector>`) is the default container for many C++ programmers. Several members of the standards committee were so enamored with it that they even proposed to replace built-in array with vectors! This decision wasn't accepted, though, for many good reasons.

In essence, a vector is a safer and cleaner version of the built-in array. However, unlike built-in arrays, its size can grow or shrink dynamically. In addition, you can insert elements in the middle of a vector. This flexibility often leads programmers to stretch this container far beyond its optimal usage. So, how do you know that vector is the right choice?

Ayes

If all you want is a "smart array" class that offers random access to elements, and perhaps the ability to append new elements to its end, then `vector` is the right choice. Because vector elements must be stored contiguously—this requirement was incorporated into C++0X (see Chapter 20, "C++0X: The New Face of Standard C++") not long ago—applications that need contiguous storage should also use `vector`.

Nays

How can you tell that `vector` is a sub-optimal choice? First, when you find yourself frequently inserting elements in the middle of a container rather than at the end. Although `insert()` will work correctly for mid-position insertions, in terms of performance it's substantially slower than appending elements to the end. If you think about inserting elements before the first element, then clearly `vector` is not the right choice because it doesn't even have a `push_front()` operation.

As a general rule, always check which unique operations a certain container supports and which common operations it disables. These should give you more than a hint regarding its optimal usage.

list

If I had to classify the "one container fits all" programmers, I'd definitely divide them into two categories: those who use `vector` exclusively and those who use `list` exclusively. No wonder then that the latter often wonder why they can't use the subscript operator to access the elements of a `list` ...

Seriously, a `list` (declared in `<list>`) offers sequential access to its elements: One element leads to the next one (or to the previous one).

Ayes

If you don't need random access (say, "15 positions from the beginning" or "three positions before the current element") and you do need to insert new elements between existing elements frequently, `list` is a good choice. Let's look at a concrete example. Suppose you need to write a task manager that displays all of the currently active windows on a user's desktop (similar to the icons that Windows displays when you press Alt+Tab). A `list` would be a preferable choice because new icons can be inserted between existing icons. You can tell that `list` deals with mid-positions efficiently because it offers the `splice()` operation, which `vector` (and other containers) don't have. Your second hint has to do with how users traverse the icons—sequentially (pressing Tab advances you to the next icon). These two criteria—frequent insertion in the middle and sequential access—indicate that you should use `list`.

Nays

When is `list` a bad choice? First and foremost, when you need random access to elements. Secondly, if you need to sort the elements frequently. Although `list` does offer the `sort()` operation, sorting lists isn't as efficient as sorting vectors.

deque

`deque` (pronounced "deck"; declared in `<deque>`), or a double-ended queue, provides random access and the subscript notation for accessing elements, just like `vector`. Yet unlike `vector`, it supports efficient insertions and deletions at both ends. In other words, you can use the `push_front()` operation to insert an element before the first element. Likewise, you can use the `pop_front()` operation to remove the first element, so that the second element effectively becomes the first. Although `list` can offer the same functionality, it's less efficient than `deque` in terms of memory usage. Therefore, when you need to insert or remove elements at either end of a container frequently but rarely use insertions and deletions in the middle, `deque` is a good choice. A classic example of using `deque` is an operating system's scheduler, which pops elements from the end once they have been allotted their CPU time slice, and inserts new tasks into the beginning of the queue. Often, a scheduler needs to remove an element from the beginning, for instance when a task has been aborted or crashed.

Adaptors

Adaptor containers change ordinary containers such as `vector` and `deque`, making them look like different container types. For example, a stack is usually implemented as a list with a different interface. Instead of `push_back()` and `pop_back()`, it has `push()` and `pop()`.

`stack`

`stack` (declared in `<stack>`) is an ideal choice when you need to a LIFO data structure. Think for example of people entering the back seat of a car that has only one door: The last person to enter is the first to exit. The four basic operations that a `stack` supports are `push()`, `pop()`, `top()`, and `empty()`.

`queue`

A `queue` (declared in `<queue>`), or FIFO, is characterized by having elements inserted into one end and removed from the other end: for example, a queue of people at a theater's box office. The `queue` adaptor container is implemented in one of two ways: either as a `deque` or as a `list`.

Summary

Premature optimization is evil, as we all know. However, this doesn't mean that programmers should neglect performance altogether or—worse yet—use a container that isn't suitable for the task at hand. In the second part of this series I will discuss associative containers and their usage.

Choosing the Right Container, Part II

Earlier, I outlined the major features of STL's sequence containers. In this section, I will continue this discussion and explain the effects of reallocation and its consequences with regards to every sequence container type.

Container Reallocation

All containers manage their storage automatically. If a container has to accommodate more elements than its current capacity, it allocates more storage as needed. Likewise, certain operations, say calling `vector::erase()` or `list::merge()`, cause a container to shrink. As much as one would like to consider this automatic storage management an "implementation detail" that shouldn't concern users, it does raise a problem: What happens to an iterator that is pointing to an element when the container reallocates? In certain cases such an iterator becomes invalid, as it is now pointing to a piece of memory that is no longer owned by the container or it is pointing to a piece of memory that contains a different object. Let's see how this can happen. Suppose you have a vector that has 256 elements:

```
vector <int> vi(256); //vi contains 256 int's
```

At this point, you define an iterator that is pointing to the first element like this:

```
for (vector<int>::iterator it= vi.begin();...)
```

Then, you call `push_back()` to insert a new element:

```
vi.push_back(99);
```

From this moment, there's no guarantee that `it` is valid because the `push_back()` call may have triggered reallocation. Of course, not every `push_back()` call does that but you can't tell with certainty whether reallocation has taken place without poking into the intimate implementation details of your STL distribution. To explain the effects of reallocation, I'll use an analogy. Shrimps have a hard shell that doesn't grow. When the shrimp's body grows, it has to shed its shell and then grow another, larger shell that fits its new size. Vectors use a similar technique when they grow: They copy their contents into a new memory block large enough to store their elements, discarding the previous memory block on which the elements were stored.

A reallocation process is actually more complicated than simply switching to a new memory block: Because vectors store objects, not raw data, they can't just copy raw memory from one location to another. Therefore, a complete reallocation cycle consists of the following steps:

- The vector allocates a new chunk of contiguous memory that is large enough for the current number of elements plus some room for extra elements. Thus, if a vector has 100 elements, it may allocate room for 128 or 256 elements, for example.
- The vector copy-constructs the current elements into the new storage (this is why STL elements must be copy-constructible).
- Once the copying operation has been completed successfully, the vector destroys the old elements by invoking their destructors (again, this is why destructors of STL elements must be accessible).
- The memory on which the destroyed elements reside is released, very much like a shrimp's old shell.

All these four stages make a single atomic operation. Therefore, a multi-threaded application must lock the entire sequence of reallocation stages so that other threads don't access a vector's elements before the reallocation has been completed. Here's the problem: Because elements may have been copied to a new memory address, iterators that were assigned before the reallocation might become dangling iterators: They are still pointing to the old memory block. Using such invalid iterators would cause undefined behavior. To avoid this, the Standard specifies which operations invalidate a container's iterators. The actual effect of each operation depends on the container type. For example, calling `push_back()` on a vector might cause reallocation and —consequently—iterator invalidation, whereas calling `push_back()` for a list object doesn't.

One way to avoid reallocation with vectors is to ensure that they have sufficient capacity in advance. This can be done by specifying the desired capacity by calling `reserve()`:

```
vi.reserve(1000); //make room for at least 1000 elements
```

If `vi` never exceeds this capacity, calling `push_back()` won't invalidate iterators. However, notice that mid-position insertion of elements could cause old iterators to point to the wrong elements, even if the vector hasn't reallocated. We can conclude that with respect to vectors, any operation that inserts new elements might invalidate iterators. By contrast, vector's const member functions don't invalidate iterators.

Capacity Versus Size

The distinction between a container's capacity and its size is crucial: Capacity refers to the actual storage that the container owns, which is equal to or larger than its size. A container's size is the actual number of elements it's currently holding. These values are always expressed as the number of elements, not bytes. Reallocation takes place only if the container's size exceeds its capacity. To see the difference between the two, let's look at a concrete example:

```
vector<int> vi; //size==0
cout<<"size: "<<vi.size()<<" capacity: "<<vi.capacity()<<endl;
```

My STL implementation produces the following output:

```
C:\Documents and Settings\Dani\My Documents\maps1.exe
size: 0 capacity: 0
```

Now let's change this program a bit:

```
vector<int> vi; //size==0
vi.push_back(1); //size==1
cout<<"size: "<<vi.size()<<" capacity: "<<vi.capacity()<<endl;
```

This time, the output is:

```
size: 1 capacity: 256
```

We can conclude that this particular implementation uses a "lazy allocation" strategy: it allocates storage only when necessary. In addition, the initial minimal allocation block consists of 256 elements. This means that you can insert 255 more elements to `vi` without causing reallocation. Notice however, that allocation policies are implementation-dependent; portable code should never rely on specific allocation policies because other implementations might work differently.

Invalidation of `list` Iterators

Lists, unlike vectors, don't use contiguous memory. Therefore, inserting new elements at any position doesn't trigger reallocation. In other words, calling `push_back()`, `push_front()`, or `insert()` doesn't invalidate list iterators. However, there are operations that invalidate list iterators. The `splice()` operation, which is unique to lists, splices a sequence into an existing list. For example, you can splice one list into another like this:

```
list<int> li, li2;
//populate the lists
li.splice(li.begin(), li2);
```

This causes the elements in `li2` to be spliced before `li.begin()`. While iterators to `li` aren't affected by this operation, `li2` becomes empty after the operation. Consequently, all references and iterators to its elements become invalid. The `pop_front()`, `pop_back()`, `clear()` and `erase()` operations invalidate iterators and references to the erased elements.

Invalidation of `deque` Iterators

Calling `insert()` in the middle of the `deque` invalidates all the iterators and references to its elements. Calling `insert()` at either end of the `deque` invalidates all its iterators but has no effect on the validity of references to its elements. The last sentence means that if you have a reference or a pointer to a certain element, say:

```
deque<int> di;
int p* = &di[5];
deque<int>::iterator it=di.begin()+5;
di.push_front(8);
```

after the `push_front()` call, the iterator `it` becomes invalid whereas the pointer p remains valid.

Similarly, calling `erase()` in the middle of the `deque` invalidates all the iterators and references to its elements. Calling `erase()` at either end of the `deque` invalidates only the iterators and the references to the erased elements.

Summary

Iterator invalidation is just as bad as plain old dangling pointers. Therefore, when using STL containers, it's important to know which operations affect the validity of its iterators and references to its elements. The most invalidation-prone container is `vector` because every insertion operation, regardless of its position, might trigger reallocation. However, if you have a rough estimate of the actual number of elements that a vector will use, you can preallocate sufficient storage by calling `reserve()`.

Choosing the Right Container, Part III

The last section of this series is dedicated to the associative containers: `map`, `multimap`, `set` and `multiset`. Here, I will show how to create and use such containers and discuss their applications.

Fundamentals of Associative Containers

Sequence containers can store any datatype. However, they offer only two retrieval methods: subscripting and searching. If the container doesn't support subscripting (`list`, for example), the only way to retrieve an element is to perform a search. Associative containers, on the other hand, store pairs of objects, where one element serves as the *key* and the other as the *associated value*. You access the associated value by using its key. What are the applications of such containers? Think of a symbolic debugger for example. It can use an associative container that maps strings (variable names) to memory addresses (the variables' addresses). This way, when you evaluate or modify a variable by its name, the debugger knows where that variable is stored in memory. Another example is a phone book, in which names serve as keys and telephone numbers are their associated values.

Unique Keys Versus Non-Unique Keys

In certain associative containers, the keys must be unique. Thus, if you want to store several telephone numbers of the same person (where the person's name serves as the key), you cannot use such a container. Instead, use a multi-key associative container.

Pairs

The concept of a *pair* is essential for understanding how associative containers work. A `pair` binds a key (known as the *first element*) with an associated value (known as the *second element*). The Standard Library defines a `pair` template, which behaves like a special `tuple` of two elements (historically, `pair` dates back to C++98, whereas `tuple` was added later to C++0x (see Chapter 20) as a generalization of the `pair` concept):

```
#include <utility> //definition of pair
#include <string>
pair <string, string> don_and_course("Horvath", "syntax101");
pair <string, void *> symbol ("mynum", 0x410928a8);
```

map

Just as `vector` serves as the default sequence container, `map` is the default associative container. The class template `map` defined in `<map>` is an associative container that uses a `pair` of types, the first of which is the index, or key, and the second is the associated value. Let's look at a concrete example of a `map` that contains a pair of strings, the first of which is a name and the second is an email address. We create the `map` like this:

```
#include <map>
#include <string>

map <string, string> emails;
```

To add an item to a `map`, use the subscript operator:

```
emails["J. Horvath"]="jhorvath@mail.com";
```

If the map already contains the key "J. Horvath," the current associated value remains unchanged:

```
emails ["J. Horvath "]="newaddr@com.net"; //has no effect
```

The subscript operator is used both for accessing an existing value and for inserting a new value. If you want to examine whether a certain value exists without inserting it into the map, use the `find()` algorithm. `find()` has two overloaded versions:

```
iterator find(const key_type& k);
const_iterator find(const key_type& k) const;
```

The following code sample searches for the key "J. Horvath" in the map:

```
typedef map <string, string>::const_iterator CIT;
CIT cit=addresses.find("J .Horvath");
if (cit==addresses.end())
 cout << "sorry, no such key" << endl;
else
 cout << cit->first << '\t' << cit->second << endl;
```

The expressions `cit->first` and `cit->second` return the key and its associated value, respectively.

multimap

A `multimap` is like a map except that it allows duplicate keys. Because multimap keys aren't necessarily unique, it doesn't support the subscript notation. To insert an element into a `multimap`, use the `insert()` member function. `insert()` takes as an argument a `pair` type. The Standard Library defines the helper function `make_pair()`, which takes two arguments, a and b, and returns `pair <x,y>`, where x is the type of a and y is the type of b. The following example inserts two pairs with the same key into a multimap:

```
multimap <string, string> emails;
emails.insert(make_pair("J. Horvath","jhorvath@mail.com"));
//duplicate keys allowed:
emails.insert(make_pair("J. Horvath","newaddr@com.net"));
```

Searching a `multimap`

Instead of `find()`, the `equal_range()`, `lower_bound()` and `upper_bound()` operations are used for accessing multiple values with the same key. `equal_range(k)` finds all of the values with the key k. It returns a `pair` of iterators that mark the first and last elements in the range. The following example displays all values whose key is "J. Horvath":

```
typedef multimap<string, string>::const_iterator CIT;
pair<CIT, CIT> range=emails.equal_range("J. Horvath");
for(CIT i=range.first; i!= range.second; ++i)
 cout<<i->second<<endl;
```

`lower_bound(k)` finds the first value whose key is k, and `upper_bound(k)` finds the first element whose key is greater than k. The following example uses `upper_bound()` to locate the first element whose key is greater than "J. Horvath" (when the key is a string, a lexicographical comparison is performed):

```
emails.insert(make_pair("M. Jones","majones@com.net"));
CIT it=emails.upper_bound("J. Horvath");
if (it!=emails.end())
 cout<<it->second<<endl; //display "majones@com.net"
```

`set`

The `set` container is similar to `map` except that it stores only keys. There are many applications for this type of a container. Think for example of a web browser that stores favorite URLs as keys to web pages. The browser needs to store only the keys; their associated values are stored on remote servers. Relational databases are another example. A database engine often performs optimizations with respect to how keys are organized, such as sorting and indexing them. In such cases, the values (the records to which the keys point) are irrelevant.

Obviously, `set` doesn't support the subscript operator because the associated value isn't stored in it.

`multiset`

A `multiset` is a `set` that allows duplicate keys. Here again, the primary means of retrieving elements is by calling the member functions `equal_range()`, `lower_bound()` and `upper_bound()`.

Summary

The Standard Library Technical Report (TR1) defines a new category of generic containers known as hashed containers, or, by their official name, *unordered associative containers*. The unordered associative containers are `unordered_set`, `unordered_map`, `unordered_multiset`, and `unordered_multimap`. They are declared in new headers: `<unordered_set>`, `<unordered_map>`, `<unordered_multiset>`, and `<unordered_multimap>`, respectively. I will discuss these containers in another section.

TIP: For more on unordered associative containers, see the DevSource article "Grok the New Features in Standard C++" at *http://www.devsource.com/ article2/0,1759,1633404,00.asp*.

Support for User-Defined Types

The generic nature of `list` enables you to define *specializations*, or instances, of user-defined types. For example, you can create lists of strings and `Date` objects like this:

```
#include <string>
#include "Date.h"
list<std::string> ls;
list <Date> ld;
```

Operations that require element comparison such as `sort()` and `unique()` use the overloaded < operator. If you intend to use any of these algorithms with lists, define a matching overloaded version of this operator for your class first:

```
bool operator < (const Date& d1, const Date& d2);
ld.sort(); // OK, using overloaded < operator
```

Note that in general, sorting a list is less efficient than sorting a vector or a queue. Therefore, if you need to sort elements frequently, you probably shouldn't use a list in the first place. The same is true for `reverse()`, which is also supported:

```
ld.reverse();
for(it=ld.begin(); it!=ld.end(); ++it)
{
 cout << *it << endl; // descending order
}
```

Algorithms

STL defines a rich set of generic algorithms that can be applied to containers and other sequences. There are three major categories of algorithms:

- Non-modifying sequence operations (algorithms that don't directly modify the sequences on which they operate)
- Mutating sequence operations
- Sorting algorithms

The various algorithms share a similar interface design, so looking at a few will give you a feel for using the STL algorithms in general.

`find()`

The generic algorithm `find()` locates an element within a sequence. `find()` takes three arguments: The first two are iterators that point to the beginning and the end of the sequence, respectively. The third argument is the sought-after value. `find()` returns an iterator that points to the first element that's identical to the sought-after value. If `find()` cannot locate the requested value, it returns an iterator that points one element past the final element in the sequence; that is, it returns `end()`. For example:

```
#include <algorithm> // definition of find()
#include <list>
#include <iostream>
using namespace std;
int main()
{
  list<char> lc;
  lc.push_back('A');
  lc.push_back('T');
  lc.push_back('L');
  list<char>::iterator p = find(lc.begin(),
```

```
    lc.end(), 'A');    // find 'A'
if (p != lc.end())     // was 'A' found?
  *p = 'S';    // then replace it with 'S'
p = lc.start();   // reset p to start of list
while (p != lc.end())   //display the modified list
  cout<<*p++;
return 0;
}
```

copy()

This algorithm copies a sequence of objects to a specified target. The first and the second arguments of copy() are iterators that mark the sequence's beginning and its end, respectively. The third argument points to a container into which the sequence is copied. The following example demonstrates how to copy the elements of a list into a vector:

```
#include <algorithm>
#include<list>
#include<vector>
using namespace std;
int main()
{
  list<int> li; vector <int> vi;
  li.push_back(1);
  li.push_back(2);
  //must make room for copied elements in advance
  vi.reserve( li.size() );
  //copy list elements into vector, starting at vector's beginning
  copy (li.begin(), li.end(), vi.begin() );
  return 0;
}
```

sort()

sort() takes two arguments of the type const iterator that point to the beginning and the end of the sequence, respectively. An optional third algorithm is a predicate object, which alters the computation of sort (predicate objects and adaptors will be discussed shortly). For example:

```
#include <iostream>
#include <algorithm> //definition of sort()
```

```
#include <vector>
using namespace std;
int main()
{
  vector <int> vi;
  vi.push_back(7);
  vi.push_back(1);
  vi.push_back(19);
  // sort vi; default is ascending order
  sort(vi.begin(), vi.end() );
  cout<< vi[0]   <<", "<< vi[1] <<",
    "<< vi[2] <<endl;   // output: 1, 7, 19
  return 0;
}
```

One way to force a descending order is to use reverse iterators:

```
sort(vi.rbegin(), vi.rend() ); // now sort in descending order
cout<< vi[0] <<", "<<vi[1]<<", "<<vi[2]<<endl; // output: 19, 7, 1
```

Function Objects

A *function object* is an object whose class overloads the function call operator. A generic function object defines the overloaded function call operator as a member function template. Consequently, the object can be used like a function call. Remember that the overloaded operator () can have a varying number of arguments, and any return value. In the following example, a function object implements a generic negation operator. (To learn more about operator overloading and templates, see Chapter 3, "Operator Overloading," and Chapter 5, "Templates.")

```
#include <iostream>
#include <vector>
using namespace std;

class Negate
{
public : //generic negation operator
  template < class T > T operator()  (T t) const { return -t;}
};
```

```cpp
//pass a function object rather than a function pointer
void callback(int n, const Negate& neg)
{
  n = neg(n);   //invoke the overloaded () operator to negate n
  cout << n;
}
int main()
{
 //Negate() creates a Negate object and passes it as
 //an argument to the callback() function
  callback(5, Negate() ); //output: -5
  return 0;
}
```

Uses of Function Objects

Some container operations use function objects. For example, a `priority_queue` uses the `less` function object to sort its elements internally. The following example demonstrates a scheduler that stores tasks with different priorities in a `priority_queue`. Tasks that have higher priority are located at the top. Tasks with identical priority are located according to the order of their insertion, as in an ordinary queue:

```cpp
#include <functional> // definition of less<>
#include <queue>  // definition of priority_queue
#include <iostream>
using namespace std;


struct Task
{
  int priority;
  friend bool operator < (const Task& t1, const Task& t2);
  Task(int p=0) : priority(p) {}
};


bool operator < (const Task& t1, const Task& t2)
{
  return t1.priority < t2.priority;
}
```

```
int main()
{
  priority_queue<Task> scheduler;
  scheduler.push(Task(3));
  scheduler.push(Task(5));
  scheduler.push(Task(1));
  scheduler.push(Task(1));
  cout<< scheduler.top().priority <<endl;    // output 5
  return 0;
}
```

Predicate Objects

A *predicate* is an expression that returns a Boolean value. Similarly, a function object that returns a Boolean value is a *predicate object*. STL defines several predicate objects that can be used to alter the computation of a generic algorithm. These predicate objects are defined in the header <functional>. In a previous example, you saw the operation of the algorithm sort(). The third argument of sort() is a predicate that alters the computation of this algorithm. For example, the predicate greater<int> can be used to override the default ascending order. Likewise, the predicate less<int> restores the original ascending order:

```
#include <functional> //definitions of STL predicates
#include <algorithm>  //definition of sort
#include <vector>
#include <iostream>
using namespace std;
int main()
{
  vector <int> vi;
  vi.push_back(9);
  vi.push_back(5);
  vi.push_back(10);
  sort(vi.begin(), vi.end(), greater<int> () );  // descending order
  cout<< vi[0] << '\t' << vi[1] << '\t' << vi[2] <<endl;  // output: 10  9  5
  sort(vi.begin(), vi.end(), less<int> () );   // now in ascending order
  cout<< vi[0] << '\t' << vi[1] << '\t' << vi[2] <<endl;  // output: 5  9  10
  return 0;
}
```

Adaptors

An *adaptor* is a component that modifies the interface of another component, thus letting you use that component in a new context. STL uses several types of adaptors:

- A *sequence adaptor* is a container that's built on another container and that modifies its interface. For example, the container `stack` is usually implemented as a `deque`, whose non-`stack` operations are hidden. In addition, `stack` uses the operations `back()`, `push_back()`, and `pop_back()` of a `deque` to implement the operations `top()`, `push()`, and `pop()`, respectively.
- The interface of an iterator can be altered by an *iterator adaptor*. The member functions `rend()` and `rbegin()` return reverse iterators, which are iterators that have the meanings of operators `++` and `--` exchanged. Using a reverse iterator is more convenient in some computations.
- *Function adaptors* modify the interface of a function or a function object. Earlier you saw the use of `greater` as a function adaptor for changing the computation of `sort()`.
  - *Negators* are used to reverse the result of certain Boolean operations.
  - *Binders* convert a binary function object into a unary function object by binding an argument to a specific value.

Specialized Containers

Chapter 5 discusses a specialized form of `vector` that manipulates Boolean values optimally: `vector<bool>`. This specialization is implemented in a way that squeezes each element into a single bit, rather than a `bool` variable, though with the familiar `vector` interface. For example:

```
#include <vector>
#include <iostream>
using namespace std

void transmit(vector <bool> &binarystream)
{
  cout<<binarystream[0]; // subscript operator provided
  vector<bool>::const_iterator bit_iter =
   binarystream.begin(); //iterators
  if (binarystream[0] == true)
```

```
{/* do something */ }
}
```

In recent years, `std::vector<bool>` has lost its appeal, mostly because it violates basic STL principles. After all, bits aren't an addressable datatype; therefore, you can't define valid iterators for them. It's likely that `std::vector<bool>` will become a deprecated feature in the next revision of the C++ standard. In the meantime, it's best to avoid using it.

Associative Containers

An *associative array* is one for which the index need not be an integer. An associative array is also called a *map* or *dictionary*. STL defines several associative containers. A `map`, for instance, stores pairs of values; one serves as the key, and the other is the associated value. The template `pair<class Key, class Value>` serves as a `map` element. In the following example, a `map` is used to translate the string value of an enumerator into its corresponding integral value. The string is the key whose associated value is an `int`:

```
#include <map>
#include <string>
#include <iostream>
using namespace std;
enum directions {up, down};
int main()
{
  pair<string, int> Enumerator(string("down"), down); //create a pair
  map<string, int> mi; //create a map
  mi.insert(Enumerator); //insert the pair
  int n = mi["down"]; //n = 1 //string used as subscript
  return 0;
}
```

A `map` can store only unique keys. A `multimap` is a `map` that can store duplicate keys.

A `set` is similar to a `map` except that the associated values are irrelevant in this case. A `set` is used when only the keys are important: for example, to ensure that a database transaction doesn't attempt to insert a record with a unique key that already exists in a table. A `multiset` is a `set` that allows duplicate keys.

Class `auto_ptr`

The class template `auto_ptr` is meant to facilitate dynamic memory management in the event of an exception. An `auto_ptr` object is initialized by a pointer to an object allocated on the free store. The destructor of `auto_ptr` destroys the object bound to that pointer. This technique simplifies certain programming tasks by sparing you the hassle of explicitly deleting every object allocated on the free store. Following is an example of using `auto_ptr` (points of possible object destruction are numbered):

```
#include <memory> //definition of auto_ptr
using namespace std;
void f() { if (condition) throw "err";}
int main()
{
  try
  {
    auto_ptr<double> dptr(new double(0.0));
    *dptr = 0.5; //overloaded * provides pointer-like syntax
    f();
  } // 1: no exception was thrown, dptr is  destroyed here
  catch(...)
  { // 2: an exception was thrown, dptr is destroyed here
  }
}
```

This way, the dynamically allocated memory is always released: If `f()` throws an exception, the `dptr` object is destroyed during stack unwinding (2) and, as a result, the memory that was allocated from the free store is released. Otherwise, `dptr` is destroyed when the `try` block exits (1).

Class `string`

`string` is a shorthand for `std::basic_string<char>`. It provides many of the operations of ordinary STL containers; for example, it conforms to the requirements of a sequence and it defines iterators. However, `string` is optimized for the use of a character string exclusively. The design considerations of `string` were based on efficiency, support for C-strings, and generality (that is, `string` is not targeted for a particular application use).

Constructors

`string` has a default constructor and five more constructors enabling you to initialize a `string` with a C-string, another string object, a part of a C-string, a sequence of characters, or part of another `string`. Following are some examples:

```
const char text[] = "hello world";
//initialization of string object with a C-style string
std::string s = text;  std::string s2(s);  //copy construction
// part of a C-string; s3 = "hello"
std::string s3(&text[0], &text[5]);
//a sequence of zero-initialized characters
std::string s4(10, 0); //initialized part of another string
std::string s5 ( s2.begin(), s2.find(' '));
                                        //s5 = "hello"
```

Conversion to a C-String

Class `string` provides two member functions that return the `const char *` representation of its object: `c_str()` and `data()`. `c_str()` returns the `const char *` representation of its object. For example:

```
std::string  s = "Hello";
if( strcmp( s.c_str(), "Hello")== 0)
 cout <<"identical"<<endl;
else
 cout<<"different"<<endl;
```

The pointer that's returned from `c_str ()` is owned by the `string` object. The user should not attempt to delete it or to modify its associated `char` array. The returned pointer is not to be used after a non-`const` member function has been called.

The member function `data()` also returns a `const char *` representation of its object, but the resulting array might not be null-terminated.

Accessing Elements

There are two ways to access a single character from a string object. One way is to use the overloaded operator `[]`. Another way is to use the member function `at()`. Similar to the class `vector`, `string::at()` performs range-checking and throws an exception of type `std::out_of_range` when an attempt is made to access an out-of-range character.

Clearing a `string`

To explicitly erase the contents of a `string`, you can use the member function `erase()`. For example:

```
char key;
string msg = "press any key to continue";
cout<<msg<<endl;
cin<<key;
msg.erase(); //clear msg
```

`string` Comparison

`string` defines three versions of operator `==`:

```
bool operator == (const string& left, const string right);
bool operator == (const char* left, const string right);
bool operator == (const string& left, const char* right);
```

This proliferation might seem redundant because `string` has a constructor that automatically converts a `const char *` to a string object. Therefore, only the first version of operator `==` is necessary. However, the overhead of creating a temporary string can be unacceptable under some circumstances; the temporary string has to allocate memory on the free store, copy the C-string, and then release the allocated memory. The standardization committee's intent was to make comparison of strings as efficient as possible. Therefore, the other versions of operator `==` were added to enable efficient comparisons.

In addition, there are three versions of the overloaded operator `+=` that support concatenation of another string, a C-string, or a single character to an existing string. For example:

```
string s1 = "ab"
string s2= "cd";
s1+=s2;
s1+= "ef";
s1+='g';
```

`string` also defines an overloaded `+` that returns a string that concatenates its operands. Similarly, the operators `<` and `>` perform a lexicographical comparison between their operands. `string` provides many additional member functions and utilities that interact smoothly with STL algorithms.

String Manipulation

Most programmers are familiar with the basic interface of `std::string`; e.g., assignment, concatenation, and case-sensitive comparison. However, serious projects often require more advanced string manipulation techniques: case-insensitive comparison, find and replace operations, and the like. Here I will explain how to get it done.

Case-Insensitive Comparison

The std::string operator == is case-sensitive. For many applications, this is the desired behavior. However, if you're designing a web server that parses HTTP requests or a compiler of a programming language that happens to be case-sensitive, you don't want to use this operator for string comparison. (And don't forget that most compilers nowadays, regardless of color, race, religion, or target platform, are written in C/C++.)

The simplest way to bypass case-sensitivity is to convert the string being compared to all-uppercase letters. However, if you don't want to modify the original string, you need to use a non-intrusive technique. Define a function that locally converts characters to uppercase without affecting the original string:

```
int nocase_cmp(const string & s1, const string& s2)
{
  string::const_iterator it1=s1.begin();
  string::const_iterator it2=s2.begin();

  //has the end of at least one of the strings been reached?
  while ( (it1!=s1.end()) && (it2!=s2.end()) )
  {
    if(::toupper(*it1) != ::toupper(*it2)) //letters differ?
     // return -1 to indicate 'smaller than', 1 otherwise
      return (::toupper(*it1)  < ::toupper(*it2)) ? -1 : 1;
    //proceed to the next character in each string
    ++it1;
    ++it2;
  }
  size_t size1=s1.size(), size2=s2.size();// cache lengths
   //return -1,0 or 1 according to strings' lengths
    if (size1==size2)
      return 0;
    return (size1<size2) ? -1 : 1;
}
```

Use the following code to test this function:

```
string s1="Me, myself, I";
string s2="me, myself, I";
int n=nocase_cmp(s1, s2); //n=0
```

As expected, the result is 0, indicating that the strings are identical even though their initial characters are in different cases. Don't be tempted to hide the `nocase_cmp()` function in an overloaded == operator, as it will clash with the case-sensitive == operator and can be very misleading.

NOTE: For more on overloading, see Chapter 3.

Finding a String Within a String

Searching a string within another string is a breeze with std::string. The Standard Library defines several specialized overloaded versions of `string::find()` that take `const string&`, `const char *`, or just `char` as a sought-after value (the substring). Here I will only show how to use the first version for locating a string object within another string object; implementing other versions should be a cinch:

```
string verse="Franco's rain in Spain";
string sought = "rain";
int pos=verse.find(sought); // pos=9
```

`find()` returns the position of the first character of `sought` with within `phrase`. This position can then be used for further manipulations such as deleting the sought-after string or replacing it with another value. Test whether the search succeeded like this:

```
if(pos!= string::npos)
  ...//success
else
  ...//not found
```

If the sought-after string wasn't found, `find()` return the constant `string::npos`. npos is an agreed-upon value that indicates an invalid position in all strings.

Substring Replacement

Suppose you want to replace the sought-after value with another substring, just as your word processor does when you use "find and replace." The `replace()` function (which also has several overloaded versions) does the trick. I will present the canonical version, which takes three arguments: the position, or offset, into which the replacement string should be written; the length of the substring to be replaced; and an overriding string. For example, the following code corrects the typo in `phrase` by replacing `rain` with `reign`:

```
phrase.replace(pos, sought.size(), replacement);
cout<<phrase<<endl;
```

Here is the output of this code:

```
Franco's reign in Spain
```

If this seems like a lot of work for replacing a substring within another string, you're probably right. There's a shorter path. The search and replace operations can be combined into a single statement like this:

```
phrase.replace(phrase.find(sought),
               sought.size(),
               replacement);
```

However, you should bear in mind that this form should be used only when you're certain that the sought-after value exists in the containing string. Otherwise, check whether the search operation succeeded before calling `replace()` or all hell will break loose.

Wonder of Wonders

You may have noticed something intriguing: `reign` is one character longer than the replaced value `rain` and yet the code above didn't extend the original string size before calling `replace()`. Did I miss something? No. `replace()` automatically increases its object's capacity to make it fit to the new size. You don't have to take my word for this; let's put it to the test. The following code uses a longer replacement string and checks the string's capacity before and after the `replace()` call:

```
cout<<"original string capacity: "<<phrase. capacity ()<<endl;
string replacement "reign in Spain should see out the forties";
```

```
string sought = "rain in Spain";
phrase.replace(phrase.find(sought), sought.capacity(), replacement);
cout<<phrase<<endl;
cout<<"new capacity: "<<phrase. capacity ()<<endl;
```

As the output shows, the new capacity is larger than the original:

```
original string capacity: 22
Franco's reign in Spain should see out the forties
new capacity: 50
```

The fat interface of std::string includes more than 100 member functions, overloaded operators and other free functions that provide various services. This diversity has encouraged programmers to use string objects for different purposes: for example, storing the content of an entire file or a comma-separated list in a string object. Another thing worth keeping in mind is that string objects are not committed to the C protocol of marking a string's end with a '\0' (null) character. Consequently, a string object may contain several nulls: for example, when you copy an .exe file into a string.

Summary

STL was designed to allow maximal reusability without sacrificing efficiency. The C++ standard specifies performance requirements with which STL containers and algorithms must comply. These performance specifications are the *minimum* requirements; an implementation may—and in most cases does—offer better performance.

STL is regarded by C++ creators as the most important addition to the language in recent years. Mastering STL is a worthwhile investment of time, effort, and energy. Other programming languages may soon follow the role model of STL and provide similar generic frameworks. Three major advantages of preferring STL to homemade containers are portability, performance, and reliability.

InformIT Articles and Sample Chapters

"The Standard Template Library: Generic Programming" (*http://www.informit.com/articles/article.asp?p=25088*) is a sample chapter from *C# Primer: A Practical Approach* (Addison-Wesley, 2001, ISBN 0201729555), by Stanley B. Lippman. This article is a good introduction to

STL's design principles and structure. Lippman was a member of the cfront project in the early 1980s. His experience in compiler writing contributes depth and clarity to the discussion. (For more on this book, visit *http://www.informit.com/bookstore/product.asp?isbn=0201729555.*)

Books and e-Books

STL Tutorial and Reference Guide: C++ Programming with the Standard Template Library (Addison-Wesley, 2001, ISBN 0201379236), by David R. Musser, Gillmer J. Derge, and Atul Saini, now in its second edition, has been my favorite STL book since 1996 or so. Although a good many other STL books have been published since this book premiered, its concise and accessible account of every STL algorithm and container is unparalleled. Note that the new edition includes all the latest extensions and modifications that took place since the first edition. (For more on this book, visit *http://www.informit.com/bookstore/product.asp?isbn=0201379236.*)

Online Resources

"Where can I find more information about the STL?" (*http://www.jamesd.demon.co.uk/csc/faq.html#C5*) is one of the questions on Bjarne Stroustrup's C++ FAQ. The answer provides useful links to exhaustive STL sites.

"Defining a Function Object" (*http://gethelp.devx.com/techtips/cpp_pro/10min/10min0100.asp*), by Danny Kalev, isn't directly related to templates. But since function objects are a fundamental feature of many STL algorithms, it's mostly useful for programmers who want to learn how to implement function objects and templatize them.

"Using auto_ptr," (*http://www.gotw.ca/gotw/042.htm*), by Herb Sutter, sheds some light on the controversial auto_ptr class and lists its do's and don'ts. Since the approval of the ANSI C++ standard in 1997, a lot of fuss has been made about its usefulness. Sadly, too many programmers still aren't fully aware of its semantics and behavior. This article may clear some of the mist surrounding `auto_ptr`, and demonstrates some valid uses thereof.

"Creating Heterogeneous Containers" (*http://gethelp.devx.com/techtips/cpp_pro/10min/10min0900.asp*), by Danny Kalev, teaches how to imitate heterogeneous containers in C++. Unlike other OO languages such as Smalltalk, C++ doesn't support this feature directly. However, it's possible to imitate this feature in STL by using containers of pointers to polymorphic objects.

The SGI STL portal (*http://www.sgi.com/tech/stl/*) provides an excellent online catalog (*http://www.sgi.com/tech/stl/stl_index.html*) and tutorial (*http://www.sgi.com/tech/stl/stl_introduction.html*) for STL. Here you'll find detailed descriptions of STL algorithms, containers, iterators, and adaptor classes, as well as a good introduction.

"Const Iterators" (*http://www.devx.com/tips/Tip/12870*) is a short tip that explains the difference between ordinary iterators and a `const_iterator` object.

"Iterator Categories" (*http://www.devx.com/tips/Tip/14191*) discusses the various types of STL iterators such as input iterators, forward iterators, bidirectional iterators, etc. Understanding the difference between these iterator types is essential for using STL algorithms correctly.

CHAPTER 11

Exception Handling

Large software applications are built in layers. At the lowest level, you usually find library routines, API functions, and proprietary infrastructure functions. At the highest level, you find GUI components.

Consider an ordinary flight-booking application. Its topmost layer consists of GUI components that display contents on the user's screen. These high-level components interact with data access objects, which in turn encapsulate database API routines. At a lower level, the database API routines interact with the database engine. The database engine itself invokes system services that deal with low-level hardware resources such as physical memory, filesystems, and security modules. In general, severe runtime errors are detected in these lower code layers, which cannot—or should not—attempt to handle them on their own. To handle an error appropriately, higher-level components have to be informed that an error has occurred. Essentially, error handling consists of detecting an error and notifying the components that are in charge. These components in turn attempt to recover from the error or terminate the program gracefully.

Traditional Error-Handling Methods

In its earlier stages, C++ didn't have a built-in facility for handling runtime errors. Instead, the traditional C methods were used for that purpose. These methods can be grouped into three design policies:

- Return a status code with agreed-upon values to indicate either success or failure.
- Assign an error code to a global variable and have other functions examine it.
- Terminate the program.

Each of these methods has significant drawbacks and limitations in an object-oriented environment. Some of these methods might be totally unacceptable, particularly in large-scale applications. For example, the `abort()`

and `exit()` library functions are never to be used in an object-oriented environment—even during debugging—because they don't invoke objects' destructors before program termination.

Exception-Handling Constructs

Exception handling is a mechanism for transferring control from a point in a program where an exception occurs, to a matching handler. *Exceptions* are variables of built-in datatypes or class objects. The exception-handling mechanism consists of four components: a *try block*, a sequence of one or more *handlers* associated with a `try` block, a *throw expression*, and the exception itself. The `try` block contains code that might throw an exception. For example:

```
try
{
 int * p = new int[1000000]; // new[] may throw std::bad_alloc
}
```

A `try` block is followed by a sequence of one or more `catch` statements (handlers), each of which handles a different type of exception:

```
try
{
 int * p = new int[1000000]; //may throw std::bad_alloc
 //...
}
catch(std::bad_alloc& )
{
}
catch (std::bad_cast&)
{
}
```

A handler is invoked only by a `throw` expression executed in the handler's `try` block, or in functions that are called from the handler's `try` block. A `throw` expression consists of the keyword `throw` and an argument:

```
try
{
 if (disaster)
    throw 5; // 5 is assigned to n in the following catch statement
}
```

```
catch(int n)
{
}
```

A `throw` expression is similar to a `return` statement in ordinary functions. An *empty throw* is a `throw` statement without an operand:

```
throw;
```

An empty throw inside a handler indicates a *rethrow*, which is discussed momentarily. Otherwise, if no exception is presently being handled, executing an empty throw causes an unconditional program termination by default.

Stack Unwinding

When an exception is thrown, the runtime mechanism first searches for an appropriate handler in the current scope. If no such handler exists, control is transferred from the current scope to a higher block in the calling chain. This process is iterative: It continues until an appropriate handler has been found. At this point, the stack has been unwound and all the local objects that were constructed on the path from a `try` block to a `throw` expression have been destroyed. In the absence of an appropriate handler, the program terminates. Note, however, that C++ ensures proper destruction of local objects only when the thrown exception is handled. Whether an uncaught exception causes the destruction of local objects during stack unwinding is implementation-dependent. To ensure that destructors of local objects are invoked in the case of an uncaught exception, you can add a `catch(...)` statement in `main()`. For example:

```
int main()
{
  try
  {
    //...
  }
  catch(std::exception& stdexc)   // handle expected exceptions
  {
    //...
  }
  // ensure proper cleanup in the case
  // of an uncaught exception
  catch(...)
  {
  }
}
```

The stack unwinding process is very similar to a sequence of `return` statements, each returning the same object to its caller.

Passing Exception Objects to a Handler

An exception can be passed by value or by reference to its handler. Exceptions that are passed by value are constructed on the stack frame of the caller. When an exception is passed by reference, the handler receives a reference to the exception object. Passing an exception by reference ensures its polymorphic behavior. For example:

```
#include <cstdio>
class ExBase {/*...*/};
class FileEx: public ExBase {/*...*/};

void Write(FILE *pf)
{
  if (pf == NULL) throw FileEx();
  //... process pf normally
}
int main ()
{
  try
  {
    Write(NULL); //will cause a FileEx exception to be thrown
  }
  //catch ExBase or any object derived from it
  catch(ExBase& exception)
  {
  //diagnostics and remedies
  }
}
```

Exception Type Match

The type of an exception determines which handler will catch it. The matching rules for exceptions are more restrictive than the matching rules for function overloading. Consider the following example:

```
try
{
  throw int();
}
// the following block won't catch the exception from
```

```
// the previous try block
catch (unsigned int)


{
}
```

The thrown exception is of type `int`, but the handler expects an `unsigned int`. The exception-handling mechanism doesn't consider these to be matching types; therefore, the thrown exception isn't caught. The matching rules for exceptions allow only a limited set of conversions: For an exception E and a handler taking T or T&, the match is valid under one of the following conditions:

- T and E are of the same type (`const` and `volatile` specifiers are ignored).
- T is an unambiguous public base class of E.

If E and T are pointers, the match is valid if E and T are of the same type or if E points to an object that's publicly and unambiguously derived from the class pointed to by T. In addition, a handler of type `array of T` or `function returning T` is transformed into `pointer to T` or `pointer to function returning T`, respectively.

Exception Objects

As you've probably noticed, the traditional convention of returning an integer as an error flag is problematic and unsatisfactory in OOP. The C++ exception-handling mechanism offers more flexibility in this respect, though. An exception can be a full-fledged object, with data members and member functions. Such an object can provide the exception handler with more options for recovery. A clever exception object, for example, can have a member function that returns a detailed verbal description of the error, instead of forcing the handler to look it up in a table or a file. It can have member functions that enable the program to recover from the runtime error after the error has been handled properly.

Exception Specifications

Several years after the addition of exception handling, the standardization committee added a complementary feature called *exception specifications*. In this section, I will present exception specifications and question their usefulness.

The Problem

Consider the following function prototype:

```
void validate(int code);
```

Third-party libraries often consist of similar declarations grouped in header files while the implementation is kept hidden from users. How can users know whether this function throws an exception and under what conditions it happens? Obviously, this declaration doesn't provide any clue. `validate()` could be a function that throws or it could even be a C function that's totally unaware of C++ exceptions.

Exception Specifications Basics

Exceptions were added to C++ in 1989. Several years of confusion of this kind convinced the standardization committee to add exception specifications to the language. An exception specification describes which exceptions a function is allowed to throw. Exceptions not listed in an exception specification should not be thrown from that function. An exception specification consists of the keyword `throw` after the function's parameter list, followed by a list of potential exceptions:

```
void validate(int code) throw (bad_code, no_auth);
```

An exception specification isn't considered a part of a function's type. Therefore, it doesn't affect overload resolution. That said, pointers to functions and pointers to member functions may contain an exception specification:

```
void (*pf)(int) throw(string, int);
```

`pf` is a pointer to a function that may throw `string` or `int`. You can assign to a function whose exception specification is as restrictive as, or more restrictive than, `pf`'s exception specification. An exception specification A is said to be more restrictive than an exception specification B if the set of exceptions A contains is a subset of B's exceptions. In other words, A contains every exception in B but not vice versa:

```
//more restrictive than pf:
void e(int) throw (string);
//as restrictive as pf:
void f(int) throw (string, int);
//less restrictive than pf:
```

```
void g(int) throw (string, int, bool);
pf=e; //fine
pf=f; //fine
pf=g; //error
```

Exception Specifications and Inheritance

An overriding virtual cannot extend the set of exceptions declared in the base class's function. However, it can narrow it. Let's look at a concrete example. Suppose you have the following class hierarchy and its related set of exception classes:

```
class clock_fault{/*..*/};
class Exception {/*..*/}; //base for other exceptions
class hardware_fault: public Exception {/*..*/};
class logical_error: public Exception {/*..*/};
class invalid_protocol: public Exception{/*..*/};

class RemovableDevice
{
public:
 virtual int
   connect(int port) throw(hardware_fault, logical_error);
 virtual int
   transmit(char * buff) throw(invalid_protocol);
};

class Scanner: public RemovableDevice
{
public:
 int connect(int port) throw(hardware_fault); //OK
 int transmit(char * buff)
    throw(invalid_protocol, clock_fault);//Error
};
```

`RemovableDevice::connect()` has an exception specification that allows it to throw `hardware_fault` and `logical_error` exceptions (as well as any exceptions derived from these classes). The overriding `Scanner::connect()` narrows this specification. Throwing any exception but `hardware_fault` from this function, including `logical_error`, isn't allowed. The exception specification of `Scanner::transmit()` is ill-formed. It includes `clock_fault`, an exception that doesn't appear in the exception specification of `RemovableDevice::transmit()`. If you try to compile this code, your compiler will complain about a conflicting exception specification.

Empty Exception Specifications and Missing Exception Specifications

A function with no exception specification allows all exceptions. A function with an *empty exception specification* doesn't allow any exceptions:

```
class File
{
public:
 int open(FILE *ptr); //may throw any exception
 int close(FILE *ptr) throw(); //doesn't throw
};
```

When you declare an empty exception specification, always check that there is no risk of violating it.

Exception Specification Enforcement

Exception specifications are enforced at runtime. When a function violates its exception specification, `std::unexpected()` is called. `unexpected()` invokes a user-defined function that was previously registered by calling `std::set_unexpected()`. If no function was registered with `set_unexpected()`, `unexpected()` calls `std::terminate()`, which aborts the program unconditionally.

Exception Specifications Theory and Practice

Seemingly, exception specifications are the best thing since sliced bread. Not only do they clearly document a function's exception policy, C++ also enforces them. At first, the C++ community greeted them enthusiastically. Many tutorials and illustrious authors started to use them all over the place. A typical class in a textbook looked like this:

```
class Foo
{
public:
 Foo() throw();
 ~Foo() throw();
 Foo(const Foo& ) throw();
 Foo& operator=(const Foo &) throw()
//...etc., etc.
};
```

It didn't take long before programmers realized that exception specifications were rather problematic. Exceptions are dynamic. It isn't always possible to predict which exception will actually be thrown at runtime. What happens if a function `g()` with an exception specification calls another function `f()` that has a less restrictive exception specification or no exception specification at all?

```
void f();
void g() throw(X)
{
 f(); //OK, but problematic
}
```

`g()` might violate its exception specification if `f()` throws any exception other than `X`.

Performance is another problem. Exceptions already incur performance overhead. Enforcing exception specifications incurs *additional* overhead because the implementation must enforce them at runtime. For these reasons and others, exception specifications soon lost their appeal. Today, you'd hardly find them in new code or textbooks. Ironically, the textbooks that were the first to adopt them were also the first to withdraw them silently.

Summary

Exception specifications are one of those features that seemed promising in theory but proved unsavory in the real world. You might wonder why I've spent our time discussing them. There are two reasons for this. First, legacy code that uses exception specifications still exists. Reading this code and—more importantly—using it correctly require familiarity with this feature. Secondly, exception specifications teach us a lesson in programming languages design. Quite a few programming languages adopted the C++ exception-handing model, including exception specifications. By the time the C++ community realized that exception specifications weren't that great, those languages had already gotten stuck with this feature for good. Today, there's pressure to add `finally` to C++. This construct is rather useful in Java, which doesn't have destructors. In C++ however, `finally` is redundant since you can perform unconditional cleanup operations in the event of an exception in a destructor. So why was `finally` proposed? Simply because Java programmers still think in Java when they're writing C++ code. Exception specifications teach us to be very cautious with adding features that haven't been tested thoroughly.

Online Resources

"Exception Handling in C++" (*http://www.informit.com/articles/article.asp?p=31537*), by Stanley B. Lippman and Josée LaJoie, provides an excellent overview of C++ exceptions and exception specifications in particular. Pay attention to the summary. It rightfully advises programmers to avoid unnecessary exceptions and consider other error-handling techniques, when appropriate. This article is a sample chapter from their book *C++ Primer, Third Edition* (Addison-Wesley, 1998, ISBN 0201824701). For more on this book, visit *http://www.informit.com/bookstore/product.asp?isbn=0201824701*.

"The `std::unexpected()` Function" (*http://www.devx.com/tips/Tip/15140*) explains how the standard function `unexpected()` works and how you can override its default behavior.

Exceptions During Construction and Destruction

Constructors and destructors are invoked automatically; in addition, they cannot return values to indicate a runtime error. The most plausible way of reporting runtime errors during object construction and destruction may seem to be throwing an exception. However, you have to consider additional factors before throwing an exception in these cases. You should be particularly cautious about throwing an exception from a destructor. The problem is that a destructor might be invoked as part of the stack unwinding. If a destructor that was invoked due to another exception also throws an exception of its own, the exception-handling mechanism invokes `terminate()`.

Global Objects

Conceptually, the construction of global objects (or more generally speaking: objects declared in a namespace scope) takes place before program outset. Therefore, any exception thrown from a constructor of a global object can never be caught. This is also true for a global object's destructor. It executes after a program's termination. Hence, an exception thrown from a global object's destructor also cannot be handled.

Advanced Exception-Handling Techniques

The simple `try-throw-catch` model can be extended even further to handle more complicated runtime errors, as I'll demonstrate in the following paragraphs.

Standard Exceptions

C++ defines a hierarchy of standard exceptions that are thrown at runtime when abnormal conditions arise:

- The standard exception classes are derived from `std::exception` (defined in the `<stdexcept>` header).
- `std::exception` is defined in the `<exception>` header.
- `std::bad_alloc` is defined in `<new>`.
- `std::bad_cast` is defined in `<typeinfo>`.
- Other exceptions are defined in `<stdexcept>`.

This hierarchy enables the application to catch these exceptions in a single `catch` statement:

```
catch (std::exception& exc)
{
  // handle exception of type std::exception as well as
  //any exception derived from it
}
```

The standard exceptions are as follows:

```
std::bad_alloc       //by operator new
std::bad_cast        //by operator dynamic_cast < >
std::bad_typeid      //by operator typeid
std::bad_exception   //thrown when an exception specification of
                     //a function is violated
```

All standard exceptions provide the member function `what()`, which returns a `const char *` with an implementation-dependent verbal description of the exception.

Exception Handlers Hierarchy

Exceptions are caught in a bottom-down hierarchy: Specific (most derived classes) exceptions are handled first, followed by groups of exceptions (base classes), and, finally, a `catch(...)` handler:

```
#include <stdexcept>
#include <iostream>
using namespace std;
```

```
int main()
{
  try
  {
      char * buff = new char[100000000];
      //...use buff
  }
  catch(bad_alloc& alloc_failure)   // bad_alloc is
                                    //derived from exception
  {
    cout<<"memory allocation failure";
    //... handle exception thrown by operator new
  }
  catch(exception& std_ex)
  {
    cout<< std_ex.what() <<endl;
  }
  // exceptions that are not handled elsewhere are caught here
  catch(...)
  {
    cout<<"unrecognized exception"<<endl;
  }
}
```

Handlers of the most derived objects must appear before the handlers of base classes. This is because handlers are tried in order of appearance. It's therefore possible to write handlers that are never executed: for example, by placing a handler for a derived class after a handler for a corresponding base class.

Exceptions and Performance

The exception-handling mechanism has to store additional data about the type of every exception object and every `catch` statement in order to perform the runtime matching between an exception and its matching handler. Because an exception can be of any type, and because it can be polymorphic as well, its dynamic type must be queried at runtime, using *runtime type information* (RTTI), which is discussed in Chapter 12, "Runtime Type Information (RTTI)." RTTI imposes an additional overhead in terms of both execution speed and program size. Yet RTTI alone is not enough. The implementation also requires runtime code information; that is, information about the structure of each function. This information is needed to determine whether an exception was thrown from a `try` block.

The technicalities of exception-handling implementation vary among compilers and platforms. In all of them, however, exception handling imposes additional overhead even when no exception is ever thrown. The overhead lies in both execution speed and program size. For this reason, some compilers enable you to toggle exception-handling support. However, turning off exception handling is rarely an option. Even if you don't use exceptions directly, you're probably using them implicitly. Operator `new`, for example, might throw a `std::bad_alloc` exception when it fails, and so do other built-in operators. STL containers might throw their own exceptions, and so might other functions of the Standard Library. Code libraries supplied by third-party vendors might use exceptions as well. Therefore, you can safely turn off exception-handling support only when you're porting pure C code into a C++ compiler. As long as pure C code is used, the additional exception-handling overhead is unnecessary and can be avoided.

Misuses of Exception Handling

Some programmers might use exception handling as an alternative to `for` loops or `while` and `do` blocks. For example, a simple application that prompts the user to enter data until a certain condition has been fulfilled can be (rather naively) implemented as follows:

```
#include <iostream>
using namespace std;
class Exit{}; //used as exception object
int main()
{
 int num;
 cout<< "enter a number; 99 to exit" <<endl;
 try
 {
   while (true) //infinitely
   {
     cin>>num;
     if (num == 99)
         throw Exit(); //exit the loop
     cout<< "you entered: " << num << "enter another number " <<endl;
   }
```

```
  }
  catch (Exit& )
  {
    cout<< "game over" <<endl;
  }
}
```

In the preceding example, the programmer locates an infinite loop within a `try` block. The `throw` statement breaks the loop and transfers control to the following `catch` statement. This style of programming is not recommended, however; it's very inefficient due to the excess overhead of exception handling. Furthermore, it's rather verbose and might have been much simpler and shorter had it been written with a `break` statement.

Summary

Exception handling overcomes the problems associated with the traditional error-handling techniques, yet incurs performance overhead. Exceptions can be grouped into categories; the standard exception classes are a good example. Exception handling is a very powerful and flexible tool for handling runtime errors effectively. However, you should use it judiciously.

InformIT Articles and Sample Chapters

"Handling Exceptions" (*http://www.informit.com/articles/article.asp?p=130360*) is a sample chapter from *Tom Swan's GNU C++ for Linux* (Que, 2002, ISBN 0789721538). This chapter teaches the basics of exception handling under the GNU compiler. Historically, UNIX C++ compilers had a hard time coping with this feature properly. I remember that in one of my projects (1997) we had to forgo exception handling altogether because the very presence of `try` and `catch` statements in our code would cause the GCC compiler to crash! Fortunately, things have improved since then, although GCC users should still pay attention to compiler-specific exception-handling quirks and idiosyncrasies. (For more on this book, visit *http://www.informit.com/bookstore/product.asp?isbn=0789721538*.)

"Exception Handling in C++" (*http://www.informit.com/articles/article.asp?p=31537*), by Stanley B. Lippman and Josée LaJoie, is a sample chapter from their book *C++ Primer, Third Edition* (Addison-Wesley, 1998, ISBN 0201824701). The article teaches all there is to know about C++ exceptions, including syntax, semantics, applications, and software design issues. (For more on this book, visit *http://www.informit.com/bookstore/product.asp?isbn=0201824701.*)

Online Resources

"Exception Handling" (*http://gethelp.devx.com/techtips/cpp_pro/10min/2002/June/10min0602.asp*), by Danny Kalev, is an introductory article that teaches the basics of exception handling. It's mostly aimed at novices; therefore, it doesn't deal with more advanced stuff such as function-try-blocks and exception specifications.

In the Q&A page "Try and Catch Me" (*http://www.gotw.ca/gotw/065.htm*), Herb Sutter addresses common exception-handling issues such as where to place a `try` block, what *exception safety* really means, and more. I liked the rules and conclusions; for example, "Using the 'resource acquisition is initialization' idiom can eliminate many `try` blocks." If only all programmers followed these guidelines, fewer bugs would occur in the first place.

CHAPTER 12

Runtime Type Information (RTTI)

Although C++ pundits have claimed for years that one can get along without Runtime Type Information (RTTI), in some frameworks and application domains it's unavoidable. The constituents of RTTI are the operators `dynamic_cast<>` and `typeid` and the class `std::type_info`. This section explores their functionality and shows the practical uses of RTTI.

Getting Along Without RTTI

Virtual-member functions can provide a reasonable level of dynamic typing without the need for additional RTTI support. A well-designed class hierarchy defines a meaningful operation for every virtual-member function that's declared in the base class. Suppose you have to develop a file manager application as a component of a GUI-based operating system. The files in this system are represented as icons that respond to a mouse right-click by displaying a menu with options such as open, close, read, and so on. The underlying implementation of the file system relies on a class hierarchy that represents files of various types. In a well-designed class hierarchy, an abstract class serves as an interface:

```
class File //abstract, all members are pure virtual
{
  public: virtual void open() =0;
  public: virtual void read() =0;
  public: virtual void write() =0;
  public: virtual ~File () =0;
};
File::~File ()   //pure virtual destructor must be defined
{}
```

At a lower level in the hierarchy, you have a set of derived classes. Each of these subclasses represents a different family of files. To simplify the discussion, assume that there are only two file types in this system: binary .exe files and text files:

```
class BinaryFile : public File
{
public:
  //implement the pure virtual function
  void open () { OS_execute(this); }
  //...other member functions
};
class TextFile : public File
{
public:
  void open () { Activate_word_processor (this); }
  //...other member functions of File are implemented here
  void virtual print();   // an additional member function
};
```

The pure virtual function `open()` is implemented in every derived class, according to the type of the file. Thus, in a `TextFile` object, `open()` activates a word processor, whereas a `BinaryFile` object invokes the operating system's API function `OS_execute()`, which runs the program stored in the binary file.

There are several differences between a binary file and a text file. For example, a text file can be printed directly on a screen or a printer because it consists of a sequence of printable characters. Conversely, a binary file with an .exe extension contains a stream of bits; it cannot be printed or displayed directly on a screen. Therefore, the member function `print()` appears only in class `TextFile`.

In this file manager, right-clicking a file icon opens a menu of options suitable for that file. This is achieved by a function that takes a `File &` parameter:

```
OnRightClick (File & file); //operating system's API function
```

Obviously, no object of class `File` can be instantiated because `File` is an abstract class. However, the function `OnRightClick()` can accept any object derived from `File`. When the user right-clicks a file icon and chooses the option Open, for instance, `OnRightClick` invokes the virtual member function open of its argument, and the appropriate member function is called:

```
OnRightClick (File & file)
{
```

```
switch (message)
{
//...
case m_open:
  file.open();
break;
}
}
```

So far, so good. Yet you might have noticed the lack of printing support. Look at the definition of class `TextFile` again:

```
class TextFile : public File
{
public:
  void open () { Activate_word_processor (this); }
  void virtual print();
};
```

The member function `print()` is not declared in `File`. It would be a design error to do so because binary files are nonprintable. Yet `OnRightClick()` has to support printing when it handles a text file. In this case, ordinary polymorphism in the form of virtual-member functions isn't enough. `OnRightClick()` only knows that its argument is derived from `File`; this information is insufficient to tell whether the actual object is printable. This is where the need for runtime type information arises. Before delving into the implementation of OnRightClick(), an overview of RTTI constituents and their role is necessary.

RTTI Constituents

The operators `typeid` and `dynamic_cast<>` offer two complementary forms of accessing the runtime type information of their operands. The operand's runtime type information itself is stored in a `type_info` object.

NOTE: It's important to realize that RTTI is applicable solely to polymorphic objects; a class must have at least one virtual-member function in order to have RTTI support for its objects.

For every distinct type, C++ instantiates a corresponding `std::type_info` (defined in `<typeinfo>`) object. The interface is as follows:

```
namespace std {
  class type_info
  {
  public:
   virtual ~type_info(); //type_info can serve as a base class
  // enable comparison
   bool operator==(const type_info& rhs ) const;
  // return !( *this == rhs)
   bool operator!=(const type_info& rhs ) const;
   bool before(const type_info& rhs ) const; // ordering
  //return a C-string containing the type's name
   const char* name() const;
  private:
    //objects of this type cannot be copied
       type_info(const type_info& rhs );
       type_info& operator=(const type_info& rhs);
  }; //type_info
}
```

All objects of the same class share a single `type_info` object. The most widely used member functions of `type_info` are `name()` and `operator==`. But before you can invoke these member functions, you have to access the `type_info` object itself. How? Operator `typeid` takes either an object or a type name as its argument and returns a matching `type_info` object. The dynamic type of an object can be examined as follows:

```
OnRightClick (File & file)
{
  if ( typeid( file)  == typeid( TextFile ) )
  {
    //received a TextFile object; printing should be enabled
  }
  else
  {
    //not a TextFile object; printing disabled
  }
}
```

To understand how it works, look at the highlighted source line:

```
if ( typeid( file)  == typeid( TextFile ) )
```

The `if` statement tests whether the dynamic type of `file` is `TextFile` (the static type of `file` is `File`, of course). The leftmost expression, `typeid(file)`, returns a `type_info` object that holds the necessary runtime type information associated with the object `file`. The rightmost expression, `typeid(TextFile)`, returns the type information associated with class `TextFile`. (When `typeid` is applied to a class name rather than an object, it always returns a `type_info` object that corresponds to that class name.)

As shown earlier, `type_info` overloads the operator `==`. Therefore, the `type_info` object returned by the leftmost `typeid` expression is compared to the `type_info` object returned by the rightmost `typeid` expression. If `file` is an instance of `TextFile`, the `if` statement evaluates to `true`. In that case, `OnRightClick` should display an additional option in the menu: `print()`. On the other hand, if `file` is not a `TextFile`, the `if` statement evaluates to `false`, and the `print()` option is disabled.

As neat as this seems, a `typeid`-based solution has a drawback. Suppose you want to add support for a new type of file, such as HTML. What happens when the file manager application is extended? HTML files are essentially text files—you can read and print them. However, they differ from plain-text files in some respects; an `open` message launches a browser rather than a word processor. By subclassing `TextFile`, you can reuse its existing behavior and implement only the additional functionality required for HTML files:

```
class HTMLFile : public TextFile
{
  void open () { Launch_Browser (); }
  void virtual print();  // perform the necessary conversions to a
                         //printable format and then print file
};
```

This is only half of the story, however. `OnRightClick()` fails badly when it receives an object of type `HTMLFile`. Look at it again to see why:

```
OnRightClick (File & file) //operating system's API function
{
  if ( typeid( file)  == typeid( TextFile ) )
  {
    //we received a TextFile object; printing should be enabled
  }
  else //OOPS! we get here when file is of type HTMLFile
  {
  }
}
```

`typeid` returns the *exact* type information of its argument. Therefore, the `if` statement in `OnRightClick()` evaluates to `false` when the argument is an `HTMLFile`. But a `false` value implies a binary file (!) in this application and disables printing. This onerous bug is likely to occur every time you add a new file type. Of course, you can modify `OnRightClick()` so that it performs another test for this type of file, but this workaround is error-prone and inelegant. Fortunately, there's a better solution.

dynamic_cast<>

`OnRightClick()` doesn't really need to know whether `file` is an instance of class `TextFile` (or of any other class, for that matter). Rather, all it needs to know is whether file *is-a* `TextFile`. An object *is-a* `TextFile` if it's an instance of class `TextFile` or any class derived from it. For this purpose, you use the operator `dynamic_cast<>`. `dynamic_cast<>` takes two arguments: a type name, and an object that `dynamic_cast<>` attempts to cast at runtime. For example:

```cpp
//attempt to cast file to a reference to
//an object of type TextFile
dynamic_cast <TextFile &> (file);
```

If the attempted cast succeeds, the second argument *is-a* `TextFile`. But how do you know whether `dynamic_cast<>` was successful?

There are two flavors of `dynamic_cast<>`: One uses pointers and the other uses references. Accordingly, `dynamic_cast<>` returns a pointer or a reference of the desired type when it succeeds. When `dynamic_cast<>` cannot perform the cast, it returns NULL; or, in the case of a reference, it throws an exception of type `std::bad_cast`:

```cpp
TextFile * pTest = dynamic_cast <TextFile *>
  (&file); //attempt to cast
          //file address to a pointer to TextFile

if (pTest) //dynamic_cast succeeded, file is-a TextFile
{
  //use pTest
}
else // file is not a TextFile;  pTest has a NULL value
{
}
```

NOTE: Remember to place a reference `dynamic_cast<>` expression inside a `try` block and include a suitable `catch` statement to handle `std::bad_cast` exceptions.

Now you can revise `OnRightClick()` to handle `HTMLFile` objects properly:

```
OnRightClick (File & file)
{
  try
  {
    TextFile temp = dynamic_cast<TextFile&> (file);
    //display options, including "print"
    switch (message)
    {
    case m_open:
      temp.open();   //either TextFile::open or HTMLFile::open
    break;
    case m_print:
      temp.print();//either TextFile::print or HTMLFile::print
    break;
    }//switch
  }//try
  catch (std::bad_cast& noTextFile)
  {
    // treat file as a BinaryFile; exclude"print"
  }
}// OnRightClick
```

The revised version of `OnRightClick()` handles an object of type `HTMLFile` properly. When the user clicks the Open option in the file manager application, `OnRightClick()` invokes the member function `open()` of its argument. Likewise, when it detects that its argument is a `TextFile`, it displays a print option.

This hypothetical file manager example is a bit contrived; with the use of templates and more sophisticated design, it could have been implemented without `dynamic_cast`. Yet dynamic type casts have other valid uses in C++, as I'll show next.

Crosscasts

A *crosscast* converts a multiply inherited object (see Chapter 9, "Object-Oriented Programming and Design Principles," for further information on multiple inheritance) to one of its secondary base classes. To see what a crosscast does, consider the following class hierarchy:

```
struct A
{
```

```
  int i;
  virtual ~A () {} //enforce polymorphism; needed for dynamic_cast
};
struct B
{
  bool b;
};

struct D: public A, public B
{
  int k;
  D() { b = true; i = k = 0; }
};

A *pa = new D;
B *pb = dynamic_cast<B*> pa;   //crosscast; access the second base
                               //of a multiply-derived object
```

The static type of pa is "A *", whereas its dynamic type is "D *". A simple static_cast<> cannot convert a pointer to A into a pointer to B, because A and B are unrelated. Don't even think of a brute force cast. It will cause disastrous results at runtime because the compiler will simply assign pa to pb; whereas the B sub-object is located at a different address within D than the A sub-object. To perform the crosscast properly, the value of pb has to be calculated at runtime. After all, the crosscast can be done in a source file that doesn't even know that class D exists! The following listing demonstrates why a dynamic cast, rather than a compile-time cast, is required in this case:

```
A *pa = new D;
// disastrous; pb points to the sub-object A within d
B *pb = (B*) pa;  bool bb = pb->b;   // bb has an undefined value
// pb was not properly
// adjusted; pa and pb are identical
cout<< "pa: " << pa << " pb: "<<pb <<endl;
pb = dynamic_cast<B*> (pa); //crosscast; adjust pb correctly
bb= pb->b; //OK, bb is true
// OK, pb was properly adjusted;
// pa and pb have distinct values
cout<< "pa: "<< pa << " pb: " << pb <<endl;
```

The code displays two lines of output: The first shows that the memory addresses of pa and pb are identical; the second shows that the memory addresses of pa and pb are indeed different after performing a dynamic cast as needed.

Downcasting from a Virtual Base

A *downcast* is a cast from a base to a derived object. Before the advent of RTTI, downcasts were regarded as bad programming practice and notoriously unsafe. `dynamic_cast<>` enables you to use safe and simple downcasts from a virtual base to its derived object. Look at the following example:

```
struct V
{
  virtual ~V (){} //ensure polymorphism
};
struct A: virtual V {};
struct B: virtual V {};
struct D: A, B {};

#include <iostream>
using namespace std;
int main()
{
 V *pv = new D;
 A* pa = dynamic_cast<A*> (pv); // downcast
  cout<< "pv: "<< pv << " pa: " << pa <<endl; // OK, pv and pa have
                                              //different addresses
}
```

V is a virtual base for classes A and B. D is multiply inherited from A and B. Inside main(), pv is declared as a V * and its dynamic type is D *. Here again, as in the crosscast example, the dynamic type of pv is needed in order to properly downcast it to a pointer to A. A static_cast<> would be rejected by the compiler in this case, as the memory layout of a virtual sub-object might be different from that of a non-virtual sub-object. Consequently, it's impossible to calculate at compile-time the address of the sub-object A within the object pointed to by pv. As the output of the program shows, pv and pa indeed point to different memory addresses.

Summary

The RTTI mechanism of C++ consists of three components: operator `typeid`, operator `dynamic_cast<>`, and class `std::type_info`. RTTI is relatively new in C++. Some existing compilers don't support it yet. Furthermore, compilers that support it can usually be configured to disable RTTI support. Even when there's no explicit usage of RTTI in a program, the compiler automatically adds the necessary "scaffolding" to the resulting executable. To avert this, you can usually switch off your compiler's RTTI support.

From the object-oriented design point of view, operator `dynamic_cast<>` is preferable to `typeid` because it enables more flexibility and robustness. However, `dynamic_cast<>` can be slower than `typeid` because its performance depends on the proximity of its target and operand, as well as on the derivational complexity of the latter. When complex derivational hierarchies are used, the incurred performance penalty might be noticeable; therefore, you should use RTTI judiciously. In many cases, a virtual-member function is sufficient to achieve the necessary polymorphic behavior. Only when virtual-member functions are insufficient should RTTI be considered.

InformIT Articles and Sample Chapters

"Friends, Exceptions, and More," Chapter 15 in Stephen Prata's book *C++ Primer Plus, Fourth Edition* (Sams, 2001, ISBN 0672322234), is a good introduction to RTTI and its syntax and applications. (For more on this book, visit *http://www.informit.com/title/0672322234.*)

Online Resources

"What Is RTTI?" is a chapter from Bruce Eckel's online book *Thinking in C++, Second Edition* (*http://www.mindview.net/Books/TICPP/ThinkingInCPP2e.html*). If you're looking for a detailed account of RTTI's constituents and issues that I didn't discuss in this chapter, such as the interaction of RTTI with templates, `void *` casts, and non-polymorphic objects, you should read this chapter of Bruce's book.

CHAPTER 13

The New Cast Operators

Originally, the C++ standardization committee wanted to deprecate C-style cast, thereby enforcing the use of the new cast operators exclusively. However, because C-style cast is widely used in legacy code and because many C++ compilers serve as C compilers, the committee decided not to do so. That said, C++ programmers are encouraged to use the new cast operators. Before I present these operators, let's see why C-style cast has fallen out of favor. Consider the following code listing:

```
void *p=&x;
int n=(int)p; //C-style cast
```

C-style cast seems harmless at first sight. Yet it has several potential dangers. First, it performs different operations in different contexts. For example, it may perform a safe `int` to `double` promotion but it can also perform inherently dangerous operations such as casting `void*` to a numeric value (as in the example above). The programmer can't always tell from the source code if the cast is safe or inherently dangerous. Worse yet, C-style cast may perform multiple operations at once. In the following example, not only does it cast `char *` to `unsigned char *`, but it removes the `const` qualifier at the same time:

```
const char *msg="don't touch!";
unsigned char *p=(unsigned char*) msg; // intentional?
```

Again, one cannot tell whether this was the programmer's intention or an oversight.

Presenting the New Cast Operators

The ailments of C-style cast have been known for years. C++ offers a superior alternative to it in the form of new cast operators that document the programmer's intent more clearly while preserving the compiler's ability to catch potential bugs as shown above. C++ has four new cast operators:

- `static_cast`
- `const_cast`
- `reinterpret_cast`
- `dynamic_cast`

The `dynamic_cast` operator is unique in this regard as it introduces new functionality that C-style cast doesn't support. I'll get to that momentarily.

static_cast

`static_cast` performs safe and relatively portable casts. For example, you use `static_cast` to explicitly document a cast that would otherwise take place automatically. Consider the following example:

```
bool b=true;
int n=static_cast<int> (b);
```

C++ automatically casts `bool` to `int` in this context so the use of `static_cast` in this case isn't necessary. However, by using it, programmers document their intention explicitly.

In other contexts, `static_cast` is mandatory. For example, when you cast `void*` to a different pointer type, as in the following example:

```
int n=4;
void *pv=&n;
int pi2 = static_cast<int *> (pv); //mandatory
```

`static_cast` uses the information available at compile-time to perform the required type conversion. Therefore, the target and the source might not be identical in their binary representation. Consider a `float` to `int` conversion. The binary representation of the floating number 10.0 is quite different from the equivalent integer value of 10. `static_cast` performs the necessary adjustments when casting one to the other.

The use of `static_cast` enables the compiler to catch programmers' mistakes such as this:

```
const char *msg="don't touch!";
unsigned char *p=
 static_cast<unsigned char*> (msg); //error
```

Here the compiler issues an error message indicating that the cast operation attempts to remove the `const` qualifier of `msg`—something that the programmer probably didn't intend to do anyway.

const_cast

The removal of `const` requires a special cast operator called `const_cast`. This operator can perform only the following operations:

- Remove the `const` and or `volatile` qualification.
- Add `const` and or `volatile` qualification.

For example:

```
struct A
{
 void func(){} // non-const member function
};

void f(const A& a)
{
 a.func(); // error, calling a non-const function
}
```

Clearly, this is a design mistake—the member function `func()` should have been declared `const` in the first place. However, such code does exist in third-party libraries and when innocent programmers try to use it, they have to resort to brute force casts. To overcome this problem, you can remove the `const` qualifier of a and then call `func()` as follows:

```
A &ref = const_cast<A&> (a); // remove const
ref.func(); // now fine
```

Trying to perform any other conversion with `const_cast` will result a compilation error. Remember also that while `const_cast` may remove the const qualifier of an object, this doesn't mean that you're allowed to modify it. In fact, trying to modify a `const` object causes undefined behavior. Therefore, use `const_cast` cautiously when it is used for the removal of `const` or `volatile`.

reinterpret_cast

As opposed to `static_cast`, `reinterpret_cast` performs relatively dangerous and nonportable casts. `reinterpret_cast` doesn't change the binary representation of the source object. Therefore, it is often used it in low-level applications that convert objects and other data to a stream of bytes and vice versa. In the following example, `reinterpret_cast` is used for "cheating" the compiler, thus enabling the programmer to examine the individual bytes of a `float` variable:

```
float f=10;
unsigned char *p = reinterpret_cast <unsigned char*> (&f);
for (int j=0; j<4; ++j)
  cout<<p[j]<<endl;
```

The use of `reinterpret_cast` explicitly warns the reader that an unsafe (and probably a nonportable) conversion is taking place. When using `reinterpret_cast`, the programmer—rather than the compiler—is responsible for the results.

dynamic_cast

As previously said, `dynamic_cast` differs from all other three cast operators. You use it when the conversion must access the runtime type information of an object rather than its static type (for more information on static versus dynamic typing, see Chapter 12, "Runtime Type Information (RTTI)"). Two common scenarios that necessitate the use of `dynamic_cast` are a *downcast*—i.e., casting a base class pointer or reference to a pointer or reference of a derived class—and a *crosscast* in which the programmer converts a multiply inherited object to one of its secondary base classes.

Summary

C-style cast is neither safe nor explicit enough, as I have shown. It disables the compiler's type-safety checks, its syntactic form doesn't express the intended conversion clearly and it cannot perform a dynamic cast. For all these reasons, you should avoid using it in new code. Instead, use `static_cast` for safe and rather portable casts, `const_cast` to remove or add only the `const/volatile` qualifiers of an object, and `reinterpret_cast` for low-level, unsafe and nonportable casts. Use `dynamic_cast` for conversions that must access the dynamic type of an object and RTTI capability-queries.

Online Resources

"Demonstrating the Differences Between static_cast and reinterpret_cast" (*http://www.devx.com/tips/Tip/13842*) is a short tip that shows the not-so-subtle differences between the operations of these two operators.

"Perform Safe Downcasts" (*http://www.devx.com/tips/Tip/12980*) is a tip that explains what a downcast is and how it should be done properly using `dynamic_cast`.

"Perform Crosscasts Properly" (*http://www.devx.com/tips/Tip/12966*) is another tip that explains the notion of a crosscast explaining why it's necessary and how it should be done properly using `dynamic_cast`.

CHAPTER 14

Miscellaneous Techniques

In this chapter, you will find "how to" style discussions that show how to implement common programming tasks using standard C++ constructs. These tasks include the implementation of persistent objects, lock files, signal processing, and so on.

Lock Files

Most operating systems provide platform-specific libraries for resource locking. A locking mechanism ensures that shared resources such as configuration files, system registry, etc., aren't accessed by multiple processes simultaneously. In this section, I will show a simple and portable technique for implementing locks without resorting to intricate platform-dependent services.

Designing a Locking Policy

To demonstrate the usefulness of the locking technique we're about to use, I'll use an example. Consider a terminal server to which multiple users can login simultaneously. The server maintains a data file called password.dat in which users' passwords are kept. The system administrator occasionally accesses this file to add new users, remove expired accounts, modify privileges and so on. The users themselves can also access this file to change their passwords. To ensure that only a single user at a time modifies the data file, we need to create a *lock file*. The lock file is essentially a disk file that has the same name as the data file and a .lck extension, indicating that it's a lock file. When the lock file password.lck exists, its associated data file is considered locked and other processes are not allowed to edit it. If the lock file doesn't exist, a process that wants to modify the data file first creates it. Only then can it access the data file. Once that process has finished updating the data file, it deletes the lock file, thereby signaling that the lock has been released. In other words, locking a resource consists of creating a file with an .lck extension in the same directory of the data file.

Implementation

The lock file creation must be *atomic*. The pre-standard <fstream.h> library used to have the `ios::noshare` flag that guaranteed atomic file creation. Sadly, it was removed from the <fstream> library, which superseded <fstream.h>. As a result, we are forced to use the traditional UNIX file I/O interface declared in <fcntl.h> (under UNIX and Linux) or <io.h> (Windows) to ensure an atomic operation.

Before a process can write to the data file, it should obtain a lock like this:

```
#include <fcntl.h> // for open()
#include <cerrno> // for errno
#include <cstdio> // for perror()
int fd;
fd=open("password.lck", O_WRONLY | O_CREAT | O_EXCL);
```

If the `open()` call succeeds, it returns a *descriptor*, which is a small positive integer that identifies the file. Otherwise, it returns -1 and assigns a matching error code to the global variable `errno`. The `O_CREAT` flag indicates that if the file doesn't exist, `open()` should create it. The `O_EXCL` flag ensures that the call is atomic; if the file already exists, `open()` will fail and set `errno` to `EEXIST`. This way you guarantee that only a single process at a time can hold the lock.

You check the return code of `open()` as follows:

```
int getlock() // returns the lock's descriptor on success
{
 if (fd<0 && errno==EEXIST)
 {
 // the file already exist; another process is
 // holding the lock
  cout<<"the file is currently locked; try again later";
  return -1;
 }
 else if (fd < 0)
 {
  // perror() appends a verbal description of the current
  // errno value after the user-supplied string
  perror("locking failed for the following reason");
```

```
    return -1;
}
// if we got here, we own the lock
return fd;
}
```

Once a process owns the lock, it can write to the data file safely. When it has finished updating the file, it should delete the lock as follows:

```
remove("password.lck");
```

At this moment, the data file is considered unlocked and another process can access it.

Lock File Applications

Thus far I've focused on one kind of resources, namely data files. However, the locking technique presented here can be applied to other system resources as well. For example, a fax application and a web browser can synchronize their access to the system's modem by using such a lock file. Remember though that this locking protocol is based on voluntary cooperation of all the processes involved. If a process fails to check whether a resource is locked before trying to access it, multiple processes might still face a *race condition*, i.e., an access clash. Another problem could occur if a process that holds the lock terminates before releasing it (e.g., due to an unhandled exception or a kill signal sent from another process). In this case, the data file will remain locked. To avoid this, you can set an expiry date after which the lock file can be deleted safely.

Summary

The main advantages of the simple locking protocol presented here are simplicity and platform independence. More sophisticated locking mechanisms such as mutexes and spinlocks are safer and offer more functionality and fine-grained access policies. For example, they allow you to grant access to a resource to four processes or less. The decision as to which locking mechanism to use should be based on the level of security needed and the availability of specialized synchronization libraries. Note that the rudimentary file lock mechanism demonstrated here can be further enhanced. For example, you can write the lock owner's pid to the lock file, thereby allowing other processes and user to know which process is currently holding the lock.

Online Resources

The manual page for the POSIX `lockf()` function (see *http://www.mkssoftware.com/docs/man3/lockf.3.asp*) explains how to use this function to lock portions of a file. Notice that on the one hand, this function provides tighter control and a higher level of safety than our file-locking mechanism. On the other hand, its interface is more complex, and, sadly, it's limited to POSIX systems exclusively.

Using the `swap()` Algorithm

Swap is one of those tricky algorithms that have several implementations, each offering its own advantages and disadvantages. In the following sections I will show why familiarity with these implementations may be beneficial, albeit for different reasons than you might think. The evaluation of these implementations will lead to an important lesson about software design and performance analysis.

Classic `swap()`

The classic implementation of the `swap()` algorithm is straightforward: take two arguments of the same type, copy the first one to a temporary variable, assign the second to the first, and finally assign the temporary value to the second. The following `vanilla_swap()` function template implements this algorithm:

```
template<class T> void vanilla_swap(T& t1, T& t2)//plain vanilla
{
 T temp=t1;
 t1=t2;
 t2=temp;
}
```

NOTE: Read more about template programming in Chapter 5, "Templates."

This implementation has a prominent advantage: It's generic. In other words, it's applicable to both built-in types and user-defined types. Not very surprisingly, this is exactly how the STL `std::swap()` is implemented in the `<algorithm>` header file. Therefore, if you want to use this implementation, there's no need to reinvent the wheel. In order to evaluate this implementation's usefulness and its performance, we need to compare it to other implementations first.

> **NOTE:** For more on the STL and generic programming principles, see Chapter 10, "The Standard Template Library (STL) and Generic Programming."

Swapping Without a Temporary Object

A common question in college exams and job interviews is: "Can you write a `swap()` function that doesn't use a temporary variable?" As the question implies, it's possible to get rid of the temporary object. The trick is to use the += and -= operators, thereby performing two operations in a single expression. Here's the complete implementation of this function template:

```
//swap with no temporary object
template <class T> void nt_swap(T& i, T& j)
{
   i -= j;
   j += i; // j gets the original value of i
   i = (j - i); // i gets the original value of j
}
```

In terms of readability, this version is more cryptic than `vanilla_swap()`. As for its generic capabilities, this implementation is applicable to all built-in types and user-defined types that define matching += and -= operators. For unknown reasons, many believe that this implementation should be faster than `vanilla_swap()` because of the omission of a temporary variable. To compare the performance of the two implementations we've encountered thus far, use two loops that call each of these functions 50,000,000 times (or more, depending on your machine's processor) and measure their speed. On my machine, the non-optimized debug version of the two loops didn't exhibit statistically significant differences when applied to integers. When applied to `double`, however, `vanilla_swap()` wins big time. Its execution speed was less than a third of `nt_swap()`'s!

Another Temporary-Free Implementation

Another common variant of `swap()` uses the bitwise operators to eliminate a temporary variable. The snag is that this version can only take arguments of integral types. For this reason, I didn't use a template in this case:

```
void nt2_swap(int& i, int& j)//no temporary, II
{
 i ^= j;
 j ^= i;
 i ^= j;
}// i and j have been swapped
```

Clearly, the type limitation of this algorithm severely restricts its usefulness. In terms of readability, it's even more cryptic than `nt_swap()`. How does it behave performance-wise? My tests show that this implementation doesn't differ significantly from the previous two in this regard.

Summary

"Cuteness hurts," says C++ guru Herb Sutter, and justly so. The previous passages have taught us an important lesson: The road to convoluted, hard-to-maintain and inefficient code is paved with naivete and programs that try to be cute. Not only does `vanilla_swap()` turn out to be at least as efficient as the other two implementations, it is also completely generic and readable. Furthermore, this implementation has another important advantage: You don't have to write it from scratch. The more general lesson to take home is that whenever you have several possible implementations of a certain component, you should prefer the one that's available in the Standard Library to any home-made solution, as it's also the most efficient implementation in most cases. Finally, if you prefer to evaluate several different implementations, base your decision on empirical tests and sound criteria rather than myths and gut feeling.

Indeed, familiarity with `nt_swap()` and `nt2_swap()` might be useful in certain cases: when maintaining legacy code or when applying for a new job. However, in production code `std::swap()` is your preferable choice.

Using Class `stopwatch` for Performance Measurements

Commercial profiling suites can be quite expensive and require some practice before you can use them effectively. In the following sections I will show how to implement a simple and effective stopwatch class that automatically calculates and reports the execution time of functions, loops, and code blocks. This class can be used for determining the efficiency of competing designs, languages features (exceptions, for instance) and so on.

Design and Implementation

The constructor and destructor of an object with automatic storage execute at a code block's beginning and end, respectively. We take advantage of this feature in the implementation of class `stopwatch`. The constructor will start counting time and its destructor will calculate and report the total execution time of a certain operation. To achieve a resolution of a millisecond (or even a more fine-grained resolution, depending on the platform in question), we will use the `clock()` function declared in `<ctime>` if your compiler is standard-compliant, or `<time.h>` for older compilers. `clock()` returns the processor's time elapsed since the program's outset in *clock ticks*. A clock tick is a platform-dependent unit of time. The macro CLOCKS_PER_SEC represents the number of clock ticks per second on your machine.

Here is the definition of class `stopwatch`:

```
#include <ctime>
class stopwatch
{
public:
 stopwatch() : start(std::clock()){} //start counting time
 ~stopwatch();
private:
 std::clock_t start;
};
```

The constructor initializes `start` with the current tick count. We don't define other member functions except for the destructor. The destructor calls `clock()` again, computes the time elapsed since the object's construction and displays the results:

```
#include <iostream>
using namespace std;

stopwatch::~stopwatch()
{
 clock_t total = clock()-start; //get elapsed time
 cout<<"total of ticks for this activity: "<<total<<endl;
 cout<<"in seconds: "<<double(total)/CLOCKS_PER_SEC<<endl;
}
```

To delay the output on the screen, you can add the following lines to the destructor:

```
char dummy;
cin>>dummy; //delay output on the screen
```

You can also write the results to a file to log performance changes among different profiling sessions, email them to your QA team—you get the idea.

Analyzing Performance Using Class `stopwatch`

To measure the duration of a code block, create a local `stopwatch` object at the block's beginning. For example, suppose you want to measure the duration of the following loop, which dynamically allocates 5,000 `string` objects:

```
string *pstr[5000]; //array of pointers
for (int i=0;i<5000;i++)
{
 pstr[i] = new string;
}
```

To measure the execution time of this code snippet, surround the relevant code in a pair of braces and create a `stopwatch` object at the block's beginning:

```
{
 stopwatch sw; // start measuring time
 string *pstr[5000];
 for (int i=0;i<5000;i++)
 {
  pstr[i] = new string;
 }
} // watch is destroyed here and reports the results
```

That's all! When the block begins, `sw` starts counting time. When the block exits, `sw`'s destructor displays the results:

```
total of clock ticks for this activity: 27
in seconds: 0.027
```

The loop took 27 milliseconds on my machine. This result may seem impressive. However, what would be the performance gain of replacing dynamic allocation with automatic storage? Let's try it and compare the results:

```
{
 stopwatch sw;
 for (int i=0;i<5000;i++)
```

```
{
  string s;
}
}
```

This time, the results are as follows:

```
total of clock ticks for this activity: 14
in seconds: 0.014
```

In other words, we achieved a 50% speed increase by using stack memory instead of allocating the strings dynamically. Considering that our dynamic allocation version didn't count the time needed for destroying the 5000 strings (as opposed to the automatic storage version), the results are even more impressive.

You probably noticed that our dynamic allocation version also had 5,000 assignment operations:

```
pstr[i] = new string;
```

By contrast, the automatic storage version didn't include an assignment expression. Could this skew the results? To answer this question, let's try a slightly different form of the dynamic allocation version:

```
{
 stopwatch sw;
 for (int i=0;i<5000;i++)
 {
   new string; // heap allocation without assignment
 }
}
```

Normally, you wouldn't write such code—it leaks memory abundantly. However, it isolates the allocation operation from other confounding variables. This is common practice in performance tuning: i.e., isolating a piece of "suspicious" code from its context. Here are the results of the dynamic allocation without assignment:

```
total of clock ticks for this activity: 27
in seconds: 0.027
```

It's safe to conclude that the assignment doesn't affect performance at all.

Summary

Performance measurements and tuning are tricky. Often, our intuition as developers can be misleading; operations that we consider expensive incur no performance penalty at all, whereas seemingly innocuous operations such as a new expression prove to be expensive in terms of CPU cycles. Without a reliable time measurement class such as stopwatch, we would not be able to discover these facts.

Signal Processing

Signals are similar to hardware interrupts. They cause a process to branch from the current execution flow, perform a specific action, and resume execution from the point of interruption. In the following sections, I will dissect the ANSI C/C++ <csignal> (<signal.h> in C) library and demonstrate how to use its interfaces. I will then discuss the POSIX signal API.

Setting a Handler

A signal is an integer value that the kernel delivers to a process. When a process receives a signal, it can react in one of the following manners:

- Ignore the signal.
- Let the kernel perform the default operation associated with that signal.
- Catch the signal, i.e., have the kernel transfer control to a *signal handler*, and resume the program from the place of interruption once the handler returns.

A signal handler is a function that the kernel automatically invokes when a signal occurs. The signal() function registers a handler for a given signal:

```
typedef void (*handler)(void);
void * signal(int signum, handler);
```

The first argument is the signal's code. The second argument is an address of a user-defined function to be called when the signal signum occurs.

Instead of a function's address, the second argument can take two special values: SIG_IGN and SIG_DFL. SIG_IGN indicates that the signal should be ignored (note however that the SIGKILL and SIGSTOP signals cannot be blocked, caught, or ignored); `SIG_DFL` instructs the kernel to perform the default action when the signal is raised.

Signaling a Process

There are three ways to signal a process:

- A process explicitly sends a signal to itself by calling `raise()`.
- A signal is sent from another process: for instance, by using the `kill()` system call, a Perl script, etc.
- A signal is sent from the kernel: for instance, when the process has attempted to access memory it doesn't own or during system shutdown.

The following program registers a handler for a `SIGTERM` signal. It then raises such a signal and thus causes it to run:

```
#include <csignal>
#include <iostream>
using namespace std;
void term(int sig)
{
  //..necessary cleanup operations before terminating
  cout << "handling signal no." << sig << endl;
}
int main()
{
 signal(SIGTERM, term); // register a SIGTERM handler
 raise(SIGTERM); // will cause term() to run
}
```

ANSI `<csignal>` Limitations

What happens when a process that is already running a handler for a `SIGx` signal receives another `SIGx` signal? One solution is to let the kernel interrupt the process and run the handler once more. To allow this, the handler must be *re-entrant*. However, designing re-entrant handlers is too complicated (for further details on re-entrancy, check out the section "Online Resources" below). The `<csignal>` solution to the recurring signal problem is to reset the handler to `SIG_DFL` before executing the user-defined handler. This is problematic, though: When two signals occur quickly, the kernel will run the handler for the first signal and perform the default action for the second one, which might terminate the process. Several alternative signal frameworks have evolved in the past three decades, each of which offers a different solution to the recurring signal problem. The POSIX signal API (see *http://www.burningvoid.com/iaq/posixsignals.php*) is the most mature and portable among them.

Introducing POSIX Signals

The POSIX signal functions operate on sets of signals packed in a `sigset_t` datatype. Here are their prototypes:

```
//Clears all the signals in pset.
int sigemptyset(sigset_t * pset);
//Fills pset with all available signals.
int sigfillset(sigset_t * pset);
//Adds signum to pset.
int sigaddset(sigset_t * pset, int signum);
//Removes signum from pset.
int sigdelset(sigset_t * pset, int signum);
//Returns a nonzero value if signum is included in pset, 0 otherwise.
int sigismember(const sigset_t * pset, int signum);
```

`sigaction()` registers a handler for a specific signal:

```
int sigaction(int signum, struct sigaction * act, struct sigaction *prev);
```

The `sigaction` struct describes the kernel's handling of `signum`:

```
struct sigaction
{
 sighandler_t sa_handler;
 sigset_t sa_mask; // list of signals to block
 unsigned long sa_flags; // blocking mode
 void (*sa_restorer)(void); // never used
};
```

`sa_handler` holds an address of a function that takes int and returns no value. It can also take one of two special values: `SIG_DFL` and `SIG_IGN`.

The POSIX API offers various services not present in the ANSI <csignal> library. These include the ability to block incoming signals and retrieve currently pending signals. Let's look at them.

Blocking Signals

The `sigprocmask()` blocks and unblocks signals:

```
int sigprocmask(int mode, const sigset_t* newmask,
                sigset_t * oldmask);
```

mode takes one of the following values:

- SIG_BLOCK adds the signals in newmask to the current signal mask.
- SIG_UNBLOCK removes the signals in newmask from the current signal mask.
- SIG_SETMASK blocks only the signals in newmask.

Retrieving Pending Signals

Blocked signals wait until the process is ready to receive them. Such signals are said to be *pending* and can be retrieved by calling `sigpending()`:

```
int sigpending(sigset_t * pset);
```

Summary

The standard <csignal> library provides rudimentary signal handling features that enable a process to install a handler for a certain signal, raise that signal and have the kernel run the specific handler for it. Although this implementation is sufficient for basic signal handling, it suffers from serious limitations such as its inability to block incoming signals or retrieve currently pending signals. For this reason, alternative signal libraries such as POSIX's are currently more widely used in production code.

Online Resources

"Signal Processing Notes" (*http://www.cs.kent.edu/~farrell/sys95/notes/examples/prog/signal/*) lists some of the OS-dependent bahviors that various POSIX systems exhibit. These notes may be useful for programmers developing cross-platform signal-based applications.

"Signal Processing" (*http://www.linux-mag.com/1999-12/compile_02.html*) is an excellent article by Erik Troan that explains how to implement signals and overcome some of the common problems associated with their implementation. This article is aimed at experienced UNIX/Linux system programmers.

"Re-entrant Functions" (*http://www.devx.com/tips/Tip/14139*) is a C++ tip that I wrote several years ago. This tip explains what re-entrant functions really are and why they are needed.

Creating Persistent Objects

Games, distributed database systems, multimedia and graphic applications use persistent objects extensively. Yet presently, C++ doesn't support persistence directly. A persistent object retains its state outside the scope of the program in which it was created. Writing an object to a file and reconstituting it later or transmitting it to a remote machine are instances of this.

> **TIP:** There are proposals for adding persistence and reflection to C++ in the future. See my interview with Bjarne Stroustrup at http://www.itworld.com/AppDev/710/lw-02-stroustrup/.

Persistence support is not as trivial as it may seem at first. The size and memory layout of the same object can vary from one platform to another. Different byte ordering, or endian-ness, complicates matters even further. In the following sections I will show how to implement persistence without resorting to third-party frameworks such as DCOM and CORBA. For small and portable applications, this is an effective and satisfactory solution.

To make an object persistent, you have to reserve its state in a non-volatile storage device. Consider an application that records and plays MP3 files. Every clip is represented as an object that contains the title, album, performer, time, bitrate, recording date and the matching MP3 file. The application displays recently played tracks on the track list. Your goal is to make MP3 objects persistent by *serializing* them—i.e., writing them to a file—and then reconstituting them in the next session by *deserializing* them.

Serializing Built-In Datatypes

Ultimately, every object consists of built-in data members such as `int`, `bool`, `char[]` and so on. Your first task is to write such datatypes to an `ofstream` (read more on `<fstream>` file I/O in Chapter 8, "Streams"). The application must store the values in their binary format. For this purpose, use the `write()` and `read()` member functions. `write()` takes the address and the size of a variable and writes its bit pattern to a file stream. `read()` takes two arguments of type `char *` and `long`, which contain a buffer's address and its size in bytes, respectively. The following example demonstrates how to store two integers in an `ofstream`:

```
#include <fstream>
using namespace std;
int main()
```

```
{
 int x,y; //mouse coordinates
 //..assign values to x and y
 ofstream archive("coord.dat", ios::binary);
 archive.write(reinterpret_cast<char *>(&x), sizeof (x));
 archive.write(reinterpret_cast<char *>(&x), sizeof (x));
 archive.close();
}
```

The use of `reinterpret_cast<>` is necessary because `write()` takes `const char *` as its first argument, whereas `&x` and `&y` are of type `int *`.

You retrieve the previously stored values as follows:

```
#include <fstream>
using namespace std;
int main()
{
 int x,y;
 ifstream archive("coord.dat");
 archive.read((reinterpret_cast<char *>(&x), sizeof(x));
 archive.read((reinterpret_cast<char *>(&y), sizeof(y));
}
```

Serializing Class Objects

To serialize a complete object, write each of its data members to a file:

```
class MP3_clip
{
private:
 std::time_t date;
 std::string name;
 int bitrate;
 bool stereo;
public:
 void serialize();
 void deserialize();
 //..
};

void MP3_clip::serialize()
{
```

```
{
 int size=name.size();// store name's length
  //empty file if it already exists before writing new data
 ofstream arc("mp3.dat", ios::binary|ios::trunc);
 arc.write(reinterpret_cast<char *>(&date),sizeof(date));
 arc.write(reinterpret_cast<char *>(&size),sizeof(size));
 arc.write(name.c_str(), size+1); // write final '\0' too
 arc.write(reinterpret_cast<char *>(&bitrate),
  sizeof(bitrate));
 arc.write(reinterpret_cast<char *>(&stereo),
  sizeof(stereo));
}
```

The implementation of `deserialize()` is a bit trickier since you need to allocate a temporary buffer for the string. Here's how you do it:

```
void MP3_clip::deserialize()
{
 ifstream arce("mp3.dat");
 int len=0;
 char *p=0;
 arc.read(reinterpret_cast<char *>(&date), sizeof(date));
 arc.read(reinterpret_cast<char *>(&len), sizeof(len));
 p=new char [len+1]; // allocate temp buffer for name
 arc.read(p, len+1); // copy name to temp, including '\0'
 name=p; // copy temp to data member
 delete[] p;
 arc.read(reinterpret_cast<char *>(&bitrate),
  sizeof(bitrate));
 arc.read(reinterpret_cast<char *>(&stereo),
  sizeof(stereo));
}
```

Performance Optimization

You might wonder why we didn't dump the entire object to a file instead of serializing individual data members. In other words, couldn't you implement `serialize()` as follows:

```
void MP3_clip::serialize()
{
 ofstream arc("mp3.dat", ios::binary|ios::trunc);
 arc.write(reinterpret_cast<char *>(this),sizeof(*this));
}
```

No, you couldn't. There are at least two problems with this approach. Usually, when the serialized object contains other objects, you can't just dump it to a file and reconstitute a valid object subsequently. In our example, the enclosing object contains a `std::string` member. A *shallow copy* (for an explanation of this term, see the resources section below) would archive `std::string` members whose values are *transient*, meaning that they can change every time you run the program. Worse yet, because `std::string` doesn't actually contain a `char` array but a pointer, it would be impossible to reconstitute the original string if you used shallow copying. To overcome this problem, the program didn't serialize the string object. Instead, it archived its characters and length. In general, pointers, arrays and handles should be treated in the same manner.

Another problem might arise with polymorphic objects. Every polymorphic object contains a `vptr`, i.e., a hidden pointer to a dispatch table that holds the addresses of its virtual functions. The vptr's value is transient. If you dumped an entire polymorphic object to a file and then superimposed the archived data on a new object, its vptr might be invalid and cause undefined behavior. Here again, the solution is to serialize and deserialize only non-transient data members. Alternatively, you can calculate the exact offset of the vptr and leave it intact when you reconstitute an object from a file. Remember that the vptr's position is implementation-dependent. Therefore, such code isn't portable.

Summary

Although C++ doesn't support object persistence directly, implementing it manually isn't a difficult task as long as you follow a few basic guidelines. First, break every composite object into its primitive datatypes and serialize them. When serializing data, remember to skip transient values. During the deserialization process, retrieve the previously stored values. String objects, arrays, and handlers are a bit trickier; always dereference them and store the values they point to. Remember to store the size of a string or an array in a separate field.

Online Resources

In my interview with Bjarne Stroustrup at *http://www.itworld.com/AppDev/710/lw-02-stroustrup*, he lists some of the features that he would like to see in the next revision round of C++, including support for object persistence.

"Deep Copy and Shallow Copy" (*http://www.devx.com/tips/Tip/13625*) is a short tip that discusses the differences between these two concepts and explains when each one of them should be used.

Bit Fields

Networking, file management, cryptography, data compression, and serial port communication are only a few of the application domains in which programmers need to manipulate bits directly. Although the smallest native datatype of C++ is char, which is equivalent to a byte, the language does enable you to manipulate bits directly without resorting to assembly programming or inefficient libraries, as I will show momentarily.

Performance Analysis

Consider a typical billing system of an international telecom company. This system monitors every telephone call and records it in a database. A typical billing record contains the customer's ID, a timestamp, codes that indicate the type of the call—e.g., local, long distance and so on—and the tariff. The database stores millions of new records every day. Furthermore, it must keep the customer's billing information for at least one year. Consequently, an entire database contains around one billion records at any given time. Backups increase the amount of stored data even further. There could be five billion records stored in the main database and backup copies at any given time. Obviously, a billing record should be as small as possible. A non-optimized definition of a billing record might look like this:

```
struct BillingRec
{
 long cust_id;
 long timestamp;
 enum CallType
 {
  toll_free,
  local,
  regional,
  long_distance,
  international,
  cellular
 } type;
 enum CallTariff
 {
  off_peak,
  medium_rate,
  peak_time
 } tariff;
};
```

`BillingRec` occupies no fewer than 16 bytes of memory on a typical 32-bit system. To detect how many bytes it occupies on your machine, use the following expression:

```
sizeof(BillingRecord);
```

The members `cust_id` and `timestamp` occupy four bytes each, as expected. However, the two enums occupy additional eight bytes when we can safely store both of them in a single byte. Remember: One redundant bit causes a waste of more than 0.5GB of storage! Clearly, this data structure needs to be optimized in order to save space.

Bit Field Usage

A bit field is a data member of a struct or a class that contains one or more bits. In the following example, we declare a struct that contains two bit fields, `f1` and `f2`, each of which occupies four bits:

```
struct A
{
 unsigned int f1: 4; // range: 0 - 15
 unsigned int f2: 4;
};
```

A bit-field declaration begins with its underlying type followed by the field's name. The underlying type can be `signed char`, `short`, `int`, `long`, their `unsigned` counterparts (an unsigned bit field cannot hold a negative value) and `bool`. The declaration ends with a colon followed by the number of bits.

Space Optimization

Our first optimization step is to check the order of `BillingRec` members. In some cases, it's possible to save space simply by changing the members' order. In this case, however, all members occupy the same size so we have to try another strategy, namely squeezing the enum values into two bit fields:

```
struct BillingRec // optimized version
{
 //...cust_id and timestamp remain as before
 enum CallType
 {
  toll_free,
  local,
```

```
    regional,
    long_distance,
    international,
    cellular
  };
  enum CallTariff
  {
   off_peak,
   medium_rate,
   peak_time
  };
  unsigned int call: 3; // range: 0-7
  unsigned int tariff: 2; // range: 0-3
};
```

The trick is that instead of creating instances of the `enum` types, we use two bit fields that have enough bits to store every valid enumerator. You treat bit fields as ordinary data members. For example, you can zero-initialize a struct that contains bit fields. The following program creates a `BillingRec` instance and fills its members with data:

```
#include <ctime>
int main()
{
 BillingRec rec;
 rec.cust_id = 1425;
 rec.timestamp = time();
 rec.call = BillingRec::cellular;
 rec.tariff = BillingRec::off_peak;
}
```

The introduction of bit fields has reduced the size of `BillingRec` to 12 bytes. Although there's still a waste of three bytes here due *member alignment* restrictions, we have shaved off four bytes, thereby shrinking the billing database to 67% of its original size. More aggressive optimizations, such as changing the first two members of `BillingRec` to `unsigned short` if possible, or replacing them with bit fields, would save more even space.

Summary

Often, programmers are concerned about optimization unnecessarily. If our database consisted of a few hundred records, there would be no reason to bend over backward and squeeze members into bit fields. Remember that almost everything about bit fields is implementation-dependent. For example, whether bits are stored left-to-right or right-to-left depends on the actual hardware architecture. Furthermore, each compiler uses a different member alignment model, which is why the size of the optimized `BillingRec` is 12 bytes rather than nine. You cannot take a bit field's address, nor can you create an array of bits. Finally, on most implementations the use of bit fields incurs speed overhead. Therefore, when you optimize your code, measure the effect of a certain optimization and its tradeoffs before you decide to use it.

Online Resources

"Member Alignment" (*http://www.devx.com/tips/Tip/12683*) is a short tip that explains what member alignment is and how you can optimize an object's layout in memory by reordering its members.

Environment Variables

An *environment variable* consists of a pair of strings: the variable itself followed by = and its *associated value*. For example:

```
PATH=C:\WINDOWS
```

Environment variables are used as a means of passing information to and from a process. In addition, they enable you to reconfigure a process while it's running without having to interrupt its execution. For example, instead of using a hardcoded IP address inside the program's source code, you can store it in an environment variable that the process will access at runtime. If you need to change that address, the program doesn't have to be changed; the next time it reads the environment variable it will obtain the new IP address. There are two types of environment variables: ones that are confined to a process, and ones that are globally accessible to multiple processes or the entire system. Each operating system defines its own security restrictions regarding the privileges required for reading and changing environment variables, so I will not discuss these issues here.

Defining Environment Variables from the Command Line

In DOS and Windows, you can define an environment variable from the command line or from a batch file using the command `SET` followed by an assignment expression. The following line creates an environment variable called `VERSION` whose value is 1.1.3:

SET VERSION=1.1.3

In POSIX systems, you omit the SET command:

VERSION=1.1.3

Reading an Environment Variable Programmatically

A program's *environment* is made available to it at startup. The environment consists of an array of C-strings, each in this form: "VAR=value". You access environment variables from a program using the functions getenv() and putenv(). The ANSI C function getenv() provides an easy and portable way for reading an environment variable. getenv() is declared in <cstdlib> and has the following prototype:

```
char * getenv(const char * name);
```

On success, it returns a pointer to a null-terminated char array that contains the variable's value. If the variable is not defined, getenv() returns NULL. For example:

```
#include <cstdlib.>
#include <iostream>
using namespace std;
int main()
{
 char * descr = getenv("PATH");
 if (descr)
  cout<<"value of PATH is: "<< descr<<endl;
 else
  cout<<"variable not defined"<<endl;
}
```

There is another quasi-standard manner of accessing a process's environment that is mostly used in POSIX systems. To access environment variables in this manner, you use a special form of main() that automatically reads the process's environment at startup and stores it in the argument envp:

```
int main(int argc, char * argv[], char *envp[])
```

At startup, the variable `envp` is set to point to the process's environment, which is in the form of an array of C-strings. Thus, you can access the first environment variable like this:

```
const char *var= envp[0]
if (var)
 cout<<"first environment variable is: "<<var<<endl;
```

The last element in the array is a null pointer indicating the end of the array. This enables you traverse the entire array easily:

```
//execute loop so long as nevp[n] isn't NULL
for (int n=0; envp[n]; n++)
 cout << envp[n]<<endl;
```

Note that under most POSIX systems you can access the process's environment by using the global variable `environ`, which is defined in <unsitd.h> (note that this isn't a standard header file and as such it might not available on all platforms). For example, the previous code sample can be rewritten like this:

```
#include <unistd.h>
int main()
{
//execute loop so long as environ[n] isn't NULL
for (int n=0; environ[n]; n++)
 cout << environ[n]<<endl;
}
```

However, using the third `main()` argument `envp` makes your intent more explicit, saves you the trouble of locating the definition of `environ`, and is more portable.

Setting an Environment Variable

To define an environment variable or change the value of an existing variable, use the `putenv()` function. `putenv()` isn't defined by the ANSI/ISO standard. In practice, however, both POSIX and Windows implementations declare it in <cstdlib> as a non-standard extension, so it's a relatively portable. `putenv()` has the following prototype:

```
int putenv(const char * var);
```

The argument var must be a string in the form "VAR=VAL". putenv() adds the variable VAR to the current environment and assigns the value VAL to it. If the variable already exists, putenv() overrides the existing value. If you prefer not to override a variable's value, check whether it already exists by calling getenv() before calling putenv(). The following example adds a new environment variable called TEMP whose value is C:\TEMP (remember that a backslash must appear as a \\ inside a quoted literal string in C/C++). On success, putenv() returns 0, and -1 otherwise.

```
int stat = putenv("TEMP=C:\\TEMP");
if (!stat)
{
 cout<<"failed to define environment variable"<<endl;
}
```

Dealing with wchar_t Strings

Certain implementations also define wchar_t versions of getenv() and putenv():

```
wchar_t * _wgetenv(const wchar_t * name);
int _wputenv(const wchar_t * var);
```

You can use these versions when you need to manipulate wchar_t environment variables.

Uses of Environment Variables

As previously said, environment variables enable you to control the program's behavior without having to make changes to its source files or recompiling it. For instance, you can control whether a program displays debug information on the screen simply by defining an appropriate environment variable. This is particularly useful if you need to enable debugging output at a customer's site without having to reinstall anything. In the following example, the program displays debug information only if the environment variable DBG is defined:

```
void func();
#include <stdlib.h>
#include <stdio.h>
int main()
{
 bool debug=false;
 if (getenv("DBG"))
  debug=true;
```

```
  if (debug)
    cout<<"calling func"<<endl;
  func();
  if (debug)
    cout<<"returned from func"<<endl;
}
```

Summary

Environment variables are a simple—albeit limited—means of passing information to and from a process without resorting to complex interprocess communication APIs or, worse yet, recompiling code. The `getenv()` and `putenv()` functions enable you to retrieve and set an environment variable. In addition, certain implementations allow you to access a process's environment through a special argument of `main()` or via a global variable. Each system sets limits on the length of an environment variable and the total number of environment variables. In addition, there are security restrictions regarding users' authorizations to read, define and override environment variables.

Online Resources

The official description of the `getenv()` function from the Minix man pages (*http://www.cs.vu.nl/pub/minix/2.0.2/wwwman/man3/getenv.3.html*) is primarily aimed at POSIX users, but this documentation is useful for all C/C++ programmers because it's based on the ANSI/ISO specification.

"Environment Variables in Windows 2000/XP" (*http://www.pcmag.com/article2/0,4149,843974,00.asp*) describes some of the environment variables that are specific to Windows 2000 and XP.

"Environment Variables" (*http://www.opengroup.org/onlinepubs/007908799/xbd/envvar.html*) lists the UNIX environment variables and explains their meanings.

Variadic Functions

A function usually takes a fixed number of arguments whose types are known at compile-time. In certain applications, however, you need to pass to the same function a variable number of arguments. Fortunately, C provides a special mechanism for defining functions that take a variable number of arguments. These are known as *variable argument list functions* or *variadic functions*. `printf()` and `scanf()` are classic examples of this. Although C++ offers superior solutions to this problem (I will get to these solutions later), familiarity with variadic functions is still advantageous because C++ implementations for embedded systems don't support templates or wchar_t streams. Furthermore, in pure C environments, variadic functions have no alternative.

Uses of Variadic Functions

A variadic function must take at least one named argument (usually, a format string). A special mechanism detects the number of the additional unnamed arguments and their types. Here's a typical variadic function declaration:

```
void printf(const char * fmt,...);
```

The ellipsis indicates that the function can take any number of arguments after the mandatory argument fmt.

Suppose you want to write a function for debugging purposes that will accept a format string indicating the type of each argument and a variable list of arguments. The function will display each argument on the screen. The function's prototype looks like this:

```
void emit(const char *fmt,...);
```

For the sake of brevity, the format codes will be 'd' for double and 'i' for int. However, you can easily extend the functionality as needed and add support for additional built-in and user-defined types.

Implementation

The standard header <cstdarg> (<stdarg.h> in C) defines the necessary macros for traversing a variadic function's unnamed arguments. A variable of type va_list traditionally named ap ("argument pointer") will refer to each argument in turn. The va_start() macro initializes ap to point to the first unnamed argument. va_start() takes ap and the last named argument of the variadic function. For example:

```
//make ap point to the first arg after fmt
va_start(ap, fmt);
```

The third macro, va_arg(), takes ap and the current argument's typename. It returns that argument by value and advances ap to the next argument (emit() relies on the format string to detect the end of the argument list).

Finally, the macro va_end(ap) is called before the function returns to perform necessary cleanup operations. Here's the complete emit() function:

```c
void emit(const char *fmt,...)
{
  va_list ap /*will point to each unnamed argument in turn*/
  int num;
  double d;
  const char *p=fmt;
  va_start(ap,fmt); /* point to first element after fmt*/
  while(*p)
  {
   if (*p=='i') /*int*/
   {
    num=va_arg(ap,int);
    printf("%d",num);
   }
   else if (*p=='d') /*double*/
   {
    d=va_arg(ap,double);
    printf("%f",d);
   }
   else
   {
    printf("unsupported format flag");
    break;
   }
   ++p; /* get the next char of the format string */
  }/*while*/
  va_end(ap) /*cleanup*/
}
```

You use emit() like this:

```c
int main()
{
 double salary;
 int id;
 // ... obtain id and calculate salary
 emit("di",salary, id);
 int age, double bonus;
 //...
 emit("diid",salary, id, age, bonus);
}
```

Object-Oriented Alternatives to Variadic Functions

As you may have noticed, the implementation of variadic functions isn't trivial. Failing to initialize ap, calling va_arg() one time too many or omitting the va_end(ap) call can crash your program. Furthermore, even if your coding practices are through and through, there is always a risk of passing an incorrect format string accidentally. For example:

```
emit("i",salary); // i used instead of d
```

If you're using a pure C compiler, this is the best you can get as far as variadic functions are concerned. C++, on the other hand, offers several alternatives to this technique that you should consider first.

Declaring a function with default parameter values enables you to control the number of actual arguments being passed to it. For example:

```
void emit(int n, const char * str=0);
```

If you want to display only one argument of type int, you can omit the second argument. emit() in turn will ignore a null pointer and display only the first argument. However, unlike with a variadic function, this solution doesn't allow you to change arguments' types.

A second solution is using a function template:

```
template <class T> void emit(const T& arg);
```

In this case, you can control the type of the argument(s) but not their number.

You can pack the arguments in an STL container and pass it to a function template:

```
template < class T > void emit(const vector< T >& args);
```

This method allows you to pass any number of arguments of any type so long as on each function invocation all the arguments are of the same type.

As neat as the previous three alternatives are, none of them offers the flexibility of variadic functions. This brings us to the fourth alternative, namely overloading the << operator. The standard objects cout, clog and cerr overload the << operator so that you can chain any number of arguments within a single output statement. For example:

```
cout << num << firstname << salary;
```

In this case, both the number of arguments and their types are flexible. In addition, you can define additional overloaded versions of << to support user-defined types. Most importantly—this technique is type-safe.

Summary

Variadic functions are considered by many a thing of the past. In most cases, C++ offers superior alternatives that are both safer and simpler. That said, in certain cases you might still need to use variadic functions or even write them. In these cases, make sure that your program follows all the rules listed above; it is easy to mess things up, thereby incurring unpredictable results at runtime.

Online Resources

"Variadic Macros" (*http://www.devx.com/tips/Tip/14815*) is a tip that explains a novel feature of C99. You wouldn't normally use variadic macros in C++—well, you wouldn't use macros in C++ in the first place! But I always advise C++ programmers to familiarize themselves with the latest developments of the sibling language C.

Pointers to Functions, Pointers to Members, and Function Objects

While the concept of pointers to data is supported by many programming languages, only few of them enable you to define pointers to code, i.e., pointers that point to functions. Originally introduced in C, pointers to functions are still widely used in C++ too, although pointers to member functions provide similar functionality in the case of class objects. C++ also introduced the concept of function objects, which are object instances of a class that overloads the ( ) operator and as such, can be used as if it were a function. This chapter discusses these three closely related concepts: pointers to functions, pointers to members, and function objects.

Pointers to Functions

Pointers to functions ("function pointers" for short) are useful in implementing callbacks, dynamic binding, and event-based applications. Unfortunately, their cumbersome syntax baffles novices and experienced programmers alike. In this section I will focus on traditional C function pointers and explain how to declare and use them effectively. This will serve as the basis for pointers to members, which I will discuss in a different section.

Declaring a Function Pointer

A callback function is one that is not invoked explicitly by the programmer; rather the responsibility for its invocation is delegated to another function that receives its address. To implement a callback you need to define an appropriate function pointer first. Although the syntax is somewhat arcane, if you're familiar with function declarations in general you'll notice that a function pointer declaration is very similar to a function declaration. Consider the following function prototype:

```
void f();
```

It declares a function called `f()` that takes no arguments and returns `void`. A pointer to such a function has the following type:

```
void (*) (); //type of f()
```

Let's parse it. The asterisk in the leftmost pair of parentheses is the *nucleus* of a function pointer declaration. Two additional elements in a function pointer declaration are the return type (`void` in this example), and a *parameter list* enclosed in the rightmost pair of parentheses (empty in this example). Note that this declaration didn't create a pointer variable yet—it only declared the *type* of such a variable. What is it good for then? You can use this type in a `typedef` declaration, in a `sizeof` expression, or as a function parameter:

```
// get the size of a function pointer
unsigned psize = sizeof (void (*) ());
// declare a typedef for a function pointer
typedef void (*pfv) ();
// used as a function parameter
void signal( void (*)() );
```

`pfv` is a synonym for "a pointer to a function that takes no arguments and returns `void`." You can use this `typedef` name to hide the cumbersome syntax of function pointers.

A pointer variable, of course, has a name. Here is an example:

```
void (*p) (); // p is a pointer to a function
```

The name of a pointer variable appears right before the nucleus, enclosed in parentheses. You can now bind a function to `p` by assigning it a name of a function that has a matching *signature* (parameter list) and return type. For example:

```
void func()
{
  /* do something */
}
p=func;
```

Chapter 15 Pointers to Functions, Pointers to Members, and Function Objects

You can bind a different value to p, so long as it's an address of a function with the same signature and return type. A function's name is not a part of its type, though.

Passing a Callback Function's Address to Its Caller

Once you've assigned a value to p you can execute the *callee* (the bound function) through it. To call a function through a pointer, simply treat it as if it were the function itself:

```
p(); //call the function bound to p
```

You can also pass p to another function that will invoke the callee without knowing its name:

```
void caller(void(*p)())
{
 p(); // call the bound function
}
void func();
int main()
{
  p = func;
  caller(p); // pass address of func to caller
}
```

Remember that the assignment to p can take place at runtime, which enables you to implement dynamic binding.

Calling Conventions

So far I've discussed function pointers without discussing compiler-specific conventions that aren't defined by the ISO standard. Many compilers have several calling conventions. For example, in Visual C++ you can precede a function's prototype with __cdecl, __stdcall or __pascal to to indicate its calling convention. Borland's C++ Builder also supports the __fastcall calling convention. A calling convention affects the compiler-generated name of a given function (i.e., its mangled name), the direction of arguments (right to left or left to right), stack cleanup responsibility (by the caller or the callee), and the mechanism for argument passing (stack, CPU registers, etc.). A calling convention is an integral part of a function's type; therefore, you can't assign an address of a function to a pointer with an incompatible calling convention. For example:

```
// callee is a function that takes int and returns int
__stdcall int signal(int);

// caller is a function that takes a function pointer
void caller( __cdecl int(*ptr)(int));

// illegal attempt to store the address of callee in p
__cdecl int(*p)(int) = signal; // error
```

`p` and `signal()` have incompatible types because they have different calling conventions, although both have the same signature and return type.

Function Pointers and Ordinary Pointers

While function pointers share many similarities with ordinary data pointers, they differ in several ways. First, you can't declare a generic pointer to function similar to `void*`. In addition, trying to store a function pointer in a `void*` isn't guaranteed to work (certain compilers tolerate this whereas others don't). Finally, you can't dereference a function pointer—there's no such thing as passing a function by value.

Summary

Function pointers are a powerful feature. In the heart of almost every large-scale application you will find them. Familiarity with this feature is therefore essential for professional programmers. To disguise the cumbersome syntax, you can use `typedef` names. As a C++ programmer you're probably wondering why you should bother about this C feature when C++ has better alternatives in the form of pointers to member functions and function objects. There are at least two compelling reasons for using them in C++: code that uses C functions (say, the `<ctime>` and `<csignal>` libraries, which have no object-oriented alternatives in C++) and static member functions. Unlike pointers to nonstatic member functions, pointers to static member functions are C function pointers, not pointers to member functions.

Pointers to Members

Pointers to members are similar to ordinary pointers to functions in that they enable you to call a member function without knowing its name. Yet unlike ordinary pointers to functions, they also enable you to manipulate data members of an object. In the following passages I will discuss pointers to members in further detail and show how to define and use them.

Chapter 15   Pointers to Functions, Pointers to Members, and Function Objects

A class can have two general categories of members: functions and data members. Similarly, there are two categories of pointers to members: pointers to member functions, and pointers to data members. The latter are less common because you rarely have direct access to data members. However, when using legacy C code that contains structs or classes that happen to have public data members for some reason, pointers to data members might be useful.

Declaring Pointers to Data Members

The syntax of pointers to members might look confusing at first but it's consistent and resembles the form of ordinary pointers to functions with the addition of the class name followed by the operator ::. For example, if an ordinary pointer to int looks like this:

```
int * pi;
```

you define a pointer to an int member of class A like this:

```
class A{/**/};
int A::*pmi; // pmi is a pointer to an int member of A
```

You can initialize pmi like this:

```
class A
{
public:
  int num;
  int x;
};
int A::*pmi = &A::num; // 1
```

Manipulating a Data Member Through an Object

The statement numbered 1 defines a pointer to an int member of class A and initializes it with the address of num. Now you can use the pointer pmi to examine and modify num's value in any object of class A:

```
A a1;
A a2;
int n = a1.*pmi; // copy the value of a1.num to n
a1.*pmi = 5; // assign the value to a1.num
a2.*pmi = 6; // assign the value 6 to a2.num
```

Manipulating a Data Member Through an Object's Pointer

Similarly, you can access a data member through a pointer to A like this:

```
A * pa = new A;
int n = pa->*pmi; // assign to n the value of pa->num
pa->*pmi = 5; // assign the value 5 to pa->num
```

Or using a pointer to an object derived from A:

```
class D : public A {};
A* pd = new D;
pd->*pmi = 5; // assign the value 5 to pd->num
```

Declaring Pointers to Member Functions

Thus far I've focused on pointers to data members, which are less in use compared to pointers to member functions. A pointer to a member function consists of the member function's return type, the class name followed by ::, the pointer's name, and the function's parameter list. For example, a pointer to a member function of class A that returns int and takes no arguments looks like this (note that both pairs of parentheses are mandatory):

```
class A
{
public:
  int func ();
};

int (A::*pmf) (); /* pmf is a pointer to some member
function of class A that returns int  and takes no
arguments*/
```

In fact, a pointer to a member function looks just like an ordinary pointer to function, except that it also contains the class's name immediately followed by the :: operator. You can invoke the member function to which pmf points like this:

```
pmf = &A::func; //assign pmf
A a;
A *pa = &a;
(a.*pmf)(); // invoke a.func()
// call through a pointer to an object
(pa->*pmf)(); // calls pa->func()
```

Pointers to member functions respect polymorphism; if you call a virtual member function through a pointer to member, the call will be resolved dynamically, as the following code shows:

```
class Base
{
public:
  virtual int f (int n);
};
class Derived : public Base {
public:
  int f (int h); //override
};
Base *pb = new Derived;
int (Base::*pmf)(int) = &Base::f;
(pb->*pmf)(5); // call resolved as D::f(5);
```

Note that you cannot take the address of constructors and destructors.

The Underlying Representation of Pointers to Members

Although pointers to members behave like ordinary pointers, behind the scenes their representation is quite different. In fact, a pointer to member usually consists of a struct containing up to four fields in certain cases. This is because pointers to members have to support not only ordinary member functions, but also virtual member functions, member functions of objects that have multiple base classes, and member functions of virtual base classes. Thus, the simplest member function can be represented as a set of two pointers: one holding the physical memory address of the member function, and a second pointer that holds the `this` pointer. However, in cases like a virtual member function, multiple inheritance and virtual inheritance, the pointer to member must store additional information. Therefore, you can't cast pointers to members to ordinary pointers, nor can you safely cast pointers to members that have different types.

To find out how your compiler represents pointers to members, use the `sizeof` operator. In the following example, the sizes of a pointer to data member and a pointer to a member function are taken. As you can see, they have different sizes, hence, different representations:

```
struct A
{
  int x;
  void f();
};
```

```
int A::*pmi = &A::x;
void (A::*pmf)() = &A::f;
int n = sizeof (pmi); // 8 byte on my compiler
int m = sizeof (pmf); // 12 bytes on my compiler
```

Note that each of these pointers may have a different representation, depending on the class in question and whether the member function is virtual or not.

Summary

Pointers to members are the third component in the trilogy of function callback constructs. The other two are pointers to functions and function objects. In the next revision of C++, a new library facility called `function` will provide a homogeneous interface to abstract the syntactic and technical differences among these three constructs, enabling the user to treat them in a uniform fashion.

One of the common mistakes made by novices is attempting to invoke a member function through a pointer to member alone. Remember that a pointer itself isn't enough; you also need an object on which the function will be called. Thus, you need to use both an object (or a pointer to an object) and a pointer to a member function to perform the call. In this regard, a pointer to a member differs from ordinary pointers to functions. You should think of it as an offset inside a class to the member in question rather than a physical memory address.

Online Resources

"Generalized Function Pointers" (*http://www.cuj.com/documents/s=8464/cujcexp0308sutter/*) by Herb Sutter is an article that discusses the `function` facility, which was recently adopted by the C++ standards committee. This facility provides a generalized way of working with arbitrary functions and function-related types—e.g., pointers to functions, function objects, pointers to members, etc.—when all you know is their signature. This article is a very interesting reading for two reasons: It prepares C++ programmers for some of the forthcoming changes and extensions in the next revision of the standard, and it also shows how to use this facility.

Function Object

Ordinary pointers to functions are widely used for implementing callbacks of C functions and static member functions. Yet C++ offers a significantly superior alternative to them, namely function objects. In essence, function objects (also called "functors") are ordinary class objects that overload the () operator. Thus, syntactically they behave like ordinary functions but under the hood they are real objects.

There are several advantages in using function objects instead of pointers to functions or pointers to members. First, they are more resilient to design changes because the object can be modified internally without changing its external interface. While the same can be said on ordinary functions whose prototypes remain intact when their implementation changes, a function object can contain data members that store its state, thereby eliminating the need for external variables and complex argument lists. Function objects offer another benefit in the form of performance. Compilers are usually able to inline a call made through a function object, thereby optimizing your code. By contrast, it is harder to inline a function call made through a pointer.

Implementing a Function Object

Suppose you want to define a function object that implements a negation operation. The first step consists of declaring an ordinary class and overloading the () operator, as follows:

```
class Negate
{
public:
  int operator() (int n);
};
```

The overloaded () might look confusing because it has two pairs of parentheses. However, remember that the first pair is always empty because it serves as the operator's name; the second pair of parentheses contains the parameter list. Unlike other overloaded operators, whose number of parameters is fixed, the overloaded () operator can take any number of parameters.

Because the built-in negation operator is *unary*—i.e., it takes a single operand—your overloaded () operator also takes a single parameter in this case. The return type is identical to the parameter's type—int in this example. The function body is trivial; it simply returns the argument's negative value.

```
int Negate::operator()(int n)
{
 return -n;
}
```

Usage of Function Object

To test this function object, let's define a test function called `test()` that takes two arguments: an `int` and a reference to `Negate`. `test()` treats the function object as if it were a function's name:

```
#include <iostream>
using std::cout;

void test(int n, Negate & neg)
{
  int val = neg(n);   //1 invoke overloaded ()
  cout << val <<std::endl;
}
```

Don't let the syntax mislead you: `neg` is an object, not a function. The compiler silently transforms the line numbered 1 into the following member function call:

```
int val = neg.operator()(n);
```

In most cases function objects do not define constructors and destructors. Therefore, they do not incur any overhead during their creation and destruction. As previously noted, the compiler can inline the overloaded operator's code, thereby avoiding the runtime overhead associated with a full-blown function call.

To complete the example, use the following `main()` driver to pass arguments to `test()`:

```
int main()
{
 test(5, Negate() );  //output -5
}
```

The program passes to `test()` the integer 5 and a reference to a temporary `Negate` object. As expected, the output is -5.

Template Function Objects

The previous example was confined to type `int`. However, one of the advantages of function objects is their generic nature. You can define the overloaded () operator as a member template (for further information about templates, read Chapter 5, "Templates") so that it will apply to all numeric datatypes: `long`, `double`, `std::complex`, and so on. For example:

```
class GenericNegate
{
public:
 template <class T> T operator() (T t) const {return -t;}
};

int main()
{
 GenericNegate negate;
 __int64 val = 10000000000i64;
 cout<< negate(5.3333); // double
 cout<< negate(val); //__int64
}
```

Now try to imagine how difficult and dangerous it would be to achieve the same functionality with ordinary pointers to functions.

Function Objects in the Standard Library

The Standard Library defines several useful function objects that can be plugged into STL algorithms. For example, the `sort()` algorithm takes a *predicate object* as its third argument (a predicate object is a templatized function object that returns a Boolean result. For further information, read Chapter 10, "The Standard Template Library (STL) and Generic Programming."

You can pass the predicates `greater<>` or `less<>` to `sort()` to force a descending or ascending sorting order, respectively:

```
#include <functional> // for greater<> and less<>
#include <algorithm> //for sort()
#include <vector>
using namespace std;

int main()
{
 vector <int> vi;
 //..fill vector
 sort(vi.begin(), vi.end(), greater<int>() );//descending
 sort(vi.begin(), vi.end(), less<int>() );  //ascending
}
```

Summary

Function objects provide the functionality of pointers to functions and pointers to member functions while offering additional benefits such as a generic interface, tighter encapsulation (by means of having internal data members that store the object's state) and enhanced performance. Predicates are a special kind of function object that return a Boolean result. They are used in the Standard Library and elsewhere to manipulate the behavior of certain algorithms.

CHAPTER 16

A Tour of C99

The new C standard officially known as ISO/IEC 9899:1999 or C99 in short contains substantial changes and extensions both in the core language and its standard libraries. These changes don't apply to C++ of course. However, familiarity with them is important for several reasons. First, it's likely that these changed will be incorporated into C++ eventually, either officially—Bjarne Stroustrup has called for merging C++ and C99 into a single language (*http://www.linuxworld.com/story/32929.htm*)—or as a de facto initiative of compiler vendors. Second, C++ programmers often work in mixed environments where C and C++ are used together.

In the following sections, I will focus on C99's new *core language* features. These include the syntax, the keywords, and built-in features.

Borrowing from C++

Some of the newly added features are direct borrowings from C++. These include `inline` functions, // comments, dispersed statements and declarations, and loop-scoped variables.

`inline` Functions

The new keyword `inline` indicates that a function should be expanded inline, if possible. Personally, I doubt that this feature is as useful as it might have been a decade ago; not only has compiler technology made a quantum leap in terms of code optimization during recent years, it's also rather easy to misuse `inline`, thereby *degrading* performance. Still, under certain conditions C programs can benefit from the performance boost of `inline` functions. For example:

```
inline void * allocate(size_t sz)
{
 return malloc(sz);
}
```

Line Comments

In addition to the traditional block comments, C now supports line-comments that start with the token // and extend up to the end of the line, just as in C++. In practice, many C compilers have supported this feature for years. Now at last it's official.

Dispersed Statements and Declarations

In earlier versions of C, declarations could appear only at a block's beginning, before any other statements. Now it's possible to place declarations freely. The following function demonstrates this. It's C99-compliant. However, pre-C99 compilers will refuse to compile it because the declaration of rank appears after a statement (and because it uses // comments):

```
void compensations(Employee *emp)
{
 double bonus=155.25;
 double salary;
 salary=employee->salary + bonus;
 int rank; //allowed only in C99
 //.. rest of the code
}
```

Scope of for Loop Variables

The scope of variables declared inside a for statement is now restricted to the loop's body. Thus,

```
for (int n=0; n<10; ++n)
{
 //statements
}
```

is equivalent to this:

```
{
  int n=0;
  for (; n<10; ++n)
  {
    //statements
  }
}
```

Novel Core Features

In addition to the borrowings from C++, C99 introduces several novel core features. These include variable-length arrays, designated initializers, variadic macros, `restrict` pointers, the `long long` datatype and the `__func__` identifier.

Variable-Length Arrays

In C++ and pre-C99 versions of C, an array's size must be a *constant integral expression* so that it can be calculated at compile-time. In C99, this restriction was relaxed. An array's size must be an *integral expression*, not necessarily a constant one. This allows you to declare a *variable-length array*—an array whose size is determined at runtime:

```
void func(int sz)
{
  int arr[sz]; // sz ins't const; allowed only in C99
}
```

The size of `arr` can be different for every `func()` call. For example:

```
int main()
{
  int size;
  printf("enter array's size: ");
  scanf("%d", &size);
  func(size);
}
```

To support variable-length arrays, C99 adds the notation [*] in a function's parameter. In addition, C99 extends the functionality of `sizeof`. When applied to a variable-length array, it calculates its size at runtime. In my opinion, this is the most daring change in C99. Not only does it alter the semantics of a built-in operator from compile-time to runtime operation, it's also a "quiet change"—there's no explicit syntactic clue to distinguish between the two forms.

Designated Initializers

Designated initializers enable you to initialize specific members of an aggregate (i.e., an array, `struct` or `union`) while leaving the rest of the members with no explicit initializers. For example:

```
int vec[5] = {[1]=10,[3]=20}; // designated initializers
```

The declaration of vec explicitly initializes the members vec[1] and vec[3] to 10 and 20, respectively, while leaving the remaining members without an explicit initializer. `struct` and `union` members can be initialized similarly:

```
struct Employee
{
 char name[20];
 int ID;
 int age;
 FILE *record;
};

Employee emp = {.ID=0, .record=NULL};
```

The declaration of `emp` contains designated initializers for `ID` and `record`. Note that when using designated initializers, members that have no explicit initializer are automatically zero-initialized. Therefore, `emp`'s members `name` and `age` contain binary zeros.

Variadic Macros

Variadic functions—functions taking a variable argument list—are rather common in C. For example:

```
int printf(const char * fmt,...);
```

C99 also supports *variadic macros*. A variadic macro looks like this:

```
#define Trace(...) printf( __VA_ARGS__)
```

The ellipsis represents a macro's variable argument list. The reserved `__VA_ARGS__` name is used for traversing the arguments passed to the macro. When you call `Trace()` like this:

```
Trace("Y = %d\n", y);
```

the preprocessor replaces the macro call with:

```
printf("Y = %d\n", y);
```

Because `Trace` is a variadic macro, you can pass a different number of arguments on every call:

```
Trace("test"); // expanded as: printf("test");
```

`restrict`-Qualified Pointers

C99 introduces a new keyword, `restrict`, that can only be applied to pointers. It indicates that, during the scope of that pointer declaration, all data accessed through it will be accessed only through that pointer and not through any other pointer. By declaring pointers as restricted, the programmer states that they do not refer to the same object. For example, C99 changes the prototype of `fopen()` to:

```
FILE *fopen(const char * restrict filename,
            const char * restrict mode);
```

`restrict` enables the compiler to employ certain optimizations based on the premise that a given object cannot be changed through another pointer. For further information about `restrict` pointers, see the original proposal at *http://www.lysator.liu.se/c/restrict.html*.

`long long` Datatype

`long long` and its unsigned counterpart `unsigned long long` are new types in C99. A `long long` variable will have at least 64 bits. Likewise, the suffixes `LL` or `ll` (and `ULL` or `ull`) can be used in constants of type `long long` and `unsigned long long`:

```
long long molecules=10000000000000LL;
```

The `__func__` Identifier

A new identifier, `__func__`, is implicitly declared if used within a function as follows:

```
static const char func[] = "func-name";
```

where *func-name* is the user-given name of the function in which the identifier is used. This provides a means of obtaining the current function's name, similar to the `__FILE__` and `__DATE__` macros. For example:

```
void myfunc()
{
 printf("you're in %s", __func__);
}
```

The output from this code should look like this:

```
you're in myfunc
```

Obsolete Features

C99 also removes several diehards such as the K&R function declaration style and the denigrated "implicit int" convention.

Obsolescing K&R Function Declaration Style

The K&R function declaration style in the form of

```
func(n, m) /* return type is unspecified */
int n; double m; /* function parameters */
{
 /*function body*/
}
```

was used in K&R. It was later replaced by the more common form:

```
int func(int n, double m)
{
/*function body*/
}
```

The K&R function declaration style is obsolescent in C99. This means that compilers are allowed to reject such code or accept it with a warning message. In either case, they aren't allowed to ignore it.

Implicit int

Until C99, if a function had no explicit return type such as

```
func(int n)
{
/*function body*/
}
```

its implicit return type would be int. Type int was assumed in other contexts where no explicit type is specified. For example:

```
const x=0; //treated as 'const int' before C99
```

The implicit int convention has its roots in the early days of C. In C++ it was removed about a decade ago. C99 follows suit by requiring that declarations shall contain an explicit type.

Summary

The changes and extensions shown here are only a representative sample. Other new features include the new keywords `_Bool`, `_Complex`, and `_Imaginary` for Boolean variables (at last!) and complex arithmetic. The standard C library has undergone a considerable overhaul too. It now includes libraries for floating-point environment support, a type-generic math, and more.

TIP: For more information about C99, see the standards page at *http://www.open-std.org/jtc1/sc22/wg14/www/standards*, or view the C99 draft rationale at *http://www.open-std.org/jtc1/sc22/wg14/www/docs/n897.pdf* (PDF).

CHAPTER 17

Dynamic Linking

Dynamic linking in its various platform-dependent forms and shapes is used in almost every nontrivial C++ project today. Yet standard C++ recognizes only static linking. Here I will explain the difference between the two, outline the pros and cons of each linkage model and discuss proposals for standardizing dynamic linking in C++.

Static Linking Versus Dynamic Linking

ISO C++ defines a *program* as a set of one or more *translation units* that are compiled into object files and then linked into a single executable called a program. This model of *static linking* was predominant until the 1970s. Today, however, every modern operating system extends it in order to support *dynamic linking*.

Dynamic linking enables an executable file to link other *linkage units* (DLLs, .so files, etc.) at runtime. This way, a *core program*, i.e., an executable file which contains the main() function, can be rather small. Additional linkage units can be loaded into the core program and unloaded at runtime. Dynamic linking in Windows is accomplished by means of creating an .exe file with one or more .dll files. In the POSIX world, *shared libraries* offer more or less the same functionality. Other operating systems use similar models: VMS for example uses *sharable images* for the same purpose.

Advantages of Dynamic Linking

The static linking model is simple to implement and use. This is its main advantage. However, it's pretty limiting. When you statically link a program, the resulting executable file must contain all the data and code that the program may ever need. Consequently, it can become ridiculously large. In addition, changing or extending a program's behavior entails recompilation and relinking.

Customers must therefore close the application and install a new version of the executable in order to reflect an update. This may not sound like a serious problem but think of your favorite web browser, word processor or even operating system. Would you agree to reinstall any of these from scratch whenever a new version, bug fix or update arrives?

Dynamic linking offers several advantages over static linking:

Code Sharing

Different programs can share identical code instead of owning individual copies of the same library. Think of the standard C or C++ libraries. They are both huge and ubiquitous—every C or C++ program uses at least a portion of these libraries for I/O, date and time manipulation, memory allocation, string processing and so on. If distinct copies of these libraries were statically linked into every executable file, even tiny programs would occupy dozens of megabytes. Worse yet, whenever a new version of the libraries is released, every executable file would have to be replaced with a newly linked executable in order to reflect the change. Fortunately, these libraries are usually implemented as shared dynamic libraries that are loaded into the core program at runtime.

Automatic Updates

Whenever a new version of a dynamically linked library is installed, it automatically supersedes the previous version. When you run a program it automatically picks the most up-to-date version without forcing the user to relink.

Security

If you want to protect your intellectual property, splitting an application into several linkage units makes it harder for crackers to disassemble and decompile an executable file, at least in theory.

Disadvantages of Dynamic Linking

Considering dynamic linking's prominent advantages, one could assume that it's superior to static linking by all means. This is not the case, though. Paradoxically, every advantage of dynamic linking can become a disadvantage under certain conditions. Let's look at these disadvantages more closely.

The "DLL Hell" Problem

While it is usually a good idea to share a single instance of a library rather than duplicate it into every individual program, this sharing can become a serious problem. Think of two different web browsers that reside on the same machine. Both browsers use the same shared libraries to access the system's modem, graphics card and I/O routines. Now suppose that you recently had to install an update of one of these shared libraries because of a security loophole found in the original version. Alas, the new version causes one of the browsers to crash. You can either wait for a new patch or revert to the previous version of the shared library. None of these workarounds is ideal. Had the library been statically linked into each browser application, this mess would have been avoided. Unfortunately, such conflicts are reconciled only when you explicitly enable multiple versions of the same shared library to coexist on the same machine. However, this workaround complicates system management and forces users to become experts. In the Windows world, this problem is called the "DLL hell" although it exists in the POSIX world too.

Aliasing

Dynamic linking enables you to share identical code, which is usually a good idea. However, sharing the same data is rarely desirable. If two processes call `localtime()`, for example, it must return a different local static `tm` struct for every process. Designers of dynamically linked libraries were aware of this necessity and devised various techniques to cope with it. However, programmers must explicitly state which components of a shared library are truly shared and which ones aren't. The result is a larger and slower shared library as well as cluttered-up source files.

Code Cracking

Windows programmers who want to thwart crackers' attempt to decompile their code often split an application into multiple DLLs. Ironically, this makes a cracker's job much easier because DLLs (and shared libraries in general) must contain *metacode*, i.e., code that documents code. This metacode (which is reminiscent of debug information) tells the runtime linker where each function and object is stored in the file, what their non-decorated names are, and so on. A hacker that knows how this information is encoded can decompile the code with less effort than required for decompiling an optimized, statically linked executable.

Summary

Dynamic linking is certainly an essential feature in today's software world. The C++ standardization committee is well aware of this. However, there are significant differences with respect to how each platform implements dynamic linking. In many ways, the dynamic linking model of Windows is the mirror image of UNIX's shared libraries, and vice versa. Consequently, defining a standard model of dynamic linking is a difficult task. The draft proposal (*http://anubis.dkuug.dk/jtc1/sc22/wg21/docs/papers/2003/n1428.html*) addresses some of these issues in an attempt to define a standardized model of dynamic linking in C++. It is hoped that future revisions of the C++ standard will define a universal model of dynamic linkage, thereby facilitating cross-platform development and simplifying learning.

Dynamic Linking by Example

Previously, I presented the principles of dynamic linking and discussed its advantages. Now it's time to see dynamic linking in action. My example is based on the POSIX `<dlfcn.h>` library. This isn't a complete tutorial; rather, my aim is to explain the implementation of dynamic linking in general. Therefore, Windows programmers should benefit from this discussion as well.

Building a Shared Library

The first step is to build a shared library. Use as an example the following simple function, `hello()`, that prints a greeting message on the screen:

```
/*hello.c*/
#include <stdio.h>
void hello()
{
 printf("have a nice day.\n");
}
```

Next, compile `hello.c` with the suitable option (e.g., -fPIC in GCC) to build an object file for a shared library and link it with the appropriate linker options to create a shared library (for the sake of brevity, I will skip these technical details because they are highly dependent on the OS, compiler and linker). The end result of the linkage process is a file called `hello.so` that can be installed either in a user's directory or in a system's default directory for shared libraries defined by the LD_LIBRARY_PATH environment variable.

The `<dlfcn.h>` Interface

The <dlfcn.h> library contains four functions for loading a dynamic library into a core program, accessing a library's components (known as *symbols*), unloading a library and error handling.

The dlerror() function has the following prototype:

```
const char * dlerror();
```

It returns a C-string describing the most recent error that occurred in the other dl functions, or NULL if no error has occurred. Each call clears the previous error. Therefore, if you need to store the error message you should copy it to the local buffer.

The dlopen() function opens a shared library. Opening a library involves finding the relevant .so file, opening it and performing additional processing. It has the following prototype:

```
void * dlopen(const char * filename, int flags);
```

If filename contains an absolute path, the function doesn't perform additional searching; if it contains only a file name, dlopen() searches for it in the default directories that contain shared libraries, the user's local directory for shared libraries and finally, the /lib directory. The function returns a non-null value serving as a handler. dlopen() returns NULL on error. The flag argument specifies the manner in which symbols are located and loaded. RTLD_LAZY indicates that symbol resolution occurs on demand. RTLD_NOW forces immediate resolution. This is the preferred option when you debug applications because it ensures that errors are reported immediately (additional flags are not discussed here).

The dlsym() looks up a symbol in a shared library. It has the following prototype:

```
void *dlsym(void * handle, const char * symbol);
```

The first argument is a value returned by dlopen(). Symbol is a C-string containing the name of a symbol you want to load. Upon success, dlsym() returns the address of the sought-after symbol, or NULL if the lookup has failed. Notice that checking whether the return value isn't NULL isn't always sufficient;

in the case of functions, a null value always indicates an error because a valid function address is never NULL. However, certain symbols may have a zero value and thus can cause dlsym() to return NULL even if it succeeds. In such cases, you should call dlerror() to determine whether the lookup has succeeded. dlsym() returns a value of type void *. You should cast it to the appropriate type before using it.

The last function is dlclose(), which has the following prototype:

```
void * dlclose(void *handle);
```

This function closes the library to which handle is pointing; if there are several open sessions of the same library, dlclose() doesn't really close the library but decrements a counter. For a complete description of all the <dlfcn.h> functions, see the manual at *http://www.opengroup.org/onlinepubs/007908799/xsh/dlfcn.h.html*.)

A <dlfcn.h> Example

The following program uses the <dlfcn.h> library to open the hello.so library, locate the symbol "hello," and call this function. Notice how the program checks for errors after each step.

```
#include <dlfcn.h>
#include <stdio.h> /*for printf() */
#include <stdlib.h> /* for exit() */

typedef void (*pf)();
int main()
{
 void *lib;
 pf greet;
 const char * err;

 lib=dlopen("hello.so", RTLD_NOW);
 if (!lib)
 {
  printf("failed to open hello.so: %s \n", dlerror());
  exit(1);
 }
 dlerror(); /*first clear any previous error; redundant
           in this case but a useful habit*/
 greet= (pf) dlsym(lib, "hello");/*locate hello() */
```

```
err=dlerror();/*check for errors and copy error message*/
if (err)
{
 printf("failed to locate hello(): %s \n", err);
 exit(1);
}
greet(); /*call hello() */
dlclose(lib);
 return 0;
}
```

Summary

Although the `<dlfcn.h>` interface is confined to the POSIX world, dynamic linking in Windows and other modern operating systems is implemented more or less in the same manner, albeit with a different set of APIs. It is hoped that a standard dynamic linkage library will materialize in the next revision round of the C++ standard.

Books

Linux Programming by Example: The Fundamentals (Prentice Hall, 2004, ISBN 0131429647), by Arnold Robbins, describes the Linux/C interface very well. Although it misses two important topics, dynamic linking and multi-threading, it's an excellent guide for programmers who are making their first steps in the Linux world. (For more on this book, visit *http://www.informit.com/title/0131429647.*)

Linux Application Development (Addison-Wesley, 1998, ISBN 0201308215), by Michael K. Johnson and Eric W. Troan, has been my favorite guide to Linux system programming. The title is somewhat out of focus—it doesn't really cover full-blown application development issues such as GUI and multimedia—but it's exactly the book every system programmer should have at his or her disposal: succinct, accurate, authoritative, and totally fluff-free. (For more on this book, visit *http://www.informit.com/title/0201308215.*)

CHAPTER 18

Tips and Techniques

Having covered a significant portion of standard C++ constructs and features (but certainly not all of them), it's time to consider some practicalities.

Using enums as Mnemonic Indexes

The ability to extend the type system of a programming language by defining new types is called *abstract data typing*, or *data abstraction*. While classes are a common data abstraction mechanism, they are not the only one. In the following sections, I will explain the properties of enum types, another data abstraction mechanism, and demonstrate some of their advanced uses.

Properties of enum Types

An enum is a set of integral constants with symbolic names called *enumerators*. For example:

```
enum ProcessState //ProcessState is an enum tag
{
//enumerators:
  stopped,
  resumed,
  zombie,
  running
};
```

By default, the first enumerator's value is 0. Each consecutive enumerator is incremented by 1. Therefore, the enumerators stopped, resumed, zombie and running have the values 0, 1, 2 and 3, respectively. You can override the default values like this:

```
enum FlightMenu
{
```

```
    standard=100,
    vegetarian=200,
    vegetarian_ovo_lacto, //default, equals 201
    vegetarian_low_fat,//equals 202
    diabetic=300,
    kosher=400
};
```

enums are strongly typed. The only values you can assign to an enum variable are its enumerators:

```
ProcessState state=stopped;//fine
state=1; //error, type mismatch
state=kosher; //error, type mismatch
```

Usually, the actual values of enumerators are immaterial. For instance, the following switch statement will function properly even if you change the values of FlightMenu's enumerators:

```
switch(menu)
{
  case standard:
    std_meals++;
    break;
  case vegetarian:
    veg++;
    break;
  //...all the rest
  .
  .
  .
  default:
    cout<<"illegal choice"<<endl;
}
```

However, when using enums as mnemonic indexes, there's less leeway.

Mnemonic Indexes Requirements

Mnemonic indexes simplify code maintenance and improve its readability. They are particularly useful in arrays of pointers to functions and in loops that iterate through an entire enumerator list. But before I demonstrate how to use this technique, there are two conditions that must be fulfilled. First, when using mnemonic indexes, all of the enumerators must have consecutive positive numbers starting at 0. In other words, you shouldn't assign explicit values to any enumerator. Second, each `enum` must contain a *counter*, i.e., a final enumerator whose value is the number of enumerators preceding it. The counter's name should clearly document its role. The common convention is to affix `Max` to the `enum` tag, as shown in the following example:

```
enum ProcessState
{
  stopped,
  resumed,
  zombie,
  running,
  ProcessStateMax // counter, equals 4
};
```

Note that C++ automatically assigns the correct value to the counter so long as it's the last enumerator. The beauty in `enum`s is that if you add more enumerators or remove some of them, the counter's value is automatically readjusted:

```
enum ProcessState
{
  stopped,
  resumed,
  zombie,
  running,
  hibernating, //added a new enumerator
  ProcessStateMax //5
};
```

Mnemonic Indexes in Action

Suppose you need to write a menu-based desktop manager that displays icons on the screen. Each icon represents a different operation: emailing, word processing, CD burning, and so on. When the user clicks on a certain icon, the desktop manager launches the corresponding application. Typically, GUI-based systems are event-driven. They invoke a callback function when notified of an event. For the sake of brevity, assume that the desktop in questions has three icons: mail, word processing and CD burning. When the user clicks on one of these icons, the desktop manager receives an event with the user's choice in the form of an `enum` defined like this:

```
enum Icons
{
  mail,
  word_processor,
  CD_burner,
  IconsMax
};
```

Each of these icons is associated with a function that launches the matching application:

```
//all functions have the same signature
int launch_mail();
int launch_wp();
int launch_CD_burner();
```

The desktop manager stores pointers to these functions in an array:

```
typedef int (*PF)(); //hide the ugly syntax with a typedef
//create an array of such pointers to functions
PF funcs[IconsMax]; //using counter as the array's size
//fill the array with matching function addresses
funcs[mail]=launch_mail;
funcs[word_processor]=launch_wp;
funcs[CD_burner]=launch_CD_burner;
```

With enumerators serving as the array's indexes, the code is very readable and easy to maintain. For example, there's no need to guess which function the following statement invokes:

```
funcs[word_processor]();
```

More importantly, a single function can handle all of the events:

```
int Process_user_request(Icons choice, PF functions [])
{
  return functions[choice](); //invoke the matching function
}
```

If that seems impressive enough, the real strength of mnemonic indexes lies in code maintenance. Suppose you need to add a new icon:

```
enum Icons
{
```

```
  mail,
  word_processor,
  CD_burner,
  Web_browser, //new
  IconsMax
};
```

You don't have to change anything in the definition of the array `funcs` since `IconsMax` automatically increased it. There's no need to change `Process_user_request()` either. All you have to do is add one line of code after the definition of `funcs` to register the function associated with the new choice:

```
funcs[Web_browsing]=launch_Web_browser;
```

To enum But a Few

The technique I've shown can be applied to pointers to members and function objects with slight modifications. Suppose you have the following class:

```
class DesktopManager
{
public:
  int launch_mail();
  int launch_wp();
  int launch_CD_burner();
//..
};
```

To store the addresses of its member functions in an array, define the following array:

```
typedef int (DesktopManager::*PMF)();

PMF mem_funcs[IconsMax]; //array of pointers to members
mem_funcs[mail]=&DesktopManager::launch_mail;
mem_funcs[word_processor]=&DesktopManager::launch_wp;
mem_funcs[CD_burner]=&DesktopManager::launch_CD_burner;
```

`Process_user_request()` also needs two tiny cosmetic changes:

```
int Process_user_request(DesktopManager &dm,
                         Icons choice,
                         PMF functions[])
```

```
{
//launch matching member function
return (dm.*functions[choice])();
}
```

Using mnemonic indexes as loop iterators is left as an exercise for the reader.

POD Initialization

Unlike `auto` objects, which are automatically initialized by their constructor, `auto` variables have an indeterminate (i.e., garbage) value by default. Explicit initialization of such variables eliminates unpleasant surprises at runtime and ensures that your code always behaves consistently. In the following sections, I will show how to explicitly initialize all sorts of automatic data: scalar types, pointers, arrays, `struct`s and `union`s.

Built-In Types

Initialization of a built-in type (`int`, `bool` and `double`, etc.) looks like an assignment expression: An assignment operator and an *initializer* appear after the variable's name. The only difference between plain assignment and an initialization is that the latter must appear in the variable's declaration. For example,

```
int func()
{
int val=100;
double price=99.99;
bool isopen=false;
Person *p=NULL;
//...
}
```

Each initializer is of the same type as the variable it initializes. As a special case, C++ allows you to use the literal 0 as a universal initializer for all built-in types, including pointers, pointers to functions and pointers to members. Therefore, you can initialize `isopen` like this:

```
bool isopen=0; // 0 is converted to 'false'
```

Similarly, all pointer types can be initialized like this:

```
Person *p=0; //converted to NULL
void (*pf)(int)=0; //pointer to function
void (A::*pmf)(int)=0; //pointer to member function
```

In fact, C++ pundits advocate the use of 0 instead of NULL in pointer initializations, as it will save you the trouble of #including a header file.

Arrays

As noted earlier, assignment and initialization look syntactically the same. Yet there are two major differences between the two. Conceptually, initializations are performed at compile-time whereas assignments take place at runtime. More importantly, you can initialize an array or an *aggregate* (I will discuss aggregates shortly) but you can't assign to them:

```
char passenger[10]="Phileas"; //OK, initialization
char passenger2[10];
passenger2 = "Fix"; //error: array assignment is illegal
```

If you provide fewer initializers than the number of elements that an array has, all remaining elements will be *default-initialized*. For example, in the following expression the array set has five elements but only the first three have explicit initializers:

```
int set[5]={0,1,2};
```

The elements set[4] and set[5] are implicitly initialized to 0 in this case. Therefore, if you want to zero-initialize a large array, simply provide a single initializer and let the compiler take care of the rest:

```
double scores[500]={0.0}; //remaining 499 elements
         //are initialized to 0.0 as well
```

The following declaration is equivalent because the literal 0 is implicitly converted to the type of the initialized object, i.e., 0.0:

```
double scores[500]={0};
```

Likewise, if you're using a char array:

```
char URL[2048]={0}; //all elements are initialized to '\0'
```

Notice how awkward and error-prone a `memset()`-based "initialization" looks in comparison:

```
#include <cstring>
char URL[2048];
memset(URL, 0, 2048);
```

Not only do you need to `#include` a special header but you also must specify the array's size. Worse yet, programmers might confuse the second and third arguments:

```
int arr[100];
memset (arr, 100, 0); //bad! actually meant (arr, 0, 100)
```

To the programmer's surprise, `arr`'s elements will contain garbage values at runtime.

Aggregates

An aggregate is a plain old data (POD) `struct`, `class`, or `union`, or an array of POD elements (as well as arrays of built-in types). To initialize a POD `struct`, provide one or more initializers in curly braces. If there are fewer initializers than the number of members, the remaining members are default-initialized:

```
struct employee
{
 int age;
 char [20] name;
 char[100] address;
 char occupation[50];
};
employee emp={45, "Passepartout", "Saville Row"};
```

The array `occupation` is zero-initialized since no explicit initializer was provided for it. You can easily zero-initialize all the members of a `struct` like this:

```
employee e={0};
```

You're probably wondering whether this would work if the first member weren't a scalar type. For example,

```
struct Book
{
```

```
char[100] title;
char [100] author;
int pages;
};
```

Yes, it would:

```
Book b={0};
```

This works because aggregate initialization rules are recursive; the initializer 0 initializes the first `Book` member, which is an array. As you already know, if an array's initialization list contains fewer initializers than the number of its elements, the remaining elements are zero-initialized. Thus, the literal 0 initializes the first element of the array `title`, letting the compiler zero-initialize all the remaining elements. Because b's initialization list doesn't provide explicit initializers for the members `author` and `pages`, they are all zero-initialized as well. Neat, isn't it?

Suppose we want to declare an array of `Book` objects. The same form of initialization will work here, too:

```
Book arr[20] ={0};
```

Even if you change the definition of `struct Book` later (by adding more data members to it, for example) or if you change the size of the array `b`, the `={0};` initializer will properly initialize every element thereof.

Unions

Union initialization is similar to struct initialization except that it can include only a single initializer. This initializer must initialize the first union member. C++ guarantees that if the rest of the members are larger than the first, they're zero-initialized as well:

```
union U
{
 int a;
 char b[4];
};

U a = { 1 }; //fine
U b = a; //fine
U c = 1; //  error
U d = { 0, "abc" }; // error
U e = { "abc" }; //  error
```

Summary

Initializing auto variables is good programming practice. Of course, you don't have to initialize all variables to zero. However, you shouldn't leave auto varaibles uninitialized. A partial initialization list initializes the entire aggregate; members for which no explicit initializer is provided are default-initialized. Unions are a special case—only their first member can be initialized.

Object Initialization

Earlier, I explained the rules of POD initialization. This was only one part of the story, as class member initialization rules are quite different. I will discuss these rules and show how to initialize ordinary data members, constants, members of base classes and embedded objects and static data members.

Assignment Versus Initialization

Novices—and even experienced programmers—sometimes confuse initialization and assignment, which are two different concepts. For example, the following constructor doesn't really initialize the data members of an object; it only assigns values to them:

```
class Person
{
private:
 int age;
 string name;
public:
 Person(int a, const string & n)
 { //the members age and name are assigned
   age=a;
   name=n;
 }
};
```

When dealing with built-in types, the performance difference between such assignments and proper initialization (which I will demonstrate momentarily) is negligible. However, when it comes to objects, as is the case with the member name for example, the difference can be rather noticeable. This is so because the object in question is first constructed and only then is it assigned.

Member Initialization Lists

A proper initialization of data members has a special syntactic construct called a *member initialization list* or mem-init for short:

```
class Person
{
//..
public:
//member initialization list:
 Person(int a, const string & n) : age (a), name (n)
 {}
};
```

Obligatory Initialization

In the previous example, the initialization of `Person`'s members was optional. Yet there are cases in which you must initialize data members: `const` members, references, and subobjects (i.e., embedded objects and base classes) whose constructors take arguments require a member initialization list. For example, a class that has a data member of type `Person` can pass an argument to its constructor like this:

```
class Foo
{
private:
 int & r; // reference member
 const int MAX; // const member
 Person p; //requires arguments
public:
 explicit Foo(int& n) : r(n), MAX(100), p (MAX,"John D."){}
};
```

The member initialization list of `Foo` first initializes the reference `r`, then the `const` member `MAX` and finally it initializes the embedded object `p`.

Notice that the member `MAX`, once initialized, serves as an initializer of another member, `p`. This is perfectly legal because members are initialized according to the order in which they are *declared in a class*. Thus, changing the initialization list into:

```
Foo(int& r) : p (MAX,"John D."), MAX(100), r(n) {}
```

doesn't change the initialization order that remains: `r`, `MAX` and `p`. The reason is that the compiler automatically transforms each member initialization list so that its members are initialized according to their declarations. Notice however that initializing a member x with a member y that is declared after x will cause undefined behavior. Consider the following class, in which the member Person is declared before MAX:

```
class BadFoo
{
private:
 int & r; // reference member
 Person p; //requires arguments
 const int MAX; // const member
public:
 explicit BadFoo(int& n)//MAX used before being initialized
   : r(n), MAX(100), p (MAX,"John D.") {}
};
```

Don't let the member initialization list mislead you; although it seemingly initializes MAX before p, the compiler actually transforms the list into this:

```
explicit BadFoo(int& n)   //actual initialization order:
  : r(n), p (MAX,"John D."), MAX(100) {}
```

Consequently, MAX has an indeterminate (i.e., garbage) value when it is passed as an argument to p's constructor. Some compilers issue a warning in this case; others don't. To be on the safe side, always check your initialization lists.

Class Constants

In earlier stages of C++, an *anonymous enum* was used as a constant shared by all instances of the same class:

```
class Heap
{
 enum { PAGE_SIZE=2048 };
//...
};
```

Anonymous enums can still be used as class constants. However, most compilers nowadays support a superior technique that achieves that same goal, namely in-class initialization of const static data members of an integral type:

```
class Heap
{
 static const int PAGE_SIZE=1024;
```

```
public:
  Heap(int pages){ p=new unsigned char[pages*PAGE_SIZE];}
//...
};
```

This kind of initialization is allowed only for `const static` members of integral types. For any other `static` members, provide an initializer in the definition itself:

```
class Trigo
{
 const static double PI;
//...
};
const double Trigo::PI= 3.14159265358;
```

Summary

A member initialization list is the primary form of initializing data members of an object. In some cases, initialization is optional. However, `const` members, references and subobjects whose constructors take arguments necessitate a member initialization list. C++ also defines a special rule for initializing `const static` members of an integral type. You can initialize such members inside the class body. All other static data members can be initialized only in their definition, outside the class body.

`const` Declarations

"const-correctness" is a key concept in large-scale software projects. Yet in order to implement it thoroughly, one has to fully understand what `const` actually means. Oddly enough, this keyword has no fewer than three different meanings in C++. In this section, I will explain each of these meanings and provide cues for coping with the baffling syntax.

`const` Objects

Declaring an object as `const` is a commitment made by the programmer that the program doesn't alter it subsequently (please note that the term *object* is used in its wider sense, namely class objects and data variables). A `const` definition (as opposed to a `const` declaration) must include a proper initializer. For example:

```
const int MAX_LINE=25;
const std::string address="203.178.156.66";
const char signage[15]="fire alarm";
const double in2cm = 2.54;
```

const **Pointers**

The second type of const refers to pointers. Declaring a pointer as const ensures that the program doesn't assign a new address to it afterward. The object bound to such a pointer can be modified, though. For example:

```
int r=10, s=0;
int *const pci = &s; // pci is a const pointer to int
pci++; // error, can't modify a const pointer
pci= &r; // error
*pci=9; //OK
```

const **Member Functions**

In addition to const objects and const pointers (which were originally introduced in C), C++ has a third type of const, namely const member functions. A class object's state consists of the values of its non-static data members. Declaring a member function as const ensures that that function doesn't change its object's state. You do that by appending const after the function's parameter list. For example:

```
class Student
{
public:
 double getAvg() const {return average;} //const member function
private:
 double average;
//...
};
```

Trying to modify a data member inside a const member function is an error:

```
int Student::getAvg() const
{
 average += 0.5; // compilation error
 return average;
}
```

Complex Declarations

Because `const` can apply to both objects and pointers, and because its exact position in a declaration is flexible, even experienced programmers find `const` declarations of compound types confusing. Consider the following example. Can you tell what the types of x and y are?

```
const char * x= "test";
char const * y= "another one";
```

x and y actually have the same type, namely "pointer to `const char`," in spite of the variation in the position of `const`. `const` may appear before or after a type name, without changing the declaration's meaning. This free ordering rule isn't unique to `const`. Consider the position of the keywords `long` and `unsigned` in the following example:

```
int long n;
long int m; //same as above
unsigned long o;
long unsigned r; //same as above
```

Now consider the following `const` declaration:

```
char * const z= "test";
```

This time, the type of z is "`const` pointer to `char`." How does the compiler know that z is a `const` pointer whereas x and y are not? More importantly, how can you distinguish between `const` pointers and pointers to `const` variables?

The secret lies in the location of `const` with respect to the asterisk. The sequence "* `const`" always indicates a `const` pointer. If however the `const` appears before the asterisk, then the object bound to the pointer is `const`. This brings us to yet another complexity.

`const` Pointers of `const` Objects

It's possible to combine `const` objects and `const` pointers in a single declaration. The result is a `const` pointer to a `const` object:

```
const int n=1;
const int * const p= &n; // const pointer to const int
```

Let's parse it together. p is a `const` pointer because its declaration contains the sequence * `const`. It points to `const int` because its declaration contains another `const` before the asterisk.

Is it possible to combine the three types of `const` in one declaration? Certainly:

```
class A
{
//...
const int * const get_scores(int id) const;
};
```

`get_scores()` is a `const` member function that returns a `const` pointer to `const int`.

operator `const_cast<>`

The operator `const_cast<>` removes the `const` quality of an object. Note that removing `const`-ness doesn't mean that you can modify the resulting object. Consider:

```
const char *msg= "hello world";
int main()
{
 char * s = const_cast <char *> (msg); // get rid of const
 strcpy(s, "bad idea!"); //undefined behavior
}
```

Any attempt to overwrite s will result in undefined behavior. The problem is that `const` objects may be stored in the system's read-only memory. A brute-force removal of `const` allows you to treat the object as if it weren't `const`, say passing it as an argument to a function that takes `char *`, but not to modify it.

`const_cast<>` performs the opposite operation as well, namely converting a non-`const` object to `const`. For example:

```
char s[]= "fasten your seatbelt";
size=strlen(const_cast<const char *> (s));// more explicit
```

You will rarely see such uses of `const_cast<>` though. C++ automatically converts non-`const` objects to `const` in a context that requires a `const` object. Therefore, using `const_cast<>` to make an object `const` is never mandatory, although it documents the programmer's intention explicitly.

Summary

The syntactic intricacies often cause programmers to give up the use of `const`, thereby producing code that is less secure and less readable. While the difference between pointers to `const` objects and `const` pointers is rather subtle, checking the position of the `const` qualifier with respect to the asterisk should resolve the ambiguity. `const` member functions are easily recognized by the presence of `const` after the parameter list.

Sample Chapters

"Object Engineering Techniques" (*http://www.informit.com/articles/article.asp?p=29043*), by Richard Dué, is a sample chapter from *Mentoring Object Technology Projects* (Prentice Hall, 2002, ISBN 0130347906). This chapter discusses some of the common object-oriented design methods such as use case modeling and class-responsibility-collaboration (CRC) modeling. (For more on this book, visit *http://www.informit.com/bookstore/product.asp?isbn=0130347906*.)

Books

Modern C++ Design: Generic Programming and Design Patterns Applied (Addison-Wesley, 2001, ISBN 0201704315), by Andrei Alexandrescu, is an excellent guide to state-of-the-art C++ design. The book discusses powerful syntactic features such as partial template specialization, along with guidelines for effective generic class design. (For more on this book, visit *http://www.informit.com/title/0201704315*.)

Project Organization Guidelines

The earlier discussion of `inline` functions subtly brought another important issue into the limelight: namely, how to organize the files of a typical C++ program or project. In this section, I will discuss this issue and the following topics: how to decide which code components should be included in a header file, which ones belong to a source file, and how many files should be used in a project.

Units

A typical program usually consists of one or more pairs of a source file and its matching header file. Such a pair is called a *unit*. (The terms *translation unit* and *compilation unit* refer more or less to this notion, too; see the MSDN article "Phases of Translation" at *http://msdn.microsoft.com/library/default.asp?url=/library/en-us/vccelng/htm/prepr_1.asp*.) Each unit can be compiled separately, the result of which is an *object file*. At link time, one or more object files that belong to the same program are linked together to produce a single executable file that you can run. Different implementations may use a slightly different program model. For example, Windows and POSIX operating systems support the concept of *dynamic linking* whereby an executable file loads components stored in a DLL (or a shared library in POSIX parlance) as needed, at runtime. However, the basic model that I've outlined still prevails on all platforms.

Header Files Versus Source Files

A header file contains declarations of entities that are *defined* in a matching source file. Typically, a header file has a .h (or .hxx) extension and a source file has a .c, .cpp, .cc or .cxx extension. For example, if a source file contains a function, its matching header file will contain the function's prototype. Likewise, a class and its members are declared in a header file whereas its member functions and static data members are defined in a corresponding source file. Here's an example:

```
// logfile.h
#include <fstream>
#include <string>
class Logfile
{
 public: //member functions are declared but not defined:
  Logfile(const std::string & path);
  ~Logfile();
  //...
private:
 std::ofstream log;
 std::string name;
};

// logfile.cpp
#include "logfile.h"
//definitions of functions declared in the .h file
Logfile::Logfile(const std::string & path) :name(path)
{
 log.open(name.c_str());
 bool success=log;
 //..
}
Logfile::~Logfile()
```

```
{
 log.close();
//..
}
```

It's customary to add *#include guards* to a header file to ensure that it isn't #included more than once during the same compilation session. Multiple inclusions of the same header file could occur if it's #included in two different source files that are compiled together. The result of multiple inclusions is a compilation error. An #include guard is a sequence of #if-#else-#endif preprocessor directives that first check whether the header has already been included. This test is accomplished by checking the value of an agreed-upon macro. If the macro isn't defined, this means that the header hasn't been #included before. In this case, the macro is defined and the rest of the file becomes accessible to the compiler. The convention I prefer is to use the header file's name and affix _H to it. For example, the previous header file with an #include guard looks like this:

```
// logfile.h
#if ! defined (LOGFILE_H)
#define LOGFILE_H  //block further #includes of this file

#include <fstream>
#include <string>
class Logfile
{
 public:
  Logfile(const std::string & path);
  ~Logfile();
  //...
 private:
  std::ofstream log;
  std::string name;
};
#endif //close the #if ! defined clause above
```

A header file template should first of all contain the following:

```
#if ! defined (filename_H)
#define filename_H
//...declarations
#endif //close the #if ! defined clause above
```

A header file and its corresponding source files are called a unit because you need to compile both of them at once. You can't compile the .cpp file alone because it doesn't contain a declaration of the class `Logfile`. You can compile a header file without the source file but at link time you'll get link errors due to undefined symbols, meaning the member functions' bodies couldn't be found.

The "One Entity" Rule

Generally speaking, each unit should contain a single C++ entity, i.e., a class, a function, a template, etc. It might seem tempting to include several related classes in one source file, and in some cases, it's perfectly okay: for example, if you have a tightly coupled set of classes derived from a common base class, say a set of exception classes. Remember, though, that in large-scale projects each class might be maintained by a different developer, team, or vendor. Therefore, it's best to pack each class in a dedicated unit. As a bonus, you get shorter compilation times because most modern IDEs are clever enough to compile only files that have changed since the last build. Thus, if class `Timer` in files `timer.cpp` and `timer.h` has been modified whereas class `interrupt_handler` in `interrupt_handler.cpp` and `interrupt_handler.h` hasn't changed, the compiler will skip the latter. If however both classes are packed in a single unit, the compiler must compile both of them. This seems like a negligible gain but in projects that consist of hundreds of units this can reduce compilation time significantly. Notice also that real-world classes are often much larger than the toy examples you see in primer books. For example, the standard `<string>` header contains a definition of the template `basic_string<>`, which has more than a hundred member functions and overloaded operators! The `<vector>` unit is also a rather bulky class template.

File Naming

As you may have guessed, I also recommend giving source files and header files the same name as the entity they contain. This way you and your colleagues can easily navigate through the project source files and know exactly where every class, function, template, etc., is located. If you're using namespaces, you want to group all of the units of the same namespace under a dedicated directory. For example, if you have a class called `mobile::Transmitter` that represents a mobile phone's embedded transmitter and a class called `space::Transmitter` that represents a satellite's transmitter, create two directories called mobile and space under the project's root tree and place each unit in its directory.

Special Cases

Header files usually contain declarations, not definitions. However, in two cases, namely templates and inline functions, they should contain complete definitions. C++ requires that definitions of inline function templates be accessible in every translation unit that uses them. The simplest way to satisfy this requirement is by implementing inline functions and templates in header files that are `#included` in every translation unit that uses them. For example, if we decide to declare all the member functions of `Logfile inline`, we can change the header file into something like this:

```
// logfile.h
#if ! defined (LOGFILE_H)
#define LOGFILE_H //block further #includes of this file
//same as before
#include <fstream>
#include <string>
class Logfile
{
 public:
  Logfile(const std::string & path);
  ~Logfile();
  //...
private:
  std::ofstream log;
  std::string name;
};
//--this section was added to the header --
inline Logfile::Logfile(const std::string & path) :name(path)
{
 log.open(name.c_str());
 bool success=log;
 //..
}
inline Logfile::~Logfile()
{
 log.close();
 //..
}
#endif
```

Once you move all the content of the source file into a header file, there's no need to have a separate source file in this case; the unit consists solely of a header file.

Summary

Poorly organized projects seldom succeed. Proper organization of project units, consistent and intelligible file naming conventions and a reliable configuration management tool (a topic that I didn't discuss here) are prerequisites for a project's successful completion. Of course, these measures can't replace talented and experienced developers and meticulous design, yet unlike the latter, project organization is rarely discussed in programming books.

`inline` Functions

The `inline` keyword was added to C++ in its inception as a means of enticing new programmers into using accessors and mutators ("getters" and "setters") instead of allowing direct access to data members. In those days, compiler technology was less advanced than it is today. C++ programmers were rather skeptical about the language's performance due to their collective experience with former object-oriented languages that were reputedly slow and bloated. Today `inline` is less and less necessary as compilers and optimizers are much cleverer. However, in certain cases it may still give your code a performance boost. I will explain the semantics of `inline` and discuss its usage and usefulness.

`inline` Basics

A function declared with an `inline` specifier is called an *inline function*. `inline` indicates that *inline substitution* of the function body at the point of call should be preferred to the usual function call mechanism. The overhead of a function call is platform dependent but it usually consists of storing the current stack state, pushing the function's arguments on the stack, performing a jump to the function's code, and then repeating more or less the same steps in reverse order when the function returns. If function's body is slim and it's called often, the performance gain can be rather noticeable. Notice however that `inline`, very much like `register`, is only a recommendation to the compiler. Compilers may refuse to inline a function altogether, or decide to inline it in a certain point of call but not in another. Furthermore, they may inline a function that wasn't declared `inline`. In short, compilers can do whatever they like but if they're polite and considerate, they might agree to inline a function that wouldn't be inlined otherwise.

Member functions defined inside their class body are implicitly declared `inline`. For example:

```
class Time
{
public:
 std::time_t current_time()//implicitly declared inline
 {
  return time(0);
 }
};
```

In pre-standard C++, `inline` affected the linkage type of a function (see the section "Linkage Types" in Chapter 4, "Memory Management"). This is not the case anymore; in standard C++ `inline` has no effect on the linkage of a function.

Usage

Unlike non-`inline` functions, an `inline` function must be defined in every translation unit in which it is used. This way, the function's body is accessible to the compiler in every translation unit. It can therefore perform inline substitution at the point of call. A common technique is to define an inline function in a header file. This header file is `#included` in every translation unit in which the function is used. As a rule, use the `inline` specifier only in a function's definition. `inline` shouldn't appear in a declaration. For example:

```
class Time
{
public:
 std::time_t current_time() const; //declaration, no inline
};

//in some .h file
inline std::time_t current_time() const
{
  return time(0);
 }
```

Compilers vary in their `inline` policies. For example, some of them will refuse to inline a recursive function or a function containing a loop.

Programmers use `inline` only in a function definition. They can't select individual points of call in which the function will be inlined. Compilers, however, have more control. They may inline a function at one point of call but refuse to inline the same function at a different point of call.

Declaring trivial accessors and mutators `inline` is almost redundant. Every decent compiler nowadays would inline these functions anyway:

```
class Employee
{
public:
 int get_rank() const;
 double get_salary() const;
//...
};

//these trivial functions are inlined by many compilers
//automatically
inline int Employee::get_rank() const
{
 return rank;
}
inline double Employee::get_salary() const
{
 return salary;
}
```

inline is useful in borderline cases, when the compiler wouldn't inline a function by default. Alas, that's exactly the problem. Most programmers know far less than their compiler which functions are better candidates for inlining. I'll return to this shortly.

inline Woes

In extreme situations, inline can really cause damage. Here are some of the more frequent problems associated with the use of inline functions.

- **Code bloat**. inline functions might increase the size of the executable. Usually, a larger executable means slower execution time because the system caches a smaller portion of the program.
- **Dynamic linking woes**. In dynamically linked libraries (DLLs and shared libraries), inline functions are a serious problem. It's nearly impossible to maintain binary compatibility between different versions of a binary file if an inline function's body has changed. In this case, you can't just drop in a new version of the DLL or shared library hoping that the application will load it automatically the next time it runs. Rather, you must recompile your code and reinstall it.
- **Premature optimization**. Most programmers' intuitions about performance are based on outdated and partial knowledge. In order to assess whether inlining a certain function improves performance, one

must use a profiler and isolate the tested code from various confounding variables such as debug versus release versions, current system loads and so on. Moreover, the "90-10" rule of optimization suggests that a typical program wastes about 90% of its execution time running 10% of its code. Therefore, focus your efforts on isolating that critical 10% and optimize it.

Summary

To be honest, it's hard to define a universal rule of thumb for `inline` usage. Sometimes, `inline` can truly boost performance. However, my feeling is that in most cases, `inline` is either redundant or even harmful. Therefore, avoid `inline` unless you truly need it. The risks are simply too high and the benefit, if any, is usually marginal.

Online Resources

"Inline Functions" (*http://www.parashift.com/c++-faq-lite/inline-functions.html*) is a chapter from C++ FAQ Lite (*http://www.parashift.com/c++-faq-lite/index.html*), a guide to inline usage that explains why and when it should be used and what the associated benefits and risks are.

Books

Inside the C++ Object Model (Addison-Wesley, 1996, ISBN 0201834545), by Stanley B. Lippman, is one of my all-time favorites. It explains in detail the inner workings of C++ compilers, including their support of `inline` functions. (For more on this book, visit *http://www.informit.com/bookstore/product.asp?isbn=0201834545*.)

All About `bool`

For too many years, C++ didn't have a built-in Boolean type. This historical accident was finally rectified a decade ago when the `bool` datatype was added to the standard. Virtually all compilers support this type nowadays; likewise, all Standard Library implementations make use this type. Yet some programmers still aren't fully aware of the benefits on the one hand, and caveats of `bool` on the other hand. I will discuss some of the properties of `bool` and give a few tips on safe and standard-compliant usage of `bool`.

The Pre-bool Era

The lack of a built-in Boolean type urged programmers to exert their creativity and resourcefulness in order to make up for it. An enumeration of the following kind was one of the better substitutes:

```
enum bool
{
 false,
 true
};
```

This solution was type-safe and efficient, although it wasn't standardized and thus forced each programmer to define it anew. Worse yet, in order to use this `enum` programmers had to `#include` a header file that contained this declaration. Since the header's name wasn't standardized either, this situation caused code maintenance problems and name clashes.

A less impressive (though faily common) alternative was macros. Many C/C++ projects used to have a header file containing macros of the following kind:

```
#define TRUE 1
#define FALSE 0
```

In some cases, a `typedef` was also added:

```
typedef int BOOL;
```

The problem with this workaround was the lack of type-safety (one could misuse a `BOOL` variable as a loop counter for example), the lack of a standardized naming convention and the need to use a header file.

The worst workaround was to use plain `int` as a Boolean type, and the literals 0 and 1 as `true` and `false`, respectively. Here is an example:

```
int done=0;
if(some_condition)
 done=1;
else
 continue;
```

While this hack didn't require the use of a header file, this coding practice has been criticized for years. Not only is the code hardly readable, it isn't type-safe and is very error-prone.

Enter `bool`

In pre-`bool` times, conditional expressions in an `if` statement, a loop or a comma-separated expression would yield a result of type `int`, with a value of zero treated as `false` and a nonzero value treated as `true`. This convention was inherited from C. For example:

```
void *p=malloc(SIZE);
//in pre-bool times,
//p's value is implicitly converted to int
if (p)
{
//..p isn't NULL
}
```

After years of hesitation and debate, the C++ standardization committee decided that a built-in Boolean type called `bool` should be added to the language along with the keywords `true` and `false`. To ensure compatibility with C code and pre-`bool` C++ code, implicit numeric-to-`bool` conversions adhere to C's convention. Every nonzero value is implicitly converted to `true` in a context that requires a `bool` value, and a zero value is implicitly converted to `false`. In addition, all logical and relational operators, `if`-conditions, loop termination conditions and the ternary ? : operator yield a result of type `bool` rather than `int`. In this regard, the semantics of the previous code snippet is slightly different under `bool`-enabled compilers:

```
void *p=malloc(SIZE);
if (p)  //p's value is implicitly converted to bool
{
//..p isn't NULL
}
```

Likewise, all the following conditions return a `bool` result, not `int`:

```
bool ready=get_status();
while (ready) //while conditions evaluate to bool
{
 //do something so long as x is true
};
bool is_five= (n==5); //relational expressions yield bool
```

Therefore, new code shouldn't use `int` or any other integral type but `bool` in such contexts.

`bool` **Properties**

The C++ standard doesn't state the underlying type of bool. However, on most implementations it's `char` or `unsigned char`. Values of type `bool` are either `true` or `false`. But under certain conditions, such as when examining the value of an uninitialized variable, a `bool` variable may have an undefined value that is neither `true` nor `false`. The following code demonstrates this case. When the `switch` statement is executed, any of the three `case` blocks may be activated, including the `default` block:

```
bool var; //uninitialized; undefined value
int n;
switch(*var)
{
 case true:
 {
 int n=0;
 }
 break;
 case false:
 {
 int n=1;
 }
 break;
 default:
 {
 int n=2;
 }
 break;
}
```

This phenomenon could cause nasty bugs that are hard to detect. Therefore, always initialize `bool` variables explicitly to ensure that they never have an indeterminate state.

Although there are no `signed`, `unsigned`, `short`, or `long bool` types or values, `bool` values behave as integral types. It is therefore possible to assign an `int` value to `bool` and vice versa:

```
bool b=0; //b is false
```

When a `bool` value is promoted to any other integral type, a value of `false` is converted to 0 and `true` is converted to 1.

```
void func(int);
int n=true; //OK, n equals 1
```

```
bool b=false;
func(b); //OK, bool promoted to int
```

In addition, the ++ operator can be applied to a `bool` variable, although this programming practice is deprecated. It was allowed only for the sake of maintaining backward compatibility with legacy code:

```
bool allowed=false;
++allowed; //allowed becomes true, poor programming style!
```

Summary

Several years after the introduction of `bool` to C++, C added a Boolean type, too. In C99, the new header file `<stdbool.h>` defines the type `bool` as well as the keywords `false` and `true`. This is a deplorable compromise because it forces users to `#include` a header file in order to use what is supposed to be a standard datatype. A program that doesn't `#include` this header may use the unwieldy `_Bool` keyword instead. Fortunately, the C++ standardization committee decided to go all the way and make `bool` a first-class citizen.

TIP: For more information about C99, see the section "A Tour of C99."

Books

The Art of UNIX Programming (Addison-Wesley, 2003, ISBN 0131429019), by Eric S. Raymond, is one of the best books I've read recently. It describes what is collectively known as the "spirit of UNIX," both in terms of programming style (and languages) and in terms of an end user's experience. The history of UNIX and C are closely interleaved. It's therefore a must-read for every system programmer, advanced C and C++ programmers, and, of course, UNIX aficionados. (For more on this book, visit *http://www.informit.com/bookstore/product.asp?isbn=0131429019*.)

Bitwise Operators, Part I

Storing and accessing bits is only one part of bit manipulation. C++ also defines a set of *bitwise operators* that manipulate strings of bits. These operators are widely used in image processing, DSP, sound-processing chips, and compression and encryption algorithms. The following sections present the bitwise operators and show how to use them.

Bitwise and Logical Operators

Beginners often confuse bitwise operators with logical operators. It's important to understand the crucial difference between the two. Logical operators such as `!`, `&&`, and `||` always yield a *Boolean value*, either `true` or `false`. You can concatenate any number of sub-expressions with one or more logical operators. The result of such an expression can always be stored in a single bit. For example:

```
bool permitted=username.isLoggedIn()
          && username.hasPrivilege()
          && system.RemoteAccessAllowed();
```

By contrast, bitwise operators yield a string of bits, typically stored in a variable of type `char`, `unsigned char`, `int`, `long long`, and so on.

Bitwise Operators

The following table lists the bitwise operators.

Operator	Name(s)
~	Bitwise NOT, or one's complement (unary)
&	Bitwise AND
|	Bitwise OR
^	Bitwise XOR (exclusive OR)

Bitwise NOT

The `~` operator flips every bit in a sequence. Applying this operator to the following bit string:

```
0111 1111 //decimal value: 127
```

produces this result:

```
1000 0000 //decimal value 128 (unsigned)
```

Usually, you don't see strings of bits in C++ programs but rather octal, decimal or hexadecimal values stored in `signed` or `unsigned` integral types. The example above would look like this in real code:

```
unsigned char c=127; //binary: 0111 1111
unsigned char flipped= ~c; //0x80, 128 or binary 1000 0000
```

Bit ordering is machine-dependent. Some hardware architectures read bits from right to left. On such machines, the rightmost bit in a sequence is the least significant bit (LSB). Other architectures use the reverse order: i.e., the LSB is the leftmost one. This is the famous little-endian versus big-endian bit ordering. In this section, I chose an order that is similar to the way humans read decimal numbers (say, 124), whereby the least significant digit is on the right. If your hardware architecture uses the reverse-bit ordering, simply read each binary string in the reverse order. Note also that for the sake of readability, I inserted a space between every four binary digits. In addition, I limited the bit strings in the code listings to `char`, although bit strings can be larger than that, of course.

Bitwise AND

The operator & *ands* every bit in a sequence with a corresponding bit of another sequence. For every such pair, the result is 1 if and only if the two bits equal 1. Otherwise, the result is 0. For example, applying & to the following bit strings:

```
0011 1111 //decimal value: 63
0100 0011 //decimal value 67:
```

produces the following result:

```
0000 0011
```

```
unsigned char c1=63; //0x3f, binary: 0011 1111
unsigned char c2=67; //0x43, binary: 0100 0011
unsigned char result=c1&c2; //0x03, binary 0000 0011
```

Bitwise OR

The | operator *ors* every bit in a sequence with a corresponding bit of another sequence. For every such pair, the result is 0 if and only if the two bits are 0. Otherwise, the result is 1.

For example, applying | to the following bit strings:

```
0011 1111 //decimal value: 63
0100 0011 //decimal value 67
```

produces the following result:

```
0111 1111 //decimal value: 127
unsigned char c1=63; //0x3f, binary: 0011 1111
unsigned char c2=67; //0x43, binary: 0100 0011
unsigned char result=c1|c2; // 0x7f, binary 0111 1111
```

Bitwise XOR

The ^ operator *xors* every bit in a sequence with a corresponding bit of another sequence. For every such pair, the result is 1 only if one of the two bits equals 1. Otherwise, the result is 0.

For example, applying operator ^ to the following bit strings:

```
0011 1111 //decimal value: 63
0100 0011 //decimal value 67:
```

produces the following result:

```
0111 1100 //decimal value: 124
unsigned char c1=63; //0x3f, binary: 0011 1111
unsigned char c2=67; //0x43, binary: 0100 0011
unsigned char result=c1^c2; // 0x7c, binary 0111 1100
```

Self-Assignment

Just like the arithmetic self-assignment operators +=, -=, and *=, C++ has self-assigning versions of the binary bitwise operators:

Operator	Name
&=	Self-assigning bitwise AND
|=	Self-assigning bitwise OR
^=	Self-assigning bitwise XOR

Using the ^= operator, the previous code listing can be rewritten like this:

```
unsigned char c1=63; //0x3f, binary: 0011 1111
unsigned char c2=67; //0x43, binary: 0100 0011
c1^=c2; // equivalent to: c1= c1^c2
```

Bit Shifting

C++ has two more bitwise operators: the left-shift and right-shift operators. They look like this:

Operator	Name
<<	Left-shift
>>	Right-shift

Although most programmers nowadays associate these operators with stream I/O, the built-in semantics of these operators has nothing to do with I/O (all the I/O classes that use these operators actually use overloaded versions thereof). A bit-shifting operation is similar to text wrapping in a word processor. When you insert more characters at a line's beginning, the characters at its end are pushed to the right (if you're typing in a language that is written left-to-right, such as English) until they fold onto the next line. Similarly, a right-shift operator shifts bits by *n* positions to the right:

```
0011 1111 //decimal value: 63
```

Shifting it by one position to the right produces the following result:

```
0001 1111 //decimal value: 31
unsigned char c1=63; //0x3f, binary: 0011 1111
unsigned char result=c1>>1; // 0x1f, binary: 0001 1111
```

To illustrate this better, I'll use a pair of bars to mark the imaginary boundaries of the original 8-bit string:

```
|0011 1111|
```

After shifting it, the leftmost bit's position becomes empty (marked by an underscore) whereas the rightmost bit is pushed outside the string's boundaries:

```
|_0011 111|1
```

The second step consists of padding empty positions with zeros and discarding bits pushed outside the string's boundaries (these rules apply to `unsigned` values; the effect of shifting `signed` values is machine-dependent):

```
|00011 111|_
```

These steps are merely didactic; they don't necessarily represent the actual operation of any processor. By the way, bit shifting is one of the most efficient instructions that processors perform. This is why time-critical code fragments use shift operators as a faster alternative to the division and multiplication operators. In the example above, the shift operation has the same effect as dividing the original value by two. The reverse is also true: If you apply the left-shift operator to the number 63, the result will be 126:

```
unsigned char c1=63; //0x3f, binary: 0011 1111
unsigned char result=c1<<1; //  126, 0x73, 0111 1110
```

Self-assignment versions of these operators also exist. The previous code can be rewritten like this:

```
unsigned char c1=63; //0x3f, binary: 0011 1111
c1>>=2; //  15, 0x0f, 0000 1111
```

Summary

Bit savviness is a crucial skill in many nontrivial applications. Unfortunately, debugging bit-oriented code is a daunting task because most debugging tools don't support individual bit inspection and assignment. However, the Standard Library offers a bitset class (see *http://www.sgi.com/tech/stl/bitset.html*) that simplifies certain aspects of bit manipulation and improves its debugging.

Books and Online Books

Stephen Prata's *C++ Primer Plus, Fourth Edition* (Sams, 2001, ISBN 0672322234) discusses bitwise operators briefly. (For more on this book, visit *http://www.informit.com/title/0672322234*.)

Effective STL: 50 Specific Ways To Improve Your Use of the Standard Template Library (Addison-Wesley, 2001, ISBN 0201749629), by Scott Meyers, dedicates a few pages to the so-called "non-container classes" of the Standard Library, including `<bitset>`. By all means, this is an excellent guide for every STL programmer, beginners and pros alike. (For more on this book, visit *http://www.informit.com/bookstore/product.asp?isbn=0201749629*.)

Bitwise Operators, Part II

In a previous section, I introduced the basic concepts of bitwise operators. In this section, I will show how to use this set of built-in operators to manipulate bit strings in a portable and efficient way.

Resetting a Bit String

Think for a moment how many times you need to initialize a certain variable to 0, or reset it to 0 after it has been used. When dealing with bit strings of an arbitrary length, such as pointers, `char`, `short`, `long long`, and bit fields, the simplest and probably the most efficient way to accomplish this task is by XORring a bit string with itself. It doesn't matter what the original value of the bit string is—after XORring it with itself, all the bits therein will have a zero value. Before looking at the first example, allow me to refresh your memory. The built-in bitwise operators of C++ are shown in the following table:

Operator	Name
~	Bitwise NOT, or one's complement (unary)
&	Bitwise AND
|	Bitwise OR
^	Bitwise XOR (exclusive OR)

Suppose you want to write a function template called `reset()` that resets all the bits of its argument to 0. A typical implementation would look like this:

```
template <class T> void reset( T & t)
{
 t^=t;
}
char c=127; //binary: 0111 1111
reset(c); //make it 0000 0000
```

If you're perturbed by this code's performance, remember that such tiny functions are inlined easily. If your compiler needs a hint to get its job done, you can declare the function `inline` explicitly. However, as I explained elsewhere, most compilers nowadays will do "the right thing" automatically.

Setting a Bit String

Setting a bit string is the opposite of resetting it. In other words, this operation turns on every bit. There are several ways to accomplish this task. However, since we already have a function that resets a bit string, let's base our implementation on this function, i.e., apply the ~ operator to the result of `reset()`:

```
template <class T> void set( T & t)
{
 reset(t);
 t=~t;
}
unsigned char s=15; //0000 1111
set(s);
int n=s;// decimal value: 255
```

There is a slightly more efficient way to accomplish this task, namely ORring the argument with a bit string whose bits are all set. The problem is that you need to use multiple constants:

```
const unsigned char C_ALL_1 = 0xff;
const unsigned short S_ALL_1 = 0xffff;
const unsigned int I_ALL_1 = 0xffffffff;
```

And so on. Not only is this approach less portable, it's also more cumbersome and error-prone.

Flipping a Bit String

Flipping a string means reversing the value of each bit thereof. For example, flipping this string:

```
0111 1111
```

produces this result:

```
1000 0000
```

Flipping is widely used in encryption and data compression algorithms. As with the previous two operations, there are several ways to accomplish this task. I'll use the simplest one, namely applying the ~ operator to a bit string. The flip function template looks like this:

```
template <class T> void flip( T & t)
{
 t=~t;
}
unsigned char s=15; //0000 1111
flip(s);
int n=s;// s is now 1111 0000 or decimal 240
```

Examining a Single Bit

Often, you need to check the value of a certain bit in a string. For example, suppose you want to test whether the third bit (from the right) in the following string is on:

```
0011 1100
```

Although you can use bit-shift operators for this purpose, the simplest solution is to AND this bit string with another string that has only its third bit set:

```
0000 0100
```

ANDing the two strings should yield a string of 0's if the third bit in the first string is 0. Otherwise, the result is a nonzero value.

```
const unsigned int FIRST_ON=1;
const unsigned int SECOND_ON=2;
const unsigned int THIRD_ON=4;
const unsigned int FOURTH_ON=8;
//..16, 32, 64, 128 and so on
```

A generic function that tests a specific bit would look like this:

```
template <class T> bool test_n( T & t, int bit_pos)
{
 return t&bit_pos;
}

unsigned char c=15; //0000 1111
bool ison = test_n(t, SECOND_ON); //true
bool ison = test_n(t, FIFTH_ON); //false
```

Summary

The set of four function templates we've defined is ideal for making a bit-manipulation class template, where auxiliary constants such as FIRST_ON, etc., are stored as private constants. When writing such a class, you may need to extend its functionality by adding more member functions. For instance, a member function that locates a sequence of bits within a bit string might be useful in certain applications. Likewise, you could add a function that compresses a large string of bits into a smaller string, a function that fills a bit string with random values, etc.

Who's this?

Many primer books will tell you that the keyword this is "a pointer holding the address of its object." This definition used to be correct until the mid 1990s but it changed later. I will show you what `this` really is, how it affects member functions and data members and discuss its historical ramifications.

Analyze `this`

In order to distinguish between traditional C functions (to which I will refer as "plain old functions" or POF for short) and member functions of a C++ object, C++ creators introduced the notion of `this`, which was at that time a real pointer containing the address of its object. `this` is passed as an implicit argument to every nonstatic member function, thereby enabling it to access its object's data members and member functions directly. Consider the following class:

```
class Point
{
private:
 int _x, _y;
public:
 explicit Point(int x=0, int y=0) : _x(x), _y(y) {}
 void set(int x, int y);
};
```

`Point::set()` assigns new values to the data members x and y:

```
void Point:set(int x, int y);
{
 _x=x;
 _y=y;
}
```

Under the hood, the compiler transforms these assignment expressions into the following:

```
//pseudo C++ code
this->_x=x;
this->_y=y;
```

Some programmers who prefer to be more explicit also use this coding style:

```
//alternative coding style
//perfectly legal though redundant
void Point::set(int x, int y)
{
 this->_x=x;
```

```
    this->_y=y;
}
```

This coding style certainly doesn't harm but it's redundant because the compiler automatically adds `this->` to every nonstatic member accessed inside a member function.

The introduction of `this` had another useful advantage. It ensured a unique signature for member functions bearing the same name of POFs. For example, if your program has the following declarations:

```
void set(int, int); //a global function
class Point
{
  int _x, _y;
public:
  explicit Point(int x=0, int y=0) : _x(x), _y(y) {}
  void set(int x, int y);
};
```

the POF `set()` and `Point::set()` are still unique signatures because the latter actually has three arguments rather than two: two `int`'s declared in its parameter list and an implicit `this` argument. This brings us to another related issue, namely, what exactly is the type of `this`?

More About `this`

As previously noted, `this` was originally a real pointer of type `X * const`, where X is the type of the class in question. In other words, `this` is a `const` pointer to a (non-const) `Point` when used inside a nonstatic member function of `Point`. The compiler conceptually transforms `Point::set()` into the following pseudocode:

```
//pseudo code
void set(Point * const _this, int x, int y); //Point::set
```

whereas the signature of the POF `set()` remains:

```
//pseudo code
void set(int x, int y); //no change
```

Notice that the C++ standard doesn't specify the exact position of `this` in a member function's argument list; some compilers insert it at the beginning while others place it at the end:

```
//pseudo code; alternative parameter ordering
void set(int x, int y, Point * const _this);
```

The introduction of `this` allowed for three more member function flavors, namely `virtual`, `const` and `volatile` member functions. `virtual` member functions are usually implemented by accessing a `vptr`, a pointer to a table of virtual function addresses. The `vptr` itself is stored as an implicit data member in every polymorphic object and is accessed through `this`.

`const` and `volatile` member functions are the more interesting cases. In order to ensure that `const` member functions are called only for `const` objects, C++ passes a different type of `this` to a `const` member function: "const X * const" that is, a `const` pointer to `const` X. Let's look at a concrete example:

```
class Point
{
public:
 int getx() const; //const member function
};
```

The compiler internally transforms the prototype of the `const` member function `getx()` into:

```
//pseudo C++ code
int getx(const Point * const __this);
```

Because the object to which `this` points is `const`, the compiler can detect attempts to modify the state of the object inside `getx()`:

```
int Pointe::getx() const
{
 _x=0; //error, can't modify a member of a const object
 return _x;
}
```

According to the C++ standard, calling a non-`volatile` member function for a `volatile` object is ill-formed. C++ uses a similar technique with `volatile` member functions to trap such ill-formed usage. When you declare a `volatile` member function, it gets an implicit `this` of the following type: `volatile X * const`. That is, a `const` pointer to `volatile` X. For example:

```
class Point
{
public:
```

```
  int gety() volatile; //volatile member function
};
```

The compiler internally transforms the volatile member function gety() into:

```
//pseudo C++ code
int gety(volatile Point * const __this);
```

Because the object *this is volatile, the compiler can detect ill-formed calls:

```
void func(volatile Point & p)
{
 int n= p.getx(); //ill-formed; getx() isn't volatile
 int m=pgety(); //OK
}
```

As you may have already guessed, when a member function is declared const volatile, its this argument is of type const volatile X *const; i.e., a const pointer to const volatile X. The hypothetical signature of such a member function looks like this:

```
//pseudo C++ code
int getx(const volatile Point * const __this);
```

Reanalyze this

As previously said, this used to be a real pointer in pre-standard C++. Consequently, users were allowed to assign to this. This technique was useful in prehistoric times as a means of allocating objects inside the constructor or for the purpose of forgoing a destructor's invocation. Today, assigning to this is a no-no. To disable such hacks, the definition of this was modified about a decade ago. Today, this isn't truly a pointer but rather an "r-value expression that returns the address of its object." In other words, you can think of this as an operator such as sizeof() that by some sort of magic returns the address of its object rather than being a bare pointer. Of course, when used inside a const or volatile member function, the result of a this expression is const/volatile qualified accordingly.

static Member Functions

static member functions were introduced only in cfront 2.0, more than 5 years after the first implementation of C++. Unlike ordinary member functions, `static` member functions don't take an implicit `this` argument. Consequently, they are characterized by the following features:

- They cannot be `virtual`, `const`, or `volatile`.
- They cannot access nonstatic members of their class.
- They can be invoked without an object of their class.

Summary

For most programmers, understanding how exactly C++ represents and enforces the semantics of `virtual`, `const` and `volatile` member functions isn't highly important. After all, that is why we have a high-level programming language and clever compilers! However, a deeper observation of the inner workings of C++ is, from my experience, an excellent way to enhance one's programming skills and produce cleaner, faster and safer code.

Books

The Design and Evolution of C++ (Addison-Wesley, 1994, ISBN 0201543303), by Bjarne Stroustrup, is an exhaustive historical account of the evolution of C++ and the design decisions that its creators made during its standardization process. This book is useful for those of you who wonder why C++ features are implemented the way they are, as well as for compiler writers who want to know the gory details of how high-level C++ features are implemented under the hood. (For more on this book, visit *http://www.informit.com/bookstore/product.asp?isbn=0201543303*.)

A Reference Guide

Unlike most other programming languages, C++ offers an unusual diversity of argument-passing mechanisms: pass by value, pass by address, and pass by reference. Additional nonstandard argument-passing mechanisms are also supported by certain compilers, such as passing arguments on a register. In this section, I will explain the semantics of the three standard argument-passing mechanisms and focus on reference variables.

A Bit of History

Most high-level programming languages offer only a single argument-passing mechanism. In Pascal and Ada, for example, arguments are passed by reference and that's it. In Java, objects are passed by reference whereas fundamental types such as int and boolean are passed by value. The crucial point, however, is that programmers cannot intervene or control the actual argument-passing mechanism that the language applies. C is different in this regard. Built on the foundations of BCPL and B, which were really nothing more than high-level assembly languages, it offered two argument-passing mechanisms: pass by value and pass by address. Oddly, it didn't offer the more common notion of pass by reference.

Pass by value is the default argument-passing mechanism of both C and C++. When a caller passes by value an argument to a function (known as the *callee*), the latter gets a *copy* of the original argument. This copy remains in scope until the function returns and is destroyed immediately afterward. Consequently, a function that takes value arguments cannot change them because the changes will apply only to local copies, not the actual caller's variables. For example:

```
void negate(int n) //buggy version
{
 n=-n;//affects a local copy of n
}
void func()
{
 int m=10;
 negate(m);//doesn't change the value of m
 std::cout<<m<<std::endl; //diplay: 10
}
```

When negate() is called, C++ creates a fresh copy of m on its stack. negate() then modifies this private copy, which is destroyed immediately when it returns. The original variable m remains intact, though. Consequently, the cout expression displays 10 rather than -10. If you want the callee to modify its arguments, you must override the default passing mechanism.

Pass by address. In C, the only way to achieve this is by passing the *argument's address* to the callee. This passing mechanism is traditionally called pass by address (in the literature it's often called *pass by reference* too, although this is a misnomer since C++ uses this term to denote a radically different passing mechanism). For example:

```
void negate(int * pn)
{
 *n=-*n;
}
```

Similarly, the caller must also be adjusted:

```
void func()
{
 int m=10;
 negate(&m);//pass m's address
 std::cout<<m<<std::endl; //diplay: -10
}
```

This is all well and good. The problem with this technique is that it's tedious and error-prone. My impression is, statistically, most C/C++ function calls don't use pass by value, so forcing programmers to override the default passing mechanism using the &, * and -> operators is an example of a bad language design choice. C++ creators were aware of this. They introduced a new type of argument passing, namely *pass by reference*. The addition of reference variables and arguments to C++ was only a means of fixing an historical accident made in C about a decade earlier rather than a genuine innovation. However, the introduction of references did affect fundamental programming idioms in C++.

Most textbooks will tell you that a reference is "an alias for an existing object." For example:

```
int m=0;
int &ref=m;
```

The reference `ref` serves as an alias for the variable m. Thus, any change applied to m is reflected in `ref` and vice versa:

```
++m;
std::cout<<ref<<std::endl;// output 1
++ref; //increment m
std::cout<<m<<std::endl;// output 2
```

In other words, `ref` and m behave as distinct names of the same object. In fact, you can define an infinite number of references to the same object:

```
int & ref2=ref;
int & ref3=m;
//..and so on
```

Here `ref2` and `ref3` are aliases of m, too. Notice that there's no such thing as a "reference to a reference"; the variable `ref2` is an alias of m, not `ref`.

Usage

In most cases, references are used as a means of passing arguments to a function by reference. The nice thing about references is that they function as pointers from a compiler's point of view, although syntactically they behave like ordinary variables. They enable a callee to alter its arguments without forcing programmers to use the unwieldy *, & and -> notation:

```
void negate(int & n)
{
 n=-n;//modifies caller's argument
}
void func()
{
 int m=10;
 negate(m);//pass by reference
 std::cout<<m<<std::endl; //diplay: -10
}
```

Advantages of Pass by Reference

Passing by reference combines the benefits of passing by address and passing by value. It's efficient just like passing by address because the callee doesn't get a copy of the original value but rather an alias thereof (under the hood, all compilers substitute reference arguments with ordinary pointers). In addition, it offers a more intuitive syntax and requires fewer keystrokes from the programmer. Finally, references are usually safer than ordinary pointers because they are always bound to a valid object. C++ doesn't have null references, so you don't need to check whether a reference argument is null before examining its value or assigning to it.

Passing objects by reference is usually more efficient than passing them by value because no large chunks of memory are being copied and constructor and destructor calls are not performed in this case. However, this argument-passing mechanism enables a function to modify its argument even if it's not supposed to. To avert this, declare all read-only parameters as `const` and pass them by reference. This way, the callee will not be able to modify them:

```
void display(const Shape & s)
{
 s.draw();
}
```

Summary

The introduction of references to C++ initially caused confusion, especially among ex-C programmers who weren't sure which passing mechanism to use when (and in those days, virtually all C++ programmers were former C programmers). Even illustrious gurus offered to use the following dichotomy: When a function modifies its arguments, pass them by address, and when it doesn't, pass them as references to `const`. Today, we can all agree that using bare pointers is a thing of the past. In most cases, C++ offers superior alternatives that are both safer and cleaner. Similarly, when you decide how to pass arguments to a function, use references by default (except when you truly need to pass them by value) and avoid passing by address, unless there's a compelling reason to do so. If the function in question shouldn't modify its arguments, they should be declared `const` and passed by reference; the lack of the `const` qualifier indicates that the function is allowed to modify an argument. When should you pass arguments by address? Only when the function deals with real pointers: for instance, a function that allocates raw storage, or when a `NULL` pointer is a valid option. Otherwise, use references.

Books

Real-Time Design Patterns: Robust Scalable Architecture for Real-Time Systems (Addison-Wesley, 2002, ISBN 0201699567), by Bruce Powel Douglass, focuses on a more specialized application domain; namely, real-time and embedded systems. Using state-of-the-art features such as advanced template programming and UML diagrams, it addresses common (and not so-common) programming tasks such as building a message queue, garbage collection, virtual machine, and many other nuts and bolts of any real-time system. (For more on this book, visit *http://www.informit.com/title/0201699567*.)

The Virtues of Multiple Inheritance

It wouldn't be an exaggeration to say that multiple inheritance (MI) has stirred more controversy and heated debates than any other C++ feature. Yet the truth is that MI, not unlike `dynamic_cast`, `auto_ptr` and other constructs, is a powerful and effective feature when used properly. In this section, I will explore its uses and debunk some of the wicked rumors that have surrounded it since its introduction.

TIP: Refer to the "Inheritance" section of "Object Oriented Design".

Rationale

Object-oriented design is meant, among other things, to enable developers to simulate real-world entities and events. The use of inheritance imitates the categorization of objects that belong to a certain semantic field. For example, a table and a chair are subclasses of a more generalized concept called *furniture*. Likewise, a text file, a program file and a database file share some commonality that is expressed by means of deriving them from a common base class. Yet in many cases, a certain object may belong to several categories at once. For example, a fax-modem card is both a fax and a modem. A cellular phone with a digital camera is a symmetric combination of two appliances that can exist independently of one another. This unification process doesn't stop here: A combined scanner, printer and fax machine is in fact three different appliances combined into one. In C++, it's easy to express this relationship by means of MI. For example:

```
class Combined: public Scanner, public Printer, public Fax
{
 //..
};
```

In many other object-oriented programming languages, it's impossible to do this because they support only *single inheritance*, whereby a class can have only one direct base class at a time. Of course, there are various workarounds in these languages but you can't express the unification of functionality so elegantly.

MI and the Deadly Diamond of Derivation

If all is so neat and dandy, why are other programming languages so wary of MI? The problem is that reckless usage of MI could lead to a problem known as the Deadly Diamond of Derivation (DDD). In the previous example, we didn't check how classes `Scanner`, `Printer` and `Fax` were implemented. What if two of them or more are derived from the same base class?

```
class USB_Device
{
public:
 virtual int transmit(int bytes, char * buff);
 virtual int receive(int bytes, char * buff);
private:
 vector <char> buff;
```

```
//..
};
class Scanner: public USB_Device
{/*..*/};
class Printer: public USB_Device
{/*..*/};
```

In this case, class `Combined` will have two different `USB_Device` subobjects, each of which is inherited from a different direct base class. Not only is this inefficient but it also causes ambiguity. If you want to use polymorphism by means of assigning `USB_Device *` to `Combined`, you're in trouble:

```
USB_Device *pdev= new Combined; //compilation error:
                        //'base class "USB_Device" is ambiguous'
```

This problem of having multiple copies of a base class within a multiply inherited object is called the DDD. The solution, however, is simple. To ensure that only a single copy of a base class exists in the entire derivation lattice, use *virtual inheritance*:

```
class Scanner: virtual public USB_Device
{};
class Printer: virtual public USB_Device
{};
class Combined: public Scanner, public Printer, public Fax
{};
USB_Device *pdev= new Combined; //now OK
```

Because `Scanner` and `Printer` are virtually derived from `USB_Device`, C++ ensures that only a single instance of the subobject `USB_Device` exists in the derivation chain, regardless of the number of intermediate base classes stacked between these classes and `Combined`.

Tackling the Ambiguity Problem

This is all well and good except that the designer of class `Combined` may not have access to the source files of the base classes. If for instance classes `Printer` and `Scanner` happen to be included in a third-party code library and they are derived from `USB_Device` using nonvirtual inheritance, the designer of `Combined` can't retrofit the inheritance model later—using both `Printer` and `Scanner` as direct base classes of `Combined` will incur the onerous DDD. Notice that applying virtual inheritance later won't work:

```cpp
class Combined: virtual public Scanner,
                virtual public Printer, //too late to use VI
                public Fax
{};
USB_Device *pdev= new Combined; //once again, an error:
                                //'base class "USB_Device" is ambiguous'
```

At this point you're probably wondering why virtual inheritance isn't the default if it averts the DDD so easily. Indeed, in certain programming languages, MI is `virtual` by default. Alas, there *are* cases in which you truly want to have multiple instances of the base class in a derived object. For example:

```cpp
class Scrollbar
{
private:
   int x; int y;
public:
   void Scroll(units n);
   //...
};
class HorizontalScrollbar : public Scrollbar
{};
class VerticalScrollbar : public Scrollbar
{};

class MultiScrollWindow: public VerticalScrollbar,
public HorizontalScrollbar {};

MultiScrollWindow msw;
msw.HorizontalScrollbar::Scroll(5);   // scroll left
msw.VerticalScrollbar::Scroll(12);    //...and up
```

Here, the problem of ambiguity is solved by using the *qualified name* of the member function `Scroll()`, thereby controlling which of the two toolbars is activated.

Virtual Inheritance and Performance

C++ doesn't specify how virtual base classes are stored in a derived object. It only requires that there shall be a single subobject of a virtually inherited base class in a derived object. Most implementations guarantee this by using pointers that refer to a single shared object. This implementation detail is user-transparent of course. However, it might affect performance in certain subtle ways. For example, compilers often need to define a complex data structure to represent a pointer to a member when the class in question has virtual base classes. Likewise, accessing a member of a virtual base class might require an additional level of indirection. Finally, when operator `dynamic_cast` is applied to such an object, its execution time might take longer.

Summary

One of the most impressive examples of MI's power is the Standard Library's `<iostream>`, `<sstream>` and `<fstream>` classes, all of which symmetrically combine input and output into a single class using MI. Some of the classic Design Patterns (e.g., Observer and Bridge) use MI as well. This only goes to show that MI is an indispensable feature that makes C++ such a powerful language when used by skilled programmers.

Books

Design Patterns: Elements of Reusable Object-Oriented Software (Addison-Wesley, 1994, ISBN 0201633612), by Erich Gamma et al., has been the ultimate pattern catalog ever since it was published in 1994. The code examples of patterns such as Bridge, Observer, and other patterns use MI. (For more on this book, visit *http://www.informit.com/bookstore/product.asp?isbn=0201633612*.)

Interfaces

Multiple inheritance (MI) in C++ has two flavors, namely *interface inheritance* and *implementation inheritance*. In this section, I will explain the notion of interfaces and present the syntactic cues that distinguish between them and concrete classes.

Interfaces Explained

A class's interface consists of its public members. Usually, these would be member functions, although in certain rare cases, local datatypes and even data members may also be included. By contrast, the non-public members of a class are said to be its *implementation*. For example:

```
class Date
{
public: //Date's interface appears in bold
```

```
  Date();
  int getCurrentDate(string & datestr) const;
  Date operator +(const Date & d) const;
private: //Date's implementation
  int day, month, year;
  bool daylight_saving;
};
```

Although `Date` has an interface, the class itself is not an interface because it contains non-public members. By contrast, the following class is an interface:

```
class File
{
public:
  explicit File(const string& name, int mode=0x666);
  virtual int Open();
  virtual int Close();
  virtual ~File();
};
```

Notice that every member function in `File` is both public and virtual (except for the constructor of course). These syntactic cues suggest that `File` should serve only as a base for other, more specialized classes. Certain frameworks mark this attribute explicitly by using the keyword `struct` instead of `class`. As you already know, the only difference between the two in C++ is that `struct` has public access by default whereas `class` entails private access. Therefore, the previous example could be rewritten like this:

```
struct File //explicitly indicates that this is an interface
{
  explicit File(const string& name, int mode=0x666);
  virtual int Open();
  virtual int Close();
  virtual ~File();
};
```

Another characteristic of interfaces is that they merely declare member functions; the classes derived from them should define, or implement these functions. The use of virtual member functions isn't sufficient for this purpose because a derived class isn't *forced* to override any of the base class's member functions. Furthermore, the author of class `File` must provide a default implementation for its members anyway, or else the linker will complain. Fortunately, there's a better way to achieve this goal.

Abstract Classes

Unlike an ordinary virtual function, a pure virtual function doesn't have to be defined. It can be declared in the class body without an implementation. C++ uses a special syntactic form to mark pure virtual functions by adding the *pure specifier* =0; to a declaration of such a function. For example:

```
struct File
{
 explicit File(const string& name, int mode=0x666);
 virtual int Open()=0; //pure virtual
 virtual int Close()=0; //ditto
 virtual ~File()=0; //a dtor may be pure virtual too
};
```

A class that has at least one pure virtual function is called an *abstract class*. An abstract class is more or less synonymous with our notion of an interface.

At last, we've turned `File` into a proper interface. Notice that the use of the pure specifier ensures two important things. First, it guarantees that users cannot instantiate an object of an abstract class:

```
File file("data.txt"); //compilation error: File is an abstract class
```

However, you can define pointers and references to an abstract class to achieve polymorphic behavior:

```
File *pfile; //OK, pfile should point to a derived object
void func(File &ref);
```

C++ ensures that classes derived from an abstract class also obey this rule—you can instantiate objects of a class derived from an abstract class only if it implements *all* the pure virtual functions it inherited from the base class(es).

Combining Multiple Interfaces

You can combine several interfaces in a single concrete class. For example, suppose you want to define a class that represents a file stored on removable media. You can combine two interfaces like this:

```
//an interface the represents an abstract removable device
struct RemovableMedia
{
 virtual int Explore()=0; //view contents
```

```
    virtual int Save(const string& file)=0;
    virtual size_t Retrieve(const string& file, void* buf)=0;
};
//public inheritance implied from 'struct':
class RemovableFile: RemovableMedia, File
{
//...implement all the pure virtual member functions
};
```

You can combine more interfaces to create a more specialized object:

```
class RemovableFile: RemovableMedia,
                     File,
                     Encrypted
{
//...implement all the pure virtual member functions
};
```

Remember that the interfaces are all publicly inherited because of the `struct` keyword. However, if you want to be more explicit about this (and to be on the safe side, should the interfaces' author decide to use `class` instead of `struct`), you can use the `public` keyword:

```
class RemovableFile: public RemovableMedia,
                     public File,
                     public Encrypted
{
 //...implementation
};
```

The DDD Strikes Again

The fact that interfaces don't have data members still doesn't prevent ambiguities. If for example one of the interfaces is inherited multiple times throughout the derivation lattice, you're in trouble:

```
class TextFile: public File, public Encrypted
{};
class NetworkFile: public File, public Encrypted
{};
class DataFile: public TextFile, public NetworkFile //DDD!
{};
File *pf = new DataFile;//error; ambiguous base class
```

DataFile happens to have two copies of File and Encrypted. To avoid this, use virtual inheritance:

```
class TextFile: public virtual File,
                public virtual Encrypted
{};
class NetworkFile: public virtual File,
                   public virtual Encrypted
{};
class DataFile: public virtual TextFile,
                public virtual NetworkFile //now fine
{};
```

Pure Virtual Functions—Final Refinements

Generally speaking, a pure virtual function needn't be implemented in an abstract class nor should it be. However, in one special case, namely a pure virtual destructor, it *must* have an implementation. The reason is that a destructor of a derived object automatically invokes its base class's destructor, recursively. Eventually, the abstract class's destructor is called too. If it has no implementation, you'll get a runtime crash. Therefore, it's important to provide a definition for every pure virtual destructor:

```
struct File
{
 explicit File(const string& name, int mode=0x666);
 virtual int Open()=0;
 virtual int Close()=0;
 virtual ~File()=0; //must have a definition
};
File::~File() {} //dummy implementation
```

In all other cases, defining a pure virtual function is optional (and rather unusual!).

Summary

The use of pure virtual functions enables you to specify only an interface, without an implementation. As a rule of thumb, an interface class should be compact, containing no more than five pure virtual functions. This way, you can define multiple specialized interfaces that a derived class can combine as needed. Lumping dozens of pure virtual functions in a single fat interface is a design mistake because derived classes will be forced to implement all of these functions, even if they intend to use only a small portion of them.

Multiple Inheritance—Construction and Destruction Order

The use of MI, either in the form of implementation inheritance or interfaces, may affect the semantics and behavior of your programs in certain subtle ways. In this section, I will show how MI and virtual inheritance affect the order of objects' construction and destruction.

Construction and Destruction of Non-Virtual Bases

When dealing with a single inheritance model, the order of construction is rather straightforward: A base class's constructor executes first. After its completion, the constructor of a derived class runs. This process is recursive. Therefore, if we have a class hierarchy such as the following:

```
class Base
{
public
 Base();
};
class Derived :public Base
{
 public Derived();
};
class Derived2: public Derived
{
public:
 Derived2();
};
Derived2 d2;
```

the construction order of d2 is as follows: `Base -> Derived -> Derived2`. In other words, the most derived object's constructor is the last to be invoked. What happens when a class has multiple base classes? In this case, the same rule applies as well. However, this time base classes are initialized in a depth-first left-to-right order of appearance in the *base specifier list*. For example:

```cpp
struct A
{
 int n;
 A(){ cout<<"A()\n"; }
 ~A() {cout<<"~A()\n";}
};
struct B
{
 int m;
 B() {cout<<"B()\n";}
 ~B() {cout<<"~B()\n";}
};
struct D:
 public A, public B // base specifier list
{
 int x;
 D() {cout<<"D()\n";}
 ~ D() {cout<<"~D()\n";}
};
struct D2: public D
{
int y;
D2() {cout<<"D2()\n";}
~D2() {cout<<"~D2()\n";}
};

D d;
D2 d2;
```

When d is constructed, the order of construction is as follows:

1. A
2. B
3. D

because A appears before B in the base specifier list of D. Here's the output of d's construction:

```
A()
B()
D()
```

Similarly, when d2 is constructed, the order of construction is as follows:

1. A
2. B
3. D
4. D2

because A and B are considered "deeper" base classes than D—they appear on the base specifier list D, which is itself a base class of D2. This is the output of d2's construction order:

```
A()
B()
D()
D2()
```

When d2 is destroyed, the destructors are called in the following order:

1. D2
2. D
3. B
4. A

Notice that the order of destruction is always the opposite of the construction order:

```
A()
B()
D()
D2()
~D2()
~D()
~B()
~A()
```

If you change the base specifier of D to the following:

```
struct D:
 public B, public A
{int x;};
```

the construction order of d2 would change accordingly to this:

1. B
2. A

3. D
   4. D2

as would the destruction order:

```
B()
A()
D()
D2()
~D2()
~D()
~A()
~B()
```

Construction and Destruction of Virtual Inheritance

When virtual inheritance (VI) is used, things become slightly more complicated. Remember that the raison d'etre of VI is to ensure that a single subobject of a virtual base class is present in the entire derivation lattice. Most compilers use some form of indirection, namely storing a pointer to the virtual base subobject, to ensure this. To guarantee that all handles or pointers indeed point to the same virtual subobject, it must be constructed before any non-virtual base classes listed on the same base specifier list. In other words, the same ordering rules that I presented in the previous section still apply except that in the presence of VI, virtual bases have a higher precedence. For example, if you change the base specifier list of D to:

```
struct D:
 public A, virtual public B //deepest base specifier list
{};
struct D2:   public D {}; /second base specifier list
D2 d2
```

the construction order of d2 will now become this:

   1. B
   2. A
   3. D
   4. D2

This is because the construction algorithm now works as follows:

1. Construct the virtual bases using the previous depth-first left-to-right order of appearance. Since there's only one virtual base B, it's constructed first.
2. Construct the non-virtual bases according to the depth-first left-to-right order of appearance. The deepest base specifier list contains A. Consequently, it's constructed next.
3. Apply the same rule on the next depth level. Consequently, D is constructed.
4. Finally, D2's constructor is called.

The destruction order, as always, is the opposite of the construction order. Therefore, B's destructor will be the last to run. Here's the complete call chain of d2's base construction and destruction:

```
B()
A()
D()
D2()
~D2()
~D()
~A()
~B()
```

What happens if D becomes a virtual base class as well?

```
struct D:
 public A, virtual public B //deepest base specifier list
{};
struct D2:   virtual public D {};
D2 d2
```

First, locate the virtual bases. This time we have B and D. Because B appears in a deeper base specifier list, it's constructed first. D should be constructed next because it's also a virtual base. However, because it has the two base classes A and B, A is constructed next (you can't construct an object without constructing its base classes and embedded objects first). Once all the base classes of D have been constructed, D's construction takes place. The construction list now becomes this:

1. B
2. A
3. D

Finally, the constructor of the most derived object, D2, is called. The result, amazing as it may seem, is the same as before.

Making B a non-virtual base would change the construction order into the following:

1. A
2. B
3. D
4. D2

This is because A and B must be constructed before D.

Summary

The seemingly complicated rules of construction order in the presence of MI aren't truly so unintuitive if you remember the following principles: Virtual bases have the highest precedence. Depth comes next and then the order of appearance—leftmost bases are constructed first. These rules aren't a C++ specific whim; in fact every programming language that supports multiple interface inheritance uses more or less the same rules.

`typedef` Declarations

A `typedef` declaration introduces a synonym for an existing datatype. Such declarations have several uses in C++: improving code readability, hiding cumbersome syntax and defining portable datatypes. I will show how to use `typedef` for all these purposed while avoiding two common pitfalls.

`typedef` Basics

A `typedef` declaration contains the `typedef` keyword followed by a *typedef name* in the position of a variable's name, and the *actual type* for which the `typedef` name serves as a synonym. For example:

```
typedef int length;
```

This declaration defines `length` as a synonym for type `int`. A `typedef` declaration doesn't create a new type; it simply defines a synonym for an existing type. You can use a `typedef` in any context that requires the actual type:

```
void allocate(length * psz);
length array[4];
length file_size = file.getlength();
std::vector<length> sizes;
```

A `typedef` can also serve as a shorthand for *compound types*, e.g., pointers and arrays. For example, instead of repeatedly declaring an array of 81 characters like this:

```
char answer[81];
char text[81];
...
```

use a `typedef`:

```
typedef char Line[81];
Line answer, text; //create 2 arrays of 81 chars each
getline(text);
...
```

If you want to avoid the intricacies of pointer syntax, a `typedef` can also prove useful:

```
typedef char * pstr;
int mystrcmp(pstr, pstr);
```

This brings us to the first `typedef` pitfall. The Standard Library's `strcmp()` takes two `const char *` arguments. Therefore, it might seem reasonable at first to declare `mystrcmp()` like this:

```
int mystrcmp(const pstr, const pstr); //wrong!
```

This is an error, though. The sequence `const pstr` actually means `char * const` (a `const` pointer to `char`); not `const char *` (a pointer to `const char`). Fortunately, the solution is almost trivial—use another `typedef`:

```
typedef const char * cpstr;
int mystrcmp(cpstr, cpstr); //now correct
```

TIP: Refer to "const declarations" section, p. 271, to learn more about `const` declarations.

Remember: When you declare a `typedef` for a pointer, adding `const` to it makes the pointer itself `const`, not the object.

Curbing Convoluted Code

As useful as they are, all of the `typedef`s we've seen so far aren't much different from `#define` macros. "So what's the big deal about `typedef`s?" you're probably asking. Unlike macros, `typedef`s are interpreted at compile-time, thereby enabling the compiler to cope with textual substitutions that are beyond the preprocessor's capabilities. Look at the following declaration as an example:

```
typedef int (*PF) (const char *, const char *);
```

`PF` is a synonym for "pointer to function taking two `const char *` arguments and returning `int`." Now look at the following function prototype:

```
PF Register(PF pf);
```

The function `Register()` takes a callback function of type `PF` and returns the address of a function with a similar signature that was previously registered. Can you imagine how the following function declaration would look without the use of `PF`? Here's the answer:

```
int (*Register (int (*pf)(const char *, const char *)))
(const char *, const char *);
```

Even experienced programmers would have a hard time figuring out what this declaration means. Needless to say, this convoluted code is also a recipe for mistakes resulting from typos or misunderstanding. Clearly, the use of a `typedef` in this case isn't just a matter of convenience but a must.

Storage Class Specifiers

Believe it or not, `typedef` is a *storage class specifier*, just like `auto`, `extern`, `mutable`, `static` and `register`. This doesn't mean that `typedef` actually affects the storage type of an object; it only means that *syntactically*, `typedef` declarations look like declarations of `static`, `extern`, etc., declarations. This peculiarity is the cause of another pitfall. Consider the following `typedef` declaration:

```
typedef register int LOOP_COUNTER; //compilation error
```

It won't compile because you can't have multiple storage class specifiers in one declaration. Because `typedef` already occupies the position of a storage class specifier, you can't use `register` (or any other storage class specifier) in a `typedef` declaration.

Facilitating Code Portability

`typedefs` have another useful application, namely defining portable datatypes. For example, you can define an abstract floating-point type REAL that has the highest precision available on the target machine:

```
typedef long double REAL;
```

On machines that don't support `long double`, this `typedef` becomes:

```
typedef double REAL;
```

And on embedded machines that don't support `double` either:

```
typedef float REAL;
```

REAL enables you to compile the same program on different target machines without changing the source file. The only thing that will change is the `typedef` itself. Even this tiny change will be totally automatic thanks to conditional compilation. The Standard Library uses `typedefs` extensively to create such platform-independent types: `size_t`, `ptrdiff_t` and `fpos_t` are a few examples. Likewise, `std::string` and `std::ofstream` are in fact `typedef` names that conceal the long and nearly unintelligible template specializations `basic_string<char, char_traits<char>, allocator<char> >` and `basic_ofstream<char, char_traits<char> >`, respectively.

Summary

`typedefs`, as we have seen, can simplify coding and improve readability. Yet programmers might misuse them by declaring unnecessary `typedefs` that have no real purpose. A good example of such misuse is a C-style `struct` declaration like the following:

```
typedef struct {} S; //never really needed in C++
```

In the olden days, C programmers would use this idiom to avoid repeating `struct` in every declaration that uses S. However, in C++ it's never needed since user-defined types are treated as built-in types:

```
struct A{};
func(S & s);
S s1;
```

State of the `union`

Unions are one of the C relics that C++ has retained; on the one hand, they are an example of the intrusive, highly implementation-dependent programming style that is the anathema of object-oriented programming. Yet even in C++ programs they can have certain useful applications, as I will show you in the following passages.

What's in a `union`?

In the olden days, when memory was scarce and static type-checking was often overlooked ("we're serious programmers and we know what we are doing!"), programming languages such as FORTRAN, PL/1 and C offered a means of storing multiple objects on the same chunk of memory. Of course, one could only use a single object at a time but this technique could save memory because the decision as to which object was needed was often delayed to runtime, whereas the objects themselves needed to be declared at compile-time. Think for example of a database query that retrieves an employee's record. The record in question can be retrieved using various criteria: the employee's name, his or her ID, telephone number and so on. Obviously, you don't need all of these keys at once, but you can't decide at compile-time which one the user will decide to use when querying the database. To solve this problem, it was customary to pack all the keys within a single data structure called a `union`:

```
union Key
{
 int ID;
 char * name;
 char phone[8];
};
```

The size of a union is sufficient to contain the largest of its data members. In the case of `Key`, it's typically eight bytes—the size of `phone`. By contrast, a `struct` containing the same data members occupies the cumulative size of its members, i.e.,

```
sizeof(ID) + sizeof(name) + sizeof (phone)
```

which is 16 bytes on most 32-bit systems (with the possible addition of padding bytes). This savings might not impress you but in those days, when a system's RAM consisted of a few kilobytes, every byte counted, especially when the program used arrays of unions. A typical program for accessing a database would determine the actual key at runtime using a type-encoding enumeration:

```
/*C style example of using type-coding enum + union*/
enum KeyType
{
 by_id,
 by_name,
 by_phone
};
```

Accessing a union's member is similar to accessing a member of a struct or a class. The crucial difference is that while objects and `structs` store each data member on a distinct memory address, all members of a union are stored on the same address. Therefore, the programmer must be careful to access the correct member:

```
Employee * retrieve(union Key * thekey, enum KeyType type)
{
 switch (type)
 {
 case of by_id:
  access_by_id(thekey.id);
 break;
 case of by_name:
  access_by_name(thekey.name);
 break;
//..
 }
}
```

This programming style has gone out of favor with the advent of object-oriented programming. Not only does it rely heavily on implementation details, it's also error-prone. If the user accesses the wrong data member of the union, the results will be meaningless, just like accessing a random piece of memory. Yet this dangerous characteristic was also an advantage in some systems that didn't support typecasting.

union-Based Typecasting

In C++, operator `reinterpret_cast` performs low-level typecasting between pointers and references that preserves the original binary layout of the source data. For example, in order to examine the bytes of an `int`, you could do something like this:

```
int num=2000;
unsigned char * p = reinterpret_cast<unsigned char *> (&num);
for (int i=0; i<sizeof (num); i++)
//display the decimal value of every byte of num
 cout<<"byte "<<i<<": " << (int) p[i] <<endl;
```

Before the days of `reinterpret_cast`, programmers would use a `union` to achieve the same effect:

```
union Cast
{
int n;
char str[sizeof (n) ];
};
Cast c=2000;
for (int i=0; i<sizeof (int); i++)
 printf("%d\n", c.str[i]);
```

Anonymous Unions

C++ introduced a special `union` type called an *anonymous union*. Unlike an ordinary union, it has neither a tag name nor a named instance. As such, it's mostly used as a data member of a class. For example:

```
class Employee
{
private:
 union   //anonymous
 {
 int key_ID;
 char * key_name;
 charkey_phone[8];
 };
 double salary;
 string name;
 int rank;
//...
public:
Employee();
};
```

The advantage of using an anonymous union is that you access its members directly, as if they were ordinary data members of the class:

```
Employee::Employee() : key_ID(0),//member of an anon. union
salary(0.0), rank(0) //ordinary data members
{}
```

Anonymous unions aren't confined to classes; you can declare an anonymous `union` in a file scope or a namespace scope. In these cases, however, it must be declared `static` and its members have internal linkage:

TIP: Read the section "Linkage types" in "Memory Management."

```
static union //declared globally, has internal linkage
{
 int x;
 void *y;
};
namespace NS
{
 static union //a namespace's scope, has internal linkage
 {
  int w;
  char s[4];
 };
}
int main()
{
x=0;
NS::s[0]='a';
}
```

A union Facelift

C++ introduced another enhancement, namely the ability to declare member functions in a `union`, including constructors, destructors, etc. Note, however, that virtual member functions (including a virtual destructor) are not allowed:

```
union Key
{
private:
 int ID;
 char * name;
 char phone[8];
```

```
public:
//ctor, dtor, copy ctor and assignment op
 Key::Key();
 ~Key();
 Key(const Key & ref);
 Key& operator=(const Key & ref);
//ordinary member functions are also allowed
 int Assign(int n)
 {
   ID=n;
 }
};
```

That said, a `union` shall not be a base class nor can it be derived from another class. Note also that only ordinary unions can contain member functions; anonymous unions can't have member functions of any kind, nor can they contain `static`, `private`, and `protected` data members.

Summary

In high-level applications, unions have limited usage nowadays, if any. Yet it's important to know how to use them because they are still widely used in legacy code and in low-level APIs. C++ creators attempted to upgrade unions into an object-oriented entity by adding the ability to declare member functions and private and protected data members in a union. An anonymous union is a special type of a union that has no tag name or instance name.

dynamic_cast Uses

Unlike other cast operators, which coerce an object to a target type at compile-time, operator `dynamic_cast` operates at runtime. In this section, I will show some of the uses of `dynamic_cast` and discuss its raison d'être.

Limitations of Static Typecasting

Seemingly, a dynamic typecasting operation can be avoided in applications that adhere to common object-oriented design principles. For example, instead of manually casting an object to a derived type, you can use virtual member functions. However, in certain frameworks where all classes are derived from a common base class, relying on inheritance and virtual member functions isn't enough. After all, a class that represents a file has very little in common with a class called `CMutex`, although both are derived from `CObject`. The following snippet in pseudocode demonstrates this problem:

```
void display(CObject & r)
{
 //need to know more about the dynamic type of r
 if(r has a member function called Show())
  r.show();
 else (if r isn't a GUI object)
  handle_differently(r);
}
```

To understand the main difference between `static_cast` and `dynamic_cast`, it's important to distinguish between an object's *static type* and its *dynamic type*. The static type is determined at compile-time and is specified in the declaration. For example, `ptr`'s static type is "`Cobject *`". By contrast, the dynamic type refers to the actual type to which `ptr` is pointing at runtime. This can be identical to its static type or it could be any type of class derived from `CObject`, such as "`CWnd *`", "`CMutex *`" and so on.

Before the advent of `dynamic_cast`, programmers resorted to an inherently dangerous operation called a *downcast*:

```
void f(CObjects * ptr)
{
//there's no guarantee that the cast will succeed;
//the results depend on the dynamic type of ptr
CWnd * p = static_cast<CWnd *> (ptr); //downcast
p->Show();
}
```

Static downcasts are inherently dangerous because the dynamic type of `ptr` can only be determined at runtime. If indeed `ptr` points to a `CWnd` object, the downcast would succeed; if, however, `ptr` happens to be a different kind of beast, all hell breaks loose and the program might as well crash.

The emergence of frameworks such as MFC in the early 1990s put tremendous pressure on C++ creators to devise a safer mechanism for downcasts. The result was operator `dynamic_cast`. `dynamic_cast` reports a failure and let the program handle it in an orderly fashion.

`dynamic_cast` comes in two flavors: a reference cast and a pointer cast. In both cases, it attempts to cast the operand to a target type using the operand's runtime type information. Let's look at a pointer cast example first.

Pointer Cast

`dynamic_cast` explicitly indicates a failure by returning a null pointer. Thus, if the result of a `dynamic_cast` expression isn't null, you can safely assume that the cast was successful and use p as a valid CWnd*:

```
void f(CObjects * ptr)
{
 CWnd * p = dynamic_cast<CWnd *> (ptr); //safe downcast
 if (p==0)
  //handle failure in an orderly fashion
 else //success, use p safely
}
```

`dynamic_cast` can only be used with polymorphic objects. This is because the compiler generates the necessary runtime type information only for objects that have one or more virtual functions. For this reason, the following code won't compile:

```
struct A//not polymorphic
{
 ~A(){}
};
struct B: A
{};
int main()
{
 A * p = new B;
 B * p2 = dynamic_cast<B* > (p);//error, A isn't polymorphic
}
```

If you make A's destructor virtual, the code will blissfully compile and run:

```
virtual ~A(){}  //make A polymorphic
```

Reference Cast

The reference version of `dynamic_cast` takes an object or a reference as an argument and casts it to a reference to T, where T is the target type:

```
void func(A& ref)
{
```

```
  B b = dynamic_cast<B & > (ref); //reference cast
}
```

Seemingly, this version is cleaner than the pointer cast notation as it avoids the hassles of `*`, `->`, and other pointer syntax idiosyncrasies. Unfortunately, this impression is misleading. Because C++ has no null references, a reference `dynamic_cast` has no way of reporting a failure. Therefore, it throws an exception of type `std::bad_cast` (declared in `<typeinfo>`) upon failure. This means that a properly written C++ app must wrap every reference `dynamic_cast` in a `try` block and provide a matching handler for the potential `std::bad_cast` exception:

```
#include <typeinfo>
#include <iostream>
void func(A& ref)
{
 try
 {
  B b = dynamic_cast<B & > (ref); //reference cast
 }
 catch(std::bad_cast & b)
 {
  std::cerr<<"can't cast ref to B&";
 }
}
```

If this seems like too much trouble for a simple `dynamic_cast` expression, my advice is to stick to the pointer cast notation.

Crosscasts

The predominant use of `dynamic_cast` in its early days was downcasts. However, the introduction of multiple inheritance made it useful for another type of cast: a *crosscast*. A crosscast converts a multiply inherited object into one of its secondary base classes. To demonstrate what a crosscast does, let's look at a concrete example:

```
struct A
{
 int i;
 virtual ~A () {}
};
```

```cpp
struct B
{
 bool b;
};

struct D: public A, public B
{
 int k;
 D() { b = true; i = k = 0; }
};
int main()
{
 A *pa = new D;
 B *pb = dynamic_cast<B*> (pa);   //crosscast; convert to the second base class
 std::cout<< "the address of pa is: " <<pa <<std::endl;
 std::cout<< "the address of pb is: " <<pb <<std::endl;
}
```

The static type of pa is A *, whereas its dynamic type is D *. static_cast cannot convert one to the other because A and B are unrelated. To perform a crosscast properly, the address of the subobject B within the complete D object has to be calculated at runtime. After all, the crosscast operation may take place in a source file that doesn't even know that class D exists! Needless to say, the classes involved must be polymorphic. The resulting pointer pb and the original pointer pa contain different memory addresses after the crosscast operation:

```
the address of pa is: 00873234:
the address of pb is: 0087323C
```

Summary

C++ encourages the use of static type checking; any checks that can be made at compile-time should not be postponed to runtime. This design decision ensures faster execution time and, typically, smaller executable files. However, in certain cases, as we have seen, the use of dynamic type checking is unavoidable. As a rule, if you find yourself using dynamic_cast extensively, you should review your design. Not only does the use of dynamic_cast incur performance overhead, it also compromises code reuse and future maintenance due to the reliance on specific types.

Books

The ACE Programmer's Guide: Practical Design Patterns for Network and Systems Programming (Addison-Wesley, 2003, ISBN 0201699710), by Stephen D. Huston et al., is a definite guide to the ACE framework. (For more on this book, visit *http://www.informit.com/bookstore/product.asp?isbn=0201699710*.) Personally, I find ACE to be an excellent example of strengths of C++: a cross-platform, reusable, extensible and efficient framework that runs "on more platforms than Java." I think I saw this quote on Bjarne Stroustrup's web site (*http://www.research.att.com/~bs/*) some time ago.

Integrating C and C++

Accessing C code from a C++ program is usually a trivial task. The opposite, however, isn't quite so. I will show how to overcome some of the obstacles when you need to integrate C++ code into a C program, both at the source file level and at the binary file level. Along the way, you will learn about the amazing world of ABIs, linkage, and name decoration.

Does C Still Matter?

From a C++ programmer's point of view, accessing C code is rarely a problem. In fact, you do this more often than you think: on many implementations every invocation of new, for example, eventually invokes C's `malloc()`. However, problems start when you try to access C++ code from a C program. Contrary to common belief, this situation isn't so rare even today. C is still the most widely used programming language in certain application domains, such as system programming and embedded systems. In the embedded systems' world, a rudimentary command-line C compiler that supports a portion of ISO C core language is often the only game in town. So, what do you do when you have to access C++ code from C?

Understanding ABI

An Application Binary Interface (ABI) specifies the binary representation of a programming language's entities, including *decorated names* of identifiers (which I will explain shortly) as well as memory layout, alignment and so on.
When you write code in a high-level language such as C++, the compiler translates your source files into binary object files. In these files, source file

constructs such as classes, objects, namespaces, overloaded operators, templates and many other goodies turn into entirely different beasts. For example, overloaded operators, member functions and function templates become ordinary `extern` functions with decorated names which are compiler-generated strings that encode all that a compiler and a linker need to know about the original identifier (function, variable, type, etc.). Take for example the following class and its member functions:

```
class Task
{
public:
 Task();
 int suspend();
 int resume();
 int run();
 int run(int priority, int cpu_timelimit);
 int get_id() const;
 virtual ~Task();
};
```

The compiler generates distinct decorated names for every member function of this class in a process called *name decoration*, or *name mangling*. The decorated name of a function encodes its parameter list, including the parameters cv-qualification, their order and their passing mechanism. Additionally, it encodes whether it's a class member or an `extern` function, whether the function is static or virtual, its cv-qualification, its enclosing namespace(s) (if there are several `Task` classes defined in different namespaces, their member functions will still have distinct decorated names) and its return type. All this information is packed into a compact set of alphanumeric symbols concatenated into a long, cryptic and unique name. Thanks to name decoration, C++ allows an `extern` function called `get_id()`, a member function called `Task::get_id()`, another member function called `Person::get_id()` and a function template called `get_id<>()` to live peacefully inside the same program in spite of their identical names. Consequently, the compiler knows that when you call:

```
Person p;
int n=p.get_id(0); //error, no arguments expected
```

the relevant function is `Person::get_id()`, that the argument 0 isn't allowed here and that it's an appropriate initializer for n.

Each compiler defines its own ABI. Thus, different compilers generate different decorated names for the same identifier. Under some conditions (e.g., when using two different versions of the same compiler), the same compiler might produce different decorated names for the same identifier.

Problems of Compiler-Specific ABIs

What are the implications of this? For starters, linking object files that were produced by different compilers is impossible. Secondly, because C compilers know very little about C++ name decoration and because C and C++ employ different ABIs, C programs can't access a function compiled by a C++ compiler unless you explicitly disable C++ name decoration. This brings us to a related concept known as *linkage*. When an identifier is said to have C++ *linkage*, it means that its decorated name is generated according to the C++ name decoration rules (linkage in this context doesn't refer to the process of linking object files produce an executable; it simply means an ABI). This is the default linkage of identifiers in C++. You can override it in some cases. For example, if you want to access a global function from a C source file, you must declare it extern "C" in the C++ source file, so that a C++ compiler will apply the C name decoration scheme. This way, a C compiler (and often compilers of Pascal, Fortran, COBOL, etc.) can call this function even if it's compiled by a C++ compiler. Notice that what matters here is which compiler actually *compiles* the source file, not its extension.

Let's look at a concrete example. Suppose you define a global function called hashval() in a C++ file:

```
int hashval(int val);
```

When a C++ compiler compiles it, its decorated name may look like this:

```
__i__hshvl_4i //a simplified hypothetical decorated name
```

The __ prolog indicates that this is a global function. The first i encodes the return type, which is int. The following __ separates the return type and the function's name (which in this decorated form often has no vowels). A single underscore indicates the beginning of the parameter list, which starts with 4, the size of the argument, and i, the argument's type.

Alas, a C compiler that encounters the following call:

```
n=hashval(x); //in a .c file
```

will look for an entirely different decorated name, something like:

```
__hashval //equivalent decorated name in C
```

At link time, the linker will complain about an unresolved symbol '`__hashval`' because the C++ compiler never generated the decorated name that a C compiler expected to find. To solve this problem you need to declare the original function like this:

```
extern "C" int hashval(int val); //force C name decoration
```

When a C++ compiler sees an `extern "C"` declaration, it uses a C name decoration for the identifier just as a C compiler would. Consequently, the decorated name will be:

```
__hashval
```

At link time, the linker will resolve the reference to this function correctly because all three tenors (the C and C++ compilers and the linker) agree on the same ABI. Lovely, isn't it?

`extern "C"` Limitations

`extern "C"` isn't a panacea. You can't apply it to member functions, templates, or even global overloaded functions. Does this mean you have to give up all the joys of generic and object-oriented programming? Not at all. Remember that a C compiler doesn't care what the body of `hashval()` contains. Inside this function you can instantiate objects, call member functions, instantiate templates, etc., because the function is still compiled under a C++ compiler:

```
extern "C" int hashval(int val)
{
std::string result;
int num=0;
std::stringstream str;
str<<val; //insert val to str
str>>result; //convert val to a string
//..play with result using hashing algorithms
return num;
}
```

So long as you declare the function `extern "C"`, all compilers agree on its ABI.

Summary

Several suggestions for standardizing a C++ ABI have been proposed. Most users and implementers alike agree that forming a universal ABI is impossible because different compilers pass arguments in different orders and even the arguments themselves vary from one machine to another. However, compiler vendors have attempted to define *platform specific ABIs* so that different Linux compilers, for example, should follow the same rules. Time will tell if this initiative succeeds.

`const` Correctness

In a previous section, (see the section "`const` declarations") I explained how to parse `const` declarations correctly. Here, I will show how to use the `const` keyword to make your code `const`-correct, and thereby enhance its durability and readability.

`const` Origins

A constant, as the name suggests, is an object that the program (or a certain component thereof, such as a procedure or a function) promises not to change. Before the advent of constants, non-modifiable objects were treated syntactically, like ordinary ones; programmers had to rely on their dexterity and good memory in hopes that they wouldn't accidentally modify these objects. In small programs this was feasible. However, in large-scale projects consisting of numerous source files and libraries, it was a serious problem. The larger a project is, the easier it is to lose track of which objects a certain module is allowed to change and which ones it shouldn't. Consequently, many programming languages introduced the notion of "read-only" variables, or constants. C++ borrowed in its early days the `const` keyword from Pascal. ANSI C borrowed `const` from C++ shortly afterward.

The Meaning of `const`

The core meaning of `const` is rather straightforward: "This object can't be changed by this program/module." This description isn't precise, though. As opposed to what many programmers think, `const` doesn't provide an absolute guarantee against changes. In fact, it's perfectly legal to change a `const` object by ways unknown to compiler. Think for example of a `const` object that is mapped to an external port or device. When the program declares it as `const`, it guarantees that *it* won't change its value; this however doesn't mean that the variable's value can't be modified by a different process, the hardware device itself, the OS kernel or a power fault. Therefore, you should consider `const` as a promise that a program makes about its own behavior regarding a certain object rather than an absolute guarantee regarding an object's value.

`const` Crush Course

As we learned before, `const` can qualify an object, a pointer, or a nonstatic member function. Here, `const` qualifies objects:

```
const int MAX=1024;
void f(const string * ps); //s is const
const char name[]="Phoebus";
```

`const` pointers are declared like this:

```
void *const p=&mem_table; //p is a const pointer
Date *const pd = &myDate
```

Of course, you can combine both types of `const` to declare a `const` pointer to a `const` object:

```
const int * const =&num;
void f(const char * const msg);
```

Thus far, C and C++ are unanimous in their interpretation of `const`. Yet C++ has a third type of `const`—a `const` member function. A const member function is one that cannot modify the state of its object (the state of an object consists of the values of its nonstatic and non-`mutable` data members). This guarantee is indicated by placing the `const` keyword after the function's parameter list:

```
int Date::getMonth() const
{
 return month;
}
```

`const` Correctness in Practice

It is customary to use libraries in the form of compiled binaries plus header files that contain only declarations. Therefore, every *observer function*, i.e., a member function that shouldn't change its object's state, should be declared `const`. This way, clients know that they can call the function safely without any unexpected surprises while implementers allow the compiler to detect violations of this guarantee. If the body of a `const` member function contains a statement that modifies its object's state, the compiler will complain:

```
int Date::getMonth() const
{
 month=APRIL; //error, attempt to change a data member
```

```
                   //inside a const member function
 return month;
}
```

By contrast, any *mutator function*, i.e., a member function that can change its object's state, isn't declared `const`. Forgetting to `const`-qualify an observer function isn't just a stylistic gaffe; it's a serious flaw because it denies clients the ability to use this member function in certain situations:

```
int Person:getAge(); //should be const, alas
void Display(const Person& p)
{
 cout<<p.getAge()<<endl; //error, getAge() isn't const
}
```

Therefore, when you design a class, dedicate sufficient time to determine which of its member functions should be `const`. You may even need to define pairs of member functions that are distinguished only by their `const` qualification. For example, class `std::vector` has two overloaded versions of `operator[]`:

```
reference vector::operator[](size_type n);
const_reference vector::operator[](size_type n) const;
```

The first version returns an iterator through which you can alter a vector's element; the second version returns a `const_iterator`, which doesn't allow you to modify the vector's data. The `const` version of `operator[]` is automatically called when the vector is `const`:

```
void f(const vector<int> & vi)
{
 vi[0]=5;//error, vi is const
 cout<<vi[0]<<endl; //fine, read-only access
}
```

Notice that there is an automatic conversion of non-`const` to `const` (but not vice versa) so the `const` version of a member function is called even if its object isn't explicitly declared `const`:

```
void assign(vector<int> & vi)
{
 vi[0]=5;//fine, using non-const []
 cout<<vi[0]<<endl; //also fine, using const []
}
```

`operator[]` isn't unique in this regard; a good many other member functions including `at()` and `front()` have two versions.

`const` Parameters

Each parameter that a function shouldn't modify is declared `const`. By contrast, the absence of `const` indicates that the function is allowed to modify this parameter:

```
void myCopy(string & dest, const string & source)
{
 dest=source;
}
```

Notice how neatly the `const` qualifier documents which string is the source and which one is the destination. Consequently, silly mistakes such as the following are detected at compile-time:

```
void myCopy(string & dest, const string & source)
{
 source=dest; //error, source is const
}
```

Summary

The term "const correctness" means that every entity that should be `const`—an object, a parameter or a member function—is indeed declared as such, whereas the lack of the `const` qualifier implies that the object can be altered. `const`-correct code documents the programmer's intentions clearly. In addition, it enables the compiler to detect human errors and design mistakes.

`const` Correctness—Advanced Issues

After covering the essential aspects of `const` correctness, I would like to discuss more advanced issues that are related to this topic: the `volatile` specifier, `volatile` correctness and `mutable` data members.

`volatile` Semantics

`volatile` is one of those keywords that you either use extensively or never use at all, depending on your application domain. The semantics of `volatile` is in many aspects platform-dependent. Furthermore, the Standard allows an implementation to ignore this keyword completely. But what does `volatile` actually do? To answer this question, we need to poke under the hood of code optimization.

When a compiler thinks a certain object will remain unchanged throughout the execution of a program or a certain code section (a function, a loop, etc.), it can store that object's value in a CPU register as an optimization measure (reading data from a register is about 1,000 times faster than accessing RAM). The problem is that compilers can't tell that an object declared `const` might still change *asynchronously*, by a different process, a signal handler, an external device to which the program's memory is mapped, etc. Consequently, nasty bugs might arise since the program might be using a stale value of said object. This problem isn't confined to `const` objects; however, such objects are likely candidates for this type of optimization. The solution is to declare objects whose value might change asynchronously `volatile`. Doing so causes the compiler to refrain from applying this optimization. If concurrent programming and code optimization are not a part of your ordinary diet, this explanation may have been over your head, so perhaps an analogy will help. Your web browser stores web pages locally on a disk so that they load faster the next time you view them. The problem is that it doesn't always know when a local copy of a certain page has become outdated. Consequently, it will display the page faster but the information therein will be useless. Web sites are aware of this and mark pages with dynamic content as *transient* (this is more or less the same as `volatile`) to indicate that these pages shouldn't be cached. Consequently, whenever you view such a page your browser loads a fresh copy from the web site. This certainly slows down browsing but it ensures accuracy. In a similar vein, `volatile` ensures esaccuracy at the cost of execution speed.

`volatile` Declarations

Generally speakinges, every syntactic rule applicable to `const` is also applicable to `volatile`. You can declare `volatile` objects, `volatile` pointers, and `volatile` member functions:

```
volatile int n=10;//built in type
volatile Time current; //object
void f(volatile ThreadContext & tc); //parameter
int *volatile p=&num;//pointer
T & vector<T>::operator[](int idx) volatile;//member function
```

In addition, you can declare `volatile` pointers to `volatile` objects:

```
volatile int *volatile p=&num;
```

`volatile` Correctness in STL

In environments that use `volatile` objects you need to define `volatile` member functions as well. Calling a non-`volatile` member function on a `volatile` object is an error:

```
void func(volatile std::list<int> li)
{
  int n= li.front();//error, front() isn't volatile
}
```

The Standard Library doesn't define `volatile` member functions at all. This is not an oversight but a deliberate decision. Adding `volatile` member functions would complicate the design of such containers, make them less portable and even worse—it would require implementers to define four(!) overloaded versions for each member function:

```
T & vector<T>::operator[](int idx);
T & vector<T>::operator[](int idx) const;
T & vector<T>::operator[](int idx) volatile; //additional
T & vector<T>::operator[](int idx) const volatile;//ditto
```

As you can see, there's a stark contrast between STL's commitment to `const` correctness and its deliberate disregard for `volatile` correctness. Developers who use `volatile` container objects therefore have to install special versions of STL or rewrite it on their own.

`mutable` Data Members

The `mutable` keyword is a *storage specifier* that can only be applied to nonstatic data members of a class. What's it good for?

When you declare a member function `const` you promise that it doesn't change its object's state. In some cases, however, there's a distinction between a *logical state* and a *physical state* of an object. Take for example a graphical image object. So long as the image hasn't changed, you would expect its state to remain intact. However, large objects often swap their memory into a file after a certain period of inactivity. Swapping an image doesn't really affect its state although some of the object's data members such as pointers and flags may consequently change. Users who call the `const` function `Redraw()` don't care how this function is implemented internally:

```
int Image::Redraw() const
{
  if (isLoaded==false)
  {
```

```
  //..read image data from a disk into a local buffer
  isLoaded=true; //changing a data member's value
 }
  //..paint image in the screen
}
```

Compiling this code will result a compilation error. `Redraw()` is `const`, and yet it modifies a data member. The solution is to declare `isLoaded` `mutable`:

```
class Image
{
public:
 int Redraw() const;
 //..
private:
 mutable bool isLoaded;//can be changed by a const function
};
```

Unlike ordinary data members, `mutable` data members can be modified by a `const` member function.

Summary

Don't use `volatile` unless you have to because it disables optimizations that most compilers apply automatically.

TIP: If you're curious about the underlying implementation of `const` and `volatile` member functions, you should read about `this`.

`mutable`, very much like `volatile`, is a patch that enables programmers to bypass the `const` mechanism in special cases. Again, use it judiciously.

Books

STL Tutorial and Reference Guide: C++ Programming with the Standard Template Library, Second Edition (Addison-Wesley, 2001, ISBN 0201379236), by David R. Musser, Gillmer J. Derge, and Atul Saini, now in its second edition, has been my favorite STL book since 1996 or so. Although a good many other STL books have been published since this book premiered, its concise and accessible account of every STL algorithm and container is unparalleled. In addition, it discusses the rationale behind the design of STL, including performance and portability. (For more on this book, visit *http://www.informit.com/bookstore/product.asp?isbn=0201379236.*)

Applied C++: Practical Techniques for Building Better Software (Addison-Wesley, 2003, ISBN 0321108949), by Philip Romanik and Amy Muntz, discusses the issue of `const` correctness and mutable members in real-world software project design. (For more on this book, visit *http://www.informit.com/title/0321108949.*)

Sprucing Up Legacy Code

Cameron Laird's article "Memory Hygiene in C and C++: Safe Programming with Risky Data" (*http://www.informit.com/articles/article.asp?p=169586*) is an excellent reminder to all of us that in many corporate businesses, classic algorithm books, academic institutes, and widely used code libraries, pre-standard C code is very much alive and kicking, and will continue to be so in the foreseeable future. The same is true for legacy C++ code that relies on pre-standard features and conventions. Here I will show how to update this code and make it standard-compliant.

K&R Style Function Declarations

In Kernighan & Ricthie (K&R) C, function definitions look like this:

```
int func(a, b, f) /*parameters' names only; type is missing */
int a,b; /* parameters' types declared here*/
float f; /*another  parameter*/
{
/*...function body*/
}
```

The parentheses following a function's name contain parameters' names without their types. After the parentheses, the parameters are declared, very much like block scope variables. Finally, the function's body appears. This is probably the most significant change between K&R C and ANSI C (1983). In ANSI C (and of course in ISO/ANSI C++ as well), you can declare a function and define it later. A standard-compliant version of this function's declaration and definition looks like this:

```
int func(int a, int b, float f); //declaration, or prototype
int func(int a, int b, float f) //definition
{
/*...function body*/
}
```

The use of function declarations, or *prototypes*, was a major contribution to C's type-safety as it enables the compiler to perform static type checking of arguments at the place of call (in K&R C, you can call a function that hasn't been declared yet). As always, delegating to the compiler the mundane task of type checking is much better than doing it on your own.

Using `char*` instead of `void*`

The generic pointer `void*` was introduced in ANSI C. Before that, `char *` was used both for strings and generic pointers. If you browse old header files and textbooks, you may find standard functions such as `malloc()`, whose return type is declared as `char*` rather than `void*`. This practice is problematic because readers can't easily tell whether the function in question expects a real C-string (with a "\0" appended to its end) or a raw memory buffer, which may or may not contain "\0". Here again, you should replace every `char*` with `void*` unless they actually refer to strings.

Compiled Binaries

In many projects, the original source files aren't available anymore. Users only have compiled binaries in the form of .lib or .obj files plus header files that contain declarations of data structures and constants. In this case, you need some sort of reverse engineering to reconstruct function prototypes from the way in which these functions are invoked in the source files. For example, if your source file contains a function call such as this:

```
FILE * infile;
int n;
n=f(infile); //f() is available in a compiled .lib file
```

you can deduce from the function call that `f()` has the following prototype:

```
int f(FILE *pf);
```

Locate all references to undeclared functions, reconstruct their prototypes and create a header file that contains them. The next time you compile your project or when you add new modules to it, turn on your compiler's ANSI C compliance option. This will ensure that it detects type mismatches from now on.

Defaulting to `int`

Until about a decade ago, incomplete type declarations defaulted to `int`. The following declarations rely on this convention:

```
static x;
unsigned y;
f(); //return type defaults to int
main() //ditto
{
}
```

These declarations were implicitly converted to:

```
static int x;
unsigned int y;
int f();
int main()
{
}
```

You can find code that uses one or more of these forms in many projects and code libraries. However, it's prohibited both in standard C and C++. If your legacy code contains such incomplete declarations, add the missing type explicitly.

Non-Tagged Data Structures

In C (but not in C++), you have to include an *elaborate type name* , i.e., `struct`, `union` or `enum`, when you refer to a user-defined type. For example:

```
enum val (struct X, union Y);
```

However, in C++ you use the following form instead:

```
val (X, Y); //no elaborate type name
```

To achieve a similar effect in C, it's customary to declare a `typedef` such as this:

```
typedef struct
{
int n;
char s[4];
}X; /*X is a typedef name, not an instance*/
```

This habit may be useful in C but in C++ it's completely redundant. Even worse, it could lead to some nasty name-hiding problems under some conditions.

Therefore, if you compile legacy C code with a C++ compiler, omit the `typedef` keyword and move the `typedef` name to the tag's position:

```
struct X//tag name; originally was a typedef name
{
int n;
}; //C++
```

Summary

C is more than 30 years old. During such a long period, revisions and extensions are inevitable. However, we can all agree that all these changes are for the best, and that C has retained its original spirit of a compact, portable, general-purpose and efficient programming language.

Books

The C Programming Language, 2nd Edition (Prentice Hall, 1998, ISBN 0131103628), by Brian Kernighan and Dennis Ritchie, isn't just the best book for learning C; it's also an exemplary programming book that has defined a standard in this category. It's certainly one of those books that sooner or later you'll come across. Although the latest edition doesn't cover the latest changes made in C99, it's still a reliable and fluff-free C tutorial. (For more on this book, visit *http://www.informit.com/title/0131103628*.)

Virtual Constructors

Syntactically speaking, constructors cannot be virtual nor can they return a value. However, in terms of functionality, it's possible to imitate the role of constructors and copy-constructors by using the "virtual constructor idiom." Here I will explain how to do it.

Rationale

In certain programming languages (but not in C++), constructors are just like any other member function: You can call them directly and they have a return value. This makes them useful in certain design patterns and frameworks, where the responsibility for creating and reduplicating objects of a certain type is delegated to the class's constructor. In C++, however, you need to use a different technique to overcome the syntactic and semantic restrictions on constructors.

Virtual Default Constructors

A virtual default constructor is a virtual member function with an agreed-upon name, `construct()` for example. Each class defines in this function the set of operations needed to construct an object of the desired type. The constructed object is then returned either as a pointer or as a reference. This way, a generic function or class can create objects of a certain type without knowing their exact type or the precise nature of their construction process. For example:

```
class Browser
{
public:
 //virtual default constructor
 virtual Browser* construct() {return new Browser;}
};
```

You use the `construct()` member function like this:

```
template <class T> void func(T & obj)
{
 T* p=obj.construct();
}
```

What about polymorphism? If `obj` happens to refer to an object derived from `Browser`, we want `construct()` to produce the correct type object. For this purpose, every class derived from `Browser` must override `construct()`. The problem is that overriding a virtual function usually requires that the original signature as well as the return type be preserved. However, C++ allows you as a special case to override the return type of a virtual function under two conditions:

- Only the return type can change; the parameter list shouldn't.
- The return type can only be changed to a pointer or reference to the derived class.

In other words, this override is legal:

```
class HTMLEditor: public Browser
{
public:
  HTMLEditor * construct() { return new HTMLEditor; }
};
```

However, this one is not:

```cpp
class HTMLEditor: public Browser
{
public:
  Notepad * construct() { return new HTMLEditor; }
};
```

This feature is known as *covariant return types*. Notice that older compilers may not support it. If your compiler refuses to compile such code then it's about time to upgrade it!

See how neatly this idiom works:

```cpp
Browser *pb = new HTMLEditor; //polymorphic pointer
func(*pb);
```

Because *pb is passed by reference, the polymorphic nature of `construct()` is preserved and as a result, `func()` produces the correct result based on the dynamic type of *pb. The virtual mechanism plus the covariant return type of `construct()` ensure that when the expression:

```cpp
T* p=obj.construct();
```

is executed, p always points to an object of the correct type.

Virtual Copy Constructors

A similar mechanism for copy-constructing an object may also be needed in certain applications. For this purpose, we use the covariant return type feature again. The only difference is in the name of the member function and its implementation:

```cpp
class Browser
{
public:
virtual Browser* clone() { return new Browser(*this); } //virtual copy constructor
};
```

Here again, every derived class must override the base class's implementation of `clone()` so that it produces an object of the correct type:

```cpp
class HTMLEditor: public Browser{
public:
  HTMLEditor * clone() { return new HTMLEditor (*this); }
```

```
};
void create (Browser& br)
{
  Browser* pnewb = br.clone();
  //...use pbr and br
  delete pbr;
}
```

Memory Management Issues

By default, `construct()` and `clone()` allocate the return value on the free store. While this isn't a major problem in general, it does incur the usual hassles of dynamic memory management. For example, you have to delete the allocated objects explicitly before the program terminates, and you need to make sure that the same pointer isn't deleted more than once. However, by using class `auto_ptr` you can simplify your code and eliminate this drudgery.

Summary

These so-called virtual constructors and copy constructors aren't needed in every class; they are required only in special frameworks and design patterns that rely on these member functions. Therefore, don't be tempted to define them in your classes "just in case." Remember that doing so incurs substantial overhead: Every derived class must override these member functions, which means more manual coding, testing and maintenance. However, when you truly have to use this idiom, stick to conventional names and use the covariant return types feature.

Naming Names

In T.S. Eliot's timeless *Old Possum's Book of Practical Cats*, the opening poem, "The Naming of Cats," starts like this:

> The naming of cats is a difficult matter
> It isn't just one of your holiday games

Choosing a name for an identifier (a variable, constant, function, macro, template and a user-defined type) is also a serious matter. Here I will explain the rules and restrictions that C and C++ impose in this area.

The Case for Case-Sensitivity

C and C++ belong to the few programming languages that are case-sensitive. This means for example that the following three functions don't clash:

```
void openFile() {} // #1
void openfile() {} // #2
void OpenFile() {} // #3
int main()
{
 OpenFile(); //#3
}
```

Of course, such a programming style isn't recommended because it confuses human readers. However, the point is to show that compilers and linkers have no problem with it.

What's in an Identifier?

An identifier must begin with a nondigit character that is followed by any number of digits and nondigits. A nondigit character is either an underscore or a letter in the range a..z A..Z. Although it's possible under certain restrictions (depending on the compiler, editor and the OS) to use universal characters as nondigits, most programmers restrict themselves to the English alphabet.

Reserved Identifiers

Every identifier that starts with two consecutive underscores, for example:

```
__exit
```

is reserved. Therefore, you shouldn't use such an identifier for class names, functions, constants, macros and so on. Many people wonder why this restriction applies to data members of a class or local variables declared at a block scope. The reason is that compilers often insert temporary variables and objects into user-written code. These compiler-generated identifiers mustn't clash with user-defined ones. To avoid such clashes, compiler-generated identifiers often start with a double underscore.

The same restriction applies to every identifier that starts with a single underscore followed by a capital letter, for example:

```
_TEMP
_Abs
```

In addition, any identifier that starts with a single underscore is reserved in the global namespace. This means that you can safely use identifiers such as

```
_value
_s
```

for local variables, class data members and so on, as long as these names aren't declared globally.

C Reserved Names

Standard C defines names that are reserved for future use. These names are divided into two categories: function names and macro names. It's important to note that these names are reserved regardless of which header files your program uses, if any.

The reserved standard C function names are as follows:

- `is` followed by a lowercase letter: `isspace`
- `mem` followed by a lowercase letter: `memset`
- `str` followed by a lowercase letter: `strcmp`
- `to` followed by a lowercase letter: `tolower`
- `wcs` followed by a lowercase letter: `wcstof`

The following macros are reserved. Don't use them in any context:

- Identifiers that start with `E` followed by a digit or an uppercase letter
- Identifiers that start with `LC_` followed by an uppercase letter
- Identifiers that start with `SIG` or `SIG_` followed by an uppercase letter

Keywords

Keywords in C and C++ are reserved. This means that you cannot use them in any other context. While this restriction certainly makes sense, it's not universal. In other programming languages, say PL/1, the statement is valid:

```
IF (IF=5) GOTO LABEL1; /*IF is used both as a keyword and as a variable*/
```

These are the reserved keywords of C++:

asm	break	char
auto	case	class
bool	catch	const

const_cast	inline	struct
continue	int	switch
default	long	template
delete	mutable	this
do	namespace	throw
double	new	true
dynamic_cast	operator	try
else	private	typedef
enum	protected	typeid
explicit	public	typename
export	register	union
extern	reinterpret_cast	unsigned
false	return	using
float	short	virtual
for	signed	void
friend	sizeof	volatile
goto	static	wchar_t
if	static_cast	while

In addition to the 63 reserved keywords listed above, standard C++ also defines *alternative representations* for certain operators and punctuators:

and	compl	or_eq
and_eq	not	xor
bitand	not_eq	xor_eq
bitor	or	

These alternative representations are also reserved so you can't use them as identifiers.

Summary

Naming conventions have been a fertile source of religious wars and debates in newsgroups and among development teams. While it's recommended that you define your own style and stick to it, there's no point in becoming dogmatic about it. One way or another, you will be exposed to different naming conventions: the one used in the Standard Library, another used in a third-party library, or ones you find when reviewing code written by others. While your compiler and linker don't care much about naming conventions, they do care about reserved keywords and identifiers. Therefore, you should familiarize yourself with the rules and restrictions listed here.

Function Calls

Earlier, I used the phrase "a full-blown function call." What other kind of function calls could there be? As you can guess, there's more than just one type. Here I will explain the subtle differences between them.

What's in a Function Call?

A typical function call in C++ consists of a set of operations that take place under the hood. Although the details depend on the hardware, operating system and the compiler, the usual steps are: storing the current stack frame, initializing a new stack frame that contains the arguments of the function, initializing these arguments as necessary (for example, if the function call includes hard-coded numbers), performing a jump statement that transfers control to the function's code and executing that code. When the function returns, the same steps are applied in reverse order. This is the ordinary function call mechanism, which I referred to as a "full-blown function call." As you can imagine, this overhead can be rather significant if the function's body is small and the function is called frequently. In this case, the program spends more time on initialization and cleanup than actually executing the function's code. Accessor member functions are a classic example of this phenomenon. This is why they are usually inlined.

Function Overhead Scale

The overhead of a full-blown function call can be completely avoided if the function is inlined. In this case, there's no need to store a stack frame, perform a jump statement and so on. However, inlining a function isn't always possible or desirable. When a function is called rarely, or when its body is too large, there's no point in inlining it. Fortunately, modern compilers are clever enough to "do the right thing" and decide by themselves which functions are viable candidates for inlining and which ones aren't. That said, inline functions and full-blown functions are the two ends of the scale. Compilers can exert several other optimizations and shortcuts that reduce some of the overhead of a full-blown function call.

Thunks

The term *thunk* dates back to the days of Algol programming language and has stuck since then. A thunk is an invisible and parameterless function returning a memory address or a similar integral value. A thunk consists of one or two assembly directives that read a CPU register or manipulate some value to return the result. For example, the implicit this pointer passed as an argument to a C++ member function is often implemented as a thunk: the object's address is stored in a CPU register and a thunk reads it from that register. Likewise, when you call delete[] to destroy an array of objects, C++ often uses a thunk to retrieve the number of the elements that the array contains. Thunks are also used in system-programming operations. The Linux kernel uses a thunk to obtain the task object associated with the current process by bitwise AND-ing the stack pointer (which is stored in the ESP register) and a magic number:

```
task_struct * p = STACK_POINTER & 0xffffe000; //pseudo code
```

Under Windows, thunks are used to convert a 16-bit address to a 32-bit address, for example.

Passing Arguments in Registers

The standard argument passing mechanism of C and C++ uses the stack, a special type of memory, to pass argument to a function and return a value from it. As efficient as it may seem, in many modern computers RAM access is a bottleneck where processes spend most of the time. Computers nowadays have plenty of RAM so swap files are less in use. Yet while a RAM access is measured in microseconds (millionths of a second), the time needed for reading a value from a CPU register is measured in nanoseconds (billionths of a second). It therefore makes sense to store data that is accessed frequently (loop counters for example) in a register rather than on the stack. The problem, however, is that CPUs have a limited number of registers. Secondly, some of the registers are reserved for special uses so you can't use them for your own functions. Still, certain optimizers and compilers enable you to play with the default passing mechanism of user-defined functions and pass arguments via CPU registers. There are several restrictions on register arguments: They cannot contain complex data structures such as structs or class objects that have multiple data members, for example.

Intrinsic Functions

Certain compilers enable you to inline Standard Library functions and APIs, say strcpy(). Remember that in this case, the compiler actually yanks compiled and optimized code from a binary file rather than copy and paste C++ statements from a C++ source file. In C++ Builder for instance you can inline every strcpy() call by using the following #pragma directive:

```
#pragma intrinsic strcpy
```

However, this directive is compiler-specific and therefore compromises code portability.

Calling Conventions

Different programming languages use various calling conventions. Calling conventions affect the way in which arguments are passed to a function: their ordering (right to left or left to right), stack cleanup (by the callee, the caller or none at all) and the name-decoration used. In some cases, overriding the default calling convention can improve performance. However, this has to be done with extra care and again, you should bear in mind that it compromises portability.

Summary

As I have shown, a full-blown function call is the most expensive type whereas an inline function is the cheapest one. Between these two extreme options, experienced programmers can play with their compiler's settings and eliminate some of the overhead associated with a function call. Remember however that each of these tweaks exacts a price in terms of portability. More importantly, always test your code to see whether these tweaks actually improve performance.

Speaking Standardese

Familiarity with *Standardese*, the language in which the official ANIS/ISO standard of C++ is written, isn't just a prerequisite for becoming a language lawyer or writing a compiler. Even experienced programmers must know a few key terms in Standardese to read advanced programming books, understand esoteric compiler errors and—most importantly—write better code. In this section, I will discuss three such key terms: side effects, sequence points and the "maximal munch" principle.

Side Effects

A *side effect* is a change in the state of the execution environment. More specifically, a side effect is one of the following operations:

- Modifying an object (in the wider sense, e.g., incrementing an `int`)
- Accessing a `volatile` object

- Calling an I/O function
- Calling a function that does any of these operations

According to the Standard, an implementation is allowed to defer a constructor call of an object defined in a namespace scope (i.e., an object with static storage type—a global object for instance) if that constructor has no side effects. Because the Standard doesn't specify how long the constructor call can be deferred, certain implementations take advantage of this leeway and "defer" it indefinitely, as an optimization measure:

```
struct S
{
 S() {} //no side-effects
};
S s; //global, ctor may be "deferred" indefinitely
```

In this example, an optimizer is allowed to remove the construction of s if it isn't used in the program and if its constructor has no side effects. In most cases, this creative interpretation of the Standard is a boon. However, sometimes you really want the constructor of such an object to be called. The easiest way to ensure this is by adding a side effect to the constructor's code, calling a dummy `volatile` member function for instance:

```
struct S
{
 S() {dummy();} //now with a side effect
 void dummy() volatile{}
};
```

Sequence Points

During a program's execution there are well-defined points in time called *sequence-points* at which the side effects of expressions that have been evaluated have all been completed and no side effects have been started for any unevaluated expressions. For example, each of the following two statements has a sequence-point:

```
++n; //a sequence point after incrementing n
y=0;//a sequence point after assigning y
```

Sequence-points are like frames in a movie: They capture a certain state of affairs for a given time frame. The compiler is free to reorder expressions and subexpressions in any order that preserves the original semantics between sequence points. Normally, you wouldn't care much about sequence points unless you have an expression that has more than one side effect within a single sequence point. For example:

```
int n=0;
n=++n-++n; //undefined behavior
```

The second line causes undefined behavior because it packs multiple side effects within a single sequence point, the result of which is undefined. By contrast, the following expression has one side effect per sequence point and is therefore well-formed:

```
n=5, ++n, n++;
```

Understanding sequence points is chiefly important when using macros. Consider the following macro:

```
#define twice(x) ((x)+(x))
```

It's well-parenthesized and performs a simple addition operation. Seemingly, it's kosher but what happens when it takes an expression with side effects as an argument?

```
int n = 1;
int sum;
sum = twice(++n);   //undefined
```

++n equals 2. One might expect (rather naively) that sum would therefore become 4. However, the expression twice(++n) is expanded to ((++n)+(++n)), which has multiple side effects in one sequence point. Note that using a function instead of a macro would resolve this issue:

```
inline int  twice(int x) { return x+x; }
```

In this case the result would be 4, without surprises. This is another good reason to avoid macros.

The "Maximal Munch" Rule

A compiler has a *tokenizer* that parses a source file into distinct tokens (keywords, operators, identifiers, etc.). One of the tokenizer's rules is called "maximal munch," which says that it should keep reading characters from the source file until adding one more character causes the current token to stop making sense (unless of course the next character is a blank or any other terminator). For example, if the letters "c", "h" and "a" have been read, and the following character is "r", the tokenizer will read it too and complete the token "char." In certain contexts, the maximal munch rule can have surprising effects, though. Consider the following declaration:

```
vector < stack<int>> vs; // error
```

Here, the tokenizer didn't parse this declaration correctly. Due to the "maximal munch" rule, the sequence >> is parsed as a single token (the right-shift operator) rather than two consecutive template argument list terminators. At a later stage, the syntactic analyzer will detect that a right-shift operator doesn't make sense in this context and you'll receive an error message.

A similar problem occurs when you use the :: operator in a template argument list:

```
::std::vector <::std::stack<int> >;
//error=====^
```

Here, the sequence <: is parsed as a digraph equivalent of the character [. Chances are low that you'll ever need to use this digraph. However, your compiler recognizes it anyway, so you need to insert a space between the opening angle bracket and the :: operator:

```
::std::vector < ::std::stack<int> >; //fine
```

Summary

Beginners' programming books usually avoid the technical language of the C++ standard. In most cases, they get away with it rather neatly. However, programmers who want to prefect their expertise and under-the-hood understanding of C++ eventually have to read more technical stuff and, in some cases, the Standard itself. In certain cases, this is the only way to resolve a professional dispute or to ensure that your code is correct.

Books

C++ in a Nutshell (O'Reilly, 2003), by Ray Lischner, is one of the better reference books that have been published recently. While it isn't 100% error-free (for example, in its description of side effects it lists "calling a function in the standard library [sic]" as the third option rather than calling an I/O function), it isn't afraid of speaking Standardese. Here you will find terms such as *l-values and r-values, storage class specifiers, argument-dependent lookup,* and so on explained in plain English. A complete reference of the Standard Library is also included, which is handy for a quick lookup.

Declarations and Definitions

Continuing our earlier brief course in *Standardese*, it's time to explain at last the differences between two similar but not identical terms, namely declarations and definitions.

A Source of Confusion

Declarations and definitions mean different things in different contexts. In the case of class objects and variables (to which I collectively refer as "objects"), a *definition* causes the compiler to allocate storage for an object whereas a *declaration* merely associates an object with a certain type, without allocating storage for it. The problem is that the two terms overlap to some extent; definitions also serve as declarations because they inject an identifier of a certain type to a scope. However, a declaration isn't a definition because it doesn't entail storage allocation for the declared object. To add to the confusion, the semantics of definitions and declarations is slightly different when applied to types and functions, as I will show momentarily. So let's look at a more detailed analysis of these two terms.

Objects

In C++, objects must be declared before you can use them. A declaration, as previously noted, merely binds an identifier to a type. For example:

```
//file1.cpp declarations
extern int num;
extern struct tm t;
extern const long val;
```

In this example, `num`, `t` and `val` are declared but their definitions appear in another translation unit. Such declarations are necessary when you access a global object from several translation units. Of course, one of the program's translation units must contain definitions for these objects:

```
//file2.cpp definitions
int num;
```

```
struct tm t;
extern const long val=100; //initialized, hence -- a definition
```

During the linkage phase, the linker resolves references to the same object that appear in separate translation units. It knows for instance that the identifier `num` declared in `file1.cpp` refers to the same `num` that is defined `file2.cpp` because the name, linkage, scope and type of the two match. This leads us to an important observation:

An object can be declared an unlimited of times within the same program (or even inside the same translation unit). However, it must be defined exactly once within the same program (later we will see that this rule has a few exceptions).

Defining (rather than merely declaring) objects before their usage is a more common scenario:

```
int main()
{
 //definitions
 int num=99;
 string URL;
 void *p=0;
 const int val=100;
 char name[12]={0};
//..
}
```

These are definitions because the compiler allocates storage for the objects (in the case of objects with static storage types, it's the linker's job to allocate storage but let's ignore these technicalities for now). Another crucial difference between a declaration and a definition is that the latter can contain an explicit initializer. That said, the definitions above are also declarations since they bind the objects num, URL, etc. to certain types. To conclude, the four objects above are declared and defined at once.

Types

A *type definition* binds an identifier to a user-defined `class`, `struct`, `union`, or `enum`. The definition includes the members of said identifier:

```
class Currency //a class definition
{
 int dollars, cents;
 Locale l;
public:
```

```
 Currency(int d, int c);
 ~Currency();
};
enum Dir  //an enum definition
{
 up,
 down
};
```

Here again, a definition also serves as a declaration because it binds a name, say `Currency`, to a user-defined type that the compiler can recognize henceforth. Type definitions don't entail storage allocation because types are a compile-time concept; they have no representation at runtime and therefore never occupy memory. By contrast, objects are a runtime concept; the executable image contains memory slots for them. Thus, you can think of a type definition as "all the information that the compiler needs in order to allow me to create an instance of the said type." For example:

```
//possible only after Currency has been defined
Currency c;
static Currency c2;
Currency *p= new Currency;
```

It is possible to declare, without defining, a type. Such declarations are often referred to as *forward declarations*. They are needed when you refer to a type before the compiler has seen its definition:

```
class Currency; //forward declaration
enum Dir; //forward declaration

class Locale
{
 Dir & d;
 Currency * c;
};

class Currency //a class definition
{
 int dollars, cents;
 Locale l;
public:
 Currency(int d, int c);
 ~Currency();
};
```

In this example, the declaration of `Currency` is necessary because `Locale` contains a reference to `Currency`. Notice that because `Currency` was merely declared but not defined, you can only create pointers and references to it. An attempt to instantiate it or use it in a `sizeof` expression will cause a compilation error.

Functions

A *function definition* contains both a *prototype* and a *body*, or implementation. For example:

```
void increment(int &n) //function definition
{
  n++;
}
```

A *function declaration* contains only the prototype followed by a semicolon:

```
void increment(int &n); //declaration
```

You can have multiple declarations of the same function but only one definition thereof must exist in the entire program. There are two exceptions to this rule, though. Inline functions (whether explicitly declared `inline` or member functions defined inside a class body) have to be defined in every translation unit that uses them. The reason is obvious: In order to inline a function, the compiler must see its definition. Templates are the second exception. A template (either a class template or a function template) must be defined in every translation unit in which it is used. Again, the reason is that the compiler must see the template's definition in order to generate code for every specialization used in a translation unit. The common practice is to define templates and inline functions in a header file and `#include` it in every translation unit that uses them. This is a common pitfall among novices, who assume that it's enough to provide declarations of templates in a header file and define them in a separately compiled translation unit. If you're concerned about the size of the resultant executable, fret not. Linkers are usually clever enough to remove redundant copies of the same specialization from the resulting executable.

Summary

Although the two terms are used interchangeably in textbooks and articles, declarations and definitions aren't the same thing. The distinction between the two is chiefly important when dealing with templates and inline functions. A special type of a declaration that I didn't discuss here is called a *using*-declaration. You can read about its uses in Chapter 6.

`finally` at Last?

Java programmers who have migrated to C++ often moan about its alleged lack of `finally`. Here I will explain the semantics of this keyword and its rationale. Then I will show why it's unnecessary in C++. Along the way, we will discuss more general issues pertaining to mastering a new programming language.

Exception Handling in C++ and Java

Java's exception handling is an adaptation of C++ exception handling. Yet there are some substantial differences between the two languages in this regard. Teaching Java is well beyond the scope of this discussion, but for those of you who haven't written any Java code before (feel more than okay about it, by the way), I will point out some of the major differences.

The first difference between the two languages is that in Java, all exceptions are ultimately derived from a common base class. In C++, an exception needn't be derived from an exception class (certain frameworks, including the Standard Library itself, do employ this idiom to some extent). In fact, a C++ exception can even be a built-in type as well, say `int` or `char *`:

```
try {//C++, not Java
if (abnormal_state)
 throw "must quit!";
}
```

Another difference between the two is that Java enforces exception specifications rigorously, i.e., every method must specify which exceptions it might throw in an exception specification. In C++ however, exception specifications are optional and quite often are completely omitted (with reason!).

Destructors Versus `finally()`

The crucial difference for our discussion isn't directly related to exceptions but to the underlying object model of the two languages. In C++, there's symmetry between a constructor and a destructor. Usually, resources allocated during construction are released in the destructor (this is the famous "resource allocation is initialization" design idiom. Class `stopwatch` is a classic example).

Because destructor execution in C++ is deterministic—you know exactly when a destructor runs—you can be certain that resources will not leak, or remain locked once an object has been destroyed. By contrast, Java has no destructors. The closest thing to this concept is the `finalize()` method, which is called when the garbage collection (GC) reclaims the storage of an object. The problem is that you can't tell in advance when the garbage collector will run. In some cases, it may take days and weeks before the JVM invokes it; some programs even disable GC altogether. Consequently, resources released in `finalize()` might remain locked. Due to the lack of this constructor-destructor symmetry, Java programmers must use a different technique for ensuring a prompt release of allocated resources. This is exactly where `finally` comes into the limelight.

When an exception is thrown in a C++ program, the stack unwinding mechanism guarantees that destructors of auto objects have executed upon entering a matching handler. You can be sure that resources have been released in any case: If an exception has occurred, the stack unwinding mechanism is responsible for invoking destructors and subsequently releasing resources; if no exception has occurred, the destructor is called normally, upon leaving the block in which the object was defined. For example:

```
try {
 std::string cat("Bustopher Jones");
 if (error)
   throw std::string ("Cat-astrophe!");
}//cat is destroyed here if no exception has occurred
catch(std::string& exc)
{
//at this point, cat has been destroyed
//during stack unwinding
}
```

In Java, things are different:

```
try {//Java pseudo-code
 myConnectionr connection= new myConnection (db_connection);
 if (connection.fail())
   //..throw an exception and leave this block
else
//continue normally
 connection.use();
}
catch(Exception ex)//..handle the connection failure here
{
}
```

```
finally
{
 connection.release();
}
```

First, you allocate a resource such as a DB connection inside a `try` block (in Java you must use a `try` block when you call a method with an exception specification). If an exception occurs, control is transferred to the `catch()` block. Releasing the resource inside a `try` block is a bad idea, though, as the exception may have occurred even before `connection` was constructed. Secondly, if no exception has occurred, the `release()` call won't take place at all. Java designers decided to solve this problem by introducing a `finally` block, which executes regardless of the existence of an exception. In other words, a `finally` block is like a destructor in C++—its execution is guaranteed. As such, it's the proper place for safely releasing resources in Java.

Evaluation

The differences between the two languages suggest that `finally` is indispensable in Java, because this language doesn't implement the C++ stack unwinding model. The second and more important conclusion, is that `finally` is completely unnecessary in C++. Using `auto` objects inside a `try` block guarantees their destruction. Since objects' destructors run whether an exception has occurred or not, they are the proper place for releasing resources.

The call for adding `finally` to C++ usually stems from inexperience in this language. For example, programmers who allocate objects dynamically in a `try` block a la Java:

```
try{//poor programming style
 std::string pstr=new std::string cat("Bustopher");
 if (error)
   throw std::string ("Cat-astrophe!");
}
```

"need" a `finally` block where they can safely delete `pstr`. However, by replacing `pstr` with an `auto std::string` object you avoid this hassle neatly. Furthermore, even if you must use a dynamically allocated object, you can always wrap it in an `auto_ptr`:

```
try{
 auto_ptr<string> pstr(new std::string ("Bustopher"));
```

```
if (error)
   throw std::string ("Cat-astrophe!");
}
```

Summary

Six years after the ratification of the ISO standard, the C++ standardization committee is in process of adding new features to the language. Undoubtedly, some of these features, including thread support and a regular expression library, are long overdue. Yet it seems that some of the newly proposed features aren't truly necessary; `finally` is one of them.

On a related note, people aren't always aware that learning a new programming language means more than just learning a few keywords and syntactic rules. As a matter of fact, the mental switch, or learning to think in the target language, is the toughest part. Another lesson to take home from this case study is that too often people look for a solution in the form of a language extension, either by means of a new keyword or a new library, when in reality the language already provides a facility that accomplishes the same task, albeit differently.

Local Classes

The good thing about C++ is that—no matter how long you've been using it—there's always a new quirky feature for you to learn. In this section, I will shed some light on such a feature: local classes.

A Local What?

"You probably mean a local object, right?" Well, no. I do mean a local class. Before explaining the usefulness of this feature (OK, it isn't *that* useful, although every weird feature has its uses, as I will show later on), let's look at the syntax. A class defined within a function definition is a local class:

```
void func()
{
 class A
 {
  public:
 A() {cout<<"I'm a local class!"<<endl;}
 };
}
```

As you can see, there are no explicit syntactic clues to indicate that this is a local class. However, notice that ordinary classes are defined at a namespace scope, typically inside a header file, whereas this class is defined inside a function's body. A local class has no linkage. This means that you can't refer to it from an outer scope. Thus, class A isn't accessible in any way from other blocks, files or linkage units:

```
void func()
{
 class A
 {
  public:
  A() {cout<<"I'm a local class!"<<endl;}
 };
 A a; //fine
 A * p = new A; //fine
}
int main()
{
 A another_a; //error: undefined symbol 'A'
}
```

You can have different classes with the same name, so long as their names don't clash:

```
class A{}; //#1
void func
{
class A {};//#2
A a;//#2
}
int main()
{
 A a; //#1
}
```

Needless to say, such coding style isn't recommended. However, the point is to show that local classes' names aren't visible outside their scope.

Restrictions on Local Classes

C++ imposes several restrictions on local class with regard to the type of members they can have, their definitions and their usage. Declarations in a local class can use only type names, static variables, `extern` variables and functions, and enumerators from the enclosing scope. For example:

```
void func()
{
 static int y;
 int x;
 void e(); //extern function
 enum {MAX=1024};
 class B
 {
//OK, y is a static variable declared in B's enclosing scope
  int f() {return y; }
  void g() { e(); }//OK
  int m() {return MAX;} //OK
  int h() {return x; } //error, x is auto
 };
}
```

Member Functions

Unlike ordinary classes, which can define their member functions inside the class body or at a different translation unit, member functions of a local class must be defined inside the class body. You cannot declare them inside the class and define them outside:

```
void f()
{
 struct S
 {
 void f() {cout<<"f() called"<<endl;}
 void g();
 };
S s;
s.f(); //fine
s.g(); //funny linkage error
}
```

Try to run this code on your computer and see how well your linker copes with the missing definition of `S::g()`. My linker issues a funny error message; it notices that the definition of a certain function is missing from the compiled binaries. However, because S has no linkage, its member functions' names aren't accessible at link time and therefore it produces a cryptic error message:

```
[Linker Error] Unresolved external
'{794}...' referenced from C:\DOCUMENTS...
```

Trying to define `S::g()` inside `f()` will cause a compilation error:

```
void f()
{
 struct S
 {
 void f() {cout<<"f() called"<<endl;}
 void g();
 };
void S::g() {} //compilation error
S s;
s.f(); //fine
s.g(); //funny linkage error
}
```

Only an in-class definition of `g()` will do.

Static Members

A local class cannot have static data members; however, as shown previously, it may access ordinary static variables declared in its enclosing scope. This restriction applies to `const` static members of an integral type, too:

```
void f()
{
 struct S
 {
  const static int MAX=1024;//error
 };
}
```

A local class may have static member functions, though. Such members (as all member functions of a local class) must be defined inside the class body:

```
void f()
{
 struct S
 {
  static void g() {cout<<"I'm g()"<<endl;}
 };
```

```
   S::g(); //fine
}
```

Summary

Admittedly, local classes are a plaything, mostly. However, they have some valid uses. For example, you can use a local class to define a function object that is accessible only from within its scope. This is the closest you can get in C++ to the concept of nested procedures that some programming languages have. Another valid use is code protection. Because ordinary classes export their names (as well as names of their member functions) to the entire program, crackers might take advantage of this and decompile the executable. With the certain .exe format and the right reverse-engineering tools, it isn't as a difficult task as it might seem, especially if the program consists of dynamically loaded modules. By using local classes that implement tiny but sensitive bits of functionality, you can protect your code from such cracking attempts, or at least make the job of a cracker more difficult. Finally, local classes are useful when you need an ad-hoc helper function that is used only once—this is the closest thing to a "disposable class," if you like. A demonstration of this practical technique can be found in the article "Use Local Classes for Proper Cleanup in Exception-Enabled Apps" (*http://www.devx.com/cplus/Article/22163*).

Complex Arithmetic

FORTRAN has had native complex datatypes for more than 50 years. Yet many other programming languages haven't considered this feature noteworthy enough to dedicate a built-in datatype or a standard library to it. C++ fixed this historical gaffe more than a decade ago with the inclusion of the `<complex>` header in its Standard Library. Here, I will explain how it works and give a few tips about its proper usage and future directions.

Complex Without Complications

Complex numbers, for those of you who haven't dealt with this mathematical oddity before, are a superset of real numbers. Real numbers in C++ are represented as one of the three built-in floating types: `float`, `double`, and `long double`. These datatypes differ in their precision and range. The larger the number of bytes each of these datatypes occupies, the larger its range. As a bonus, the precision of the fraction part increases as well.

While we're on the subject, it may be a good opportunity to step up on my soapbox and advise all programmers to refrain from using `float`. The only reason for the existence of this datatype is compatibility with embedded hardware and *el cheapo* processors that cannot chew more than four bytes at once. Use `float` only when there's no other choice; otherwise, `double` or `long double` should be your default floating-point datatype.

The set of real numbers contains all the positive and negative numbers (including zero), with or without a fraction. Thus, you can think of a real number as a pair of two integers: one containing the main value and the other one representing the fraction. The real number 3.34 can thus be represented as:

```
int real[2];
real[0]=3;
real[1]=34; //hundredths
```

This technique of representing floating-point values as *scaled integers* is widely used in financial systems and in hardware environments that don't support floating datatypes natively.

A complex number contains two constituents: a *real part* and an *imaginary part*. Both parts are floating-point values of the same type. In a language such as C++, which doesn't have a built-in complex datatype, the common workaround is to pack two floating-point variables, very much like the scaled integers I've just shown. For example, to represent the complex value 9.67 and an imaginary part 3.26 you can do the following:

```
double complex[2];
complex[0]=9.67; //real
complex [1]=3.26; //imaginary
```

This is in fact how programmers dealt with complex numbers before the advent of STL. Fortunately, the `<complex>` library defines a class template `complex` that implements this trick and wraps it in a user-friendly interface. The reason for choosing a template rather than an ordinary class is, as you may have guessed, the need to support different precision levels. When you create a complex object, you have to specify which specialization you're using:

```
#include <complex>
using std::complex;
complex <double> val;
```

Constructors and Initialization

The constructor of `complex` isn't `explicit` by design, so that automatic conversions to and from a floating-point variable can take place:

```
complex <double> num=5.6;
```

The default constructor creates a complex object initialized to 0.0,0.0, where the first number is always the real part and the second one is the imaginary part. However, you can initialize a complex object with any other pair of values:

```
complex<double> num(0.1); //0.1, and a default value of 0.0
complex<double> num2(-10.8, 0.8);
```

Overloaded Operators

This class defines overloaded versions of unary and binary operators:

```
//binary +
template <class T> complex<T> operator+ (const complex<T>&, const complex<T>&);
template <class T> complex<T> operator+ (const complex<T>&, const T&);
template <class T> complex<T> operator+ (const T&, const complex<T>&);
//..similar declarations of -, *, /, == and !=
//unary + and -
template <class T> complex<T> operator+ (const complex<T>&);
template <class T> complex<T> operator- (const complex<T>&);
```

Using these operators, you can combine complex objects and native floating-point variables in the same expression:

```
complex <double> val, val2;
val=val2+9.5;
val2-=.5;
```

Additional Functions

The standardization committee recently discussed the usefulness of exposing complex's "implementation details," allowing direct access to its data members. To be honest, the zeal with which which OOP pundits have pursued this for decades has led to some ridiculous, over-protective design idioms. After all, a complex number can't be implemented in a reasonably efficient and reliable manner other than by grouping two floating-point variables of the same type. Therefore, some members suggested that direct access to the real and imaginary data members be granted. There's still a debate on whether the two members should be represented as an array:

```
template <class T> class complex <T>
{
 T arr[2];
};
```

or two data members:

```
template <class T> class complex <T>
{
 T re;
 T im;
};
```

However, for the time being, the safest and most portable approach is to use the real() and imag() function templates to access a complex number's constituents:

```
complex<double> num(-10.8, +0.8);
double real_part=real(num);
double imaginary=imag(num);
```

The standard I/O stream classes support complex objects. They output a complex in the format (x,y) and read it in the formats x, (x) and (x,y). For example:

```
cout<<"insert a complex, e.g., 10,(0) or (10,0)"<<endl;
cin>>val;
cout<<"val is: "<<val<<endl;
```

A typical input session looks like this:

```
insert a complex, e.g., 10,(0) or (10,0)
(-99,8)
val is: (-99,8)
```

Implicit Conversions

An implicit conversion of two distinct complex specializations is allowed only in one direction—upward. You can convert complex<double> to complex<long double> but not vice versa. Likewise, complex<float> can be converted implicitly to complex<double> or complex<long double> but complex<double> cannot be converted to complex<float>—you get the idea.

Summary

Complex arithmetic is widely used in scientific applications and simulations. The C99 standard also added a complex arithmetic library <complex.h> and even two new keywords: complex and imaginary.

TIP: For more information about C99, see the section "A Tour of C99."

Floating-Point Woes

The earlier discussion about complex arithmetic entered another notable issue through the back door: floating-point woes. Here, I'll explain the problem and its causes and suggest a few workarounds.

The Problem

Computer hardware is incapable of dealing properly with the mathematical notion of real numbers. It's not your CPU that's to blame nor is it the programming language, the compiler, the math coprocessor, etc. It's because computers squeeze real numbers into a finite number of bits. For example, the value of the expression 10/3 is 3.3333 . . . with an infinite number of 3s after the decimal point. When you store it in a datatype that has a fixed number of bits, the result is *approximated*. It can be truncated to 3.333 or it could be rounded to 3.3330, perhaps 3.3334, and so on.

Using a datatype with a higher precision level minimizes this distortion, so the result becomes 3.333333333, 3.333333330 or 3.333333334 instead. This asymptotic approximation reduces the relative distortion of the original value (to which I refer as "digital noise") but it doesn't eliminate it. For many purposes, a close-enough approximation is sufficient. For instance, if you're a professor at the department of linguistics and you need to calculate the average grades of all students listed to the "Introduction to Indo-European Languages" course, it doesn't really matter whether the result of 87.8888 . . . is truncated into 87.88887.

There is one serious problem with this imprecise nature of floating-point numbers though: you can never use operator == reliably. Let's look at a concrete example:

```
double cost=293.14;
cost*=1.073333; //add tax
double before_tax=cost/=1.073333; //deduct tax for invoice
bool b=
 (before_tax==cost);//surprise!
```

You would expect that after adding and deducting the tax, `before_tax` should have the same value as `cost`. However, the results are slightly different. The imprecise representation of irrational fractions causes the two values to differ. Consequently, operator `==` returns `false`. The use of a more precise datatype, `long double`, or tampering with your compiler settings so that it would compensate for the alleged buggy processor (and you know which processor I'm referring to!) wouldn't work:

```
long double cost=293.14;
cost*=1.073333;
long double before_tax=cost/1.07333;
bool b= (before_tax==cost); //same old story
```

This is truly a serious problem. In fact, I'm surprised that many programmers aren't aware of this, wasting precious hours debugging their code and trying to find faulty `if-else` statements, until they realize where the problem really lies. So, the first lesson is this: Never use `==` to compare floating-point values. This means that `!=`, `<=`, etc., are also out of the question.

Relative Operators

The relative operators and `<`, `>` are seemingly less dangerous because they function as expected in the majority of cases:

```
cost*=1.073333;
long double before_tax=cost/1.07333;
bool b= (before_tax<cost); //fine
```

Although `before_tax` and `cost` contain only approximate values, the difference between them is sufficiently large to overcome the digital noise. And yet, it is still possible to get wrong results even here:

```
long double cost=293.140000001;
//cost actually equals 293.140000000999976
bool b= (cost<293.140000001); //false!
```

The value 293.140000001 can't be represented accurately. On my computer it's approximated as 293.140000000999976. Therefore, one might expect that this expression:

```
293.140000000999976<293.140000001
```

should evaluate as `true`. It doesn't, though. The problem is that the constant 293.140000001 is also approximated. Therefore, applying any of the relative operators to these approximated values produces unpredictable results.

In my opinion, this situation is even worse than the onerous equality operator. A program that produces correct results 99.99% of the time and fails 0.01% is much worse than one that gets wrong results all of the time because it misleads you into thinking that it's totally reliable. If these calculations were applied to medicine doses at an ICU, you certainly wouldn't want to rely on "low failure probability."

Remedies

There are several workarounds for this onerous problem. The "scaled integers" technique presented in complex arithmetic can be a simple and efficient workaround in many cases. A meteorological service that uses a telemetric device to measures temperatures doesn't need absolute accuracy; a precision of a tenth of a degree is usually acceptable. In this case, you can use integers that represent tenths of a degree:

```
int tenths=1034;  //103.2 Fahrenheit
```

If you choose to use this technique, you will need a library that includes conversion, formatting, and calculation services.

In scientific applications, you can use specialized math libraries. These libraries include classes that simulate infinite precision. The downside is that such libraries are often slow and pretty costly.

A third solution is to overload mathematical and relative operators for a certain class. The overloaded versions can compensate for the digital noise of floating-point data. For example, an overloaded == may return `true` even if the two operands are very close but still not identical.

Summary

Acknowledging a problem is a major step toward a solution. When you need to deal with real numbers, you should first determine whether the imprecise nature of floating-point datatypes is tolerable. As noted above, in many cases it is. If however it isn't, you should consider one of the workarounds described here.

The Object Model, Part I

The "object model" is a set of implementation specifications and semantic properties that define how objects are represented in a C++ program and how they manage to provide services such as member function calls, automatic initialization and destruction, copying, encapsulation, inheritance and so on. In this series, I will present the underlying C++ object model.

Memory Layout of Data Members

Most object-oriented programming languages implement objects as references or some other type of an alias to the actual object. This indirect-access model was originally introduced with Smalltalk. Other programming languages have adopted this concept because it facilitates the implementation of a built-in garbage collector and because of its rather straightforward implementation—as long as the language is restricted to the single inheritance model. In C++ however, objects are represented as chunks of memory that contain their data members, very much like good old C structs. Take a look at the following class:

```
class Time
{
private:
  int hours, minutes, seconds;
public:
  explicit Time(int h=0, int mins=0, int secs=0);
  int getHour() const;
  void setHour(int h);
//..additional member functions
};
```

The memory layout of such an object is identical to that of the following struct:

```
struct S
{
  int a;
  int b;
  int c;
```

```
};
Time t;
S s //t and s have identical binary layouts
```

This raises the first question: Shouldn't there be a difference in the memory layout of members with different access types?

Indeed, the C++ Standard allows an implementation to store members with different access types in non-adjacent memory chunks. Thus, in theory at least, the data members of the following two classes may not be binary-compatible:

```
struct A
{
public:
  int a;
protected:
  int b;
};
class B
{
private: //as opposed to public in A
int a;
protected:
int b;
};
```

The idea behind this leeway was to enable implementations to store data members with different access types in different memory regions, assuming that each region could provide hardware-controlled access checking or similar functionality. In practice, however, I'm not aware of a single implementation that doesn't store members with different access types contiguously. Thus, even though the Standard doesn't guarantee binary compatibility between A and B, practically all compilers treat them in the same manner, regardless of their members' access type.

Non-Virtual Member Functions

Another question that the comparison between t and s raises is: Where are the member functions of class Time stored? Some programmers believe that member functions are represented as pointers to members stored in each object. This model could be useful in toy languages and didactic tools. However, real programming languages never use it because it's terribly inefficient. Think of class Time. Every instance thereof must have at least six pointers to members if this model were used: four for the special member functions, and two more for `setHour()` and `getHour()`. In most cases, classes have many more user-defined member functions, which means that more space would be required per object. Things get much worse when you create a large array of objects under this naive model. Clearly, the "one pointer to member per member function" model is unacceptable. In reality, member functions are represented like ordinary C functions: A single copy of the function's body is shared by all objects. To ensure that a member function can access the data members of the object for which it is called, C++ automatically inserts a hidden `this` argument into every nonstatic member function call. You can think of a nonstatic member function as an ordinary C function that takes a pointer to the actual object that invokes it. This trick enables an implementation to share a single copy of a member function among all objects of the same class (as well as objects derived from it) while giving you the impression that each object calls its own copy of the member function.

Static Member Functions

Static member functions are even closer to C-style functions. Here again, a single instance of the function is shared by all objects except that this time, the hidden `this` argument isn't passed as an argument. Consequently, static member functions cannot access an object's data members. To conclude, a nonstatic member function call is performed in the context of a certain object, whereas a static member function is called for a class. This means that you can call a static member function even if there are no objects of a certain class.

Virtual Member functions

How are virtual member functions represented? Oddly enough, they are identical to non-virtual, nonstatic member functions: A single instance of the same function is shared by all objects. There is, however, a crucial difference with respect to their invocation process. Every polymorphic object (i.e., an object that has at least one virtual member function, either directly or indirectly) contains an additional hidden data member, traditionally called `vptr`, which stores an address of the `vtbl`—a per-class table of the virtual functions' addresses. Thus, the space overhead is one `vptr` (typically a four-byte pointer) per object, regardless of the number of virtual member functions in a given class. This isn't as costly as storing a distinct pointer for every member function, although in certain situations, e.g., when you have a large collection of polymorphic objects with no data members, the space overhead can be noticeable. Note also that the Standard doesn't require that a `vptr` member be included in each object; technically, there are other ways to implement the virtual function mechanism, although in practice, all compiler use the same method.

Ideally, C++ creates a single `vtbl` that is shared by all objects of the same class. In some complicated (and rare) inheritance lattices, it isn't always possible to avoid the reduplication of the virtual table, though.

To implement dynamic binding, a virtual function call made through a reference or a pointer to a polymorphic object is performed in two steps. At compile-time, the compiler replaces each call with a stub that refers to the relevant table entry. The content of this entry is determined only at runtime. So you can think of a virtual function call as two consecutive calls: the first one retrieves the actual address of the virtual function and the second one invokes the member function through the address obtained in the previous step. As you may have suspected, the additional level of indirection incurs runtime and space overhead. However, you pay for this (rather small) overhead only when you're truly using dynamic binding. If the call can be resolved at compile-time, this extra overhead is eliminated, as shown in the following example:

```
struct S
{
 virtual int func();
};
S s;
s.func(); //resolved statically
```

In this case, the compiler has all the type information necessary for invoking `func()`. Therefore, it doesn't defer the resolution to runtime but bypasses the virtual call mechanism and treats the function as a non-virtual one. This is perfectly safe because the static type of s, which is "S," can't change at runtime. By contrast, in this case the call must be resolved dynamically:

```
void f(S *ps)
{
 s->func(); //what's the dynamic type of *ps?
}
```

In this case, the compiler can't be certain about the dynamic type of *ps. It could be S or it could be any other type derived from S. Consequently, the call resolution is deferred to runtime, with the inevitable overhead associated with dynamic binding.

Summary

A C++ object is in many aspects compatible with C structs. This design decision enables C++ code to use C code directly, without incurring performance penalties or compatibility problems. In the second part of this series I will show how more advanced features such as object embedding, inheritance, multiple inheritance, and virtual inheritance affect the C++ object model.

The Object Model, Part II

Part I of our discussion of the object model presented the basic implementation details of the underlying C++ machinery. Now I'll discuss inheritance in its various flavors.

Single Inheritance

Every object-oriented programming language supports at least one type of inheritance: ordinary, single inheritance. Deriving a class from a base class causes the data members of the latter to be copied into the derived class. Here again, there is a lot of leeway in the Standard with respect to the underlying layout of the resulting object. However, it is agreed that the base class subobject should be located before the data members of the derived class. If we have the following class hierarchy:

```
class Base
{
private:
 int a;
 char b;
 void * p;
public:
 explicit Base(int a);
};
class Derived : public Base
{
private:
 double d;
public:
 Derived: Base(0) {}
};
```

the memory layout of `Derived` should be identical to that of the following struct:

```
struct S
{
 int a;
 char b;
 void * p; //last member of base subobject
 double d; //first member of derived
};
```

As noted before, the Standard requires that data members declared without an intervening *access-specifier* (i.e., `public`, `protected` and `private`) are allocated so that later members have higher addresses within a class object. By contrast, the order of allocation of nonstatic data members separated by an access-specifier is unspecified. In practice, however, all compilers ignore access specifiers with respect to members' order. Therefore, it doesn't matter if `Base` declares `a` as `protected` or `public`—the resulting `Derived` object will still have the same memory layout of struct `S` above. That said, there's no guarantee that members will be allocated on adjacent memory addresses. Alignment requirement might cause the compiler to insert *padding bytes* between members that don't fit into the hardware's native alignment requirements. This is why most compilers allocate the member `p` on a memory address that is four bytes farther than `b`'s address, even though `b` occupies only a single byte. The three padding bytes inserted after `b` contain garbage.

Inheritance and Polymorphism

In the previous examples, I used a slightly contrived inheritance model in which the base class doesn't declare any virtual member functions. In practice, base classes usually have at least a virtual destructor. In that case, the memory layout of a derived object is slightly different. The compiler must insert the `vptr` into the object. Compilers can be divided into two categories with respect to their `vptr` handling policy. UNIX compilers typically place the `vptr` after the last user-declared data member, whereas Windows compilers place it as the first data member of the object, before any user-declared data members:

```
class A
{
int x;
public:
```

```
virtual int f();
};
A a;
```

The memory layout of a is either as that of S1 or S2:

```
struct S1 //UNIX style vptr location
{
int x;
void * vptr;
};
struct S2 //Windows style vptr location
{
void * vptr;
int x;
};
```

Each of these policies has its pros and cons. Placing the vptr at offset 0, a la Windows, ensures that its relative position in a polymorphic object is always the same as this. This premise enables the compiler to apply certain optimizations. The UNIX tradition of placing the vptr at the end necessitates that its precise location must be calculated for each object. However, it ensures backward compatibility with C structs. This may not seem like a boon today but many UNIX applications use C libraries that have undergone an object-oriented facelift, e.g., by adding member functions to data structures that were formerly POD structs.

What happens when a class inherits from a polymorphic class? Obviously, the resulting object can't have multiple vptrs. Depending on the compiler, the vptr is moved into the correct offset in the resulting object:

```
class Derived: public A
{
 double y;
public:
 virtual int g();
};
struct D1 //UNIX style vptr location
{
int x;
double y;
void * vptr; //pushed to the end
};
struct D2 //Windows style vptr location
```

```
{
void * vptr;//always at offset 0
int x;
double y;
};
```

Multiple Inheritance

When a class has multiple base classes, the compiler inserts each base class subobject into the resulting object according to the bases' declaration order:

```
class A
{
 int one;
};
class B
{
 double two;
};
class D: public A, public B
{
 void * three;
};
```

The memory layout of a D object is as follows:

```
struct D
{
int one;
int two;
void * three;
};
```

If any of the three classes declares a virtual function, the compiler will insert the `vptr` either before `one` or after `three`.

Virtual Inheritance

When virtual inheritance is used, all hell breaks loose. The problem is that the compiler tries its best to ensure that the resulting object shall have only a single subobject of a virtual base. The common strategy employed by virtually all compilers is to use a pointer to the virtual (shared) subobject. However, the exact location of that shared subobject is compiler-dependent.

Summary

Ideally, programmers should rarely care about the underlying representation of objects, let alone the virtual dispatch machinery. However, in low-level applications such as an object-oriented database engine, object serializers and compiler writing, you have to be familiar with these intimate details. Furthermore, even if this information isn't required for your daily programming tasks, it can certainly help you understand the way things work in C++ and how to exert the full potential of your compiler.

The Object Model, Part III

In this section, I will discuss the last two issues regarding the underlying C++ object model, namely embedded objects' representation and the handling of empty base classes.

Embedded Objects

Embedded objects are stored as ordinary data members in their enclosing class. However, they are constructed before the enclosing class's constructor runs. Their order of declaration affects their relative location within the resulting object. For instance, the following `Transaction` class contains an embedded object as its first data member:

```
struct Rec
{
int id;
time_t timestamp;
};
class Transaction
{
 Rec rec;
 uid_t user_id;
 //...
};
```

The memory layout of a `Transaction` object looks like this:

```
class Transaction
{
 int id;
```

```
  time_t timestamp;
  uid_t user_id;
};
```

As you can see, there are no clues that mark the embedded object's boundaries. In fact, this very memory layout could represent the following class as well:

```
class Flat_transaction
{
 int id;
 time_t timestamp;
 uid_t user_id;
//..
};
```

However, when an embedded object is polymorphic, the enclosing object has a boundary marker either at the beginning or the end of its embedded object in the form of a `vptr`. If the containing object is also polymorphic, you will find two `vptrs` and so on—each embedded object retains its own `vptr`. Unlike in the case of inheritance, the compiler doesn't collapse the embedded objects' `vptr`(s) into one, as can be seen in the following example:

```
class A
{
 char * buff;
public:
 virtual int f();
};
class B
{
  int n;
public:
 virtual int g();
};

class C
{
 A a;
 B b;
public:
 virtual int h();
};
```

The memory layout of C is platform dependent; under Windows, each vptr marks the beginning of a subobject, whereas in UNIX, it marks the end:

```
struct C //Windows memory layout of class C
{
 void * _C_vptr;   //enclosing object first

 void * A_vptr; //members of a
   char * buff;

 void * B_vptr; //members of b
   int n;
};
struct C //UNIX memory layout of class C
{
char * buff; //members of a
  void * A_vptr;

 int n; //members of b
  void * B_vptr;

void * _C_vptr;   //enclosing object's vptr
};
```

As complicated as this may seem, there's no simple and efficient way to collapse all the embedded objects' vptrs into one because member functions of such objects are called through their respective objects:

```
C c;
c.a.f();
c.g(); //error, no such member in class C
```

Advice

This property of composite objects often surprises programmers who believe that each object contains no more than one vptr. Things get even worse when you declare an array of embedded objects in an enclosing class; in this case, every element in the array has its own private vptr. Therefore, when you design composite classes, you should take these issues into consideration. It is perfectly OK to declare an array of string objects, for instance, because std::string isn't a polymorphic class. By contrast, an array of fstream objects could bloat your classes unduly.

Empty Base Classes

Classes that contain neither virtual functions nor nonstatic data members are said to be *empty classes*. As such, they should—at least in theory—occupy no memory at all. However, the Standard requires that the size of a complete object shall not be zero. Therefore, compilers insert at least one or more dummy bytes into each such object:

```
class WinterWeather
{
void Rain();
void Snow();
};

WinterWeather   ww;
cout<<sizeof ww <<endl;
```

The precise value that the `cout` statement displays is platform-dependent. However, it must be a positive integer larger than zero. The reason for this requirement is obvious: Every object must have a distinct memory address. If objects were allowed to occupy no memory at all, you wouldn't be able to create arrays of such objects because their addresses would overlap. However, this restriction applies to *complete objects*. By contrast, a subobject serving as a base class of another class may have a zero size. This is an optimization measure employed in many compilers nowadays, although it isn't a Standard requirement. Consider the following example:

```
class Forecast: public WinterWeather
{
 int flags;
 time_t timestamp;
public:
 Forecast();
//..additional non-virtual member functions
};
Forecast fc;
```

The memory layout of `fc` may include a `WinterWeather` subobject as its first member or there could be no trace of this base class subobject inside `fc`. If you're curious to see how your compiler behaves in this regard, you can use it to compare the address of `fc` with that of `fc.flags`:

```
if ((void *)&fc == (void *)&fc.flags)
{
//empty base class optimization in use
}
else
{
//it isn't
}
```

Remember, though, that this optimization applies to base classes; embedded objects must have distinct memory addresses within their enclosing object for the same reason given above.

Summary

At first glance, poking into the underlying memory layout of objects might seem like the hair-splitting of lawyers' language. As I have shown here though, this theoretical discussion has practical implications that affect the design of composite classes.

The "Object Model" trilogy has exemplified the differences between base classes and embedded objects, as well as the subtle details of each class's components. For instance, whether a class is polymorphic or not could be a decisive factor when choosing between an embedded array and a pointer. Likewise, if you're using interfaces and empty base classes, the way your compiler handles empty base classes could also affect your design—or the compiler you choose to work with.

Temporary Objects

In this section, I will discuss the concept of temporary objects, or temporaries for short. Temporaries differ in several aspects from ordinary objects with respect to their lifetime and assignment. Here I will explain why and when they are introduced and how you can minimize their creation and thus optimize your code.

Calling All Temps

The notion of temporary objects isn't new. It dates back to the early days of FORTRAN, when programmers were able for the first time to incorporate expressions that looked like mathematical formulae in their programs. Things haven't changed much since then; in the evaluation of complex expressions, the compiler has to store intermediary results in a temporary location. Here's an example of an expression that necessitates a temporary:

```
int n;
read(n);
int x= 2+(4/n); //necessitates temporaries
```

The evaluation order of this expression is as follows: First, the result of 4/n is computed. Obviously, it has to be stored somewhere. Therefore, the compiler introduces a temp int for storing it. Next, the expression 2+temp is evaluated and stored in another temporary object. Finally, the second temporary is assigned to x. Note that clever compilers can elide the second temporary by writing the result directly into x. However, eliding the first temporary isn't always possible.

You can break this complex expression into several steps. This way, instead of letting the compiler introduce temporaries, you will manage them explicitly:

```
int temp = 2/n;
int x=2+temp;
```

In terms of performance and size, there's no difference between the two forms. However, when you let the compiler introduce temporaries as it sees fit, it can apply certain optimizations. For example, if n's value is known at compile-time, the expression 4/n can be calculated at compile-time and thus the entire expression can be replaced with the result.

Temporaries' Anonymity

One of the characteristics of temporaries is that they are nameless. As such, you can't refer to them explicitly, nor can you assign a value to them, but you can copy their values to a named object:

```
int func(); //result is stored in a temporary
int c= func(); //copying temporary's value to c
```

The function call returns a temporary int whose value is copied into a named int called c. However, you can't access the temp variable directly:

```
func()=5; //error, can't assign to a temp
```

This is the major difference between temporaries and named objects: A temporary is an *r-value*; i.e., something that may appear on the right-hand side of an assignment expression, whereas a named object is an *l-value*, which is a piece of memory to which you can write a value.

Temporaries' Lifetime

Temporaries differ from ordinary objects with respect to their lifetime. When you define an `auto` object, it remains alive until its scope is exited. For example:

```
void func()
{
 int n=5;
 if (something)
 //..
 else..
 //..
}//n is destroyed here
```

By contrast, temporaries are destroyed as the last step in evaluating the full expression that contains the point where they were created. This Standardese phrasing means that temporaries are destroyed when control reaches the terminating semicolon of the full expression in which they were created. In the following example, the temporary `string` object remains alive conceptually until the first semicolon that terminates the entire expression:

```
string s1,s2,s3;
string s =
        s3+(s2+s1)
      ; //temporaries destroyed at this point
```

Let's evaluate it. First, a temporary `string` is introduced that stores the value of `s1+s2`. This temporary is then added to `s3`. The result is then assigned to `s`. Finally, all the temporaries that have been introduced in the evaluation of this line of code are destroyed in reverse order of the completion of their construction. Notice that the Standard guarantees the automatic destruction of temporaries at this point even when an exception is thrown during the stack unwinding process.

There is one exception to this rule, though. When you bind a reference to `const` to a temporary, the bound temporary persists for the lifetime of the reference. For example:

```
int main()
{
 string s1;
 const string& sr = string("a")+string("b"); //#1
 string s2;
}
```

The expression `string("a")+string("b")` in the line marked #1 creates three temporary `string` objects. The first temporary `__t1` contains the result of the subexpression `string("a")`, the second temporary `__t2` stores `string("")` and finally, a third temporary `__t3` stores the result of the addition of these two expressions. The order of the construction of the first two temporaries is unspecified because the compiler is allowed to evaluate the expression `string("a")+string("b")` in either direction. `__t1` and `__t2` are destroyed at the end of the full expression, as usual. However, the temporary `__t3` bound to the reference `sr` is destroyed at the end of `sr`'s lifetime, that is, at the end of the program. This exception is meant to guarantee that `sr` doesn't turn into a dangling reference silently.

Summary

Temporary objects are usually harmless and—in some cases—unavoidable. However, when dealing with complex objects whose construction and destruction are expensive in terms of performance, you want to minimize their introduction. There are several guidelines that can help you. First, break complex expressions into autonomous subexpressions and store their results in a named object. If you need to store multiple intermediary results sequentially, you can reuse the same object. This is more efficient than letting the complier introduce a new temporary in every subexpression. In the following example, a single string object is used for storing two intermediate values:

```
//original expression was : string s= s1+s2+s3;
string temp=s1+s2;
temp+=s3;
string s=temp;
```

Another useful technique is to use `+=` for self-assignment instead of `+`:

```
//original expression was : temp=temp+s3
temp+=s3;
```

Remember that the expression `temp+s3` yields another temporary object; by using `+=` you avoid this.

Temporary Objects—Advanced Techniques

Earlier I presented the basic concepts of temporary objects. In this section, I will explain under which circumstances the explicit instantiation of temporary objects may be useful and how it's done. In addition, I will clear the air regarding the quirky syntax of auto object's instantiation.

Explicit Instantiation of Temporaries

Earlier, I may have given you the impression that temporaries are always created behind your back. This isn't always so. In fact, there is a way to create such objects explicitly. The syntax looks confusingly similar to that of an ordinary auto object instantiation, except that in the case of a temporary object, you don't name it. The following minimal pair shows the difference between the instantiation of a named object and a temporary object:

```
string s("hello"); //ordinary auto object
string  ("hello"); //#2 nameless, hence: temporary
int x; //temporary created in #2 has been destroyed at this point
```

As usual, the temporary object remains alive until the end of the full expression in which it was created. In the line marked as #2 above, the temporary string object is destroyed immediately before the declaration of x. However, if you bind a reference to `const` to that temporary, it will remain alive as long as the reference to which it is bound remains alive:

```
string s("hello"); //ordinary auto object
const string &sr =string("hello"); //
int x; //
sr.clear(); //fine, temporary is still alive
```

This example, though contrived, demonstrates one of the uses of an explicit instantiation of a temporary instantiation: namely, binding an object to a reference when the reference itself is to be used in the program instead of an actual object.

An explicit temporary instantiation is also useful when you need to pass an argument to a function. In the following example, a temporary `Date` object is created as an argument passed to the `push_back()` member function. By using a temporary you ensure that the argument cannot be used elsewhere in the program:

```
vector <Date> vd;
vd.push_back(Date());
```

NOTE: The vector *copies* the argument into its own storage; it never stores the original argument. Therefore, using a temporary is perfectly safe.

Explicit instantiation of a temporary may also be needed when you want to assign a new state to an existing object at once. Suppose you want to assign a new value to a `complex` number. You can use its setter member functions to assign each of its data members explicitly. Alternatively, you can use the following shortcut:

```
complex <double> d(1.0, 0.5);
//suppose you want to change d's value to (10, 0.9)
d=complex(10,0.9);
```

Here, a temporary `complex` object with the desired value is created and assigned to d. The full-blown instantiation of a `complex` object might seem inefficient. However, many compilers are clever enough to optimize this code and elide the actual construction of a temporary. Secondly, this notation is shorter and more readable. In some cases, it is even more efficient than explicitly invoking a sequence of member functions that clear the current object's state and subsequently assign a new value to it.

Syntax Musings

An explicit instantiation of a temporary object always includes an argument list, although the list itself may be empty:

```
void func (const string & s);
func (string() ); // invoking string's default ctor
```

When the non-default constructor is to be invoked, the argument list of the temporary contains the constructor's arguments:

```
func (string("Test"));
```

However, when you instantiate an ordinary `auto` object, you have to distinguish syntactically between a default constructor invocation and a non-default constructor invocation. Here is how you create an `auto` string object without the constructor's arguments:

```
string s;   //note: no parentheses in this case
```

By contrast, if you want to pass arguments to the constructor, use parentheses:

```
string s("welcome!");
```

Using an empty argument list to instantiate an auto object is not a syntactic error—it's much worse:

```
string s(); //compiles OK; expect a surprise
```

As opposed to what many programmers think, this line of code doesn't instantiate an `auto` string object called `s`. Instead, it declares a function s that takes no parameters and returns a string object by value. Compilers can't guess that the programmer actually meant to define an `auto` string object here rather than declare a function prototype. To overcome the syntactic ambiguity, C++ distinguishes between these two cases by omitting the parentheses when instantiating a named auto object. This decision has historical significance, too: In C++, a declaration of the following form:

```
type identifier();
```

declares `identifier` as a function that takes no parameters and returns `type`. C++ creators didn't want to alter the semantics of legacy C code compiled under a C++ compiler. Therefore, C++ retains the original C interpretation of such declarations.

Summary

An explicit instantiation of a temporary object may have several advantages: The object in question lives only during the evaluation of the expression in which it was created and therefore can't be tampered with in other parts of the program. In addition, it enables you to assign a new state to an existing object instantly. As for the baffling syntax, remember to omit the empty pair of parentheses in an instantiation of a named object that uses the default constructor.

Over-Engineering

In the past 16 months, I've focused mainly on techniques and features that enhance code safety, reliability, readability and performance. Interestingly, quite a few textbooks and gurus who also acknowledge the importance of these issues sometimes lose the distinction between the goal and its means. It is not unusual to see whole articles dedicated to the "academicization" of simple programming tasks and to hair-splitting. This isn't just a waste of time; it leads programmers (especially novices) to the wrong conclusion that C++ is an impossible programming language that no one can ever truly master or fully understand. The golden rule, as always, is to know where to draw the line. To paraphrase a common idiom, I believe in "good-enough engineering" rather than dwelling indefinitely on the same poor algorithm that has been beaten to death, especially if it is going to be used only once or twice in a project. Here I will show some of the common symptoms that might typify over-engineering, and discuss their potential damage.

Exceptions

What I'm about to say here would shake the foundations of every decent C++ tutorial, but the more I look at it I can't avoid this honest conclusion: Exceptions are, almost without exception (pun unintended), more of a problem than a solution. Yes, they are unavoidable in some rare cases, and yes, they are widely used in the Standard Library. However, when you closely examine large-scale projects that use exceptions proactively you soon realize that exceptions are just lip service. The best example of this comes from Java. Consider the following example:

```
try //inevitable; mymethod() has a non-empty exception spec
{
 myobj.mymethod();
}
catch(Exception e)
{}//just to make to compiler shut up
//...
```

This idiom is very common in every Java-based application. In this particular language, it's not the poor programmers' fault, because Java forces them to enclose every call to a method that might throw in a `try` block and provide a matching `catch`-clause. More often than not, the dummy handler does absolutely nothing; it's there just to pacify the compiler. Thus, exceptions are just a nuisance that gets in the way in the majority of cases. You could argue that under some extreme conditions exceptions have no alternative: If the system has run out of heap memory or if a hardware fault of some sort disables the application from running normally, you can't ignore the exception as if nothing happened. This is true but, frankly, what can your exception handler do in such catastrophic situation other than write a laconic error message to a log file before giving up the ghost? More importantly, *should* it try to do anything at all when it's usually best to let the application terminate gracefully? In C++ things are slightly better because the C++ community unanimously agrees that exception specifications are a misfeature that should be ignored. However, you can still see naively implemented libraries and textbooks that obsessively include an empty `throw()` (i.e., no-throw) specification in every member function, including the canonical four. The Standard Library's designers were aware of this and tried to minimize the use of exceptions. For example, when the `find()` algorithm fails to find the sought-after value, it returns an iterator with an agreed-upon value rather than throwing an exception; similarly, `vector` forgos range checking when you use the `[]` overloaded operator.

If you examine specialized variants (*http://www.caravan.net/ec2plus/*) of C++ targeted at embedded systems, you will see that they don't support exceptions—with good reason. By contrast, such implementations do support use of classes, inheritance and virtual functions—as expensive and complicated as they can be in terms of runtime overhead and compiler writing.

Over-Genericity

Another acute symptom of over-engineering is over-genericity. Generic containers and algorithms are unquestionably the best thing that happened to C++ since the advent of classes. And yet, people often exaggeratedly pursue genericty. Indeed, a general-purpose standard library of a widely used programming language has to be generic enough to suit the needs of as many users as possible. But does a simple object viewer class that is used in a single project really have to meet the same requirements as would a Standard Library class? It's obvious that not every class and algorithm can be generic. Think of a string class for example. A string, as opposed to `vector`, knows a little more about the type of elements stored in it. For instance, it knows that they may be written to the screen or printed; it also knows that there are *collating rules* that define how its elements (i.e., characters) should be sorted. The fact that a string class knows a little more about its elements' properties is a two-edged sword: On one hand, it enables the implementer to write specialized algorithms such as `find()` and `assign()` that are more efficient than their generic versions; on the other hand, a string isn't truly a generic class nor should it be.

Excessive Operator Overloading

When Java designers decided to disallow operator overloading, they cited C++ as an example of the inherent woes of this feature. As usual, they got it wrong and that is why operator overloading is slowly but surely creeping into Java just as generics recently did. That said, operator overloading *can* be misused. In classic cases such as math libraries, strings and perhaps time and date libraries, defining an overloaded version of almost every operator makes sense; in many other cases, it doesn't. Consider the following example:

```
template <class T, void(T::*F)()>
class Dispatcher
{
private:
 T & obj;
//..
public:
 void execute () const { (obj.*F)(); }
};
```

Seemingly, one could argue that `execute()` should be replaced with an overloaded version of operator ():

```
void operator ()() const { (obj.*F)();}
```

This implementation might look sexier and more generic and might even impress your colleagues. The problem is that under certain situations, an overloaded operator leads to confusion and also imposes certain limitations that an ordinary member function doesn't. One such example is static member functions. If you needed for some reason to make `execute()` a static member function, it wouldn't be a problem. Alas, if you're using an overloaded version of operator (), you're confined to a nonstatic member function.

In terms of readability (especially in a project that combines development teams that use diverse programming languages), a member function with a self-evident name such as `execute()` might look less confusing than two consecutive pairs of parentheses. Remember also that overloaded operators—except ()—take a fixed number of parameters, whereas ordinary member functions aren't limited in this regard. Finally, turning a quasi-generic dispatcher class into a totally generic function object might be another example of over-engineering—after all, this class might be confined to a well-defined set of member functions in a certain project. While it is a good idea to plan ahead and make your classes resilient to changes, making a class more generic than necessary exacts a price in terms of testing, debugging, documentation and maintenance.

Summary

In a way, over-genericity is just as bad as premature optimization. Remember: Not every class you write is meant to be incorporated into the C++

Standard Library or win the first prize in the Most Ingenious C++ Class Design Competition. Therefore, your goal is usually to meet crazy deadlines while providing reasonably correct, reliable and efficient implementation. To achieve this goal, it may be necessary to relax some of the rigid academic restrictions you often see in posh textbooks. In other words, know when to draw the line between quality-of-design issues and academic hair-splitting and over-engineering.

Online Resources

"Error and Exception Handling" (*http://www.boost.org/more/ error_handling.html*), by Dave Abrahams, provides many useful tips about the do's and don'ts of exception handling. Sadly, more than 16 years after the introduction of this mechanism, exceptions are still very much compiler and OS dependent. As such, it's nearly impossible to write an exception-based application that is both portable and reliable. While I disagree with some of Abrahams' recommendations, this article presents pretty well the inherent complexities and woes of exceptions (and it still doesn't mention exception specifications!). Here are some of the guidelines with which I disagree:

Avoiding catch(...) sounds like a good idea, but since the C++ Standard doesn't guarantee that the stack be unwound without it (and after all, the primary reason for throwing an exception in the first place, as Abrahams notes, *is* to unwind the stack!), the omission of catch(...) could be dangerous. So my recommendation with respect to catch(...) is: Check your implementation's behavior and determine whether to use it accordingly. Likewise, while it is nice to believe that all exception objects should be derived (using virtual inheritance!) from `std::exception`, there are many projects that prefer to define their own exception classes for various good reasons. Similarly, expecting programmers to use virtual inheritance when deriving from `std::exception` is wishful thinking in terms of overhead, debugging and design complexity; this policy—while certainly justifiable under certain circumstances—isn't always adequate nor is it always necessary.

An interview (*http://www.builderau.com.au/program/work/ 0,39024650,39129961,00.htm*) with Miguel de Icaza, a Linux guru and the founder of the Mono project (*http://www.mono-project.com/*), is an instructive lesson about the potential damage that over-engineering might cause: "The problem with J2EE really is that it became very, very academic and the complexity of all these perfectly designed systems in schools does not necessarily map when you have deadlines and all kinds of other things . . ." Although de Icaza doesn't specify which features exactly are the culprit, the ubiquitous inane exceptions exemplified above are surely one of them.

Migrating to 64-Bit Environments

It is likely that 32-bit architectures will remain predominant in the near future. However, developers should bear in mind that their applications may sooner or later be ported to 64-bit environments, as these are becoming increasingly widespread. In this section, I will discuss the ramifications of migrating to 64-bit environments and explain the major differences between the object models of these two environments.

Compatibility Issues

The good news is that in the majority of cases, migrating your 32-bit apps to a 64-bit environment should be simple. All that it would take is recompilation and relinking. In practice, however, there are a few issues that need special attention.

When speaking of the portability of C++ code, one usually means *source file portability*. By contrast, the binaries are rarely portable even among different compilers on the same platform. Porting 32-bit code to a 64-bit environment means that there could be substantial differences between the binaries produced from the same source file under the two environments. Let's look at some of these differences more closely.

Built-in Types

C++ programmers who started their career in the DOS heyday learned to use `long` whenever they needed a 32-bit integer. However, in certain 64-bit systems, `long` is now a 64-bit integer. If your code depends on the actual number of bits that a datatype occupies, you should use the standard `typedef` names:

```
//defined in the C99 <inttypes.h>
int8_t     int16_t     int32_t     int64_t
uint8_t    uint16_t    uint32_t    uint64_t
```

Unfortunately, these typedefs are defined by C99 but not by C++98. In practice, however, most C++ compilers support C99 extensions including `<inttypes.h>`. Alternatively, you can define your own `typedef` names and use conditional compilation to ensure platform-independence.

TIP: For more information about C99, see Chapter 16, "A Tour of C99."

Another problem that may arise is that new processors sometimes don't support 8-bit types at all. C++ requires that the smallest addressable datatype should be `char`. Such platforms represent `char` as a 16-bit type. Again, if the underlying number of bytes is not an issue, you can safely ignore this difference since all the standard `char *` functions and data structures will work as expected. If however you truly need an 8-bit datatype, you will have to use bit fields or other kludges. Should that be the case, it's always advisable to hide the low-level details in a class such as `std::bistet` or a similar custom class.

Pointers

In 32-bit systems, a data pointer is represented as a 32-bit integer; 64-bit systems have 64-bit pointers in addition to or instead of 32-bit pointers. This duality enables users to run 32-bit programs under an emulator. Ideally, however, programs should use the default addressing mode, which relies on 64-bit pointers. This difference affects pointers to freestanding functions as well. Pointers to members are a different story, though. Under 32-bit architectures, they may have various sizes, depending on compiler settings, the member function in question, and their class's inheritance lattice. In most cases, a typical pointer to member is represented as a struct that packs two ordinary pointers. This means that under a 64-bit system a typical pointer to a member will have twice as many bits compared to its 32-bit counterpart. There could also be differences with respect to the actual *values* of pointers to members due to the alignment scheme of 64-bit environments.

Member Alignment

Member alignment is affected by the addressing mode of the target platform, the hardware's alignment requirements and compiler switches. In 64-bit systems, you should expect a *quadword* (eight bytes or 64 bits) alignment scheme or higher, as opposed to the typical *dword* (four bytes) alignment of 32-bit systems. Consequently, the sizes of user-defined types—i.e., structs, classes, unions, and enumerations—could increase due to the extra padding bytes inserted between members.

ABI

A platform's ABI defines a binary protocol for naming symbols and other layout issues. These symbols include the *decorated names* of functions, external objects, static data members and so on. The decorated names of functions with C++ linkage encode, among other things, their parameter types and their stack offset. Because the parameters' size may change when migrating to a 64-bit environment, the decorated names of functions, member functions, templates, structs, classes, and so on may change accordingly. Let's look at a concrete example:

```
struct S
{
void * p; // 4/8 bytes under 32/64-bit systems
int n; // 4 bytes
}; //sizeof (S)==8/16 under 32/64-bit envs, respectively
void func (S& );
```

The decorated name produced by a 32-bit compiler for the function `func()` could look like this:

```
v__func@@struct_S8@
```

A 64-bit compiler may produce this decorated name instead:

```
v__func@@struct_S16@
```

This difference eliminates the risk of inadvertently linking incompatible binaries. However, it also means that if you have a library or a DLL only as a binary file, you will have to get an updated 64-bit version thereof. Tools that convert pure .exe and other binary formats are available on some 64-bit platforms. However, the best solution is to recompile the original source files.

Summary

The advent of 64-bit systems demonstrates once more the importance of separating low-level, platform-dependent implementation details from the interface. Code that doesn't rely on hard-coded magic numbers and specific sizes of datatypes is easier to port. Therefore, even if the migration to a 64-bit environment still seems remote, it's best to design your new apps so that this migration will be as smooth and automatic as possible, necessitating only recompilation and relinking.

Online Resources

"Porting to a 64-Bit Platform" (*http://www.devx.com/Intel/Article/27237*) discusses the reasons for porting to 64-bit computing and how this process is actually carried out. In spite of its heavy commercial bias, it does provide useful insights, such as why 64-bit is required and which problem it solves.

Security Enhancements

Those of you who have followed reports about security vulnerabilities and patches must have déjà vu: The majority of these vulnerabilities result from buffer overflows. In this section, I will explain how buffer overflows are caused and what you can do to eliminate them. I will also show how to ensure automatic initialization of dynamically allocated storage, both in C and C++.

C++ and Security

It wouldn't be an exaggeration to say that a through-and-through C++ program should rarely deal with pointers directly, if at all. Standard facilities such as `std::string`, `stringstream` objects, `auto_ptr`, `std::vector`, and reference variables drastically reduce the need to use bare pointers. Once you get rid of pointer fiddling, your code has fewer security loopholes.

What About C?

C code isn't doomed to be a security hazard. The recent C99 standard provides plenty of improvements in this regard that reduce the risk of buffer overflows.

TIP: For more information about C99, see Chapter 16.

`memset()` and Security

The `mem-` `str-` and `printf-` families of functions are notoriously bug-prone. Yet there are more secure versions of these functions, or you can avoid them altogether. Let's look at a concrete example. The `memset()` function, declared like this:

```
//in <string.h> or <mem.h>
void *memset(void *s, int c, size_t n);
```

is often used in this manner:

```
struct Point {
 int x;
 int y;
};

struct Point p;
memset(&p, 0, sizeof(Point));
```

This code, though seemingly secure, still has a potential security problem. Suppose we make this tiny change:

```
struct Person p; //note: not Point anymore
memset(&p, 0, sizeof(Point)); // compiles OK
```

The programmer mistakenly left the original `memset()` call as is. Honestly, even the most experienced programmers make such mistakes. The code will compile and link blissfully. However, at runtime anything can happen. `memset()` is even more dangerous than that because it takes three parameters that can be easily confused:

```
void *memset(void *s, int c, size_t n);
```

One can mistakenly misplace the arguments:

```
memset(&p, sizeof(Point), 0); //2nd and 3rd args reversed
```

This code actually leaves p uninitialized.

The solution? Avoid `memset()`. Let's see how C programmers can get along without it. When instantiating POD types, always provide explicit initializers. This way, your data is always in a determinate state. In addition, changes to a struct definition (say adding new members) won't be a problem:

```
struct Point p ={0};//OK, p is zero initialized
```

If this code later changes to:

```
struct Person p ={0};//OK, p is zero initialized
```

All is still well and good.

However, when you allocate data dynamically, an explicit initializer won't work:

```
struct Point *p=malloc(sizeof(Point));
```

Here, the pointer p refers to a chunk of raw memory. The C standard doesn't require that `malloc()` should return initialized memory. Seemingly, there's no escape from calling `memset()` after `malloc`, right? Not necessarily. If you must allocate POD types, I recommend using `calloc()` instead of `malloc()`:

```
void *calloc(size_t n_items, size_t item_size);
```

`calloc()` returns is zero-initialized memory. Indeed, it was originally designed for allocating arrays of objects. However, who says you can't allocate a single element array? Let's see how:

```
struct Point *p= calloc(1, sizeof(Point)); //allocate 1 element
```

After this call, `p` points to a single zero-initialized `Point` object. Neat, isn't it?

C-Style String Manipulation

The `str`-family of functions—`strcpy()`, `strcmp()`, and so on—is another painful problem. C++ programmers should never use these functions in new C++ code. However, C is here to stay and so are thousands of libraries and applications written in this language. Luckily, there are a few cosmetic touches that can significantly enhance its security. In short, this means replacing every `str` function with its `strn` equivalent. For example, instead of `strcmp()`:

```
int strcmp(const char *s1, const char *s2);
```

use `strncmp()`:

```
int strncmp(const char *s1, const char *s2, size_t maxlen);
```

C99 defines a set of sibling functions that offer the same functionality as the classic `str-` functions: for example, `strncpy()`, `strncat()`, `strncmp()`, and so on. The new functions, unlike the vintage `str` functions, always take an explicit size limit. `strncpy()`, for example, will stop copying characters when the first of these conditions is met:

- A '\0' terminator of the source string has been detected.
- The function has copied *n*-1 characters, where *n* is the specified limit.

In interactive applications that read passwords, names, etc., it's chiefly important to limit the number of characters read because crackers exploit this loophole frequently.

Let's look at two versions of the same code:

```
int copy_passwords(const char * pwd1, const char * pwd2)
{
 return strcpy(pwd1, pwd2); //dangerous
}
```

In this example, `pwd2` may have been read from a terminal or a web form. There's no guarantee that it contains a '\0' terminator. Should that be the case, an overflow is imminent. The secure version of this code looks like this:

```
int copy_passwords(const char * pwd1, const char * pwd2)
{
 return strncpy(pwd1, pwd2, maxchars); //safer
}
```

Here, `strncpy()` will copy up to `maxchars-1` characters from `pwd2` even if it's longer than `maxchars`.

Summary

C++ programmers rarely face these bugs because they use constructors to ensure that objects are always properly initialized. If you're porting legacy C code to a C++ environment and you don't need to retain compatibility with C, you can always add a constructor to the original C structs and remove initialization code from the program. Similarly, instead of using the `str-`functions, always use their `strn-` equivalents. Finally, prefer `calloc()` to `malloc()` (and `new`) if you really have to allocate raw memory dynamically. Oddly enough, with respect to arrays of POD types, `calloc()` is even safer than `new[]`.

Drop the (Automatic) Pilot

To keep up with the pace of new design trends and techniques, software developers are constantly looking for the latest books and hottest courses. These are all wonderful ways to improve one's programming skills and acquire knowledge. However, software quality doesn't depend solely on novelties. Sometimes, the "automatic pilot" mode of thinking, which leads us to repeat the same design practices whether relevant or not, has more impact on code quality than any posh design pattern or sleek algorithm. In this section, I will present a handful of such bad-yet-prevalent habits that impair code quality in terms of maintenance, performance and readability.

Embedded Literals

Quoted text and hard-coded numeric values (collectively known as *literals*) should never be used in production code. Instead, use symbolic constants or variables:

```
//bad habit: embedding literals in code
beep_frequency(2000);
CApp myapp("testapp");
//correct forms
const int DEF_FRQUENCY=2000;
const char APP_NAME[]="test_app";
beep_frequency(DEF_FRQUENCY);
CApp myapp(APP_NAME);
```

Although this is a trivial rule of thumb, programmers often violate it. In nonsensical code examples, it isn't a major problem. In fact, some of the code listings that I include in my articles also use literals for the sake of brevity. However, in production code, you should never use literals directly. There are at least three good reasons why:

- **Maintenance**. Future changes of code that contains literals require extensive search-and-replace operations with a high likelihood of missing a few spots or introducing typos. The use of constants localizes the change to one place, thereby simplifying future maintenance immensely.
- **Readability**. A meaningful constant documents the programmer's intent more clearly than an arbitrary numeric value does.
- **Error detection**. When you use a symbolic constant the compiler is able to detect typos that it can't detect otherwise. For example, your compiler won't notice that you typed 200 instead of 2000. However, if you misspell DEF-FRQUENCY, this error won't pass unnoticed.

Avoid "Unnecessary Journeys"

During WWII, a poster cautioning the public to avoid unnecessary journeys was posted in British railway stations. Although it's not exactly related to the topic at hand, it's a reminder of the automatic choices that we make without giving much thought to their real necessity and costs. Two of such common "automatic pilot" decisions are multithreading and internationalization (i18n). As useful as they are in certain applications, neither is mandatory or portable.

Multithreading

Even today most computers have only one CPU. Consequently, multithreading comes at a price: context switching between threads and synchronization. In poorly designed apps, this overhead can be overwhelming. It's not unusual to see a single-threaded code fragment executing 10 times slower once you make it multithreaded. Even in applications in which concurrency is absolutely necessary, there are more alternatives to consider: multi-processing for instance. An application that reads data from two or more tables can spawn child processes that read from each table. These in turn will signal the parent process once they've completed their task. Such a design is usually simpler to implement, debug, and optimize than a multithreaded solution. And yet, multi-processing is often overlooked because programmers are either unaware of it or because they mistakenly believe that multithreading is always "more efficient."

Internationalization

Think for a moment: How many of your applications have ever supported more than a single locale at once? How many of them have been localized to a different language? My impression is that in the majority of cases, applications are never deployed outside the premises of a single office, or—at most—a single country. In such cases, making your app i18n ready "just in case" is a terrible waste of money. Don't get me wrong: i18n is a wonderful thing, but only when it's truly needed. Otherwise, it complicates the design unnecessarily, compromises portability and consumes precious system resources. Still, programmers opt for this "unnecessary journey" too often for no justified cause.

The interesting question is not how much overhead these features incur but why programmers use them even if their apps don't really need them. If the answer is one of these:

- "That's the boilerplate code that my wizard generates."
- "I copied the examples from my textbook/MSDN/guru and never gave much thought to it."
- "I never knew I could use ASCII/ `spawn()` / `exec()`."

then this is most likely an unnecessary journey (and quite an expensive one). If these features are truly needed, however, always examine alternative options.

Summary

Good programmers should always ask themselves: "Why am I doing things this way? What are the alternatives and how much would they cost?" These questions should be an integral part of every design review. If you can justify your design choices, then you know that you're on the right track. Otherwise, it might be yet another unnecessary journey.

Books

Parallel and Distributed Programming Using C++ (Addison-Wesley, 2003, ISBN 0131013769), by Cameron Hughes and Tracey Hughes, is one of my favorite guides to concurrent programming. Although the book focuses on the POSIX specification (which means that Windows developers might find it less useful than would Linux and UNIX developers), it presents the basic concurrency concepts such as synchronization, cooperation, deadlocks, and rendezvous very clearly. As such, it can serve as a platform-independent concurrency primer. The authors also dedicate a thorough discussion to the pros and cons of both multithreading and multiprocessing. (For more on this book, visit *http://www.informit.com/title/0131013769*.)

Arrays and Pointers

One of the first things that C programmers learn is that arrays are essentially pointers in disguise. This idiosyncrasy (at least for programmers of other high-level programming languages) is maintained in C++ as well. In this section, I will explore the resemblance between pointers and arrays, show some subtle differences between the two and present refactoring techniques for improving code safety with respect to arrays.

When Arrays Behave Like Pointers . . .

Functions in C/C++ can't returns or receive array arguments. The common workaround in C is to pass the address of an array and an additional argument indicating its size:

```
void fillArray(int [], size_t sz);
int myArr[100];
fillArray(myArr, sizeof(myArr));
```

You can use the subscript notation on a pointer, assuming that that pointer is originally an array that decayed into a pointer:

```
char arrc[2];
char p=&arr[0];
p[0]=0; //ok
void func(char * pc)
{
pc[0]='a';
```

}

In C++, you would normally use a vector instead of a built-in array:

```
void fillArray(vector<int> &);
vector <int> vi;
fillArray(vi);
```

Later on, I will show a different C++ technique for safe and efficient array handling that doesn't incur the overhead of vector's dynamic memory allocation and deallocation.

. . . and When They Don't

Although arrays decay into pointers in certain contexts, they aren't really pointers. For example, if you try to assign to an array you will get a compilation error:

```
char arr[10];
char c;
arr=&c; //error
```

However, assigning an array's name to a pointer is well-formed:

```
char *p=arr;
```

In this case, the rvalue arr decays into a temporary pointer to char containing the address of the first element of the array. This assignment expression is therefore equivalent to the following:

```
char * p=&arr[0];
```

The fact that arrays decay into pointers shouldn't mislead you: The compiler treats every array as a distinct type. The type of an array consists of the elements' scalar type (e.g., char) as well as the array's size and its cv qualifications. Therefore, each of the following arrays has a distinct type:

```
char arr1[10];
char arr2[11];
cout<<typeid(arr1).name()<<endl; //output: 'char [10]'
cout<<typeid(arr2).name()<<endl; //output: 'char [11]'
```

`sizeof` Expressions

Operator `sizeof` returns the size of an array in bytes. However, the ice here is thin because when the array decays into a pointer, `sizeof` returns the size of the *pointer* instead. For example:

```
int func(int [] a)
{
 return sizeof (a); // returns the size of the pointer p
}
int main()
{
 int num[2];
 cout << sizeof (num); //output 8 (on most platforms)
 func(num);
}
```

Array Wrapping

As mentioned above, C++ programmers should use a vector instead of a built-in array. This way, the inherent pitfalls of built-in arrays are avoided. The problem is that in some situations, using a vector is undesirable or simply impossible—a vector object entails at least one constructor call and one destructor call. In addition, it's impossible to have vector allocate its storage statically, as opposed to built-in arrays. As a workaround, you can wrap a built-in array in a high-level class without altering the array's low-level properties. The following `array_wrapper` class template wraps a built-in array in a lightweight struct that has no additional data members except for the array itself. Unlike ordinary STL containers, this wrapper class allocates its array on the stack statically. More importantly, it provides the standard member functions of other STL containers. This way, it can be used with standard algorithms:

```
template <class T, int _size> struct array_wrapper
{
 //typedef names used in STL algorithms and containers
 typedef T value_type;
 typedef T* iterator;
 typedef const T * const_iterator;
 typedef T& reference;
 typedef const T& const_reference;

 T v[_size]; //the actual array
 // member functions of STL containers
 operator T* () {return v;}
```

```
reference operator[] (size_t idx) {return v[idx];}
const_reference operator[] (size_t idx) const {return v[idx];}

iterator begin() {return v;}
const_iterator begin() const {return v;}

iterator end() {return v+_size;}
const_iterator end() const {return v+_size;}

size_t size() const {return _size;}
};
```

You can initialize an `array_wrapper` object as you would a built-in array. The resulting object can be used in C-style code that expects a built-in array:

```
void func(int *, int sz); // C function
//wrap an array of 20 int's initializing its members to 0
array_wrapper<int, 20> arr={0};
func(arr, arr.size()); //using T* conversion operator
```

Such a wrapper is particularly useful for bridging between the Standard Library's containers, algorithms and iterators, and a built-in array. The following examples uses the `copy()` algorithm and `ostream_iterator` iterator class to display the contents of `arr` on the screen:

```
copy(arr.begin(), arr.end(),
  ostream_iterator<int>(cout, " "));
```

The `array_wrapper` class isn't included in the C++98 Standard Library. However, it is likely that a similar wrapper class template will be added to it in the next revision round.

Summary

The close resemblance between arrays and pointers dates back to the pre-C age, with mid-level languages such as BCPL and B. In the early days of STL, some of the C++ standards committee members proposed that C's built-in arrays would cease to exist in C++. Instead, the compiler should convert under the hood every array into a vector object. This proposal was rejected for several good reasons, such as performance and compatibility with C. However, if you find yourself using built-in arrays in new C++ code, you should probably consider refactoring. Even if replacing every array with a vector isn't a practical solution (and I admit that it isn't), the use of a wrapper class can be an acceptable compromise.

Low-Level File I/O, Part I

C's original file I/O library used low-level concepts such as descriptors and direct `read()` and `write()` calls. Surprisingly, this antiquated library is still widely used, especially in the POSIX world and networking protocols. In this section, I will walk you through the main functions and concepts of this library.

Back to the Source

Although it may not be everyone's cup of tea, C's original I/O library (henceforth, I will refer to this library as <fcntl.h>) is still alive and kicking. There are two major reasons for this. First, many networking protocols such as sockets and ftp were originally developed for UNIX. The advent of the Internet has made these protocols virtually ubiquitous. Secondly, UNIX treats almost everything as a file—be it a keyboard, a serial port, a screen or a disk file. Consequently, almost every library that uses some sort of I/O relies on the <fcntl.h> interface, even when ported to Windows.

When the ANSI C committee endorsed <stdio.h> in the 1980s, it was believed that the low-level <fcntl.h> library would vanish shortly afterward. As a result, <fcntl.h> was never officially incorporated into the C standard (C99 standard, for example, completely ignores it). And yet, unofficially, this library is supported on every major platform. One of its major advantages over <fstream> is its tighter control over file I/O operations. For instance, you can use flags that open a file in exclusive mode, or open a file only if it already exists. Another advantage is performance. Because of its low-level nature, <fcntl.h> can be optimized for specific hardware architectures and network topologies.

open(), creat(), close(), and unlink()

Except for the standard input, the standard output and the standard error, which are automatically opened at program's startup, you need to open any other file explicitly before performing any I/O operation. The `open()` function has the following prototype:

```
int open(char * name, int flags, int perms);
```

This function returns a non-negative integer if the call was successful; a return value of -1 indicates an error. The first argument is a file name or a path name. The second argument contains one or more flags indicating how the file should be opened. Only one flag from the following list can be used, and there must be at least one of them:

```
O_RDONLY // read only
O_WRONLY // write only
O_RDWR // combined read and write
```

Additional flags can be ORed with one of the previous three flags. These optional flags are:

```
O_APPEND // open and advance to the end of the file
O_CREAT // create a new file if one doesn't exist
O_TRUNC // if the file exists, truncate its length to 0
O_EXCL // used only with O_CREAT. If the file already exists, an error is returned
O_BINARY // open the file in binary mode
O_TEXT // open the file in text mode
```

The combination of O_CREAT and O_EXCL is used for opening a file in exclusive mode. This can be useful for implementing lock files, for instance (`<fstream>` doesn't offer this feature). The third argument indicates the file's permissions. Its values are implementation-defined.

To create a new file, use the `creat()` [sic] function:

```
int creat(char * name, int perms);
```

The function returns a positive value (the file descriptor) upon success or -1 if an error has occurred.

The `close()` function closes an open file:

```
int close(int fd);
```

A return value of 0 indicates success and -1 otherwise. The argument must be a descriptor of an open file.

To delete a file, use the `unlink()` function:

```
int unlink(char * name);
```

The function's name betrays the UNIX origins of this library. This function takes a file name as an argument. You cannot use wildcards. The return value is 0 on success, -1 otherwise.

`read()` and `write()`

Input and output use the `read()` and `write()` functions. Both functions take a file descriptor as their first argument:

```
int read(int fd, char * buf, int n);
int write(int fd, char * buf, int n);
```

The second argument is a buffer into which the data is written, or from which data is read. The third argument is the number of bytes to be transferred. The return value is the number of bytes that were actually transferred. A return value of 0 implies end of file and -1 indicates an error has occurred.

Platform-Specific Issues

C borrowed the `const` keyword from C++. This is why K&R libraries don't use `const` parameters. However, some vendors rectified this by refurbishing the original prototypes of the aforementioned functions. For example, the Windows version of `unlink()` has the following prototype:

```
int _unlink(const char *); //Windows and DOS
```

Notice the underscore at the beginning. Similarly, certain DOS and Windows variants of `open()` omit the third parameter:

```
int open(const char *path, int access); //Windows and DOS
```

Windows NT and its successors also define a `wchar_t` version of each function that originally takes `char *` arguments. For example:

```
int _wunlink(const wchar_t * name); //Windows NT only
int _wopen(const wchar_t * name, int access); //Windows NT only
```

The precise headers in which these functions and constants are declared are also platform-dependent. In System V UNIX the constants (macros, actually) O_RDONLY, O_WRONLY, etc. appear in `<fcntl.h>`, whereas in BSD they are declared in `<sys/file.h>`. The functions' prototypes appear in `<io.h>` (for DOS and Windows) or `<fcntl.h>` in POSIX systems.

Low-Level File I/O, Part II

I've already presented the main constituents of the <fnctl.h> library. In this section, we'll be looking into the rest of this library's functions and see how to use it to perform random file access.

Buffered I/O and Non-buffered I/O

File I/O is usually divided into two major categories: buffered I/O and non-buffered I/O. Under the non-buffered I/O model, data is immediately transferred into its destination. By contrast, buffered I/O uses an intermediary buffer to store the data before actually transferring it to its destination. For example, if you write several records into a file by using consecutive output operations, the underlying I/O bus may store the data of these operations in a temporary buffer until that buffer is filled. Only then does the implementation actually write the data from the intermediary buffer to its destination. In the olden days, when the average seek time of a magnetic disk was terribly long, buffered I/O was almost used exclusively. Think for example of editing a document that is stored on a floppy disk. If every character you type were written directly to the disk, you'd have to spend hours in order to write a few sentences.

The advantages of using buffered I/O are noticeable. However, there are cases in which its latency is unacceptable. Two common scenarios are real-time data transfer and exceptions. When an exception occurs, buffering might cause a data loss because the application may exit before its partially filled buffers have been flushed. This is why `stderr` and `cerr` use non-buffered I/O.

tell(), lseek() and eof()

As I explained previously, UNIX uses the file abstraction to represent every source of input or output. This generalization enables you to tie the standard input to a physical file easily, or to redirect the output on the screen to a different terminal, printer, etc. When you open a file, the system creates a pointer that is referring to a specific position in that file. By default, the file pointer is positioned at the beginning of the file. However, each I/O operation changes its position by advancing it farther. The function `tell()` reports the current position of the file pointer. It returns the offset in bytes from the file's beginning:

```
long tell(int fd);
```

Let's see how it works. First, create a new file using `creat()` and check the file pointer's position:

```
int offset=0;
int fd=creat("mytextfile.txt", O_BINARY);
if (fd)
 offset=tell(fd); //value: 0
```

Because we didn't use any I/O operation yet, the value of `offset` should be 0 at this time.

Next, let's write a few bytes to the file using `write()`:

```
int num=100;
if (write(fd, &num, sizeof(num)))
 offset = tell(fd); // offset equals 4
```

On most platforms, the above write call advances the file pointer by four bytes. More precisely, it advances the file pointer by `sizeof(int)` bytes. Subsequent output operations will advance the file pointer farther.

Random Access: `lseek()`

Simple databases use flat files to store fixed-size records. As each record occupies exactly the same size, calculating the relative position of each record is easy. For this purpose, use the `lseek()` function. This function moves the file pointer to a random position. It has the following prototype:

```
long lseek(int fd, long offset, int whence);
```

The return value is the new offset of the file pointer, or -1 upon failure. The second argument contains the number of bytes beyond the location specified in whence. whence must be one of the following constants:

```
SEEK_CUR //current file pointer position
SEEK_END //end of file
SEEK_SET // file's beginning
```

`lseek()` doesn't take an absolute offset value; rather, the second argument is always relative to the third argument. This may seem confusing at first. However, the advantage is that you can advance the file pointer without having to know its current position. For example, to advance the file one byte ahead without having to know the file pointer's current position, you can do something like this:

```
lseek(fd, 1, SEEK_CUR);
```

To rewind a file:

```
lseek(fd, 0, SEEK_SET);
```

Likewise, to forward it to the end:

```
lseek(fd, 0, SEEK_END);
```

Let's see how to use `lseek()` for random-access I/O. Suppose you have a file of fixed records of the following type:

```
struct record
{
 int id;
 time_t timestamp;
 long val;
};
```

This example reads the 15th record from a file:

```
record rec;
lseek(fd, 14*sizeof(record), SEEK_SET);//skip the first 14 records
read(fd, &rec, sizeof(record));
```

Similarly, if you want to overwrite an existing record, point the file pointer to the correct offset and use `write()`. The following example updates the timestamp field of the last record in the file:

```
//point to the beginning of timestamp in the last record
int offset=sizeof (record)-sizeof (int);
lseek(fd, -offset, SEEK_END);//negative offset
time_t t=time(0);//obtain a new timestamp
read(fd, &t sizeof(t));//overwrite previous timestamp
```

Notice that the remaining fields of the record remain intact.

`eof()` and Error Handling

To detect an end-of-file condition use the `eof()` function:

```
int eof(int fd);
```

`eof()` returns the value 1 if the current position is the end of file; otherwise, it returns 0. A return value of -1 indicates an error.

The <fcntl.h> library doesn't define its own error codes. Therefore, detecting an error consists of two phases: First, check the return value of each function call. If it indicates an error of some sort, check errno's value immediately. Any subsequent call overrides the previous errno value.

Summary

Familiarity with the low-level <fcntl.h> concepts is important for another reason: Many high-level class libraries use <fcntl.h> system calls under the hood. You may come across these system calls during debugging or profiling your apps.

static Declarations, Part I

The static keyword is context dependent. It can indicate not fewer than four different concepts:

- Internal linkage of namespace-scope identifiers
- Local variables that remain in existence throughout the program's execution
- Static data members of a class
- Static member functions

In this section, I'll discuss the semantics of static declarations of the C subset of C++; namely, local statics and namespace scope statics.

Local statics

The following sections describe the semantics of static objects of POD types exclusively. The rules of static objects of non-POD types are different and will be discussed later. The terms *variables* and *objects* are used interchangeably in this section, as are *function* and *block*.

static variables declared inside a block are local to that block, similarly to auto variables. The following function uses the local static variable calls to track the number of its invocations:

```
int count_calls()
{
 static int calls=0; //local static
 return ++calls;
}
```

Unlike `auto` variables, local `statics` aren't destroyed upon leaving their function; they remain in existence until the program terminates. As such, they provide private and permanent storage for a function. When that function is invoked again, it will access the same `calls` variable.

How does this feat work? `static` objects aren't allocated on the stack but on a permanent storage section that remains active throughout the program's execution. Implementations usually allocate a special block in each `.exe` file for objects that remain in existence as long as the program is running. Namespace-scope objects (e.g., globals) and local `statics` are stored in this block. If you have the address of `calls`, you can manipulate it even when the name `calls` is not in scope:

```
int count_calls(int *& rpi)
{
static int calls=0;
rpi=&calls;
return ++calls;
}
int main()
{
int *pi;
int n=count_calls(pi);
cout <<n<<endl; //output 1
*pi=5; //modify calls, although it's not in scope
n=count_calls(pi);
cout <<n<<endl; //output 6
}
```

This property of static objects can lead to race conditions in multithreaded apps, e.g., when one thread is assigning a new value to a static variable while another thread is reading its value. The solution is to use synchronization objects that selectively grant access to static variables.

Initialization

As opposed to `auto` and dynamic variables, static variables—either local or external—are zero-initialized by default, unless their declaration contains an explicit initializer with a different value:

```
int count_calls(int *& rpi)
{
static int calls=1; //non-zero initialization
return calls++; //postfix
}
```

The explicit initializer of `calls` in this case:

```
int count_calls(int *& rpi)
{
static int calls=0;
...
```

is therefore redundant. However, it's still a good idea to use an explicit initializer in every static declaration to document your intention explicitly.

Local static variables are conceptually initialized before their block is first entered. *Aggregates*—i.e., POD structs, POD unions and arrays of POD elements—are initialized to binary zeroes, unless the declaration contains an explicit initializer with a different value:

```
struct Date
{
 int d;
 int m;
 int y;
};
void func()
{
 static Date d; //zero-initialized by default
 static int num[10]; //all elements are zero-initialized
 static Date Xmas={25,12,2004};
}
```

Namespace Scope `static` Declarations

When applied to a namespace scope object or function, `static` restricts their scope to the rest of the translation unit, thereby enabling a programmer to implement the information hiding principle even in a procedural language such as C:

```
//inaccessible from other translation units
static void decrypt(char *msg)
{
//...
}
```

If `decrypt()` is to be used solely by one function in the program, move that function into the same translation unit of `decrypt()`. Similarly, you can restrict access to namespace scope objects by declaring them static:

```
static char CRC[5]; //internal linkage
static Date d; //ditto
int main()
{
//..
}
```

This technique can be used for reducing the risk of name conflicts across translation units and for implementing the information hiding principle.

In standard C++ this type of `static` declarations is deprecated. In normative C++ programs you should use an unnamed namespace instead:

```
namespace //unnamed
{
 char CRC[5];
 Date d;
}
```

Although the underlying machinery differs, the effect of declaring objects and functions in an unnamed namespace is the same—they can only be accessed from within their translation unit.

Readers have asked me several times why the C++ standards committee frowned at namespace scope static declarations. The first problem was didactic. The keyword `static` was already overloaded in C; C++ added to this confusion the concept of static data members and static member functions. The committee felt that `static` was becoming a Swiss army knife—a single keyword that does too many different things. Another problem was more subtle. Not all implementations truly support internal linkage. Therefore, the "internal-linkage" promise couldn't be fulfilled in certain environments—hackers familiar with the inner workings of such implementations could access allegedly invisible functions and data declared in other translation units. An unnamed namespace of course doesn't cure broken linkers; however, it is more honest about its capabilities. Article 7.3.1.1/1 of the C++ standard says: "[a]lthough entities in an unnamed namespace might have external linkage, they are effectively qualified by a name unique to their translation unit and therefore can never be seen from any other translation unit." Put differently, an unnamed namespace restricts the visibility of its members to the scope of the translation unit by means of name mangling; it doesn't necessarily guarantee internal linkage, though.

Do these arguments sound convincing? In the next installment I will show that standard C++ itself forces programmers to violate this normative recommendation in one case. Additionally, I will discuss the initialization phases of non-POD objects with static storage type, as well as static class members.

`static` **Declarations, Part II**

After reviewing the C legacy of `static` declarations in Part I, I will show here how C++ "embraced and extended" this keyword. The widely known static data members and static member functions aren't the only novel uses of this keyword that C++ developed, as you will shortly see.

Initialization of Non-POD Objects

The initialization rules of non-POD object with static storage type is different from that of POD types. It consists of two phases: *static initialization* and *dynamic initialization*. Static initialization means zero-initialization or initialization with a constant expression. In essence, it's the same type of initialization that POD objects with static storage type undergo, as we saw in the previous part. This static initialization phase is followed by a subsequent dynamic initialization phase, whereby the constructor of the non-POD object executes. An object is considered initialized only after the successful completion of the dynamic initialization phase. If the initialization exits by throwing an exception, the initialization is not complete, so it will be tried again the next time control enters the declaration. For example:

```
void func(bool error)
{
try
{
 if (error)
  throw my_exception();
 //initialization is aborted in the first invocation of func
 static std::string s("test");
}
catch(my_exception& exc)
{}
}
int main()
{
 func(true); //raises an exception
 func(false); //no exception this time
}
```

The dynamic initialization of s is aborted when func() is first invoked due to an exception. Consequently, C++ marks this object as uninitialized. When func() is invoked for the second time, s's constructor will run.

The initialization order of objects with static storage duration that are defined in different translation units is unspecified. For example, if an object a defined in translation unit x attempts to access a global object b defined in another translation unit, there's no guarantee that the latter has already been constructed at that time. I will present a technique for solving this problem in a different section.

Static Data Members

Static data members have external linkage, unless their class name has a different linkage type. Static data members declared in different classes don't collide, even if the members have identical names. As usual, name mangling ensures uniqueness of names:

```
class Dynamically_loaded_image
{
 static bool loaded;
};
bool Dynamically_loaded_image::loaded=false;
class Dynamically_loaded_class
{
 static bool loaded; //distinct from Dynamically_loaded_image::loaded
};
bool Dynamically_loaded_class::loaded=false;
```

Under the hood, static data members are nothing but global objects disguised by mangled names. However, they obey the access rules of C++. Private static data members are accessible only to their class (or its object instances). Similarly, protected static data members are accessible only to their class and its derived classes. As with other data objects of static storage type, static data members undergo static initialization; if they are of non-POD types, they undergo a subsequent dynamic initialization phase that invokes their constructors.

Static Member Functions

The concept of static member functions wasn't new in the early days of C++ (other OO programming languages such as Smalltalk had already implemented similar constructs in the early 1970s). And yet, the initial implementations of C++ didn't support this feature. Static member functions were first implemented only in cfront 2.0 (1988). How did programmers cope with the lack of static member functions before that? To call the member function `instances()` of the following class:

```
struct C
{
public:
//a static-like member function vintage 1987
 int instances() {return count;}
private:
 static int count;
};
```

you would do something like this:

```
((C*) 0)->instances(); //pre-cfront 2.0 hack
```

This cryptic syntax wasn't only unreadable—it was dangerous as well because you could accidentally apply it to nonstatic member functions.

Static member functions are useful in several cases:

- **Compatibility with C**. A static member function has the same type of a freestanding C function. This property is particularly useful in multi-threaded apps that use a C thread library.
- **Design idioms**. Certain design idioms mandate that there shall be no object instances of a class.
- **Accessing static data members**. You want to be able to call the `instances()` member function of a reference counting class even when no object instances of that class exist.

Static Member Function Implementation

Static member functions differ from nonstatic ones in that they don't take a `this` argument. Consequently, they are subjected to the following restrictions:

- They cannot access nonstatic data members of their class.
- They cannot be `const`, `volatile`, or `virtual`.
- They cannot be bound to a pointer to a member of their class.

Static member functions have external linkage, unless their class has a different linkage type. Here again, name mangling ensures name uniqueness:

```
struct A
{
 static void func();
};
struct B
{
 static void func(); //distinct from A::func
};
```

Deprecated—Alas, Unavoidable

Recall that namespace scope static declarations are deprecated in C++. Normative code should use unnamed namespaces instead. However, standard C++ *forces* you to use this deprecated feature in one case. An *anonymous union* has the following form:

```
union  //no tag name
{
int x;
char c[4];
}; //no named instances or pointers
x=5; //members of an anonymous union are accessed directly
int first_byte=c[0];
```

Anonymous unions' members have internal linkage. Standard C++ requires that a global anonymous union be declared `static` (hence, such a union can never be truly global).

NOTE: Although the C++98 standard speaks of "global anonymous unions" (7.1.1/1), it appears that the text probably means *namespace-scope anonymous unions*, as implied in (9.5/3). Note also that anonymous unions don't exist in C; they are unique to C++.

Is it possible to declare such a union in an unnamed namespace, as prescribed by the Standard? Yes and no. Although you can do so, that union must still be declared `static`:

```
namespace { //unnamed
  static union { //anonymous, must be declared static
    int x;
    void* p;
  };
```

```
}
p=malloc(1);
```

This loophole in the standard hasn't been fixed yet, as far as I know.

Afterthoughts

The "extend and embrace" policy with respect to the `static` keyword demonstrates how deeply intertwined C and C++ are. In my opinion, too many C features were deprecated in C++ hastily—sometimes without compelling reasons or satisfactory alternatives. The case of anonymous unions is particularly interesting. To fix this loophole, a core language change may be required: Either anonymous unions should have external linkage, or unnamed namespaces should guarantee internal linkage. Of course, "undeprecating" namespace-scope `static` could do the trick, too.

NOTE: More information about static member functions, their underlying implementation and usage can be found in the "Object Model" series. "POD Initialization" and "Object Initialization" provide further information about the initialization rules of POD data and non-POD objects, respectively.

Online Resources

Even if unions seem at first like a recondite feature, they have useful applications: e.g., enforcing compile-time constraints in generic programming. My article "Enforcing Compile-Time Constraints" (*http://www.devx.com/cplus/ 10MinuteSolution/24908*) exemplifies some of the advanced uses of unions in generic programming.

Bjarne Stroustrup's "C++ Glossary" (*http://www.research.att.com/~bs/ glossary.html*) addresses, among other things, the various uses of the `static` keyword and its context-dependent semantics.

Books

Inside the C++ Object Model (Addison-Wesley, 1996, ISBN 0201834545), by Stanley B. Lippman, discusses the inner workings of static data members and member functions and their history. Although the book is several years old, it's still one of the best sources for learning how C++ really works. (For more on this book, visit *http://www.informit.com/bookstore/product.asp?isbn=0201834545*.)

The C Programming Language, 2nd Edition (Prentice Hall, 1998, ISBN 0131103628), by Brian Kernighan and Dennis Ritchie, isn't just the best programming book ever written (and I'm not the only one who thinks so). It's also an essential guide for any C++ programmer pondering why certain things in C++ are the way they are—the origins of static declarations, for instance. (For more on this book, visit *http://www.informit.com/title/ 0131103628.*)

Static Initialization Order

In the static declarations series I briefly mentioned an onerous problem pertaining to initialization order of objects with static storage duration: In standard C++, the initialization order of such objects is unspecified if they are declared in different translation units. In this section, I will discuss the consequences of this problem and show techniques for averting it.

Initialization Order Dependency

A properly organized C++ program consists of multiple source files and corresponding header files. A *compilation unit*, or *unit* for short, is a pair of a source file and its matching header file. Each unit can be compiled separately. Wouldn't it be better to group multiple classes and functions in one unit? Not really. In large-scale projects, each class or function may be maintained by a different developer, team, or vendor. Splitting projects into separate compilation units is therefore inevitable. Even when it is possible to bundle declarations in one unit, the separate compilation model offers another advantage, namely reducing compilation time. Many compilers nowadays use *incremental builds*, which means that only units that have changed since the last compilation session are actually compiled.

TIP: "Project Organization Guidelines" provides additional info about units.

Recall that non-POD objects with static storage type are considered initialized only after the successful completion of the dynamic initialization phase. The problem is that you can't predict (in a platform-neutral manner, at least) the initialization order of objects that are declared in separate translation units. Here's an example:

```
// #1:Bar.h
struct Bar
{
 explicit Bar(int val=0): _data(val) {}
 int data() const {return _data; }
private:
 int _data;
```

```
//..
};

// #2: Foo.h
#include "Bar.h"
struct Foo
{
 explicit Foo(const Bar & b) :m(b.data()) {}
private:
 int m;
};

// #3: foo_file.cpp
#include "Bar.h"
#include "Foo.h"

extern Bar bar; //global object defined in a separate file
Foo foo(bar); //no guarantee that bar has been initialized!

// #4: bar_file.cpp
#include "Bar.h"

Bar bar;
```

foo's initialization uses a value returned from bar.data(). Therefore, bar must be initialized before foo. However, since foo and bar are defined in separately compiled translation units, there's no such guarantee. Put bluntly, there's a 50% likelihood that bar hasn't been initialized by that time, so foo might be accessing an object with an indeterminate state. Woe unto this program!

Note that this problem applies to objects declared in a namespace-scope, e.g., globals. By contrast, local static objects are initialized the first time control passes through their declaration (or earlier). This difference between local statics and namespace-scope objects with static storage type is the key to our solution.

Working Around the Initialization Order Problem

Before taking any radical measures, remember that for simple cases there is a quick workaround: Move the definitions of foo and bar into the same translation unit. Consequently, their initialization order will match their declaration order:

```
//foobar.cpp
Bar bar; //initialized first
```

```
Foo foo(bar); //initialized after bar
```

For small projects, this workaround can be satisfactory. However, it's unsuitable for large-scale projects. Furthermore, if you're designing a new project from scratch you want to use a systematic and reliable solution to this problem.

Eliminating Initialization Order Dependency

Instead of forcing all users to guess the precise initialization order, you want a mechanism of *controlling* it. Fortunately, such a mechanism is readily available: Replace every global object with an *accessor function* that returns a reference to a local static object. For example, instead of a global `bar` object, use the following:

```
//getbar.cpp
#include "Bar.h"
Bar& getbar() //accessor function
{
//create a local static object when this function is
//called for the first time
 static Bar bar;
 return bar;
}
```

The `getbar()` function is now the sole mechanism for accessing `bar`. Create a matching header for every accessor function, too:

```
//getbar.h
#include "Bar.h"
Bar& getbar();
```

NOTE: For the sake of brevity, I omitted the `#include` guards from the `.h` files.

In a similar vein, replace `foo` with a matching accessor function and a header file:

```
//getfoo.cpp
#include "getbar.h"
#include "Foo.h"
```

```
Foo& getfoo() //accessor function
{
 static Foo foo(getbar());//safe
 return foo;
}

//getfoo.h
#include "Foo.h"

Foo& getfoo();
```

This technique solves the order dependency problem elegantly. The first invocation of an accessor function initializes the local static object and returns a reference to it. Subsequent invocations return a reference to the same local static object, so the value returned from such a function is always valid. The use of accessor function has another bonus: It rids you of global objects.

Final Notes

The curious among you may have noticed something peculiar here. The standard objects cin and cout are also declared in a namespace scope. Aren't they subjected to the same initialization order conundrum? Consider:

```
struct A
{
A() {cout<<"constructing A"<<endl;}
~A() {cout<<"destroying A"<<endl;}
};
A obj;
int main()
{}
```

obj is conceptually constructed before main() starts. During its construction, it uses cout, which is another object with static storage type. Is it safe to assume that cout (and its siblings wcout, cin, wcin, clog, wclog, cerr and wcerr) has been initialized at this time? Yes, it is. C++ guarantees that <iostream> objects are initialized before any other user-defined objects with static storage type. Because objects are always destroyed in the opposite order of their construction, you can safely use the <iostream> objects in the destructors of objects with static storage type as well.

CHAPTER 19

Design Patterns

Design Patterns became famous relatively recently, yet they're hardly new. Their origins can be traced back to the early days of Smalltalk, when users noticed that different and complex programming tasks consisted of smaller, recurrent design idioms serving as the building blocks of large-scale designs. They decided to formalize these recurrent idioms so that they could be reused later by other programmers, in very much the way standard algorithms and containers are used today. The main difference between Design Patterns and standard libraries of algorithms is that the former are mere *concepts*, not actual code. This is advantageous because patterns aren't bound to a specific programming language or a platform, at least in theory. Alas, this is also Design Patterns' main weakness: In order to use a Design Pattern, programmers must write it from scratch. Another problem associated with Design Patterns is that programmers who have learned a few of them start to use them excessively. For example, an application that happens to use a single data file all of a sudden wraps it in a Singleton object, even if a Singleton object isn't really necessary in this case. That said, Design Patterns are an essential tool in every professional programmer's arsenal; ignoring them altogether would be a mistake. In this chapter, I will introduce some of the more widely used Design Patterns that have been implemented in C++.

Monostate Pattern

Design Patterns were the hottest commodity of the 1990s, promising a cure to almost every ailment of the software industry. The tremendous hype led programmers to believe that a catalog of a few dozen recipes was all they needed to accomplish every programming task painlessly and swiftly. As usual, unrealistic expectations led to a bitter disappointment afterward. Today, as the pattern enthusiasm has abated, a more down-to-earth analysis is possible. Patterns will not solve all the problems of software developers nor will they replace resourcefulness, experience, skill and intelligence. Yet they offer a few shortcuts that simplify certain recurring programming tasks, very much like standard algorithms. In this section, I will explore the monostate pattern and its applications.

Problem Analysis

Sharing a single resource among multiple users or processes is a common scenario. Different applications on the same machine need to share a single modem; a single exchange rate table is shared by different departments of the same department store; a weather report is shared by different workstations of flight controllers at the same airport, and so on. How can you ensure that all users access the shared data safely? More importantly, how can you ensure that changes propagate immediately and automatically to all users?

Let's look at a concrete example. Suppose you have a weather report table containing the max and min temperatures, wind velocity, visibility conditions, etc., of a certain resgion. These data are constantly updated and need to be shared by all flight controllers of a certain airport. A naive programmer might be tempted to use a file to store these data. Although this solution could work, it suffers from several shortcomings: Accessing a physical file by multiple users could cause deadlocks and bottlenecks; the application in question must know where the file is located and how it's formatted. Worse yet, granting dozens of users direct access to a file could incur security problems and network congestion. Finally, how are end users informed of changes made to the file?

A better solution is to encapsulate the weather report in a class. You want to ensure that every user and application module gets a private object instance of that class while ensuring that these objects always share the same state. Furthermore, any change in the state of the class should propagate to other objects automatically and immediately. This is exactly what the monostate pattern provides.

Enter Monostate

A monostate class contains only `private` static data members and public non-static member functions to access these members. This way, all objects of this class share the same state.

Here's a class that represents the current weather conditions at a certain region:

```
class Weather
{
private:
  static int max_temp; //all temperatures are in Fahrenheit
```

```
    static int min_temp;
    static int current_temp;
    static int wind_velocity; //mph
    //...
};
```

The definitions of the static members outside the class also initialize them:

```
int Weather::max_temp=53;
int Weather::min_temp=36;
int Weather::current_temp=50;
int Weather::wind_velocity=14;
```

In the real world you'd probably use a function that reads the current weather conditions from a remote meteorology server or an external telemetry device that measures temperatures, humidity, etc.:

```
int Weather::current_temp=thermometer.get_current_temp();
```

Obviously, class `Weather` also defines member functions to access these values:

```
class Weather
{
//
public:
  int get_max_temp() const { return max_temp;}
  int get_min_temp() const { return min_temp;}
  int get_current_temp() const { return current_temp;}
  int get_wind_velocity() const { return wind_velocity;}
//
};
```

Putting It to Work

Each controller's desktop runs a module of the same flight control application that uses its own `Weather` object. This means that there are several live `Weather` objects at any given time:

```
Weather weather1, weather2;
```

However, they all share the same state, thereby ensuring that every controller gets exactly the same weather report:

```
//first controller's desktop
int current1=weather1.get_current_temp();
//second controller's desktop
int current2=weather2.get_current_temp();
```

It doesn't matter which object is queried; the same member function will return an identical result even if it's called from different objects. This solves the problem of data sharing neatly. That said, I haven't shown the real strength of the monostate pattern yet. What happens when the weather conditions change and Weather's data members need to be updated accordingly? To change the weather conditions, add another class called Admin, which is a friend of Weather. The new weather conditions propagate immediately to all instances of Weather like this:

```
class Admin;
class Weather
{
friend class Admin;
//
};
class Admin
{
public:
 Admin(const string &password) {} //authorize
 void set_min_temp(int min) {Weather::min_temp = min;}
 void set_max_temp(int max) {Weather::max_temp = max;}
 void set_current_temp(int temp)  {Weather::current_temp = temp;}
//
};
```

Suppose the current temperature is now 42. The system administrator (or a deamon process) updates it like this:

```
Admin admin("mypassword");
admin.set_current_temp(thermometer.get_current_temp());
```

After calling set_current_temp(), every Weather object knows that the current temperature is 42 degrees. If any of the flight controllers performs the following query,

```
//controller 1
current1=weather1.get_current_temp(); //42
//controller 2
current2=weather2.get_current_temp(); //42
```

all existing `Weather` objects will report the new `current_temp` value. Thus, we have accomplished the second design requirement: ensuring immediate and automatic propagation of state changes to every object.

Summary

In terms of its goals, monostate is similar to the Singleton pattern, though is much simpler to implement and use. Using static data members exclusively ensures that the same state is shared by all objects of the same class, regardless of their creation time. By changing a static member's value, you update the state shared by all objects immediately and automatically. Notice however that the implementation shown here isn't thread-safe; slight modifications (that are beyond the scope of this discussion) will make it thread-safe, if necessary.

Books

Design Patterns: Elements of Reusable Object-Oriented Software (Addison-Wesley, 1994, ISBN 0201633612), by Erich Gamma et al, has been the ultimate pattern catalog ever since it was published in 1994. Although many patterns have been developed after its publication (monostate, for instance), and many of the patterns it depicts have been revised, it's still one of the most influential programming books ever written. (For more on this book, visit *http://www.informit.com/bookstore/product.asp?isbn=0201633612*.)

Real-Time Design Patterns: Robust Scalable Architecture for Real-Time Systems (Addison-Wesley, 2002, ISBN 0201699567), by Bruce Powel Douglass, focuses on a more specialized application domain: namely, real-time and embedded systems. Using state-of-the-art features such as advanced template programming and UML diagrams, it addresses common (and not-so-common) programming tasks such as building a message queue, garbage collection, virtual machine, and many other nuts and bolts of any real-time system. (For more on this book, visit *http://www.informit.com/title/0201699567*.)

`Singleton` Pattern

`Singleton` is perhaps the most familiar design pattern. Its intent is to ensure that a class only has one instance, and provide a global point of access to it. In this regard, it isn't much different from a `monostate` class, although there are many situations in which a true `Singleton` class is required. In this section, I will present the guidelines of writing such a class and demonstrate its usefulness.

Rationale

There are many scenarios in which you need exactly one object in a system, application or device. Think of a printer spooler as an example. Although there can be many printers in a system, there should be only one printer spooler. Similarly, your operating system uses only one file system, and if it's connected to the Internet, it usually has only one active Internet connection at a time. Ensuring uniqueness without the use of a `Singleton` class is difficult and error-prone. The `Singleton` pattern provides a skeletal template for such a class, which you can extend and modify according to your specific needs.

Implementation

`Singleton` ensures that only a single instance of its type can be created by intercepting requests to create new objects. In addition, it provides a means of accessing the sole instance (also known as the *Singleton object*). To ensure that clients cannot create objects directly, `Singleton` has a protected constructor. In addition, it contains a static member function called `Instance()` that returns a pointer to its sole instance:

```
class Singleton
{
public:
  static Singleton* Instance();
protected:
  Singleton();
private:
  static Singleton* _instance;
};
```

The `private` static data member `_instance` is a pointer to the sole instance. `Singleton` uses *lazy initialization*, meaning that the value returned from `Instance()` isn't created until this member function is first called:

```
Singleton* Singleton::_instance = 0;
Singleton* Singleton::Instance ()
{
  if (_instance == 0)
  instance = new Singleton;
  return _instance;
}
```

Design Considerations

The constructor is responsible for all the initialization operations of the `Singleton` object. For example, if we're creating a `Singleton` printer spooler, it will create an empty job queue, check the status of all the currently active printers, etc. Because the constructor is `protected`, a client that tries to instantiate `Singleton` object directly will get a compilation error. Note that this constructor will get called on the first call to `Instance()`.

Storing a pointer rather than an actual object has two advantages. First, it enables `Singleton` to use lazy instantiation. Secondly, it supports polymorphism—you can assign the pointer to a subclass of `Singleton`.

The Design Patterns literature elegantly ignores the issue of a `Singleton`'s destructor. This isn't as trivial as it may seem at first. Remember that if you intend to derive classes from `Singleton`, you must declare its destructor `virtual`. Alternatively, you can forgo destructors both in the base class and its descendants. However, if you do define a destructor, don't be tempted to use it to destroy the `Singleton` object. The problem is that calling will invoke the destructor:

```
delete _instance;
```

which in turn will try to delete `_instance` once more, infinitely. That said, you can't ignore the fact that `Instance()` allocates an object on the free store and that that object must be deleted explicitly to avoid a memory leak. The simplest solution is to `delete _instance` at the end of the program:

```
int main()
{
 Singleton *p = Singleton::Instance();
 //..use p
 delete p;
}
```

This is however, a violation of basic OOD principles. Imagine what would happen if another thread calls `Instance()` one again. A better solution is to define another static member function that explicitly destroys the `Singleton` object and resets `_instance`:

```
void Singleton::Destroy()
{
   delete _instance;
   _instance=0;
}
```

This way, a subsequent call to `Instance()` will work as expected because it checks whether `_instance` is 0 before returning. Another solution that is suitable for single-threaded environments is to use a local static object:

```
//using a static Singleton object
//not suitable for multithreaded apps
Singleton* Singleton::Instance ()
{
 static Singleton s;
 return &s; //  _instance isn't needed in this case
}
```

Applications

Suppose you have a network card through which different applications access a local network. To ensure uniqueness, you choose to implement the network card as a `Singleton` class. Because there are several types of network cards used on different machines, you decided to derive different classes from `Singleton`, each of which represents a different brand. `Instance()` determines at runtime the actual network card type by examining an environment variable. It then constructs an object of the right type and returns its address to the caller:

```
class NetCard // a Singleton class
{
public:
   static NetCard * Instance();
protected:
   NetCard ();
private:
   static NetCard * _instance;
};
NetCard * NetCard::_instance=0;

NetCard* NetCard::Instance()
{
  if (_instance == 0)
  {
    const string* type = getenv("CARDTYPE");
    if (type == "Rockwell")
      _instance = new RockwellNetCard;
    else if (type == "Samsung")
      _instance = new SamsungNetCard;
    // ... other types
```

```
    else
       _instance = new NetCard; //default card
  }
  return _instance;
}
```

Summary

Singleton is not a panacea. The implementation of `NetCard::Instance()` already pushes the design to its limits; it provides some level of dynamic typing but if you add more derived classes, you'll need to modify `Instance()` accordingly. If you need a mechanism for dynamic type creation, consider using the Abstract Factory pattern instead.

Books

Design Patterns: Elements of Reusable Object-Oriented Software (Addison-Wesley, 1994, ISBN 0201633612), by Erich Gamma et al., has been the ultimate pattern catalog ever since it was published in 1994. Although many patterns have been developed after its publication (monostate, for instance), and many of the patterns it depicts have been revised, it's still one of the most influential programming books ever written. (For more on this book, visit *http://www.informit.com/bookstore/product.asp?isbn=0201633612*.)

Real-Time Design Patterns: Robust Scalable Architecture for Real-Time Systems (Addison-Wesley, 2002, ISBN 0201699567), by Bruce Powel Douglass, focuses on a more specialized application domain; namely, real-time and embedded systems. Using state-of-the-art features such as advanced template programming and UML diagrams, it addresses common (and not-so-common) programming tasks such as building a message queue, garbage collection, virtual machine, and many other nuts and bolts of any real-time system. (For more on this book, visit *http://www.informit.com/title/0201699567*.)

Anti-Patterns

Design Patterns are recommended solutions to recurring problems. The pattern movement also identifies and catalogs *anti-patterns*. Unfortunately, anti-patterns are more widespread than patterns and their impact on software projects is much more noticeable. In this section, I will explain what anti-patterns are and present some of them.

What Is an Anti-Pattern?

According to Jim Coplien, "An anti-pattern is something that looks like a good idea, but which backfires badly when applied." In other words, it's a recipe for doing things the wrong way. Unlike patterns, anti-patterns aren't restricted to design and implementation phases. They may stem from personal, organizational, and financial factors.

The History Book on the Shelf . . .

It's no secret that the majority of software projects fail. Assuming that the causes of failure aren't unique to each project, why aren't we witnessing a decline in the failure rate? It appears that people can't always put their finger on the ultimate cause of the problem. Developers and project managers can consult the anti-pattern catalog, identify these problems and learn how to cope with them effectively.

. . . Is Almost Repeating Itself

It is possible to come up with high-quality software solutions even if you don't use patterns; however, the very presence of anti-patterns in a software project usually entails poor-quality and problematic maintenance, or even an utter failure. Thus, identifying and averting anti-patterns pays off more than would throwing in a few normative patterns.

Anti-patterns can be classified into subcategories, e.g., language-specific anti-patterns (for example, template- and exception-related anti-patterns), analysis and design anti-patterns, and organizational anti-patterns. Let's look at a sample of such anti-patterns. Does any of these look suspiciously familiar?

Language-Specific Anti-Patterns

Certain coding practices and language-specific features lend themselves easily to misuse. *Exception funneling* is one such example.

Exceptions usually occur in low-level routines that should not try to fix the problem. These routines propagate the exceptions upward until an appropriate handler catches the exception. In a large-scale project, designers may be tempted to collapse various exception types into a single general exception either because they don't want to confuse the users with technical details or because the design phase deals only with the best-case scenarios so during the implementation phase, exception handling is only done to ensure that the code doesn't crash. Programmers who conceive exceptions as rare and hopeless runtime errors tend to use this anti-pattern frequently. As a result, when an exception occurs, users can't tell what exactly happened. They need to debug the application, reconstruct the call stack and locate the code section that threw the exception.

In some cases, avoiding exceptions altogether and using an alternative method for reporting failures is preferable. For example, STL algorithms such as `find()` return an agreed-upon iterator value that indicate "not found." In other scenarios, a thorough design of exception types and the responsibility for handling them is necessary to avert this anti-pattern.

Analysis and Design Anti-Patterns

The following anti-patterns depend on the analysis and design phases rather than the actual programming language used.

A *God Object* is an object that knows too much or does too much. Procedural programmers making the migration to an object-oriented environment tend to treat the notion of a class as the equivalent of a complete program: They design a class that knows everything about everything and has dozens of data members. Often, such poor design leads to the instantiation of a single (usually global) object of this class. Every function call and if-condition has to use this object, update its state and depend on its gigantic interface.

The *Analysis Paralysis* anti-pattern is a pathological state in which a team of analysts begin the analysis phase but never finish it. In many cases, this leads to the project's cancellation. What are the causes of this? Sometimes, the analysts have no experience in developing software. Consequently, they never soar beyond the diagrams-and-charts stage. In other cases, the project's requirements aren't clear, or they conflict. One solution is to employ developers who are also analysts, not analysts who haven't developed before.

Organizational Anti-Patterns

Poor managerial skills, egotism, and lack of collaboration lead to recurring delays, additional costs, and poor-quality software.

The *Heir Apparent* management anti-pattern occurs when the boss seems to have chosen a successor. Although this decision isn't publicized officially, everyone mutters the successor's name. Consequently, senior team members leave the project as an act of protest. The subversive undercurrents stirred by other disgruntled team members also shift the focus from the development phase to a political campaign.

Managers should realize that "clandestine coronations" become common knowledge very quickly. It's therefore better to appoint a successor in an open process that gives other candidates a fair chance. Remember: Even when the successor is elected in an open process, other team members might leave. If you can't afford to lose them, perhaps the best idea is to postpone the coronation until a less critical phase in the project.

Summary

The small number of anti-patterns (a few dozen) compared to the huge number of failed projects suggests that on average, each anti-pattern has occurred hundreds of times before. Familiarity with the anti-pattern catalog can thus teach managers and developers alike which mistakes they should avoid.

Online Resources

"The Anti-Patterns Catalog" (*http://c2.com/cgi/wiki?AntiPatternsCatalog*) is an incomplete list of some of the more popular and documented anti-patterns. Although the items are presented in fluctuating levels of depth and details, this catalog is pretty exhaustive.

Wikipedia also provides a detailed catalog (*http://en.wikipedia.org/wiki/Anti-pattern*) of anti-patterns.

Refactoring

Extreme Programming (XP) is a relatively new discipline of software development. It advocates simplicity, pair programming, and direct customer involvement. However, refactoring is probably the most popular doctrine introduced by XP. Here, I will explain the motives behind refactoring and some of its principles.

TIP: For more on extreme programming, visit *http://www.extremeprogramming.org/*.

What Is Refactoring?

XP believes that programmers hold on to their software designs long after they have become unwieldy. From my experience, there's more than a grain of truth in this claim. Look at your own infrastructure code. Wouldn't you come up with a simpler and neater design, possibly with fewer lines of code, if you were to write from scratch? Look at class `string` of your operating system's APIs—I have no doubt that if these were to be redesigned from scratch today, they would be rid of the useless fluff and excess baggage that they have been carrying for years.

Programmers are afraid of changing code that is no longer maintainable because it still works. But is it really cost effective to do so? XP believes that it is not; instead, it advocates *refactoring*: i.e., removing redundancy, eliminating unused functionality, and rejuvenating obsolete designs.

Refactoring usually consists of renaming member function, moving data members from one class to another, and splitting a large member function into two separate functions. However, refactoring isn't restricted to classes and member function. Renaming variables and user-defined types so that they conform to a certain coding standard are also instances of refactoring.

Refactoring by Example

Take for example a loop that transforms a string to uppercase letters. A naive implementation would use a `for` loop such as this one:

```
void uppercase(string &s)
{
  for (int j=0; j<s.length(); ++j)
    s[j]=toupper(s[j]);
  return; // s now contains uppercase letters
}
```

Though functionally correct, this loop is a maintenance headache. To apply a different type of transformation to the string (say converting it to lowercase or transliterating its characters to their Cyrillic equivalent) you'll have to rewrite the loop's body or create another function. To improve the design, separate the string transformation into two operations: one that iterates through the string's elements and one that actually transforms every element. You gain more flexibility by decoupling these operations and simplify future maintenance. You can achieve this decoupling by using the `transform()` algorithm instead of a `for` loop:

```
transform(s.begin(), s.end(), s.begin(), ::toupper);
```

Even this design can be improved by replacing the hard-coded operation (passed as the fourth argument) with a pointer to function. This enables you to control the precise transformation type at runtime (changing a string to lowercase letters, Cyrillic letters, or encrypting it), simply by assigning a different address to the pointer argument:

```
int(*pf)(int));
pf= ::toCyrillic;
transform(s.begin(), s.end(), s.begin(), pf);
```

However, even this design can be further improved by replacing `pf` with a function object. This will enable you to use not just bare functions, but algorithms and function objects, without having to modify the code. At this point you're probably wondering when this iterative process stops. Indeed, one of the problems with teaching programmers to use refactoring is that they get carried away and constantly look for design improvements. There's no rule of thumb here—stop when you feel that the new design is simpler, cleaner, and more efficient and conforms to the project's coding standard. For example, in a project that migrates C code to C++, you are likely to replace `qsort()` calls with `std::sort`. Later, you may discover that the Standard Library has specialized sorting algorithms such as `stable_sort()` and `partial_sort()` that have slightly different semantics, so you may decide to replace some of the `std::sort` calls with either `stable_sort()` or `partial_sort()`. You may also discover later that by using a self-sorting container such as `priority_queue`, you can eliminate sorting altogether. To conclude, refactoring is an iterative process that proceeds gradually on a continuous basis, rather than a wholesale code surgery.

TIP: Check out these specialized topics:

Topic	More Info
Function objects	See the section "Function Objects" in Chapter 10
stable_sort	*http://www.sgi.com/tech/stl/stable_sort.html*
partial_sort	*http://www.sgi.com/tech/stl/partial_sort.html*
priority_queue	*http://www.sgi.com/tech/stl/priority_queue.html*

Refactoring Patterns

Design Patterns sell well. It's no wonder then that every recurrent theme that can be molded into a template or a recipe is referred to as a *pattern* these days. In this respect, XP is no exception: It also has *Refactoring patterns*, which are recipes for replacing obsolete, incoherent, verbose, or inefficient constructs with prescribed design norms that don't alter the code's functionality. Let's look at a couple of examples.

The *Extract Method* pattern tackles a common scenario: a member function (a method in XP parlance) is too big. The recommended solution (see *http://c2.com/cgi/wiki?ExtractMethod*) is as follows:

- Take a part of the member function that seems useful on its own. (To check this, see if you can find a good name for it.)
- Turn it into a separate member function.
- Change the original member function to use the new one.

The *Move Method* pattern tackles another common scenario: While refactoring, you discover a member function that is tightly bound to another class, but not to its own. The prescribed solution is to create a new member function with a similar body in the class it uses most. Then, either turn the old member function into a simple wrapper that invokes the new member function, or remove it altogether.

Summary

The "Refactoring to Patterns Catalog" (*http://www.industriallogic.com/xp/refactoring/catalog.html*) contains dozens of such recipes. Indeed, some of these patterns are language-specific. For instance, the *Chain Constructor* pattern deals with the reduplication of code in separate constructors of the same class. In Java, the solution is to chain constructors. In C++ you would instead define a private `init()` member function that performs the recurrent initialization operations and have every constructor call it. This is in fact what the Extract Method pattern does.

CHAPTER 20

C++0X: The New Face of Standard C++

The current C++ standard, officially known as ISO/IEC 14882, is already seven years old. The C++ standards committee is currently working on extending and enhancing C++. Most of the work focuses on additions to the Standard Library, with very minimal core languages changes. In this series, I will explore some of the novel features added to the Standard Library.

Rationale

Extensions and enhancements are the best indicator that a programming language is being used heavily in the real world rather than being confined to esoteric academic niches. Therefore, it's no surprise that the current standard is undergoing an overhaul. There's no need to panic, though: it will still remain the same C++ as you've known for years, except that it will include many new facilities that are long overdue. As always, the standardization process is long-winded but in the long run, it will pay off. When you consider the frequent wholesale upheavals that new programming languages undergo with every new release, I'm sure you'll agree that it's better to make a good standard right from the start (even if it takes longer) than to rush the standardization process only to discover later that "My goodness, we forgot generics!"

As I showed before, adding a half-baked feature at the last moment is never a good idea. The committee is well aware of this. Therefore, proposals for new features are always based on existing implementations. For instance, the regular expressions library of C++ (to which I will dedicate a separate section) is based on the `boost::regex` library (see *http://sourceforge.net/project/ showfiles.php?group_id=7586*). This way, the feedback of users can help the designers fine-tune their implementation, and add new features to it. Only then is the refined implementation proposed to the committee. The official paper that specifies the newly added features is called *The Standard Library*

Extensions Technical Report 1 (known as the "Library TR1"). The committee in turn reviews the TR, suggesting improvements, proper Standardese and implementation guidelines. There is no obligation to accept the facilities described in the TR as is; in fact, it is more than likely that the final version will look different. Namespace issues, naming conventions, exception-safety, interaction with existing Standard Library components and other factors will affect the final version of the proposed features. Therefore, all the code listings, class and function names, and other design and implementation details provided in this section are subject to change.

The `<tuple>` Library

The Library TR includes the new header file `<tuple>`, which contains a tuple class template and its helper functions. A tuple is a fixed-size heterogeneous collection of objects. Several programming languages, e.g., Python and ML, have tuple types. Tuple types have many useful applications, such as packing multiple return values for a single function, simultaneous assignment and comparison of multiple objects, and grouping related objects (such as a function's arguments). A tuple's size is the number of elements stored in it. The current specification supports tuples with 0-10 elements. Each element can be of a different type. The following example creates a tuple type that has two elements: `double` and `void *`:

```
#include <tuple>
tuple <double, void *> t(2.5, &x);
```

If you omit the initializers, default initialization will take place instead:

```
tuple <double, std::string> t; //defulat initialized to (0.0, string())
```

Helper Functions

The `make_tuple()` function simplifies the construction of tuple types. It detects the types of its arguments and instantiates a tuple type accordingly:

```
void func(int i);
make_tuple(func); // returns: tuple<void (*)(int)>
make_tuple("test", 9); // tuple< const char (&)[5], int>
```

To examine a tuple's size, use the `tuple_size()` function:

```
int n=tuple_size < tuple <int, std::string> >::value;//2
```

To obtain the type of an individual element, use the `tuple_element()` function.

`tuple_element()` returns the type of an individual element. This function takes an index and the tuple type. The following example uses this function to retrieve the type of the first element in a tuple:

```
typedef tuple_element <0, tuple<float, int, char> >::type
  T1;// T1 is a synonym for float
```

To access the element itself, either for reading its value or to assign a new value to it, use the `get<>()` function template. The template argument (the argument passed in the angle brackets) is the index of sought-after element, and the argument in parentheses contains the tuple type:

```
tuple <int, double> tpl;
int n=get<0>(tpl); //read 1st element
get<1>(t)=9.5; //assign to the 2nd element
```

Applications

Functions with a dual interface can use tuples to pack two or more return types. Some of the better candidates for dual interfacing include Standard Library functions that return only `char *` but not `std::string`. For example, the `getenv()` function retrieves an environment variable and returns its value in the form of a C-string. In this case, overloading can do the trick:

```
char * getenv(const char * name); //existing version
//hypothetic overloaded version
const std::string& getenv(const std::string name);
```

However, if the function can't use different arguments to play this trick, tuples can save the day. For example, a function that translates a file name to its equivalent `FILE *` *and a file descriptor* can't rely on overloading because its parameter doesn't change, only the return type. POSIX often solves this problem by defining multiple functions with slightly different names:

```
int traslatefile(const char * path);
FILE * ftraslatefile(const char * path);
```

Using a tuple can solve this problem neatly:

```
typedef tuple <int, FILE *> file_type;
file_type translatefile (const char *);
```

Summary

Tuple types are only one of many new facilities that are being added to the Standard Library. The fact that very minimal core changes, if any, are needed to support the new proposals shows the foresight of C++ designers. Consequently, the new facilities can be neatly integrated in existing code without causing conflicts or design changes.

Reference Wrapper Class

Continuing our journey into the new C++ standard, this time I will present another proposal that has been incorporated into the Library Extensions Technical Report: the reference wrapper class.

Rationale

In certain contexts, built-in reference types cannot be used as first-class citizens in C++. For example, you can't define a container of references:

```
std::vector <int &> vri; //won't compile
```

In this respect, reference types are different from bare pointers, which can be used as container elements. Additionally, it is sometimes necessary to pass references as arguments to algorithms and functions that would usually create a copy of their arguments.

A reference wrapper class template enables you to wrap a reference in the guise of an object. The object can then be used in contexts in which built-in references won't work. Consider the following example:

```
void func(int & r)
{
 r++;
}

template<class F, class T> void g(F f, T t)
{
```

```
  f(t);
}

int main()
{
  int i = 0;
  g(func, i);
}
```

The second parameter of g() is passed by value. If you want to force g() to take a reference instead, a reference wrapper can do the trick.

The reference_wrapper Class Template

reference_wrapper<T> is a *copy-constructible* and *assignable* wrapper around an object of type T&. The copy-constructible and assignable properties ensure, among other things, that reference_wrapper objects can be used as an element of STL containers.

The reference_wrapper class and its helper functions are declared in the <utility> header. This header, as you probably know, already contains several other facilities such as auto_ptr. (For more on auto_ptr, see Chapter 4, "Memory Management.")

There are two helper functions: ref() and cref(), which create a reference_wrapper object that wraps their argument. cref() returns a const T& wrapper object, whereas ref() returns a T& wrapper object.

When dealing with plain references and references to const objects, people often use the term "const reference" when they actually mean a reference to a const object. Notice that there's no point in having a const reference in C++ in the first place because a reference, once initialized, can't be bound to a different object.

Notice how the use of a reference_wrapper helps us ensure that the function template g() behaves as if it took a reference rather than a copy of its argument:

```
int main()
{
  int i = 0;
  g(f, i); //pass i by value
  cout << i << endl; //as expected, 0
  g(f, ref(i)); //bind a reference to i and pass it as arg
  cout << i << endl; // output: 1
}
```

Let's look at what this program does. First, the function g() is called with two arguments that are passed by value: a function pointer and a copy of i. g() in turns invokes the function bound to f, which increments the copy of i. As expected, when g() returns, the change to the local copy of i isn't reflected in the i that was declared in main(). Therefore, the first cout expression displays 0. In the second call to g(), the ref() helper function creates a temporary reference_wrapper() that is bound to i. The side effects of func() are therefore reflected in i after the call and the second cout expression displays 1.

reference_wrapper can be used where ordinary references cannot, such as in containers:

```
std::list<int> num;
std::vector<reference_wrapper<int> >
 num_refs; // a list of references to int

for(int i = 0; i < 10; ++i)
{
  numbers.push_back(2*i*i^4 - 8*i + 7); //ordinary copy semantics
  num_refs.push_back(
//create a reference to the last element in nums
  ref(numbers.back()));
}
```

A reference_wrapper enables you to pass T& as an argument to algorithms that expect the underlying type, i.e., T:

```
std::sort(num_refs.begin(), num_refs.end());
```

Using reference_wrapper with Tuples

reference_wrapper also enables you to create tuples of references and references to const in cases where the tuple class would use the underlying, non-cv-qualified type instead:

```
void f(const A& ca, B& b)
{
 make_tuple(ca, b); // returns tuple<A, B>
}
```

To override the default behavior of `make_tuple`, use `ref()` and `cref()` like this:

```
A a; B b; const A ca=a;
make_tuple( cref(a), b); // tuple <const A&, B> (a,b)
make_tuple( ref(a), b); // tuple <A&, B> (a,b)
make_tuple( ref(a), cref(b) ); // tuple <A&, const B&> (a,b)
```

Summary

The `reference_wrapper` utility class and its helper functions exemplify how a small library can be neatly incorporated into C++ to fill a few syntactic lacunae. This type of solution is preferable because it guarantees that existing compilers can cope with new C++ code without requiring upgrades and—more importantly—without causing existing code to break.

CHAPTER 21

The Reflecting Circle

This chapter will discuss programming theory and practice in general and bring you analyses and views that may not be directly related to C++ (e.g., the latest changes in the Solaris API or digital audio compression), interviews, and miscellaneous tidbits.

The Future of Programming

Elsewhere I referred to Herb Sutter's views (see *http://www.devsource.ziffdavis.com/article2/0,1759,1684840,00.asp*) about the programming languages of the next decade: "[T]op future programming languages will blend existing 'concrete' languages with virtual platforms. They will likely include garbage collection, security and verifiability," he said. This led me to reflect on predictions about the future of programming in general. How many of them turn out to be true eventually? Is there a litmus test that can be applied to sift viable predictions from mere wishful thinking and hyperbole? To answer these questions I decided to look at some predictions that were made 20 years ago and others that were made relatively recently. In 2000 and early 2001, I conducted several interviews with industry experts including Dennis Ritchie and Bjarne Stroustrup. In all of these interviews I asked for their opinions about the future of programming. Four years later, it's interesting to look at these predictions. However, before I do that, let's look at older predictions first.

Analysts' Views—Early 1980s

It's hard to believe that in the early 1980s, analysts were all but certain that the sun was setting on conventional programming languages. Ada, launched in 1983 after more than a decade of research and design, was considered by many as the last programming language. Experts deemed conventional programming "too complicated and open to risk." (See "Hard Coding Is In" at *http://startechcentral.com/tech/story.asp?file=/2004/11/2/corpit/9192130&sec=corpit*.) They complained that its interfaces to third-party software had to be constantly maintained. Application generators, they claimed, would replace conventional programming "soon." They couldn't have been more wrong, though. During the past two decades, the software industry has spawned an unprecedented number of programming languages, whereas application generators vanished. Even hybrid products that combine automated boilerplate code generation with manual programming (Delphi and C++ Builder, for example) show the opposite trend, of moving from proprietary languages that purportedly facilitate the development process toward conventional, general-purpose programming languages such as C++ and Java. Indeed, the programmer's job today is less arduous than it was 20 years ago: Syntax highlighting, auto-completion, and good old copy-and-paste allow us to use fewer keystrokes and make fewer typos. However, hardcore programming is still the primary means of application development today, just it was 20 or 30 years ago.

Perhaps it would be more interesting to look at what analysts in the early 1980s *didn't* foresee. They didn't predict that object orientation would sweep the software world, turning into the leading paradigm in less than a decade. They also missed the Internet revolution and its impact on the availability of knowledge and information. This begs the question: How seriously should we treat predictions? It depends on who makes them.

Experts' Views—2000–2001

In December 2000, I interviewed Dennis Ritchie, the father of UNIX and C. One of my questions was this: "Five or ten years from now, will C still be as popular and indispensable as it is today, especially in system programming, networking, and embedded systems, or will newer programming languages take its place?"

You can read his complete answer in the interview at *http://www.itworld.com/Comp/3380/lw-12-ritchie/*. Here's the bottom line:

"The kind of programming that C provides will probably remain similar absolutely or slowly decline in usage, but relatively, JavaScript or its variants, or XML, will continue to become more central. For that matter, it may be that Visual Basic is the most heavily used language around the world. I'm not picking a winner here, but higher-level ways of instructing machines will continue to occupy more of the center of the stage."

Dennis, as always, was right.

Five months later, I presented the same question to Robert C. Martin. Martin's opinion was that the long build cycles required by statically compiled languages such as C++ and Java were a major drawback. He predicted that dynamically (though strongly) typed languages like Python and Smalltalk would be the mainstream languages of the future, rather than C++-like languages.

Unfortunately, this interview is no longer available online. However, its "echoes" are found in a later interview with Bertrand Meyer (the designer of Eiffel) and Robert C. Martin. (See "Point/Counterpoint: Does Extreme Programming Deliver on Its Promises?" at *http://www.itworld.com/AppDev/1246/ITF010425meyer/*.)

While Python has gained a small market share particularly in the Linux realm, static type-checking is still the predominant paradigm even among the newest general-purpose programming languages (e.g., C#). Dynamic typing hasn't become a major player in mainstream application development—not yet at least.

Revolution? What Revolution?

"It is hard to make a prediction, especially about the future," said Mark Twain. And yet, by contrasting the predictions that turned out to be correct with those that didn't, we can draw at least two important conclusions.

Revolutions don't happen overnight. Consider the two most conspicuous changes in the software world of the last 20 years: object-orientation and the Internet. The roots of object-oriented programming date back to the 1960s with languages such as Simula (*http://www.engin.umd.umich.edu/CIS/course.des/cis400/simula/simula.html#apparea*) and its successors. It took more than 20 years for this technology to mature and become the predominant paradigm. Similarly, the Internet's seeds were sown in 1969 in the form of Arpanet. More than 20 years elapsed between the first Arpanet network and Al Gore's High Performance Computing Act of 1991, which in my opinion signaled the shift from a mere academic trifle into a universal public network. Thus, visions of overnight revolutions are less likely to materialize.

The Conservative Party

The second generalization is that the software world that we consider as the culmination of cutting-edge technology is in fact very conservative. I believe that industries such as printing or home entertainment advance more rapidly than programming. Much of the success of object-orientation is attributed to the success of C++; C++ succeeded due to its reliance on C. Had C++ creators designed a new language from scratch, both C++ and object-orientation would have remained a footnote in the history of programming. This phenomenon isn't unique to C++. Consider other new programming languages: As innovative as they seem, they rarely offer genuinely original features and concepts. Furthermore, writing a C++ or Java application isn't significantly different from writing an Ada application 20 years ago. And frankly, why should there be a difference? Generics, encapsulation, exception handling, default arguments, operator overloading and other wonderful constructs that we use today were already present in Ada 83. As Bjarne Stroustrup put it succinctly in an interview (*http://www.itworld.com/AppDev/710/lw-02-stroustrup/*): "The future is usually more like yesterday than we like to believe."

Characters and Strings, Part I

Standard C++ supports two native character types: `char` and `wchar_t`. In addition, strings are represented either as zero-terminated arrays of characters or as a specialization of the `basic_string` class template. Although these standards are widely used in other programming languages and environments, there are plenty of other character-encoding schemes and string representations. Here, I will discuss some of these coding standards and list their pros and cons.

What's in a Character?

The invention of semaphores and telegraphs in the 18th and 19th centuries, respectively, led to the development of coding systems whereby letters of the alphabet were mapped to detailed semaphore shapes, electrical pulses and numbers. The early electronic computers borrowed the concept of representing characters as small numbers. A *code set* defines a collection of characters (say, the Latin alphabet) and their matching numeric codes. Thus, a North American code set may map the letter 'A' to the decimal value 65 whereas a Hebrew code set would map the same value to the letter *shin*. In the early 1960s IBM developed two coding standards: ASCII and EBCDIC. These standards were originally designed for the use of teletypewriters and punched cards, respectively. The ASCII standard consists of 127 or 255 (in its extended form) characters that are encoded in 7 or 8 bits. The archaic nature of this standard is manifested by the presence of codes for obsolete symbols such as CR (carriage return) and FF (form feed), as well as the lack of modern keyboard codes for Page Down and Print Screen, etc. EBCDIC is even more peculiar. Its forerunner, BCDIC, was used before the era of digital computers, when key-punchers and tabulator machines were used. EBCDIC, which stands for Extended BCDIC, was designed for IBM's mainframes and mini-computers. It consists of 225 symbols whose precise interpretation requires a special code page that maps codes to characters.

Double-Byte Coding

The quirks and limitations of ASCII and EBCDIC are well-known and too numerous to be repeated here. No one was really content with them but various workarounds and hacks made their usage tolerable—so long as they were used in locales with no more than a few dozen characters. For Asian languages and syllabic orthographical systems (e.g., Amharic), which contain hundreds, thousands and even tens of thousands of letters and ideograms, a single-byte encoding system is unsuitable. This led to the development of Double-Byte Coding Systems (DBCS). The name *double-byte* is misleading because it implies that every character is represented as two bytes. In reality, DBCS uses a single byte to represent frequently used characters and certain *extension codes*, indicating that the current character consists of two bytes. Thus, DBCS uses the entire 256-character range of the ASCII standard minus 3 extension signs in the first byte. The extension codes, when set, indicate that the current character stretches to the next byte. Such a system supports 1,021 characters: 256 distinct values for each extension byte * 3 plus 256-3 characters of the ASCII system. DBCS solves some of the problems of single-byte codes. However, it introduces a plethora of other problems. First, this system can't handle more than 1,021 characters. For languages such as Chinese and certain Japanese orthographical systems, this number is too small. Secondly, string manipulation algorithms usually rely on the assumption that each character has a fixed size. Therefore, they can't cope with DBCS strings properly. For example, a string length function has to scan a DBCS string byte by byte and look through each character of the string to locate any extension values. Another serious problem has to do with pointer arithmetic. C/C++ programmers are used to advance a pointer to the next character by a ++ operation; in DBCS, pointer arithmetic is unpredictable because it uses variable size characters.

Unicode

In the late 1980s, engineers at Apple and Xerox started to develop a new coding standard called Unicode that was meant to overcome the limitations of both single-byte coding and DBCS. Unicode uses a 16-bit word to represent each character, supporting up to 65,536 different characters. The lower range of Unicode codes coincides with the ASCII codes, making conversion between the two standards relatively simple. Unicode has been adopted and supported by every leading computer manufacturer and every major OS. Thus far, approximately half of its 65,536 possible characters have been defined.

String Representation

A string is essentially a sequence of characters. As simple as this definition sounds, almost every programming language and framework implements strings differently. These differences result from two causes: the different underlying representation of characters, and the different representations of strings implemented by each programming language and framework.

C/C++ and several other languages represent strings as an array of characters with a terminating binary zero. Zero-terminated strings (ZTS) offer several advantages: They can represent any practical length with only one byte overhead, they are simple to implement and they are relatively portable. However, they raise several problems:

- There's no escape from traversing the entire string to detect its size.
- It's impossible to create strings with embedded binary zeros.
- When the string's terminating zero isn't present (say due to a buffer overflow/underflow bug)—all hell breaks loose.

Standard C++ fixed this problem by introducing a string object. Such an object keeps track of its internal string buffer. Therefore, computing a string's length is a fast, constant-time operation. In addition, the internal string can contain binary zeros, unlike ZTS. And yet, this solution introduces new problems: lack of compatibility with C and other languages, and a more complicated serialization/deserialization procedure.

In the next part of this series I will explore other models of representing strings, such as seven-bit strings, length-prefixed strings, and descriptors.

Recommended Books

Write Great Code (No Starch Press, 2004), by Randall Hyde, teaches important concepts of machine organization in a language-independent fashion, discussing among other things the notion of character representations and standards, string types and other under-the-hood topics such as binary arithmetic, floating-point representation, CPU architecture and so on. Today's programmers can hardly keep up with the race against inhumane deadlines and new technologies; therefore, they rarely have a chance to learn the basics of computer architectures and the inner workings of their programming languages. This book fills in the gaps. I strongly recommend it. (For more on this book, visit *http://www.nostarch.com/frameset.php?startat=greatcode*.)

Characters and Strings, Part II

In the first part of this series, I explained how C and C++ implement strings. Other programming languages and environments implement strings in various different ways. In this section, I will present some of these alternative string implementations and discuss their benefits and drawbacks.

Seven-Bit Strings

The ASCII standard uses seven bits to encode 128 symbols. This leaves one free bit in every unsigned byte. It's possible to use this redundant bit as a flag; all but the last characters in a string have their high-order bit clear (or set, as the implementer decides), whereas the last character in the string has its high-order bit set (or clear). This contrast between a final-position eighth bit and a non–final-position eighth bit eliminates the need to cache the string's length elsewhere. However, this technique has several disadvantages:

- You can't have zero-length strings in this format.
- You need to scan the entire string to determine its length.
- Most programming languages don't support seven-bit literal constants.
- Your code set can't contain more than 128 symbols.

This implementation has one conspicuous advantage: It doesn't rely on extraneous data structures. As such, it's ideal for assembly languages.

Length-Prefixing

Certain C++ implementations use *prefixing* to cache the size of a dynamically allocated array, so that operator `delete []` can tell how many elements that array contains. This technique was originally implemented in Pascal to cache the length of a string. Pascal strings consist of an unsigned byte that stores the number of characters in a string, followed by an array of characters. For example, the following string:

```
"Bill"
```

is implemented in Pascal as (each byte is marked by a pair of brackets):

```
[0x04] [0x42] [0x69] [0x6c] [0x6c]
```

The first byte, known as the *cookie*, contains the binary value 4, which is the number of characters in the string. The rest of the bytes contain the ASCII codes of letters. This implementation has several advantages:

- It's possible to store null characters in a string.
- Detecting a string's size is a fast, constant-time operation because you have to read a single byte at a fixed position.

There is an obvious limitation, though: A string cannot have more than 255 characters. Although increasing the size of the cookie to two or four bytes solves this problem, the cost is a waste of space. Another problem with this technique is byte ordering. If the cookie contains more than a single byte, the sender and the receiver must agree on the cookie's byte ordering.

Once you open the floodgate of caching information in a prefixed cookie, it is possible to stretch this technique further and prefix additional information. For example, an implementation may store two adjacent cookies that indicate the string's capacity and its actual length. This way, the application can always tell how many more bytes it can append to the strings safely. Imagine how many buffer overflows could have been averted if C strings were implemented this way!

With prefixing, a zero-terminator character isn't needed. However, several implementations use a hybrid design whereby the string's size is prefixed and the final character is set to zero. This ensures compatibility with C/C++, for instance. Microsoft's proprietary BSTR format uses a 32-bit cookie that stores the string's size, followed by a zero-terminated array of Unicode characters. In this format, the cookie contains the number of characters (not bytes) in the string, excluding the terminating zero. The following string in BSTR format:

```
L"Bill"; //wchar_t literal string
```

consists of a four-byte cookie followed by five Unicode characters of the string, namely the four letters plus a zero terminator:

```
cookie              'B'          'i'          'l'          'l'        L'\0'
[0x00000004]+ [0x0, 0x42] [0x0, 0x69] [0x0, 0x6c] +[0x0, 0x6c] [0x0, 0x0]
4 byte cookie +4 Unicode letters, each occupying 2 bytes + 2 byte zero terminator
```

Consequently, this string occupies no less than 14 bytes!

Other Microsoft frameworks such as OLE use variations on this theme, with the ability to switch between Unicode and ASCII via macro magic.

Descriptors

A *descriptor* is a data structure that contains information about another object. For example, a file descriptor may contain a handle that uniquely identifies a file in a program. The simplest string descriptor contains two data members: the string's size and its address. For example:

```
struct DESC
{
 size_t length;
 char * pc;
};
char str[MAX];
DESC d;
d.length=MAX-1;
d.pc=str;
```

Descriptor-oriented frameworks and programming language pass a descriptor (usually by reference) instead of passing the address of the character buffer. This technique is safer than zero-terminated strings because the string's size is kept separate from the actual buffer. As a bonus, calculating the length of such a string is a fast, constant-time operation. Yet descriptors have a few drawbacks:

- An extra level of indirection, which incurs slight runtime overhead.
- Space overhead. Each string is associated with a matching descriptor. The smallest descriptor occupies eight bytes; when more data members are added (say for reference counting, etc.), this size increases accordingly.

In programming languages that use this technique, descriptors are automatically maintained. Usually, the descriptor is implicit; under the hood, the compiler rewrites the code, replacing seemingly direct string access operations with *thunks* that access the relevant descriptor. The main problem with this technique is compatibility with other languages. If programmers can't access the actual implementation of a string, it's more difficult to export and import strings to and from other sources.

Summary

Using string descriptors instead of ZTS would have made C a much more secure programming language. However, ZTS offered two major advantages: It enabled C, and subsequently C++, to plug in different string types by using different libraries. Even in C, you can override the default string implementation, using custom-made string types and APIs. Other programming languages rarely offer that level of flexibility. Another advantage is that ZTS is one of the simplest and most platform-neutral string implementations extant.

Online Resources

"Guide to BSTR and C String Conversions" (*http://www.codeproject.com/string/bstrsproject1.asp*), by Robert Pittenger, presents the string-Babel of the Windows world. The combination of several programming languages (VB and C++), frameworks (OLE, MFC, STL, etc.) and coding standards (ASCII versus Unicode) makes navigation among the plethora of Windows string types very confusing. This section shows how each format is implemented and how you can convert one format to another.

Sound Bytes

After many discussions about elaborate type specifiers, linkage units, and a good many other issues, I have a surprise for you. In this section, I will discuss something that has little to do with C++, though not entirely unrelated. Welcome to wonderful world of digital audio and video! Here, I will explain the basic concepts of digital recording, encoding and decoding, compression and data reduction, sound quality and MP3 files.

Overture

The first commercial digital audio appliances for home users were compact disc players. They appeared on the market in 1983. Their success is still a mystery since in terms of value for money, they offered very little at a very expensive price. In 1984, a high-quality CD player could cost $3,000 in today's value. In terms of sound quality, they were beyond the pale: Harsh, metallic, off-beat, ear-fatiguing and flat sound was marketed as the "perfect sound." Yet people must have had it with huge vinyl records that would collect dust and scratches; the market was ripe was for a technological change. The CD standard itself was formulated in the late 1970s. Considering the technological limits of that time, digital audio discs were, at best, a compromise with which we have to live today. Undoubtedly, had the CD standard been formulated 20 years later, it would have been immeasurably superior in terms of sound quality, compactness, durability, costs and features. So, the next time you hear a media player that offers "CD quality"—frown at it. Here's why.

Crescendo

The CD standard encodes digital audio at a *sampling rate* of 44,100 Hertz and at a *quantization rate* of 16 bits. A digital recording, unlike an analog recording, is based on sampling whereby a recording device takes a discrete snapshot X times every second. These snapshots are similar to the frames of a movie, except that in this case the rate is much higher: 44,100 times per second for each audio channel (left and right). While this number sounds very impressive, remember that many of the sounds we hear, such as cymbals, flutes, a window-crashing soprano, etc., have a high frequency that is measured between 1,000–10,000 Hertz. This means that only four frames in the digital recording represent the high-pitch sound of cymbal because there are only four frames within the time slot of each wave:

```
44,100 / 10,000=~4
```

To demonstrate this problem, think of a helicopter propeller that revolves 20 times each second. In order to view each revolution in slow motion, you need at least 40 frames per second. The same thing applies to digital audio—the higher the sound frequency, the lower the number of frames per each wave. The 44,100 sampling rate is therefore acceptable for human speech or bongo drums. However, high frequencies are represented in a much less accurate manner. This was the first compromise that digital audio designers had to come up with. The second deplorable compromise was a 16-bit quantization rate. Quantization is the process in which the loudness is represented digitally. Because sound recordings (especially in classic music) may include abrupt changes in volume—switching from the lowest whispering notes to the noisiest rumble—a digital recording device splits the volume range into discrete units of voltage. Each unit is represented as a numeric value, with the value 0 representing absolute silence and the value 2^16, or 65,5535 representing the loudest possible sound. Again, while this range seems impressive in theory, the human ear can actually cope with a much larger range of 10,000,000 different values. To represent this fine-grained resolution, a quantization rate of 24 bits or higher would be required. Alas, the technology of the late 1970s could hardly cope with 12- or 14-bit quantization rate, so no one dared moaning at a "state of the art" quantization rate of 16 bits in 1983.

Recitative

To conclude, the sampling frequency is the equivalent of frames in a movie that capture a certain moment. The quantization rate is the number of bits used for representing each individual frame. Finally, remember that the digital audio format supports two channels, so you need at least 1,411,200 bits *per second* to encode music:

```
16 * 44,100 * 2 =1,411,200
```

Since additional bits for error corrections and metadata are also necessary, the typical rate is even higher. Yes, your compact disc player crunches at least 2,000,000 bits per second! In fact, it's very likely that the actual number is dramatically higher due to sophisticated noise-reduction algorithms used in CD players.

Diminuendo (Data Compression Versus Data Reduction)

Stop for a minute and try to think: What was the bitrate of the last .mp3, .ogg, .wma, or .asf clip you listened to? 128kbps? 160kbps? These rates are significantly lower than the 1,411,200 figure mentioned above. Media streaming formats count bits per second (bps), not bytes. Let's do the math together:

```
128 * 1024 =131,072
```

This rate is less than a tenth of the standard CD bitrate! Where have more than 90% of the bits gone? The sad answer is that they are truly, irretrievably lost. Unlike data-compression algorithms such as ZIP, which are called *lossless compression algorithms* because they enable you to reconstitute every bit of the original file from the compressed file. (Imagine what a terrible situation it would be if your source files were to lose lines of code randomly!) This is not the case with media streaming, though. Lossless compression can shrink a typical file to half of its original size. In certain cases, it can even reduce it to 40% of the original. However, any compression beyond this means that some of the data must be removed. MPEG-layer 3 (MP3), WMA, and other codecs perform data reduction rather than compression. Without getting into the gory details—trust me, they *are* gory!—they rely on several assumptions: Most people don't hear beyond the 15,000 Hertz threshold, and some don't even hear beyond the 10,000 Hertz barrier. In addition, silent passages in a musical piece, or monotonous sounds that last even a few hundredths of a second, can be represented in a compact form. Going back to the visual domain, it's very much like encoding the static background of a picture in a few bits rather than repeating the same information for every pixel.

Finale

So far so good; however, music is rarely a monotonous piece of a single instrument playing at a constant frequency. Therefore, no matter how clever the algorithm is, at a certain point it has to remove some of the original data. The result, as the hi-fi connoisseurs among you know too well, is poorer sound quality—and I mean much, much poorer. Human vocals sound muffled, the three-dimensional illusion of a stereo recording is reduced to 2.5 dimensions or less, high-frequency sounds are removed, and the overall sound is less detailed. Admittedly, this is a reasonable compromise in many applications. Without such data-reduction algorithms, a typical three-minute audio clip would occupy 30–40MB (!) of data instead of the average 3MB size. Video conferencing, Internet phone, and live media streaming would be impossible without aggressive data-reduction algorithms. However, if you're looking for high-quality sound, settle for no less than the magic number 1,411,200. If you're fanatical about sound quality, throw into the dustbin every digital format and revert to good old vinyl records. Yes, the best digital encoding standard today still can't compete with analog formats.

Aspect-Oriented Programming

There's a new game in town, and it's called *aspect-oriented programming* (AOP). You can't participate in it—not yet, at least—and perhaps it's just as well; once you've grasped the rules of this game, you might question whether it's really worth the trouble. Curious? Here are the details.

AOP and ISO C++

C++ in its present state doesn't support AOP directly, nor are there any plans to incorporate AOP facilities in C++0x (see Chapter 20, "C++0X: The New Face of Standard C++")—at least, not if judged by the draft proposals submitted to the Evolution Working Group. Although there have been a few attempts to ship proprietary AOP variants of C++ (*http://aosd.net/2004/tutorials/ aspectcpp.php*) that rely on nonstandard extensions, the main interest in AOP usually comes from other programming languages, notably Java.

At present, there are several Java-based AOP IDEs (*http://www-106.ibm.com/ developerworks/java/library/j-aopwork1/?ca=dgr-lnxw09AOP*) that support more or less the same concepts, although each of them implements AOP constructs differently, sometimes extending the core language with new nonstandard keywords and syntactic constructs.

Another Silver Bullet?

Object-oriented programming purportedly simplifies and automates large parts of manual coding. In large-scale systems, this claim doesn't always hold true. Ideally, when a new requirement triggers code changes, it's localized to a single member function or a class. This is the optimistic scenario. Sometimes, however, such a new requirement may involve a wholesale code rewriting. Take for example a requirement to log every invocation of every function that takes a `void *` argument. This isn't such a capricious requirement as it may first appear; think of testing a library's 64-bit compliance, for example. Such a requirement is called a *cross-cutting concern*—it cannot be isolated or encapsulated in one or two isolated code spots, but rather involves changes in many places across the system. Even if the logging operations are implemented as a single coherent class, this isn't very helpful because you still need to add the logging functionality to every piece of code that meets this criterion. From my experience (and yours as well, I'll wager), this is exactly the kind of last-minute requirement that bosses and hysterical customers like to throw at you three days before the project's finishing line. Quite a nightmare, isn't it?

Join-Points, Point-Cuts, and Advices

AOP tackles this problem by means of *join-points* and a matching *point-cut*. A join-point is a well-defined point in the code at which our concern cross-cuts the application. In plain English, a join-point is one of many spots in the code that are affected by the new requirement. Typically, there are many join-points for each concern (otherwise, we could fix the code manually). AOP IDEs enable you to define a single *point-cut*, a rule that characterizes all of the join-points. For example, here's how you define (in a hypothetical variant of C++) a point-cut called `pc1` that affects "every `SQLQuery` member function that begins with `set`, ends with `Table`, and takes an argument of type `const std::string &`":

```
pointcut pc1: call( // associated event is a function call
  int SQLQuery::set*Table ()) //define applicable functions
    && args(const std::string&); //filter by argument's type
```

AOP IDEs offer a rich set of syntactic constructs that allow you to define various criteria. In the following example, I numbered the join-points that are included in this point-cut:

```
class SQLQuery
{
//..
public:
int getIndexTable(const std::string &tablename) const;
int  setDataTable(const std::string &tablename); //1
int setViewTable(const std::string &tablename); //2
int setTextTable(const std::string &tablename); //3
int resetViewTable(const std::string &tablename);
int setLookupTable(const std::string &tablename); //4
int setTextTable(int idx);
int setTableSize (long n_items);
};
```

Even with such a small number of member functions, it's easy for a human programmer to mistakenly skip a join-point or include a false join-point. Try to imagine a more realistic scenario: making the Standard Library thread-safe, for example.

An *advice* defines the actual change that applies to a join-point. I'm not particularly keen about this term because it implies that the advice is optional, which it isn't. Perhaps the closest analogy would be a C++ exception handler: Whenever a certain join-point is met, the implementation automatically invokes the matching advice (handler), just as an exception handler is invoked automatically when a certain runtime condition is met.

Let's summarize what we've learned thus far. A cross-cut concern is a requirement that affects many specific places in the code. These places are called join-points. A point-cut is a formal definition (often using special syntax and regular expressions) of a cross-cut concern. Finally, an advice is the operation that takes place when control reaches a join-point. There are three different types of advice: before, after, and around. They execute before the join-point, after the join-point, and instead of the join-point, respectively. It's possible to combine two or more advices per point-cut, and vice versa. An *aspect* is a type similar to a class that defines point-cuts and their matching advice(s).

Back to our example. We can define a *before advice* that writes to a log just before any of the following member functions is called:

```
int  SQLQuery::setDataTable(const std::string &tablename);   //1
int  SQLQuery::setViewTable(const std::string &tablename);   //2
int  SQLQuery::setTextTable(const std::string &tablename);   //3
int  SQLQuery::setLookupTable(const std::string &tablename); //4
```

Defining an *after advice* for the same point-cut will cause the logging operation to take place after each function returns. An *around advice* is particularly useful for debugging and profiling purposes—say when you want to check how many times certain member functions that update a database are called—without actually accessing the database.

Around the Bend?

Thus far, AOP seems like a magic spell. However, it has a few disturbing aspects (pun intended) that have to be considered.

- **Gaps between source file code and runtime behavior**. When your IDE compiles an aspect, it doesn't re-edit your source files to reflect the new behavior. Rather, the new aspect is *woven* into intermediary files that you normally don't see. Thus, if all member functions of a certain project have an advice associated with them, the sources are actually very misleading. Java AOP IDEs weave the advice into the bytecode so the only way to see what's really happening is to decompile it. For a C++ programmer, this weaving is very reminiscent of macro magic—a feature we've learned to abhor, with reason.
- **Testing**. Because the changes entailed by an aspect aren't localized to a specific place, every slight modification of a point-cut or its matching advice could affect a varying number of join-points, possibly incurring time-consuming testing and debugging. Think about changing `pc1` as follows:

```
pointcut pc1: call(   //"slightly" modified
  int SQLQuery::set*Table () const) //only const member functions
    && args(const std::string&);
```

  This "minor" change has in fact reduced the number of join-points to zero!
- **Exceptions**. Suppose you want to modify almost every function with certain properties, save in one or two special cases. Alas, when the changes aren't reflected in the source files, it's easy to miss these exceptions. In C++, a similar phenomenon occurs with templates. However,

there are mechanisms for overriding the default behavior of a primary template, namely partial specializations and explicit specializations. (See the section "Template Specializations" in Chapter 5, "Templates," for details.)
- **Lack of standardization**. This isn't really a problem because, at some point, the industry will have to agree about the precise syntax and semantics of AOP-enabled IDEs. Presently, however, AOP constructs are very implementation-dependent.
- **Encouraging bad programming practices**. Although it's too early to evaluate the merits of AOP, I suspect that it might lead to sloppy coding practices, whereby programmers are tempted to patch poorly designed code by means of aspects instead of going back to the drawing board.

Epilogue

For better or worse, C++ programmers don't have to worry about any of these issues for the time being. Let other languages be the guinea pigs of AOP; if and when this technology matures, it will reach C++ as well.

Index

& operator, 289, 294
[ ] operator, 128
^ operator, 295
| operator, 290, 294
<< operator, overloading, 104–105
64-bit environment migration, 399
   ABI, 401
   built-in types, 399–400
   compatibility, 399
   member alignment, 401
   pointers, 400
<complex> header, 371, 377
   constructors, 372, 378
   functions, 379–380
   implicit conversions, 380
   initializing, 372, 378
   overloaded operators, 373, 379
<csignal> limitations, 212
<deque>, 147
<dlfcn.h> interface, 255–256
<fstream> library, 107
<iostream>, user-defined type support, 102
<list>, 147
<sstream> library, 106
<tuple> library, 448–449
<vector>, 146

A

ABI (Abstract Binary Interface), 335–336
   64-bit environment migration, 401
   troubleshooting, 336, 338
abstract classes, interfaces, 310
abstract datatyping (ADT), 110, 259
access
   elements
      containers, 128–130
      string class, 169
      information hiding, 110–111
      random, 420–421

ACE Programmer's Guide, The: Practical Design Patterns for Network and Systems Programming, 331
"Ada 95 Reference Manual, The," 121
adapters, 148, 163, 166
add operator, 91
ADT (abstract datatyping), 110, 259
aggregates
   arrays, 266–267
   initializing, 266–267
algorithms, 158
   copy(), 159
   find(), 158
   generic programming, 7
   lossless compression, 466
   sort(), 159
   STL, 125
   swap(), 204–206
aliases
   dynamic linking, 253
   namespaces, 86
alignment of members, 49–50, 401
allocation
   arrays, 39
   dynamic memory, 54–55, 59
   new operator, 42
alternative representations, 351
ambiguity, tracking, 306
analyzing
   design anti-patterns, 441
   this keywords, 297–299
   bits, 218
AND (bitwise operator), 289, 294
anonymous unions, 324–325, 429–430
ANSI, <csignal> limitations, 212
ANSI/ISO Professional Programmer's Handbook, The, 8–9
anti-patterns, 440–441
"Anti-Patterns Catalog, The," 442
AOP (aspect-oriented programming), 467–471

applications
   lock files, 203
   Singleton patterns, 438–439
   <tuple library>, 449
applying
   delete operator, 52
   environment variables, 225, 229
   function objects, 240–241
   inline functions, 281–282
   namespaces, 83–89
   new operator, 52
   nothrow new, 48–49
   variadic functions, 229
argument-dependent lookups, namespaces, 87
arguments
   class templates, 71–72
   manipulators, 4
   passing, 354
   values, 2
arithmetic, <complex> headers, 371, 377
   constructors, 372, 378
   functions, 379–380
   implicit conversions, 380
   initializing, 372, 378
   overloaded operators, 373, 379
arrays
   allocating/deallocating, 39
   associative, 167
   initializing, 265–266
   new operator, 42–44
   pointers
      behavior, 409
      sizeof expressions, 410
      troubleshooting, 410
      wrapping, 411–412
   variable-length, C99, 245
Art of UNIX Programming, The, 287
aspect-oriented programming (AOP), 467–471
assigning bitwise operators, 295
assignment operators, 22
associative arrays, containers, 167
associative containers, 153

audio, 464–467
"Automating Type Conversions with stringstream Objects," 108
auto ptr class (automating memory management), 54–62, 168
automatic memory storage, 35
automatic storage, 65
automatic updates, 252

B

back operations, 129
base classes, inheritance, 112–114
bidirectional iterators, 132, 136–137
binary files, compiling, 347
binding, dynamic, 115–116
bit fields, 218
    declaring, 219–220
    performance, 218
    spacing, 220
bits, seven-bit strings, 461
bitwise operators, 288, 293
    AND, 289, 294
    assigning, 295
    NOT, 289, 293–294
    OR, 290, 294
    shifting, 296
    strings
        flipping, 299
        resetting, 298
        setting, 299
        viewing, 300
    XOR, 295
blocking signals, 213
blocks, analyzing stopwatch class, 208–209
bool datatype, 284–292
boolalpha flag, 101
buffered I/O, 415, 419
built-in datatypes, serializing, 215
built-in types, 2
    64-bit environment migration, 399–400
    initializing, 264–265
    pseudo–constructors of, 13
    streams, 102–103

C

C
    C++, integrating, 335–338
    comparisons to C++, 1–2
    reserved names, 350
    stings, manipulating, 404–405
C Programming Language, The, 426
C++
    C, integrating, 335–338
    exception handling, 363
    overview of, 1–2
    reserved keywords, 350–353
    security, 402
"C++ Boost Timer Library," 98
"C++ Glossary," 426
"C++ Memory and Resource Management," 45
C++ in a Nutshell, 357
C++ Primer Plus, 292
C++ Programming Language, The, 8
"C++ Templates: Metaprograms," 81
C++ Templates: The Complete Guide, 82
C++0X, 447–449
C99
    designated initializers, 246
    dispersed statements and declarations, 244
    for loops, 244
    func identifiers, 247
    inline functions, 243
    line comments, 244
    long long datatype, 247
    obsolete features, 248
    restrict-qualified pointers, 247
    variable-length arrays, 245
    variadic macros, 246
caching, 462
callback functions, passing, 233
calling functions, 352
    conventions, 354
    intrinsic functions, 353–354
    overhead scale, 352
    passing arguments, 353
    pointers, 233–234
    thunks, 352–353
capacity, containers, 151–152
capacity() function, 127–128
case-sensitivity, 171, 349
cast operators, 195
    const, 197
    dynamic, 198
    reinterpret, 198
    static, 196
    categories
        of constructors, 14–15
        of pointers, 132
char*, 343
character strings, 458–459
    descriptors, 463
    double-byte coding, 459
    length prefixing, 461–462
    representation, 460
    seven-bit strings, 461
    Unicode, 459
cin, 102, 105
classes
    auto ptr, 54–62, 168
    constants, 270
    containers, STL, 124–130
    declaring new/delete as members, 50–51
    destructors, 22–23
    dynamic binding, 115–116
    encapsulation, 111–112
    file streams, 107
    generic programming, 7
    information hiding, 110–111
    inheritance, 112–114
    interfaces, 308–310
        abstract classes, 310
        combining multiple, 310–311
        pure virtual functions, 312
    local, 367–368
        member functions, 369
        restrictions, 368
        static members, 370
    member alignment, 49–50
    objects, serializing, 215
    queue container, 129

Index

std::auto ptr, 60–62
stopwatch, 207
    analyzing, 208–209
    implementing, 207–208
string, 168
    accessing elements, 169
    clearing, 170
    comparing, 170
    constructors, 169
    converting to C-strings, 169
    manipulating, 171
templates, 67–72
virtual base, 307
wrapper, references, 450–452
clearing strings, 170
close() function, 413–414
code
    ABI, 335–338
    AOP, 467–471
    cracking, 253
    double-byte, 459
    encapsulation, 111–112
    information hiding, 110–111
    inheritance, 112–114
    legacy, 346
        char*, 343
        compiled binaries, 343
        int type, 343–344
        K&R function declarations, 342–343
        non-tagged data structures, 344–345
    reuse, 119
    runtime, 181
    sharing, 252
    typedef
        declarations, 320
        portability, 321
    Unicode, 459
collating rules, 396
combining multiple interfaces, 310–311
comment lines, C99, 244
comparing
    dynamic and static linking, 251
    strings, 170

compatibility, 64-bit environment migration, 399
compilation
    exported templates, 78–80
    units, 276
compiled binaries, 347
compilers
    ABI, troubleshooting, 336, –338
    external "C" limitations, 338
compound types, 319
compression algorithms, 466
configuring
    environment variables, 224, 228
    handlers, signals, 210
const keyword, 339–341
    cast operator, 197
    correctness, 342–345
    declaring, , 271–274
    parameters, 342
constant integral expressions, 245
constants, classes, 270
constituents, RTTI, 187–190
constructors, 11–12
    <complex> headers, 372, 378
    built-in types, 13
    copy, 20–21
    exceptions, 178
    explicit keyword, 14–16
    implicit keyword, 16
    member initialization lists, 17–20
    nontrivial, 36
    string class, 169
    trivial, 13
constructs, exceptions, 170–173
containers
    adapters, 148, 163, 166
    algorithms, 158
        copy(), 159
        find(), 158
        sort(), 159
    associative arrays, 153, 167
    function objects, 160–165
    invalidating, 152
    iterators, 133–134
    keys, 154

map templates, 154
multimap templates, 155–156
multiset, 157
pairs, 154
predicate objects, 162, 165
queues, 148
reallocating, 149–150
selecting, 146–147
set, 156
sizing, 151–152
specialization, 163, 166–167
stacks, 148
std::list, 139, 144–145
STL, 124–130
user-defined types, 157
conventions, calling, 233, 354
conversion operators, 32
converting
    <complex> headers, 380
    crosscasts, 192–193
    strings, 169
cookies, 462
copy constructors, 20–21
copy() algorithm, 159
core programs, 251
correctness, const, 342–345
cout statements, 102–104
cracking (code), 253
create() function, 413–414
crosscasts
    dynamic cast operators, 330–334
    RTTI, 192–193
current time, retrieving, 95–96
customizing new operators, 51

D

data abstraction, 259
data members
    memory layout of, 384–385
    static keywords, 427–428
data structures
    non-tagged, 348
    unions, 322–323
        anonymous, 324–325
        optimizing, 326
        typecasting, 324

datatypes
    ADT, 110
    bool, 284–287, 292
    long long, 247
    typedef, 318–321
DDD (Deadly Diamond of
        Derivation), 305
deallocation, arrays, 39
dec flag, 101
declarations, 359
    bits, 219–220
    C99, 244
    class templates, 68–69
    const, 271–274
    functions, 362–363
        pointers, 231–232
    K&R functions, 248, 346
    new/delete operators, 50–51
    objects, 360
    pointers, to data members,
        235–237
    static keywords, 422–423
    typedef, 318–321
    using-declarations, 85
    volatile keyword, 343
"Declaring Classes and Member
        Functions in a
        Namespace," 94
decorated names, 335–336
"Deep Copy and Shallow Copy,"
        217
defaults
    argument values, 2
    constructors, 11, 14
    type arguments, 72
defining, 359
    associative arrays, 167
    environment variables, 222
    functions, 362–363
    primary templates, 73–74
    template specializations, 74–76
    types, 361–362
    user-defined types, 157
"Deitel Introduces Polymorphism
        in C++," 121
delete operator
    declaring, 50–51
    overloading, 50
delete() function, 38

delete[], 39
"Demonstrating the Differences
        Between static_cast and
        reinterpret_cast," 198
dependency, initialization orders,
        432
dependent names, 78
deque, 130
descriptors, 463
*Design and Evolution of C++,
        The,* 24, 300
design. *See also* configuring
        patterns, 431
        anti-patterns, 440–441
        monostate, 431–433, 435
        Singleton, 436–439
        stopwatch class, 207–208
*Design Patterns: Elements of
        Reusable Object-Oriented
        Software,* 308, 435, 439
designated initializers, C99, 246
destructors, 22
    exceptions, 178
    explicit invocation, 22–23, 44
    finally keywords, 364–365
difftime() function, 97
directives, using-directives, 85
documentation, C++ standard, 9
double-byte coding, 459
downcasts, RTTI, 193
dynamic binding, 115–116
dynamic cast operator, 198, 327
    crosscasts, 330–334
    pointers, 328–331
    references, 329–333
    static type casting, 327–331
dynamic_cast<>, RTTI, 190–191
dynamic initialization, 426
dynamic linking, 276
    <dlfcn.h> interface, 255–256
    implementing, 251–252
    shared libraries, building,
        254
    static linking, comparing, 251
    troubleshooting, 252–253
dynamic memory, 36–37
    allocation, 54–59
    auto ptr class template, 168
dynamic types, 116

E

*Effective STL: 50 Specific Ways
    to Improve Your Use of the
    Standard Template
    Library,* 292
efficiency, of class templates, 71
elaborate type names, 348
elements
    containers, accessing, 128–130
    string class, accessing, 169
embedding
    literals, 406
    objects, 392–394
empty exception specifications,
        176
encapsulation, 111–112
"Enforcing Compile-Time
        Constraints," 426
enforcing exception
        specifications, 176
enum types, 31, 259–264
"Environment Variables," 225
environment variables, 222
    applying, 225, 229
    configuring, 224, 228
    defining, 222
    reading, 222–224, 226–228
"Environment Variables in
        Windows 2000/XP," 225
eof() function, 416, 420
erase() function, 141
"Error and Exception Handling,"
        398
errors
    handling, 169, 422
    runtime, try-throw-catch
        model, 179–180
evaluation, finally keywords, 366
"Exception Handling," 183
"Exception Handling in C++,"
        177–178
exceptions, 40–41, 395–396
    auto ptr class template, 168
    constructors, 178
    constructs, 170–173
    destructors, 178
    error-handling methods, 169
    funneling, 441

handling, 363
misuses of, 181
performance, 181
specifications, 174–177
throwing, 54–55, 59
try–throw–catch model, 179–180
excessive operator overloading, 397–398
explicit constructors, 14–15
explicit destructor invocation, 22–23, 44
explicit instantiation, temporary objects, 392–393
explicit keyword, 16
explicit specializations, templates, 76–77
exported templates, 78–80
expressions
 new, 46–47
 sizeof, 410
 throw, 170
extending
 cin, 105
 cout, 104
 namespaces, 88–90
external "C" limitations, 338
external linkage, 63–64

F

fields, bit, 218
 declaring, 219–220
 performance, 218
 spacing, 220
file I/O library, 412–422
 buffering, 415, 419
 platforms, troubleshooting, 415, 418
files
 binary, compiling, 347
 header (STL), 124–125
  managing, 276–279
  naming, 93
 lock, 201
  applications, 203
  implementing, 202
 naming, 279

source, managing, 276–279
streams, 107
finally keyword, 363
 destructors, 364–365
 evaluation, 366
 exception handling, 363
find() algorithm, 158
fixed flag, 101
flags, formatting, 101
flexibility of class templates, 71
flipping, bit strings, 299
floating-point types, 381–382
 relative operators, 382
 troubleshooting, 383
flushing, 100
for loops, C99, 244
format flags, 101
formatting
 flags, 101
 lists, 140, 144
 locking policies, 201
 memory layout of data members, 384–385
 persistent objects, 214
  optimizing, 217
  serializing classes, 215
  serializing datatypes, 215
forward declarations, 362
forward iterators, 132
free store memory, 36–37
free() function, 38
Frequently Asked Questions (Bjarne Stroustrup Web site), 24
"Friends, Exceptions, and More," 194
front operations, 129
fully qualified names, 84
func identifiers, C99, 247
functions
 adapters, 163, 166
 calling, 353
  conventions, 355
  intrinsic functions, 355
  overhead scale, 353
  passing arguments, 354
  thunks, 354
capacity(), 127–128
close(), 413–414

<complex> headers, 379–380
const, declaring, 272
create(), 413–414
declaring, 362–363
definition, 362–363
delete(), 38
difftime(), 97
eof(), 416, 420
free(), 38
helper, 448
inline, 280–281
 applying, 281–282
 C99, 243
 troubleshooting, 283
iterators, 139, 143
K&R, declaring, 248, 346
lseek(), 416, 420–422
main(), 3
malloc(), 38
members, 119
 local classes, 369
 static, 428–429
memset(), 403–404
mutator, 341
new(), 38
non-virtual member, 385
objects, 160–165, 239
 applying, 240–241
 implementing, 239
 STL, 241
 templates, 241
observer, 340
open, 413–414
overloaded operators, 5–6
pointers
 calling, 233
 declaring, 231–232
 passing, 233
prototypes, 3
pure virtual, 312
read(), 414
sigprocmask(), 213
size(), 127–128
static member, 305, 386
tell(), 416, 420
templates, 77
time(), retrieving current time, 95–96
unlink(), 413–414

variadic, 229
virtual member, 386–387
write(), 414
funneling (exceptions), 441
future of programming, 455–458

G

"Generalized Function Pointers," 238
generate on demand policy, 70
generic containers, 125
generic programming (STL), 7, 123–124
iterators, 130–134, 136–143
"Generic Programming and the C++ Standard Library," 8–9, 121
global objects, exception handling, 178
globally overriding new and delete, 52–58
guidelines
memory management, 64–65
operator overloading, 26–31
"Guide to BSTR and C String Conversions," 464

H

handlers
exception objects, passing, 172
signals, configuring, 210
"Handling Exceptions," 182
headers
<complex>, 371, 377
constructors, 372, 378
functions, 379–380
implicit conversions, 380
initializing, 372, 378
overloaded operators, 373, 379
files
managing, 276–279
STL, 124–125
naming, 93
heap memory, 36–37
helper functions, 448

hex flag, 101
hierarchies, exceptions, 180
history, of new operators, 46–47
"How to Use <fstream> for File I/O," 108

I

I/O
file libraries, 412–422
buffering, 415, 419
troubleshooting platforms, 415, 418
file streams, 107
identifiers, 349–350
decorated names, 335
func, C99, 247
implementing
constructors, 12
dynamic linking, 251–252
function objects, 239
lock files, 202
new operator, 51–58
singleton patterns, 436
static member functions, 429
stopwatch class, 207–208
"Implementing a Stopwatch Class for Performance Measurements," 23
implicit conversions of <complex>headers, 380
implicit int types, 248
implicit keyword, 16
indexes, mnemonic, 259–264
information hiding, 110–111
inheritance, 112–114, 120
exception specifications, 175
MI
construction and destruction orders, 313–315
DDD, 305
object models, 388–393
VI, construction and destruction orders, 316–318
initializers, designated, for C99, 246

initializing
<complex> headers, 372, 378
arrays, 265–266
built-in types, 264–265
member lists, 17–20
non-POD objects, 426–427
objects, 268–270
POD, 264–267
static keywords, 424–427
static initialization order, 431–432
zeroes, 65
"Inline Functions," 283
inline functions, 280–281
applying, 281–282
C99, 243
troubleshooting, 283
input iterators, 133
insertion operators, 4
Inside the C++ Object Model, 34, 283, 426
instantiation
class templates, 69–70
explicit, temporary objects, 392–393
int type
implicit, 248
legacy code, 347–348
integral expressions, 245
integrating, C and C++, 335–338
interaction, namespaces (languages), 91–92
interfaces
ABI, 335–336
64-bit environment migration, 401
troubleshooting, 336–338
classes, 308–310
abstract classes, 310
combining multiple, 310–311
pure virtual functions, 312
dynamic linking, <dlfcn.h> interface, 255–256
nothrow new, 48
internal flag, 101
internal linkage, 63–64, 92
internationalization, 407

Interprocess Communications in Linux: The Nooks and Crannies, 45
interviews
    Bjarne Stroustrup, 217
    Miguel de Icaza, 398
intrinsic functions, 355
invalidating containers, 152
invocation, explicit destructors, 22–23, 44
iostream objects, 100
iterators, 130–131
    adapters, 163, 166
    bidirectional, 136–137
    categories of, 132
    containers, 133–134
    functions, 139, 143
    input, 133
    output, 133
    pointers as, 130
    random-access, 138, 142
    reverse, 137
    STL, 125

J

Java, exception handling, 363
join-points, 468, 470

K

K&R function declaration style, 248, 342
keys, containers, 154
keywords
    const, 339–341
        correctness, 342–345
        parameters, 342
    explicit, 16
    finally, 363
        destructors, 364–365
        evaluation, 366
        exception handling, 363
    implicit, 16
    mutable, 344–345
    reserved, 350–353
    static, 422
        anonymous unions, 429–430
        data members, 427–428
        initializing, 424–427
        local, 423
        member functions, 428–429
        namespace scope, 425–426
    template, 68
    this, 301–304
        analyzing, 301–302
        static member functions, 305
    typedef, 318–321
    volatile, 342–343
        declaring, 343
        STL, 344

L

languages (interaction), namespaces, 91–92
left flag, 101
legacy code, 346
    char*, 343
    compiled binaries, 347
    int type, 347–348
    K&R function declarations, 346
    non-tagged data structures, 348
length prefixing, 461–462
libraries
    dynamic linking
        <dlfcn.h> interface, 255–256
        building shared, 254
    <fstream>, 107
    numeric (STL), 125
    <sstream>, 106
    STL, 123. *See also* STL
    <tuple>, 448–449
lifetimes, temporary objects, 390–391
limitations
    <csignal>, 212
    external "C", 338
    static typecasting, 326–331

lines, comments, C99, 244
linkage, 337
    internal, 92
    types, 63–64
    units, 251
linked lists
    std::list class, 139, 144–145
linking, dynamic
    building shared libraries, 254
    <dlfcn.h> interface, 255–256
    comparing to static linking, 251
    implementing, 251–252
    troubleshooting, 252–253
Linux Application Development, 257
Linux Programming by Example: The Fundamentals, 257
lists
    member initialization, 17–20, 269
    std::list container class, 139, 144–145
    template parameter, 68
literals, embedding, 406
local classes, 367–368
    member functions, 369
    restrictions, 368
    static members, 370
local objects, instantiating, 65
local static keywords, 423
lock files, 201
    applications, 203
    implementing, 202
logical state, 344
long long datatype, C99, 247
lookups, argument-dependent, 87
lossless compression algorithms, 466
lseek() function, 416–422

M

macros, variadic, C99, 246
main() function, 3
maintenance, memory, 65
malloc() function, 38

management
    automatic memory storage, 35
    automating memory, 54–62
    containers (STL), 125–130
    files
        header and source, 276–279
        naming, 279
    free store memory, 36–37
    header files (STL), 124–125
    memory, 2, 64–65, 168
    one entity rule, 278
    static memory storage, 36
    units, 276
mangling names, 332
manipulating
    bits, 218
        declaring, 219–220
        performance, 218
        spacing, 220
    members, pointers, 235
    strings, 171, 404–405
manipulators, 4
map templates, containers, 154
matching, types, exceptions, 172–173
mathematics, <complex>
    headers, 371, 377
    constructors, 372, 378
    functions, 379–380
    implicit conversions, 380
    initializing, 372, 378
    overloaded operators, 373, 379
maximal munch rules, 358
measurements, stopwatch class, 207
    analyzing, 208–209
    implementing, 207–208
"Member Alignment," 221
members
    64-bit environment migration, 401
    alignment, 49–50
    const, declaring, 272
    data, static, 427–428
    declaring new/delete as class, 50–51

functions, 119
    local classes, 369
    non-virtual, 385
    static, 386, 428–429
    virtual, 386–387
initialization lists, 17–20, 269
memory layout of, 384–385
mutable keyword, 344–345
namespaces, 88–89
pointers, 234
    declaring, 235–237
    manipulating, 235
    representations, 237–238
    referring to namespaces, 91
    static functions, 305
    static local classes, 370
memory
    auto ptr class template, 168
    automatic storage, 35
    automating management, 54–62
    dynamic allocation, 54–55, 59
    exceptions, 40–41
    free store, 36–37
    management, 2, 64–65
    new operator, 42, 44
    nothrow new, 49
    object models, 384–385
    POD objects, 37–38
    static storage, 36
    vector container class, 126–127
"Memory Hygiene in C and C++: Safe Programming with Risky Data," 342
memset() function, 403–404
Mentoring Object Technology Projects, 275
messages, polymorphism, 114–115
methods, error-handling, 169
metrics, stopwatch class, 207
    analyzing, 208–209
    implementing, 207–208
MI (multiple inheritance)
    ambiguity, tracking, 306
    construction and destruction orders, 313–315

DDD, 305
virtual base classes, 307
migration of 64-bit environments, 399
    ABI, 401
    built-in types, 399–400
    compatibility, 399
    member alignment, 401
    pointers, 400
Minix man pages (Web site), 225
missing exception specifications, 176
misuses of exceptions, 181
mnemonic indexes, 259–264
models
    objects, 383
        embedding, 392–394
        formatting memory layout of data members, 384–385
        inheritance, 388–393
        non-virtual member functions, 385
        static member functions, 386
        virtual member functions, 386–387
    separate compilation (templates), 78
Modern C++ Design: Generic Programming and Design Patterns Applied, 275
monostate patterns, 431–435
multimap templates, containers, 155–156
multiple inheritance (MI)
    ambiguity, tracking, 306
    construction and destruction orders, 313–315
    DDD, 305
    virtual base classes, 307
multiple interfaces, combining, 310–311
multiset containers, 157
multithreading, 407
mutable keyword, 344–345
mutator functions, 341

Index

N

names
  decoration, 335–336
  dependent, 78
  elaborate type, 348
  files, 279
  fully qualified, 84
  headers, 93
  linkage types, 63–64
  mangling, 336
namespaces
  aliases, 86
  applying, 83–89
  argument-dependent lookups, 87
  extending, 88–90
  language interaction, 91–92
  members, 88–89
  properties, 84–85
  referring to members, 91
  static keywords, scope, 425–426
new operator, 42, 44
  declaring, 50–51
  history of, 46–47
  implementing, 51–54, 57–58
  nothrow new interface, 48. *See also* nothrow new
  overloading, 50
  standard-compliant, 47–48
new() function, 38
new[], 39
non-buffered I/O, 415, 419
non-POD objects, 37–38, 426–427
non-tagged data structures, 348
non-virtual member functions, 385
nontrivial constructors, 36
NOT (bitwise operator), 289, 293–294
nothrow new
  applying, 48–49
  interface, 48
numeric libraries, STL, 125

O

"Object Orientation: C++ Specifics," 121
object-oriented programming
  concepts of, 118–120
  overview of, 1–2
  support for, 6
objects
  allocating/deallocating, 39
  assignment operators, 22
  auto_ptr, 168
  const, declaring, 271–274
  constructors, 11–12
  conversion operators, 32
  copy constructors, 20–21
  declaring, 360
  destructors, 22–23
  dynamic binding, 115–116
  exceptions, 172–173
  explicit constructors, 14–15
  explicit keyword, 16
  freestore memory, 36–37
  functions, 160–165, 239
    applying, 240–241
    implementing, 239
    STL, 241
    templates, 241
  global, exception handling, 178
  implicit keyword, 16
  initializing, 268–270
  instantiating local, 65
  iostream, 100
  lists, creating, 140, 144
  member initialization lists, 17–20
  models, 383
    embedding, 392–394
    formatting memory layout of data members, 384–385
    inheritance, 388–393
    non-virtual member functions, 385
    static member functions, 386
    virtual member functions, 386–387
  operator, 42, 44
  non-POD, initializing, 426–427
  persistent, 214
    optimizing, 217
    serializing, 215
  POD, 37–38
  polymorphism, 114–115
  predicate, 162, 165
  pseudo-constructors of built-in types, 13
  returning by value, 29–30
  semantic support, 38
  state, 344
  streams, 99–101
    format flags, 101
    <iostream>, 102
    types, 102–103
  temporary
    explicit instantiation, 392–393
    lifetimes, 390–391
    syntax, 393–394
    swap() algorithms without, 205–206
  trivial constructors, 13
observer functions, 340
obsolete features of C99, 248
oct flag, 101
one entity rule, 278
open() function, 413–414
operator const_cast<>, 274
"Operator Overloading + the Right Way," 34
operators
  <<, overloading, 104–105
  add, 91
  assignment, 22
  bitwise, 288, 293
    AND, 289, 294
    assigning, 295
    flipping strings, 299
    NOT, 289, 293–294
    OR, 290, 294
    resetting strings, 298
    setting strings, 299
    shifting, 296
    viewing strings, 300
    XOR, 295

cast, 195
    const, 197
    dynamic, 198
    reinterpret, 198
    static, 196
const_cast<>, 274
conversion, 32
dynamic cast, 327
    crosscasts, 330, 333–334
    pointers, 328–331
    references, 329–333
    static typecasting, 327–331
insertion, 4
new, 42–46. *See also* new
    operator
overloading, 5–6, 26–31
    <complex> headers, 373,
        379
    excessive, 397–398
    relative, floating–point types,
        382
    scpe resolution, 91
    [ ], 128
"Optimize Abstract Operations
    with Function Templates,"
    82
optimizing
    persistent objects, 217
    unions, 326
OR (bitwise operator), 294
organizational anti-patterns,
    442
ostream objects, cout,
    overloading, 104
output iterators, 133
output pointers, 133
over-engineering, 395
    exceptions, 395–396
        excessive operator
            overloading, 397–398
        over-genericity, 396–397
over-genericity, 396–397
overhead scale, 353
overloading
    cin, 105
    cout, 104
    new/delete operators, 50
    operators, 5–6, 26–31

<complex> headers, 373,
    379
excessive, 397–398
"Overloading Operator << for a
    User-Defined Type," 108
overriding
    delete operator, 53–58
    new operator, 51–58
    new/delete operators globally,
        52, 57

P

padding bytes, 49
pairs, containers, 154
*Parallel and Distributed
    Programming Using C++,*
    408
parameters
    class templates, 71–72
    const, 342
    template parameter lists, 68
partial template specializations,
    75–76
pass-by-references, 2
passing
    arguments, 354
    exception objects, 172
    functions, pointers, 233
patterns
    design, 431
        anti-patterns, 440–441
        monostate, 431–435
        Singleton, 436–439
    refactoring, 445
pending signals, 213
"Perform Crosscasts Properly,"
    199
"Perform Safe Downcasts," 199
performance
    bits, 218
    exceptions, 181
    persistent objects, 217
    stopwatch class, 207
        analyzing, 208–209
        implementing, 207–208
    virtual base classes, 307
persistent objects, 214

classes, serializing, 215
datatypes, serializing, 215
optimizing, 217
physical state, 344
placement new, 42, 44
Plain Old Data (POD) objects,
    37–38
platforms, file I/O libraries,
    troubleshooting, 415, 418
POD (Plain Old Date) objects,
    37–38, 264–267
point-cuts, 468–470
pointers
    64-bit environment migration,
        400
    arrays, behavior, 409
        sizeof expressions, 410
        troubleshooting, 410
        wrapping, 411–412
    const, declaring, 272–274
    dynamic cast operators,
        328–331
    functions
        calling, 233
        declaring, 231–232
        passing, 233
    iterators, 130
    members, 234
        declaring, 235–237
        manipulating, 235
        representations, 237–238
    restrict-qualified, C99, 247
policies, locking, 201
polymorphism, 114–115, 389–393
portability, code, 321
"Porting to a 64-Bit Platform,"
    401
POSIX signals, 212–213
POSIX lockf() function (Web site
    manual), 204
predicates, objects, 162, 165
prefixing, 461–462
primary templates, defining,
    73–74
priority_queue, 130
processes, signals, 210–211
    ANSI <csignal> limitations,
        212

blocking, 213
configuring handlers, 210
pending, 213
POSIX, 212–213
programming
   AOP, 467–468, 470–471
   concepts of, 118–120
   double-byte coding, 459
   future of, 455–458
   generic, 7, 123–124
   object-oriented, 1–2, 6. *See also* object-oriented programming
   Unicode, 459
"Programming Languages: The Early Years," 8
programs, structure of, 3–4
properties
   bool datatypes, 286–287, 292
   enum types, 259–260
   namespaces, 84–85
prototypes, functions, 3
pseudo-constructors of built-in types, 13
pure virtual functions, 312

Q

quadword, 401
qualified names, 4
queues, containers, 129, 148

R

race conditions, 203
random access, 420–421
random-access iterators, 132, 138, 142
read() function, 414
reading environment variables, 222–228
reallocating containers, 149–150
Real-Time Design Patterns: Robust Scalable Architecture for Real-Times Systems, 435, 439
"Re-entrant Functions," 213
refactoring, 442–445

references, 306–307
   dynamic cast operators, 329–333
   namespace members, 91
   pass-by, 2
   wrapper classes, 450–452
registers, arguments, passing, 354
reinterpret cast operator, 198
relative operators, floating-point types, 382
representations
   pointers to members, 237–238
   strings, 460
requirements, mnemonic indexes, 260–261
reserved identifiers, 350
reserved keywords, 350–353
reserved names, C, 350
resetting, bit strings, 298
restrict-qualified pointers, C99, 247
restrictions, local classes, 368
retrieving, current time, 95–96
returning objects by value, 29–30
reuse (code), 119
reverse iterators, 134, 137, 141
right flag, 101
RTTI (Runtime Type Information), 181, 185–187
   constituents, 187–190
   crosscasts, 192–193
   downcasts, 193
   dynamic cast<>, 190–191
rules
   collating, 396
   maximal munch, 358
   one entity, 278
runtime
   errors, try-throw-catch model, 179–180
   overhead, 65
Runtime Type Information (RTTI), 181, 185–187
   constituents, 187–190
   crosscasts, 192–193
   downcasts, 193
   dynamic cast<>, 190–191

S

safety, memory, 65
scientific flag, 101
scope, namespaces, static keyword, 425–426
scope resolution operators, 91, 156
security, 402
   C++, 402
   C-style string manipulation, 404–405
   dynamic linking, 252
   memset() function, 403–404
selecting containers, 146–147
self-assignment operators, 295
semantics
   object support, 38
   volatile keyword, 342–343
separate compilation models (templates), 78
sequence containers, 125
sequence-points, 357
sequences
   adapters, 163, 166
   algorithms, 158
      copy(), 159
      find(), 158
      sort(), 159
   lists, 145
serialization
   built-in datatypes, 215
   class objects, 215
set containers, 156
setting. *See also* configuring
   bit strings, 299
   formatting, 299
seven-bit strings, 461
sharable images, 251
shared libraries, 251
sharing
   code. 252
   libraries, dynamic linking, 254
shifting bitwise operators, 296
showbase flag, 101
showpoint flag, 101
side effects, 356
"Signal Processing," 213

signal processing, 210–211
    ANSI <csignal> limitations, 212
    blocking, 213
    configuring handlers, 210
    pending, 213
    POSIX, 212–213
"Signal Processing Notes," 213
sigprocmask() function, 213
single inheritance, object models, 388–393
Singleton patterns, 436–439
size() function, 127–128
sizeof expressions, 410
sizes, members, 49–50
sizing containers, 151–152
skipws flag, 101
sort() algorithm, 159
sound, 464, 466–467
source files, managing, 276–279
spacing bits, 220
specializations
    class templates, 69–70
    containers, 163, 166–167
    defining, 157
    explicit, 76–77
    templates, 72–76
specifications, exceptions, 174–177
stacks
    containers, 148
    memory, 35
    unwinding, 171
standard exceptions, 179
Standard Template Library. *See* STL (Standard Template Library),
standard types, streams, 102–103
standard-compliant new, 47–48
Standardese, 355
    sequence-points, 357
    side effects, 356
    tokenizers, 358
state, 344
statements, dispersed, C99, 244
static, internal linkage, 92
static cast operator, 196
static initialization, 426–432

static keywords, 422
    anonymous unions, 429–430
    data members, 427–428
    initializing, 424–427
    local, 423
    member functions, 428–429
    namespace scope, 425–426
static linking, comparing to dynamic linking, 251
static members
    functions, 305, 386
    local classes, 370
static memory storage, 36
static typecasting, dynamic cast operators, 326–331
static types, 116
std::list container class, 139, 144–145
std::auto ptr class template, 60–62
"std::unexpected() Function, The," 178
STL Tutorial and Reference Guide: C++ Programming with the Standard Template Library, 341
STL (Standard Template Library)
    adapters, 163, 166
    algorithms, 158
        copy(), 159
        find(), 158
        sort(), 159
    auto ptr class template, 168
    containers, 125–130
        accessing elements, 128–130
        adapters, 148
        associative, 153
        associative arrays, 167
        invalidating, 152
        keys, 154
        map templates, 154
        multimap templates, 155–156
        multiset, 157
        pairs, 154
        queues, 148
        reallocating, 149–150

        selecting, 146–147
        set, 156
        sizing, 151–152
        specialization, 163–167
        stacks, 148
        user-defined types, 157
    function objects, 160–165, 241
    generic programming, 123–124
    header files, 124–125
    iterators, 130–139, 141–143
    predicate objects, 162, 165
    std::list container class, 139, 144–145
    string class, 168
        accessing elements, 169
        clearing, 170
        comparing, 170
        constructors, 169
        converting to C–strings, 169
        manipulating, 171
    volatile keyword, 344
stopwatch class, 207
    analyzing, 208–209
    implementing, 207–208
storage
    automatic memory, 35
    class specifiers, 320
    specifiers, 344–345
    static memory, 36
streams, 99–101
    files, 107
    format flags, 101
    <iostream>, 102
    strings, 106
    types, 102–103
strings, 168
    bit
        flipping, 299
        resetting, 298
        setting, 299
        viewing, 300
    C-strings, converting to, 169
    C-Style manipulation, 404–405
    characters, 458–459
        descriptors, 463

Index

double-byte coding, 459
length prefixing, 461–462
representation, 460
seven-bit strings, 461
Unicode, 459
clearing, 170
comparing, 170
constructors, 169
elements, accessing, 169
manipulating, 171
streams, 106
wchar_t, 226
structure, of programs, 3–4
support
exported templates, 79
<iostream>, user-defined types, 102
for object-oriented programming, 6
object semantics, 38
swap() algorithm, 7, 204–206
symbols, 255
syntax, temporary objects, 393–394

T

tell() function, 416, 420
templates
auto ptr class, 168
classes, 67–72
explicit specializations, 76–77
exported, 78–80
functions, 77, 241
generic programming, 7
map, 154
multimap, 155–156
reference wrapper class, 451
specializations, 72–76
std::auto ptr, 60–62
STL, 123. See also STL
"Templates and Inheritance Interacting in C++," 81–82
"Template Specializations," 82
temporary objects
explicit instantiation, 392–393
lifetimes, 390–391

swap() algorithms without, 205–206
syntax, 393–394
this keyword, 301–304
analyzing, 301–302
static member functions, 305
threads, multithreading, 407
throw expressions, 170
throwing exceptions, 54–55, 59
thunks, 354
time, difftime() function, 97
Time and Date.com, 98
time() function, retrieving current time, 95–96
tokenizers, 358
tools, STL, 125
"Tour of C++, A," 7
tracking, ambiguity, 306
translation units, 251, 276
trivial constructors, 13
troubleshooting
ABI, 336, 338
DDD, 305
dynamic linking, 252–253
file I/O libraries, 415, 418
floating–point types, 383
inline functions, 283
pointers, 410
"Try and Catch Me," 183
try blocks, 170
try-throw-catch model, exceptions, 179–180
tuples, reference wrapper class, 452
type parameters, class templates, 71–72
typecasting
static, limitations of, 327–331
union, 324
typedef declarations, 318–321
types, 2
ADT, 110
bool, 284–292
built-in
64-bit environment migration, 399–400
initializing, 264–265
compound, 319

definition, 361–362
destructors, 22–23
dynamic, 116
enum, 31, 259–264
exceptions, 172–173
floating-point, 381–382
relative operators, 382
troubleshooting, 383
int
implicit, 248
legacy code, 347–348
linkage, 63–64
long long, C99, 247
operator overloading, 31
pseudo-constructors of built-in types, 13
RTTI, 185–187
constituents, 187–190
crosscasts, 192–193
downcasts, 193
dynamic cast<>, 190–191
serializing, 215
static, 116
user-defined, 31, 157

U

Unicode, 459
unions, 322–323
anonymous, 324–325, 429–430
arrays, 267
initializing, 267
optimizing, 326
typecasting, 324
units, management, 276
unlink() function, 413–414
unwinding stacks, 171
updates, automatic, 252
uppercase flag, 102
user-defined specializations, 74–75
user-defined types, 2, 31
containers, 157
<iostream> support, 102
using-declarations, 85
using-directives, 85
utilities, STL, 125

V

values
    arguments, 2
    returning objects by, 29–30
variable-length arrays, C99, 245
variables
    environment, 222
        applying, 225, 229
        configuring, 224, 228
        defining, 222
        reading, 222–228
    for loops, C99, 244
    free store memory, 36–37
variadic functions, 229
variadic macros, C99, 246
vector container class, 126–127
VI (virtual inheritance), construction and destruction orders, 316–318

viewing, bit strings, 300
virtual base classes, 307
virtual functions, 312
virtual inheritance (VI), construction and destruction orders, 316–318
virtual member functions, 386–387
volatile keywords, 342–343
    declaring, 343
    STL, 344

W

wchar_t strings, 226
"What Is RTTI?," 194
Wikipedia, 442
wrapper classes, references, 450–452
wrapping arrays, 411–412
write() function, 414
Write Great Code, 460

X

XOR (bitwise operator), 295

Z

zero-initialization, 65, 422
zones (time), difftime() function, 97